Cognitive Behavioural Approaches to the Understanding and Treatment of Dissociation

Edited by Fiona Kennedy, Helen Kennerley and David Pearson

 Routledge
Taylor & Francis Group

LONDON AND NEW YORK

First published 2013
by Routledge
27 Church Road, Hove, East Sussex BN3 2FA

Simultaneously published in the USA and Canada
by Routledge
711 Third Avenue, New York, NY 10017

Routledge is an imprint of the Taylor & Francis Group, an informa business

British Library Cataloguing in Publication Data
A catalogue record for this book is available from the British Library

Library of Congress Cataloging in Publication Data
Cognitive behavioural approaches to the understanding and treatment of dissociation / [edited] by Fiona Kennedy, Helen Kennerley, and David Pearson.
pages cm
Includes bibliographical references and index.
1. Dissociative disorders--Treatment. 2. Cognitive therapy. I. Kennedy, Fiona (Fiona Clare) II. Kennerley, Helen. III. Pearson, David (David C.)
RC553.D5C64 2013
616.89'1425--dc23
2012046958

ISBN: 978-0-415-68776-8 (hbk)
ISBN: 978-0-415-68777-5 (pbk)
ISBN: 978-0-203-50208-2 (ebk)

Typeset in Times
by Fakenham Prepress Solutions, Fakenham, Norfolk, NR21 8NN

Cognitive Behavioural Approaches to the Understanding and Treatment of Dissociation

The study of dissociation is relevant to anyone undertaking research or treatment of mental health problems. *Cognitive Behavioural Approaches to the Understanding and Treatment of Dissociation* uses a cognitive approach to de-mystify the processes involved in linking traumatic incidents to their effects.

The editors present a full and comprehensive understanding of mental health problems involving dissociative disorders and their treatment, bringing together an international range of experts. Each chapter addresses a single topic in full, including assessment of previous research from a cognitive perspective, recommendations for treatment and case studies to illustrate clinical approaches. Using an evidence-based scientific approach combined with the wisdom of clinical experience, the chapter authors make the relevance of dissociation immediately recognizable to those familiar with PTSD, dissociative identity disorder, eating disorders, hallucinations, and a wide range of psychological and non-organic physical health disorders.

Designed to provide new perspectives on both research and treatment, *Cognitive Behavioural Approaches to the Understanding and Treatment of Dissociation* includes a wide range of material that will appeal to clinicians, academics and students.

Fiona Kennedy, Consultant Clinical Psychologist, was formerly an NHS Director of Psychology and is now MD of GreenWood Mentors Ltd. She has published on dissociation and specializes clinically in adult survivors of trauma, personality disorder and dissociation.

Helen Kennerley, Consultant Clinical Psychologist, is a founder member of the Oxford Cognitive Therapy Centre and Director of the Diploma/MSc in Advanced Cognitive Therapy Studies. She is an experienced clinician specializing in childhood trauma, dissociative disorders and self-injurious behaviours.

David Pearson, Consultant Clinical Psychologist, is a specialist in child and adolescent mental health, formerly an NHS Head of Psychology and Honorary Tutor at the University of Southampton. He has published in a number of peer-reviewed journals.

We dedicate this book to all of our lovely children:
Eva, Noah, Lorna, Marie, Adam, Jude, Bibi, Joanna and Simon.
Thank you for being part of our lives.

Contents

Contributors

Richard J. Brown is Senior Lecturer in Clinical Psychology and Programme Director of the Clinical Psychology Doctorate at the University of Manchester. He also works clinically for Manchester Mental Health and Social Care NHS Trust within the Complex Primary Care Psychology service. He has a long-standing interest in the psychological mechanisms and treatment of dissociative and somatoform phenomena, and has numerous empirical, theoretical and clinical publications in this area.

Timothy A. Carey is Associate Professor in Mental Health at the Centre for Remote Health in Alice Springs, Australia and also works as a clinical psychologist in the public mental health service. He uses the principles of control theory (Perceptual Control Theory) to understand and help people deal with the experience of dissociation.

Vivia A. Cowdrill is a Consultant Clinical Psychologist in acute inpatient care; a cognitive behaviour therapist and dialectical behaviour therapist. Her clinical and research interests are in personality disorders and the psychological consequences of childhood trauma and dissociative disorders.

Katharine Donnelly earned her PhD in Clinical Psychology at Hofstra University. Her areas of interest include acceptance-oriented therapies and obsessive-compulsive spectrum behaviours. She is the co-author of the book *Overcoming Depersonalization Disorder: A Mindfulness and Acceptance Guide to Conquering Feelings of Numbness and Unreality.*

Martin J. Dorahy is Associate Professor in the Department of Psychology, University of Canterbury, Christchurch, New Zealand. He also maintains a private practice focused primarily on complex trauma disorders.

Paul Gilbert OBE is Professor of Clinical Psychology at the University of Derby and Consultant Clinical Psychologist at the Derbyshire Health Care Foundation Trust. He has researched evolutionary approaches to psychopathology for over 35 years, with a special focus on shame and the treatment of shame-based difficulties – for which compassion-focused therapy was developed. In 2006 he established the Compassionate Mind Foundation (www. compassionatemind.co.uk).

Vegard Øksendal Haaland is dipl.psych from Christian-Albrechts-University of Kiel, Germany and PhD from the University of Oslo, Norway. He is working as a clinical psychologist at the Department of Psychiatry, Sørlandet Hospital in Kristiansand, Norway and as an Associate Professor at the Department of Psychology, University of Oslo. His main research interest is the association between cognition and symptomatology in disorders of affect regulation.

Elaine C. M. Hunter is a clinical psychologist and researcher based at the Institute of Psychiatry and Maudsley Hospital in London. She has been conducting research and treating people with depersonalization disorder since 1999.

Rafaële J. C. Huntjens is Assistant Professor in the Department of Clinical Psychology, University of Groningen, the Netherlands. She has published on memory and attentional processes in trauma-related disorders.

Fiona C. Kennedy, Consultant Clinical Psychologist, worked as Head of Psychology Services for the Isle of Wight NHS until 2006. She has published and presented nationally and internationally and now provides training, supervision, therapy and business coaching privately. Her interest in dissociation was stimulated after seeing several clients with unusual and difficult to treat symptoms. She produced a CBT formulation of dissociative symptoms, and designed and researched a new measurement scale in collaboration with University of Southampton and the Wessex Group of Clinical Psychologists. Together with David Pearson she provides pro bono work for an Indian NGO, teaching Indian volunteers to work with disadvantaged children, and designing outcome measures for their programs.

Helen Kennerley is a Consultant Clinical Psychologist with the Oxford Health NHS Foundation Trust and the Oxford Cognitive Therapy Centre (OCTC). She is a founder member of OCTC and Director of the University of Oxford–OCTC Diploma/MSc in Advanced Cognitive Therapy Studies. Clinically, she has specialized for 25 years in working with adult survivors of childhood trauma and through this work has become experienced in helping patients manage dissociation and self-injurious behaviours. She has published academically and has also written a popular self-help text: *Overcoming Childhood Trauma*.

Udo Kischka is a Consultant in Neurological Rehabilitation at the Oxford Centre for Enablement. He is both a psychologist and a medical doctor. In both his clinical and his academic work he has combined his interests in psychology and neurology, which has led to the development of his workshops on the brain, emotion, memory and cognitive therapy. He has always been active in brain research, taking up research posts at Harvard, MIT and the University of Basel. He has published extensively. He is a visiting professor at Oxford

Brookes University, the University of Hertfordshire and the University of Basel in Switzerland, and an honorary senior lecturer at the Department of Neurology at the University of Oxford.

Nils Inge Landrø is Professor of Neuropsychology at the Department of Psychology, University of Oslo. His main research areas are cognitive impairments and brain function in affective and personality disorders, as well as identification of vulnerability markers for mood and impulsivity disorders in healthy people.

Warren Mansell is a Reader in Clinical Psychology and author of over 100 publications in the field of mental health. In 2011 he received the May Davidson Award from the British Psychological Society for his outstanding contribution to the field in the first ten years since qualifying as a clinical psychologist.

Victoria A. Mountford is Principal Clinical Psychologist at the Eating Disorders Service, South London and Maudsley NHS Foundation Trust and Visiting Research Associate at the Institute of Psychiatry, King's College London. Her research interests include treatments for the eating disorders, therapeutic processes – particularly in CBT, and body image. She has published and taught widely on the subject of eating disorders.

Katherine Newman-Taylor works as a Consultant Clinical Psychologist in the NHS, and as a Lecturer in CBT at the University of Southampton. She works with people with severe and enduring mental health needs, to develop ways of living well with complex problems. Her research focuses on understanding the cognitive and meta-cognitive factors associated with distressing psychosis, and the implications for therapeutic work, including process-based interventions such as mindfulness.

Fugen Neziroglu is a board certified behaviour and cognitive psychologist. She is Clinical Director of the Bio Behavioral Institute in Great Neck, New York. Dr Neziroglu has published over 100 papers in scientific journals, and fifteen books. Her three most recent books are *Overcoming Depersonalization*, *Overcoming Body Dysmorphic Disorder* and *A Treatment Manual on Body Dysmorphic Disorder*.

David Pearson is a Consultant Clinical Psychologist with the NHS UK, specializing in children and adolescents, where he has been head of service and specialism head. He has been an honorary tutor at the University of Southampton. Research interests include the behavioural effects of food additives, hyperactivity, child hallucinations and the impact of poor child experiences. He is author of numerous journal papers and the *Dream Mentoring Manuals* (India).

Suzanne Sambrook is a Consultant Clinical Psychologist working within an NHS forensic low secure unit. Her areas of specialist interest are personality disorder and recovery-based interventions with service users. Current research projects include developing interventions for those with psychosis and complex trauma.

Kathy Steele is a practicing psychotherapist and Clinical Director of Metropolitan Counseling Services, a psychotherapy and training centre in Atlanta, Georgia. She frequently publishes and teaches about trauma, dissociation, and attachment.

Lusia Stopa is a Senior Lecturer at the University of Southampton and she directs the post-graduate cognitive therapy programmes run in the Psychology Academic Unit. Imagery is a key research interest, particularly the way in which images of the self can contribute to and maintain disorders. Her clinical practice includes a special interest in PTSD and in the role of dissociation in trauma.

Onno van der Hart is Emeritus Professor of Psychopathology of Chronic Traumatization at the Department of Clinical and Health Psychology, Utrecht University, the Netherlands. He is a clinical consultant on the diagnosis and treatment of complex trauma-related disorders. He has for many years pioneered research, writing and teaching on the topic of dissociation and its treatment.

Rineke van Wees-Cieraad is a PhD student in the Department of Clinical Psychology, University of Groningen, the Netherlands. She is also a psychologist-in-training for Healthcare Psychologist in the Department of Psychotrauma at PsyQ Groningen, the Netherlands.

How to use this book

We have worked to make this book as accessible as possible for all readers. It should be possible to pick it up and begin with any chapter, although the chapters are ordered to tell the dissociation story from start to finish if that is your preference. There is a glossary to explain terms you may come across in the course of your browsing. We hope you become as entranced as we are by this fascinating subject.

Foreword

Arnoud Arntz

This book offers timely and necessary help for clinicians, researchers and students who are *not* specialists in the field of dissociation to improve their understanding of the wide range of dissociative symptoms and how to treat them. Among the attractive qualities of the book is the use of contemporary theories from the cognitive sciences to explain problematic dissociation, and to guide therapists in how to treat it. Dissociation can obstruct treatment or be a major problem by itself that needs to be addressed. This book takes the normalizing and practical stance of providing understanding and treatment guidance by applying contemporary cognitive theories and therapies. Dissociation is acknowledged as common across a wide range of disorders and clinical problems, encouraging therapists to be alert to identifying and addressing its manifestations in different contexts.

The editors have brought together contributors who provide a radical and revolutionary approach to dissociation and mental health problems. They debunk and demystify the language and the assumption that only experts can understand it. Drawing upon rich and disparate areas of research and clinical skills, treatment guidelines are presented that are accessible to therapists treating a wide range of mental health problems.

Dissociation is one of the most intriguing yet controversial issues in our field. Many clinicians fear that only specialists can handle dissociation, and that they will damage patients showing dissociative symptoms if they try to treat them with their usual approaches.

Some have criticized the concept of dissociation itself, pointing out that it has become over-inclusive and therefore meaningless. Others focus on the possibility of inducing dissociative symptoms in vulnerable patients, and the lack of solid scientific research evidence. On the other hand, some writers' and therapists' specialist knowledge has been couched in complex terminology which can create barriers to learning about their insights and practices – they may use different paradigms and language. Between critics and specialists yawns an unbridged chasm, so that the field has remained in a disconnected state.

This book demystifies many dissociative problems, helping clinicians understand and respond in a calm and decisive way, instead of panicking! Students coming to this area will find it a gentle, well-structured and up-to-date introduction.

The book will help to reduce the 'dissociation' between mainstream psychological interventions and specialist treatments of dissociation, and has an extremely important function in our field.

Preface

Fiona C. Kennedy
Helen Kennerley
David Pearson

If you are flicking through this preface you might well be one of many clinicians whose therapeutic intervention has been thwarted by untreated dissociation, or one of many who have been frustrated by the lack of interest taken by clinicians and researchers in the applied cognitive field. In the light of recent advances in the understanding of dissociation, we aim to gather recent findings and to help you achieve more in your therapeutic interventions.

Cognitive Behavioural Approaches to the Understanding and Treatment of Dissociation is Fiona Kennedy's brain-child. She recognized the need for a clinician-friendly text which would guide the reader through what is fast becoming a maze of information and ideas about dissociation. This was by no means a new thought on her part – she had begun this mission in 1998 when she started to develop a cognitive model that could embrace the multitude of presentations that fall under the umbrella term of dissociation. Helen Kennerley had been trying to make clinical sense of the phenomena for some time and produced clinical guidance in a paper back in 1996. So it was very easy to persuade her that she would make an ideal editor or writer of this text. Soon afterwards Dave Pearson was drawn in – his work with children and young people brought an invaluable insight into the development of dissociative disorders.

None of us had any doubt that this would be a relevant text and our conviction has been strengthened by the increasing research on the topic and the increasing numbers attending our various workshops and training events. Dissociation seems no longer to be a poor relative of proper psychological disorders, but is gaining a following of interested and critical researchers and clinicians. Amongst them are the contributors to this book.

The book's authors represent the diverse clinical and academic fields in which dissociation is relevant. Contributors have different perspectives on dissociation and different clinical interests, yet all have consistently told us that the more they considered the role of dissociation in relation to psychological problems, the more fascinating they found it – so we hope you will too.

What to expect from this book and how to get the most out of it

Our main aim was to produce a text which would be of practical value and thus would provide a usable guide for the clinician. In order to achieve this we set ourselves several tasks. Firstly we set out to debunk the misconception that dissociation is only relevant to dissociative disorders per se and we encourage readers to consider dissociation as a basic and universal psychological process that initially might protect the individual, but that can sometimes become dysfunctional and result in, or contribute to, mental health problems of many kinds. Each author has described this in relation to his or her own field of interest or work and you will be able to see how the continuum of severity from 'normal' to pathological is evident across many disorders.

Secondly, we aimed to demystify the therapy of dissociative disorders. Each chapter contains clinical illustrations showing how even basic cognitive and behavioural techniques can help to combat the problems associated with dissociation, and each contributor provides 'top-tips' and specific guidelines for working with certain clinical populations. We hope to give you confidence that you can understand and support patients with dissociative disorders rather than assuming that it is outside your capability.

You will find that the book begins with 'foundation' chapters which set the scene. There is a general introduction to dissociation, which means that subsequent writers have not needed to detail the history and phenomenology of dissociation but have been able to focus on their clinical and academic areas of expertise. Kennedy presents an empirically based model of dissociation to help with formulation and beginning to understand cognitive perspectives on dissociation. Pearson outlines dissociation's developmental foundations. Kennerley and Kischka offer a simple (or as simple as we could make it) overview of relevant neuro-psychology as this is so very pertinent to understanding dissociation and making sense of the dissociation literature. This has allowed other contributors to focus on the more practical aspects of various clinical presentations of dissociation, or on particular theoretical models and methods.

The next section of the book describes the roles of imagery (Stopa), and memory (Huntjens, Dorahy and Van Wees-Cieraad), and basic cognitive processes essential in the maintenance and treatment of dissociation.

Subsequent chapters focus on the role of dissociation in specific mental health problems: eating disorders (Mountford), psychosis (Newman-Taylor and Sambrook); borderline personality disorder (Haaland and Landrø); somatoform disorders (Brown); and depersonalization disorder (Hunter). Although there is no chapter entitled post-traumatic stress disorder, PTSD is examined in detail in many chapters, in particular those by Kennerley and Kischka. Next, working with dissociative identity disorder is illustrated using a chapter-length case example (Cowdrill).

Finally, other theoretical-therapeutic approaches relevant to a cognitive orientation are presented along with their clinical implications: an evolutionary psychology approach (Gilbert); a structural approach (Van der Hart and Steele);

perceptual control theory and the method of levels (Mansell and Carey); and acceptance and commitment therapy (Neziroglu and Donelly).

So you can see that we've covered a broad base, illustrating the relevance of dissociation in a wide range of clinical presentations and bringing authors from around the world to focus their expert gaze on the puzzles and problems it poses.

The advent of DSM-5 (*Diagnostic and Statistical Manual, 5th Edition, American Psychiatric Association*) will bring some changes to the categorization of dissociative phenomena and, we hope, further contribute to our understanding of them, and thereby enhance what we are able to offer as clinicians. In our final chapter we consider future directions for dissociation from a cognitive perspective.

By now you realize that we find dissociation fascinating and believe that clinicians can bring significant relief to patients suffering from the consequences of dissociative symptoms. Our hope now is that we can instil in you an eagerness to know more and do more.

Chapter 1

The development of our understanding of dissociation

Fiona C. Kennedy
Helen Kennerley

We have both presented workshops about dissociation and the topic seems to evoke an unusual level of both intrigue and clinical concern. Intrigue because it is fascinating, curious and even rather exotic in some of its presentations and concern because we still lack good guidance on recognizing and managing dissociative symptoms, some of which can be life threatening, so that clinicians are justifiably wary of working with patients with such presentations. This chapter presents an overview of the construct of dissociation. We recognize the wide variety of presentations but bring them together to help clinicians understand and formulate dissociative phenomena and provide researchers with an historical context to their endeavours. In doing this, we review ideas spanning centuries and phenomena which have links with sorcery and celebrity. We also highlight ongoing controversies, as the term dissociation itself and its relevance is still far from clear.

Defining dissociation

Dissociation is described as a 'disruption of the usually integrated functions of consciousness, memory, identity or perception of the environment' (*Diagnostic and Statistical Manual*, text revision edition (DSM IV-TR) American Psychiatric Association, 2000, p. 811). A simple example of 'integrated functions' is a mother hearing a buzzing sound as she pushes her infant in its buggy. She immediately 'sees' an image of a wasp in her mind's eye, accesses memories of wasps and the knowledge that they can sting. She has a frisson of alarm and she looks down to check her baby is safe. In an instant, perception, memory and emotion are *integrated*, leading to rapid and appropriate action. In dissociation, this integration is disturbed. DSM IV-TR states that dissociative phenomena should not be considered inherently pathological, recognizing that we all experience a degree of normal and benign dissociation. For example, the mother might later smell the heavy scent of honeysuckle and for a moment be transported back to a pleasant childhood memory – she will have had a pleasurable flashback – or she might have day-dreamed and not realized that she had walked the length of the park.

The current DSM definition captures many of the qualities of dissociation, but debate around definition continues. A great variety of seemingly disparate

Table 1.1 Phenomena which have been considered dissociative

Memory

amnesia for past events (e.g. a childhood trauma)
amnesia for the recent past (e.g. yesterday's therapy session)
amnesia for important personal information (e.g. one's address)
fugue states (where the person lives for a time as a another person with no
memory of the past)
'reliving' of traumatic events (where a memory is experienced as if here and now)

Sense of Self

depersonalization (feeling like an alien, or disconnected from the body)
derealization (the sense that the environment is not real)
age regression (the person experiences him/herself as a child)
identity confusion (e.g. sexual orientation, political affiliation, opinions, are
unclear/undecided)
identity alteration (e.g. changes from a peace-loving to an aggressive personality)
multiple personalities (two or more 'selves' alternately/simultaneously control the
body) (Dissociative Identity Disorder)
possession states (e.g. angelic/demonic possession)
intermittent loss of skills (e.g. one day the individual can drive, the next day she
says she has no idea how to)

Consciousness/Perception

hallucinations and pseudo-hallucinations (seeing, hearing, smelling or feeling things
which are not actually there)
absorption (e.g. reading a book with reduced awareness of one's surroundings)
hypnotic and other trance states such as automatic writing and medium trance
states
'losing time' (where the person 'comes to' in a given time and place and cannot
remember the immediately preceding events)
flashbacks (where an individual re-experiences past events vividly and emotionally)

Somatic/Bodily Symptoms

non-organic pain
auto-anaesthesia (being unable to feel pain)
somatic symptoms such as gait disturbances, problems urinating
some unexplained medical symptoms (not all unexplained symptoms are
dissociative)
motor inhibition (e.g. being unable to perform certain actions, being rooted to
the spot)
'made behaviors' (automatic behaviors carried out without feeling in control)
non-epileptic seizures

Other Phenomena

emotional numbness
mental blanking (inability to think)
inability to speak

psychological phenomena have been described as dissociative (not all recognized by DSM). Table 1.1 summarizes some of the phenomena which have been described as dissociative: you can see the diversity.

Dissociative states also occur in other psychological disorders, for example: acute stress disorder, PTSD, somatization disorder, panic disorder, schizophrenia, major depressive disorder, eating disorders, borderline personality disorder (BPD) and other personality disorders.

Understanding (and treatment) of dissociation has been hampered by factors such as:

• lack of conceptual clarity: different researchers and clinicians may not use the same language in referring to their work
• isolated study of disparate disturbances associated with dissociation: thus general conclusions are hard to draw
• a dearth of testable models of dissociation undermines understanding and classification of relevant psychological or neurological processes

The function of dissociation

Despite the above debate, research indicates dissociation has well-established links with traumatic events (Van der Kolk, McFarlane, and Weisaeth, 1996), and that dissociation mediates the relationship between trauma and psychopathology (Becker-Lausen, Sanders, and Chinsky, 1995; Griffin, Resick, and Mechanic, 1997; Zatzick, Marmar, Weiss, and Metzler, 1994). It is thought that it serves to reduce awareness of intolerable (traumatic) information (both internally- and externally-derived): exactly how this is achieved is just beginning to be explored, particularly through neurobiological approaches (see Kennerley and Kischka chapters, this volume).

A common view is that dissociation is a defence preventing emotionally unacceptable material from entering consciousness, but there are other views. Brown (2006a, and in this volume) proposes that memory, rather than current experience, may 'over-determine' perception and activate a 'program', a built-in response to a past situation, although the current situation does not warrant that response. Many factors can influence whether rogue memories dominate responses, only one of which is a traumatic past. Worrying about one's health can increase one's vulnerability to rogue representations and produce somatoform symptoms; or traumatic past memories can cause a woman to freeze when having to squeeze past a stranger in a doorway. Mansell and Carey (this volume) show how our perceptual hierarchy naturally splits to allow us to use our imagination and planning capacities, as well as different aspects of ourselves in different situations.

Brown, Gilbert, Kennedy, Mansell and Carey, Pearson and Van der Hart and Steele (all in this volume), and others argue that the fragmentation of the sense of self in dissociative identity disorder (DID, American Psychiatric Association,

2000) and other dissociative presentations may function to resolve conflict between a child's need to *attach* and the need to *protect themselves* from harm which arises when a caregiver is dangerous. The function of dissociation may change and develop over time. For example, a child might have learnt to 'space out' when abused by her father but as an adult finds herself doing so when her therapist invites her to review emotionally painful material. In both situations this detachment is negatively reinforced (because it provides escape) but its function has subtly changed.

The next section of this chapter describes the evolution of thinking about dissociation, emphasizing recent cognitive approaches to provide a context for the book. Keen historians can find a more detailed review in Van der Hart and Dorahy (2009).

From possession to hysteria: the sixteenth–nineteenth century

Early cases of possession and witchcraft

'Possession' and 'witchcraft' can be interpreted, with hindsight, as instances of extreme dissociation, as these cases illustrate (Van der Hart, Lierens, and Goodwin, 1996):

> *In the 16th century Jeanne Fery, a French Dominican nun, claimed identities including Mary Magdalene, and 'devils' Namon and Bélial. An eating disorder seemed related to Jeanne's sexual abuse, aged 4, by a 'demon' named Cornau who gave her sweets. She described self harm caused by a 'devil', Sanguinaire, who wanted pieces of her flesh. The devil Garga protected her from feeling pain but re-enacted childhood beatings by head-banging, throat-cutting and self-strangulation. She suffered seizures, rage attacks, age regression, sleep disturbance, conversion blindness, mutism, intermittent loss of knowledge, skills, and amnesia.*
>
> *In 1623 Sister Benedetta of Italy was 'possessed' by 'boys' who caused chronic pain and spoke in different dialects. One, a nine year old, Splenditello, had a sexual relationship with another nun. She also self-mutilated and suffered eating problems.*

Although classified as 'possession' you can see that these accounts reflect many dissociative phenomena, along with other responses which typically occur alongside dissociation, such as self-harm, suicidal gestures, aggression, mood lability and disordered eating.

Multiple personality

More familiar clinical terminology appeared in the eighteenth and nineteenth century when cases of 'double' personality, with two self-states, were reported by Gmelin in Germany (1791), Mitchell in America (1888) and Azam in France (1876). Myer's case of Louis Vivet (1886) is reported by Faure, Kersten, Koopman and Van der Hart (1997) as the first explicitly described case of multiple personality.

> *Vivet was born of a 'child mother', neglected, beaten, abandoned at the age of seven. He showed many personality states, 'hysterico-epileptic seizures', intermittent paralysis, varying food preferences (e.g. either craving or disliking wine), aggression and stealing interspersed with calm politeness.*

At that time (Camuset, 1882) and recently (Hacking, 1995) authorities questioned whether some or all 'personalities' were the iatrogenic result of treatment in the asylum, and there was questioning by authority of the genuineness of the symptoms, a theme which recurs throughout history. Notable here is the prevalence of somatic symptoms, which commonly occur in dissociation. A further recurring theme is a background of severe child abuse and neglect.

Mediums, automatic writing, hypnosis and hysteria

From the late eighteenth century interest grew in non-pathological dissociation, and in 'hysteria', a pathological disorder (now called conversion or somatoform disorder). Alternating states of consciousness were observed and investigated and our understanding of dissociation moved forward considerably.

Puységur, (1751–1825) a student of Mesmer, noted that when he used magnetism to induce convulsions, some people entered a state which he called 'artificial somnambulism' (later 'hypnosis'). Subjects seemed to have two separate streams of consciousness which were divided from each other during this state, and subsequent amnesia (Van der Hart and Dorahy, 2009).

Moreau de Tours first used the term 'dissociation' (*'désagrégation'*) in France in 1845, understanding it as a lack of integration of ideas, causing a split in the personality. Gros-Jean (1855) and Taine (1878) applied his ideas to automatic writing and to possession states in spiritualist mediums, claiming that two personality states existed concurrently while a 'trance' was occurring. Later, Charcot (1887) used artificial somnambulism/hypnotic states as a model to explain 'hysterical' symptoms such as paralysis, claiming that these symptoms occurred in separated-off states of consciousness.

In summary, by the late nineteenth century scientists had noticed the connection between divided states of consciousness and psychopathology in terms of 'hysteria' and multiple personality.

The late nineteenth–early twentieth century: vehement emotions and repression

Janet, Binet and James

Pierre Janet (1859–1947) made a huge contribution to the study of dissociation, describing flashbacks perhaps for the first time. A contemporary of Freud, Breuer and Charcot, his theoretical model described 'idées fixes' or traumatic memories, with associated 'vehement emotions' as well as images, movements and physiological 'phenomena'. These could alternate with an apparently normal personality state and cause intrusions when triggered by traumatic reminders. While accessing one personality state a person seemed not to experience the trauma, but when accessing the other personality state experienced nothing but the trauma (Janet, 1889, 1907, 1928).

Janet identified secondary idées fixes, or 'hysterical psychosis' such as trauma-related dreams, fantasies or hallucinations. These have since been re-named dissociative psychosis (Van der Hart, Witzum, and Friedman, 1993). He distinguished 'mental accidents' (positive symptoms) namely, intrusions such as pain, automatic movements and perceptions and 'mental stigmata' (negative symptoms) which included loss of sensation, inability to move, amnesia (Nijenhuis and Van der Hart, 1999).

Janet reflected that the sense of self was fragile and that a fragile self could be seen in many disorders, not just those classed as dissociative.

Alfred Binet (1857–1911), best known for his work on intelligence measurement, provided experimental support for Janet's model. He also noted that exchange of information can take place between dissociated personality states even when the person is unaware of the different states (Van der Hart and Dorahy, 2009).

William James in America also spoke of dissociation as a division of consciousness, with normal and abnormal manifestations. He used this to explain hysteria, dreams, hypnotism and multiple personality (Taylor, 1983).

Thus, by the early nineteenth century, links had been made between trauma and dissociative states, and a sophisticated view of the fragility of the self had been developed.

Freud and the disappearance of dissociation

Breuer and Freud developed the idea of hypnotic or dissociated states as divisions in consciousness underlying hysteria (1893). Freud gave childhood trauma a central role in the development of 'hysterical' psychopathology (1896), but soon changed his formulation, developing his theories of intrapsychic pressures between id, ego and superego, with the concept of repression gradually replacing that of dissociation (Erdelyi, 1994). As a result, reports of child abuse and trauma received less attention, such reports often being interpreted as manifestations of repressed sexual wishes, rather than actual events. In the early twentieth century the great influence of psychoanalysis may have contributed to the relative disappearance of thinking about dissociation.

The twentieth century: wars, Hollywood and DSM

The Great Wars: shell shock

Two World Wars resulted in much military trauma, or 'shell shock', some of it well documented by army psychiatrists (e.g. Myers, 1940). Overwhelming traumatic experiences were seen as not psychologically integrated but held in an 'emotional personality': in this state the patient acted as if the trauma were re-occurring. In an 'apparently normal personality' state the patient lacked trauma awareness and would suffer hysteria. Pseudo-epileptic seizures or headaches seemed to precede the emergence of the 'emotional personality', which might be in a state of stupor or terror.

'Shell shock' has been replaced with the terms 'post traumatic stress disorder' (PTSD), acute stress disorder (ASD) and complex PTSD (Herman, 1992a). The structural and various cognitive models of dissociation described in this book converge with and diverge from Myers's work. The structural model follows Myers, conceptualizing all PTSD, complex and simple, as divided personality; the cognitive models see simple PTSD as a failure in integration involving detached states of consciousness and compartmentalized self-states, but not necessarily involving separate personalities with different senses of self.

A re-emergence of interest: the 1960s and 1970s

The case of Eve (Osgood and Luria, 1954), later a film, attracted public attention in the 1950s, yet only in the 1960s did work on drug-induced altered states revive academic interest. Could all altered states of consciousness be described as dissociative (even meditation and yoga) or should the term be reserved for a subset of states? This debate continues today (Van der Hart and Dorahy, 2009). Public interest was further stimulated by the publication of the case of Sybil (Schreiber, 1973) – also made into a film – followed by several popular biographies of apparent DID sufferers.

In the academic world, Hilgard (1977) published his neo-dissociation theory. Hypnotized students reported no pain with their arms in freezing water – but he accessed another state of consciousness in which they could feel the pain (Hilgard, 1974). He christened this the 'hidden observer'. He conceptualized a hierarchical 'central control system' normally controlling many cognitive processes. In overwhelming conditions, this system lost control and other 'control centres' emerged, functioning in parallel. Many cognitive control systems are not accessible to consciousness: Hilgard gave us the example of performing complex driving tasks whilst thinking about other things. Being absorbed in reading, whilst screening out other things was another example of parallel functioning. Thus a broadened definition now included absorption and day-dreaming as examples of non-pathological dissociation. Hilgard's focus on cognitive structures and processes is echoed in modern-day cognitive accounts, e.g. using Perceptual Control Theory (Mansell and Carey, this volume), the Integrated Cognitive Model (Brown, this volume) and Kennedy *et al.*'s levels model (2004 and this volume). So, by the 1970s, information-processing models were having an impact on our thinking about the self, trauma and dissociation.

The late twentieth century: new thinking, new models

The late twentieth century saw revised thinking about dissociation reflected in diagnostic classification systems, new work on the theoretical modelling of dissociation, and revived interest from the psychoanalytic community and others.

Diagnostic confusion

In 1980 DSM-III (APA) re-conceptualized its classification of dissociation. Conversion 'hysteria' shifted to 'somatoform disorders', placing these alongside other conditions which are not considered dissociative. In doing so, the more physical subset of dissociative phenomena lost its connection with the rest. The remainder of the 'hysterical neuroses' were re-classified as 'Dissociative Disorders'. These changes may have contributed to a modern lack of attention to the part dissociation plays in somatic disorders. Separating off 'dissociative disorders' may also have led us to neglect dissociation in a number of trauma-related problems, notably PTSD, but also eating disorders, BPD and anxiety disorders. These changes were continued in DSM-IV (APA, 1994).

ICD-10 (International Classification of Diseases 10, World Health Organization (WHO) 1992) had a 'dissociative (conversion) disorders' category, which included pseudo-neurological symptoms such as paralysis, non-epileptic seizures, sensory loss and gait disturbance. It included trance and possession disorders, which are categorized as 'dissociative disorders not otherwise specified' (DDNOS) in DSM-IV. DSM-IV had a separate category for DID, whereas ICD-10 included it in 'other dissociative (conversion) disorders'.

Depersonalization disorder is not included in the ICD-10 dissociative (conversion) disorders category because it does not involve loss of control over sensation, memory or movement and only minor changes in personal identity (WHO, 1992). PTSD is not categorized as a dissociative disorder in either system, and dissociative symptoms are not a *necessary* criterion for diagnosis of PTSD, yet dissociative symptoms frequently occur in PTSD (Ehlers and Clark, 2000; Foa and Hearst-Ikeda, 1996; Holmes, Grey and Young, 2005). This confusion reflects the disparate phenomena included under the term 'dissociation' and the lack of theoretical understanding as to how they are inter-related.

Ross, Anderson, Fleisher, and Norton (1991) suggested dissociation is part of a hierarchy of diagnostic categories, with DID at the top level, personality disorders and psychoses next, and disorders such as anxiety and depression at the bottom. Thus, people with a diagnosis of DID are likely to also receive diagnoses such as schizophrenia, BPD and depression.

Continuum or category?

Dimensional models (e.g. Hilgard, 1977; Ross, Joshi, and Currie, 1990; Putnam and Carlson, 1996) propose that dissociation becomes a problem at the extreme end of a *continuum*, as found in clinical groups (Kihlstrom, Glisky, and Angiulo, 1994). This view is reflected in the DSM IV-TR definition of dissociation. This has been described as the 'unitary model' (Brown, 2006a), reflecting the idea that one psychological mechanism, 'dissociation', underlies all the phenomena in Table 1.1, the differences between them being due to the 'amount' of dissociation involved. Figure 1.1 illustrates this.

The unitary model formed the basis of the Dissociative Experiences Scale (DES; Carlson, E. B. and Putnam, F. W. 1993), the most commonly used measure, and is supported by research showing that DES scores vary in accordance with the severity of clinical presentation (Van Ijzendoorn and Schuengel, 1996).

Frankel (1994) argued that the concept of dissociation had become over-inclusive and some categories should be excluded; similarly, Cardeña (1994) argued that absorption should not be included. He also distinguished between the following *categories*:

- *Non-integrated mental systems*: a dysfunction in perception, memory or action that (a) cannot be reversed by an act of will (b) occurs in the presence of preserved functioning of the apparently disrupted system (c) is reversible, at least in principle.

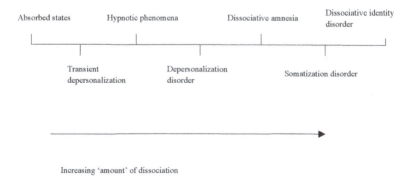

Figure 1.1 The unitary model continuum of dissociation
From Brown (2005), reproduced with permission

- *Altered consciousness* involving a disconnection from the self or the world (e.g. depersonalization, derealization).

Other categorical models included Putnam's (e.g. 1988, 1997): abrupt state-switches can be understood as traumatic experiences producing failure to achieve the major *developmental* task of integrating discrete states of consciousness. Ryle (1995) stated that 'self states' elicit reciprocal reactions from others, (e.g. 'abused child' elicits 'rescuer'). Traumatic experiences can produce dissociation between self states.

Van der Hart, Van der Kolk and Boon's (1996) hierarchical categorical model involved:

- 'primary' dissociation: fragmented processing of threatening aspects of events (e.g. a knife), and reduced processing of other information
- 'secondary' dissociation: perceiving an event without emotion (e.g. recounting a rape with no affect)
- 'tertiary' dissociation: developing separate identities (e.g. abused child self and business person self)

Psychodynamic formulations (e.g. Fonagy, 1991; Mollon, 1996) argued that dissociative processes reflected intra-psychic *defences*. Repeated 'pretending' that trauma is not occurring (denial) and acting 'as if' there is more than one self lessens the impact of trauma.

Nijenhuis (e.g. 2000, 2004) and colleagues introduced a somatoform dissociation category, arguing that conversion disorder symptoms reflect a psychobiological freezing response. There is an excellent body of research around this concept, a summary can be found in Nijhenuis (2009).

So, although it seems natural and attractive to think of a dissociative continuum, the majority of models have been categorical, and the psychological processes underlying the dissociative categories still require elaboration.

Cognitive approaches

In the 1970s and 1980s, there was a great refinement of cognitive theory (see Williams, Watts, Macleod, and Matthews (1997)). Understanding of information processing and emotional processing progressed, offering new ways of conceptualizing dissociation. For example, cognitive and behavioural *avoidance* may slow information processing (Foa and Kozak, 1986) or prevent full inspection of stimulus features (Williams, Watts, MacLeod, and Mathews, 1997). These processes have been shown to occur without conscious awareness (Dixon, 1981; Patton, 1992), and are believed to involve both classical (Nijenhuis and den Boer, 2009) and operant conditioning (Kennerley, 1996). Braun (1988) proposed the cognitive BASK (behaviour, affect, sensation and knowledge) model, suggesting that any or all aspects of experience could be separated off, or dissociated, at any one time (e.g. numbing of affect or mental blanking).

Kennerley (1996) provided a rare practical paper on cognitive approaches to treatment, recommending formulating dissociative reactions in terms of our cognitive understanding of emotion, recognizing the role of classical and operant conditioning (see glossary). Conditioned stimuli often trigger dissociative reactions; dissociative states may negatively reinforce self-harm or eating-disorder behaviours, offering escape from aversive emotions; self harm may be conditioned behaviour to escape from aversive detached states or to induce pleasant dissociative states. She emphasizes the utility of even simple cognitive strategies such as 'grounding' techniques, including using a squeeze ball, devising a 'safe place in mind' as well as agreed prompts (finger click or safe word) to help patients regain a sense of 'here and now'. Throughout the book, contributing authors provide more specific formulations of different types of dissociation and offer practical guidance.

The construct of schema avoidance (Young, 1999), has clear parallels with dissociation. Unbearable affect may be associated with a pathological schema (a cognitive framework or concept that helps organize and interpret information); the individual makes strenuous efforts to avoid the unbearable affect, e.g. consciously avoiding new challenges if they have a 'failure to achieve' schema, unconsciously orienting attention away from threatening written material describing failure. Young's later work on 'modes' (self states) in personality disorders (e.g. 'abused child', 'angry protector') provides a potential framework for working with disso-ciated self states.

These cognitive accounts addressed dissociative symptoms rather than syndromes, and so were applicable to a range of mental health problems. Yet, these processes were not yet articulated as a coherent model, nor elaborated within a broader cognitive perspective.

Cognitive and structural approaches in the twenty-first century

The 'dual representation' model of PTSD proposed by Brewin and colleagues (1996), described two levels of information processing: situationally accessed memories (SAMs) and verbally accessed memories (VAMs). SAMs were driven by stimulus similarity (e.g. a man with blue eyes triggers memories of an abuser, also with blue eyes); VAMs were integrated with autobiographical (personal) memory, with a sense of location in time. Failure to integrate SAMs into VAMs was held to produce flashbacks: the emotionally laden SAM retained a sense of 'here and now' – it was dissociated in time. Brewin, Gregory, Lipton, and Burgess (2010) revised the model to embrace imagery across psychological disorders (see Stopa, 2009 and this volume), retaining the theme of failure to integrate infor-mation processing systems.

In 2000, Ehlers and Clark published a cognitive model of PTSD: in cognitive models, anxiety generally results from appraisals of impending threat, yet PTSD relates to an event which has *already happened*. So they proposed that PTSD occurs if trauma processing results in a sense of current threat – if it is dissociated in time. Whilst PTSD sufferers often struggle to recall voluntarily traumas such as a car accident, they have *involuntary* recall in the form of intrusive sensory impressions (images of an approaching car, sounds of screeching tyres, smell of burning rubber). Like Brewin, Ehlers and Clark proposed that trauma memories are poorly integrated into autobiographical memory, which would provide context in time and place. Trauma memories remain in implicit memory (see glossary), with strong classically conditioned links, easily triggered by environmental cues. Ehlers and Clarke provide a treatment protocol for re-processing trauma memories through therapeutic re-living strategies, allowing traumatic recollections to be 'properly' stored in autobiographical memory. Ehlers and Clark mention dissociation (depersonalization and derealization) as a poorly understood cognitive response that might inhibit integration of trauma memories into autobiographical memory. So, they include dissociation as a factor but do not elaborate what processes might be involved and how these might interact with the rest of the model.

In 2005 Holmes and co-workers published a most helpful paper following Cardeña's (1994) and Allen's (2001) work, arguing that there is convincing evidence for a dichotomy between two qualitatively different phenomena; 'detachment' and 'compartmentalization'.

- Detachment incorporates depersonalization and derealization, out-of-body experiences, 'spacing out' and feelings of unreality, with little disturbance to sense of identity. It often occurs peri-traumatically (during the trauma) and during recollections of the trauma. Different types of detachment often occur together, reflecting a possible common neurobiological mechanism (see Kennerley and Kischka chapters, this volume). Detachment may prevent encoding of information, leading to fragmented recall. This amnesia *would not be reversible*, since it involves an encoding failure.
- Compartmentalization is 'a deficit in the ability to deliberately control processes or actions that would normally be amenable to such control' (Holmes *et al.*, 2005, p. 7). It includes inability to bring normally accessible information into conscious awareness (e.g. past experience of child abuse). Compartmentalization deficits cannot be overcome by an act of will but *are* reversible in principle, because material has been encoded in memory. Functions no longer amenable to control (e.g. the walking function in loss of gait) are seen as compartmentalized. So somatoform symptoms or conversion disorders are included in this category in line with Janet's (1907) view that hysterical symptoms are produced by the separation of traumatic material from consciousness. Compartmentalized processes continue to operate normally and can influence emotion, cognition and action (Brown 2002a, b, 2004; Cardeña, 1994; Kihlstrohm, 1992). Detachment and compartmentalization are distinct processes typically occurring in isolation but, in certain conditions such as PTSD, they may occur together.

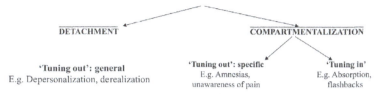

Dissociation can occur at differing points in information processing

DETACHMENT   COMPARTMENTALIZATION

'Tuning out': general   'Tuning out': specific   'Tuning in'
E.g. Depersonalization, derealization   E.g. Amnesias,   E.g. Absorption,
                                   unawareness of pain   flashbacks

Each of these presentations can be experienced along a spectrum of severity
from non-pathological to extremely dysfunctional and can be psychological
or physical

Figure 1.2 The dichotomy model of dissociation
Reproduced from Kennerley (2009), with permission

Figure 1.2 illustrates this concept, but also reminds us that any specific presentation of dissociation can be experienced along a continuum of severity. The treatment implications are that when detachment is a problem, the therapist works towards preventing detachment being triggered, and terminating the state when it occurs; in compartmentalization, the therapist works towards reactivation and reintegration of compartmentalized elements of an experience. Formulating the problem with the patient and addressing their *interpretation* of their symptoms is also vital. This body of work helps us to organize our thinking, treatment and research from a cognitive perspective. Yet we still need to address disturbances to identity, the sense of self, involved in problems such as personality disorders and DID.

The self and its discontents: cognitive approaches in the twenty-first century

Cognitive theorists have written little about the self, except to focus on the negative content of self-beliefs. Useful self theories have been borrowed from social psychology, where the most advances have been made in understanding how the self is constructed and regulated (Stopa, 2009). Several cognitive theorists have used the notion of a 'working self-concept', a schema for organizing information about the self, stressing the link between autobiographical memory and the self (e.g. Conway and Pleydell-Pearce, 2000). Working self-concept may be represented through self-images: for example, someone with social phobia having images of sweating and trembling whilst giving a presentation. Stopa (this volume) explores the importance of imagery in dissociation and how to use imagery to address problems including negative or unhelpful self-schemas.

People are motivated to maintain a positive sense of self (Sedikes and Gregg, 2003) but those with an abuse history tend to hold negative self-views which persist and are difficult to change (Stopa, 2009). People with personality disorders and DID fail to integrate different aspects of the self into one over-arching self schema: we see a continuum of identity disturbance, from dis-jointed to dis-integrated. This is particularly the case when trauma is superimposed on developmental processes, and when the threat comes from carers, though single events can also disturb the sense of self. PTSD patients frequently feel they have lost their 'old self'; in depersonalization disorder there is a feeling of disconnection from self. Where a sense of self has been built *before* the trauma, it is generally easier to restore it. Gilbert (this volume) describes the use of compassion-based interventions to aid the healing or re-construction of the self.

The theory of structural dissociation of the personality, outlined by Van der Hart and Steele in this book, holds that detachment phenomena (altered states of consciousness) are related to, but separate from, dissociation. For them, the term dissociation is equivalent to compartmentalization of the personality, or multiple selves. They describe effects of PTSD on personality structure (following Myers,1940): an 'apparently normal person' (ANP) negotiates with the outside world, an 'emotional personality' (EP) holds the trauma memory separate. This division of consciousness is responsible for many of the symptoms of PTSD. In DID, there can be many EPs and also several ANPs as consciousness divides to cope with repeated and severe childhood trauma. Nijenhuis (2011) outlines a philosophical analysis of what constitutes a 'self' in terms of relationships with objects in the world and ability to reflect on one's own experience.

Developmental approaches have much to offer the understanding of the effects of trauma on the self. Putnam's (1997) approach has already been mentioned, and Pearson's (this volume) contribution shows how neglect and abuse during development obstruct essential developmental tasks required for cognitive, emotional and relational maturity. Disorganized attachment patterns in adult dissociation (Liotti, 2006, 2009) as well as the neurobiology of attachment (Schore, 2009) deserve more attention from cognitive theorists looking to elaborate the development of self from a cognitive perspective and the impact of trauma on this development.

Kennedy *et al.*'s (2004) dissociation model is based on Beck's (1996) model of personality. This has three levels of information processing: automatic (threat) perception and response schemas; strategic information-processing modes including thoughts, feelings, physiological and behavioural responses; and personality structure, linked to autobiographical memory, consisting of integrated self states (clusters of modes of responding which have evolved over an individual's lifetime). When this 'normal' information-emotional processing system is overwhelmed by trauma, the typical associative style of processing may switch to a dissociative or inhibitory style. This can result in damage to the *formation* of the self, including changed personality structure, as in personality disorders and DID. This altered structure may be maintained because it offers advantages to the child in extremis, such as allowing attachment to a carer and reduced awareness of danger when that carer is *not* dangerous, yet self-preservation when the carer is abusive (see Kennedy, this volume). Cowdrill (this volume) describes a cognitive approach to working with severe disruption to the self in a DID patient.

In summary, cognitive thinkers are beginning to make the leap from theory to practice in the complex area of understanding the self and consciousness, as well as in specific trauma reactions such as PTSD. Understanding dissociation is central to many of these formulations.

Forgetting important things: understanding dissociative amnesia

An obvious lay conclusion is that a traumatic event is burnt into one's consciousness forever. The counter-intuitive nature of dissociative amnesia and highly charged emotions around 'recovered' memories have produced fierce debate. Amnesia may result from failure to encode material during periods of detachment; *dissociative* amnesia occurs in compartmentalization where there is encoding but inhibition of retrieval. A substantial minority of individuals reporting childhood sexual abuse also report a period of partial or complete forgetting of these experiences (Brown, Scheflin and Whitfield, 1999). Therapists might be familiar with the patient who seems disturbed, showing patterns of behaviour, such as re-victimization, consistent with an abuse history, but denies anything but a happy childhood. The dilemma is having a duty of care not to suggest an abusive history, along with the imperative to assist patients in making sense of their problems. The False Memory Syndrome Society was established in the US, to defend, among other things, the rights of parents falsely accused of abuse. This led to a public perception that a syndrome exists, although of course there is no such diagnostic category.

The literature on 'lost' memories questions the extent and deliberateness of forgetting and stresses the dangers of memory recovery techniques (Lindsay and Briere (1997), Lindsay and Read (1995), Loftus (1993) McNally (2003)). The American Psychological Association (1996) and the British Psychological Society (Morton *et al.*, 1995) strongly advise against the use of suggestion techniques, hypnotic regression, guided imagery or 'truth drugs' in efforts to recover memories. Schachter (1999) reviews the evidence that a pseudo-memory may be created through suggestion, post-event misinformation and other processes. Kennerley and Kischka (this volume) describe the psychobiology of normal memory. Huntjens, Dorahy and Van Wees-Cieraad (this volume) provide a detailed review of the interactions between memory and dissociation.

In summary, the study of dissociation can help clinicians and patients understand the many different kinds of amnesia and memory disturbances we see following trauma, and the profound effects on identity amnesia can have.

Conclusion

The term dissociation has been used since Moreau de Tours's coining, and the themes of lack of integration and divided consciousness remain. A better understanding of the term has begun, assisted by systematic psychological research and new neurobiological information. The dichotomy between detachment and compartmentalization, along with focus on specific psychological states and disorders, allows us to begin formulating the information-processing systems producing dissociative phenomena. These systems seem primarily to involve abnormal processing of traumatic information within memory systems. This affects autobiographical memory, the seat of our 'personal story', and thus our sense of self (Conway, 2005).

During trauma, the individual's response may include detachment, allowing more effective coping (thinking calmly without affect), but *preventing encoding* of information and leading to fragmented memory. Trauma response may also include compartmentalization, where there *is* encoding of information but it *cannot be accessed by an effort of will*, preventing elaboration and integration of traumatic memories. The inability to retrieve compartmentalized information at will is accompanied by intrusions or unintentional retrieval (whether of images in the broadest sense; of affect, thoughts, behaviour and physiological responses; or of 'personalities'). Strong classically conditioned associations to threat may trigger these intrusions. An individual's identity is vital to their mood, relationships and functioning. Traumatic memories with 'meanings' that would destroy self-respect or conflict with essential developmental needs may remain unintegrated to preserve a functional sense of self.

More is written about understanding dissociation than treating it. Dissociation is only ever part of the clinical picture: eating disorders, anxiety, personality disorders, simple and complex PTSD, psychosis, somatoform as well as dissociative disorders, can all involve dissociation. This book aims to provide up-to-date information and guidance for the academic and clinician alike, so that we can identify dissociation in the many contexts in which it is found, and deliver best practice to fellow human beings who dare to trust us to help ameliorate their suffering.

Chapter 2

Dissociation, personality and psychopathology

A cognitive approach

Fiona C. Kennedy

Frequently Asked Questions

- What might I see in therapy to make me think I'm dealing with dissociation?
- What do I do if my client seems not to be able to remember anything about the traumatic event?
- What should I do if my client seems to be different 'people'? Can this really happen?
- How does dissociation affect personality?
- Does my client have schizophrenia or dissociation? He hears voices and has a history of abuse.
- My client can walk one day but seems to need a wheelchair the next. She must be malingering, mustn't she?
- What do I do if I think my client may be dissociating?
- What exactly is dissociation?

This chapter presents a revised theory of dissociation (Kennedy *et al.*, 2004) to help with these questions. It builds on Beck's (1996) and Beck and Clark's (1997) model of three levels, or stages of information-processing and personality systems.

Dissociation may affect any or all of these levels (Figure 2 below):

1 'Automatic dissociation' (during pre-conscious processing of incoming stimuli);
2 'Within-mode dissociation' (thoughts, feelings, behaviours and physical responses which become inaccessible to conscious awareness);
3 'Between-mode dissociation' (dissociated self-states, or aspects of the personality).

The chapter shows how the theory helps in formulating mental health problems and constructing treatment.

What is dissociation?

This chapter follows Allen (2001) and Holmes *et al.* (2005), using the concepts of *detachment* and *compartmentalization*. It acknowledges a continuum from 'normal' detached states of consciousness (e.g. day-dreaming, planning ahead, being absorbed in music) to pathological or problematic dissociation.

Detachment is characterized by **alterations in consciousness**. It is thought to be a consequence of the fight/flight/freeze response, when the brain and body are flooded with hormones such as adrenaline and cortisol (Holmes *et al.*, 2005). Symptoms include: depersonalization (feeling detached from one's body, including out of body experiences); derealization, (feeling the environment is unreal); and numbing of emotions.

In detachment, information is not fully stored (encoded) and so cannot be accessed later either by an act of will or through hypnosis (Kuyk, Spinhoven, and Van Dyck, 1999). *Compartmentalization* is the **inaccessibility of information** which is actually encoded and stored in the brain. Neurological systems underlying skills such as walking, for example, remain intact but are inaccessible however much the individual wants to use them. Similarly with memories when information is stored but not available.

Compartmentalization involves abnormal processing of traumatic information, so that it is stored without being integrated into the normal memory systems which provide context in space and time for a given event. This may lead to intrusive images or 'flashbacks' being experienced as if they are re-occurring here and now. Dissociation may *prevent* normal processing and integration of memories (Ehlers and Clark, 2000; Huntjens, Dorahy and Van Wees-Cieraad, this volume). In 1994 this author suggested that dissociation (compartmentalization) could be produced by the firing of nerve cells to *actively inhibit* the normal associative neural connections (Dixon, 1981; Kennedy, *et al.*, 2004). 'Accidental' consequences of detachment and compartmentalization, such as not integrating information about trauma, may negatively reinforce (strengthen) inhibitory activation of neurones, providing *escape* from and *avoidance* of, unbearable experiences.

For example, a child assaulted by a parent experiences a 'fight/flight/freeze' response to the threat: adrenaline courses through her blood and prevents memory storage of much of the attack (detachment). Some information is stored, but separately from her normal memory systems (compartmentalization). When as an adult she tries to remember this information, she finds it cannot be recalled with an act of will. Each time she tries to remember and fails, she (unwittingly) escapes from re-experiencing the awfulness of the event, as well as the possible consequences of recalling the event, such as family disintegration. So, the dissociative response becomes stronger and more established. All of this is of course happening outside her conscious awareness. Consciously, she may feel trepidation but also frustration that she cannot 'make sense' of her life, and concern about her poor memory.

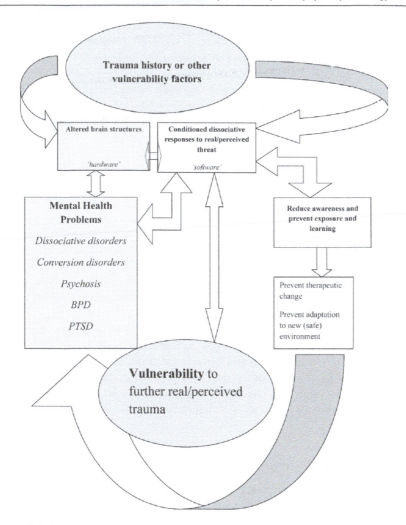

Figure 2.1 Dissociation and mental health problems

Figure 2.1 shows a general formulation of the role played by dissociation in mental health problems. Dissociation in response to trauma results in classically conditioned or paired associate learning: previously innocent stimuli become labelled (conditioned) as threatening.

These stimuli can trigger an (inappropriate) threat response at any time in the future: dissociation then re-occurs as a learned (conditioned) response. Dissociation prevents exposure to the emotion of fear and so prevents learning that there is now no need to be afraid, thus maintaining mental health problems.

A woman inpatient collapsed unconscious at seemingly unpredictable times. Some staff regarded this as 'attention-seeking', since it resulted in care-giving. Recording of the behaviour revealed she turned pale and felt sick just before she collapsed. The collapses were triggered by people talking about abuse of any kind. As a child she had been severely beaten by her father, these attacks only ending when she lost consciousness. The problem now was that, because she collapsed at any mention or reminder of abuse, she was unable to learn that the threat was no longer present.

The levels of dissociation theory

Background: Beck's model of personality

Beck (1996) proposed that personality is constructed of a collection of 'modes'. A mode is a set of schemas responsible for encoding cognitive, affective, behavioural and physiological information and for generating responses. Orienting schemas encode internal and external *events* and activate modes in response. This orienting process occurs *automatically*, without conscious effort or volition (Beck and Clark, 1997).

Beck formulates a phobia of lifts thus: the personality contains a mode, (set of schemas) with information about how to feel (scared), think ('I can't cope'), react physically (sweat, shake) and behavioural urges (avoid, run away), when travelling in lifts. This mode is only activated when the orienting schemas process relevant input (e.g. my friend suggests dinner at the top of the Eiffel Tower). In the absence of threats, the mode remains inactive and the person quite untroubled.

Dissociation in the context of Beck's model.

Normally, there is information exchange (associative processing) between schemas and throughout the system. According to the 'levels' model, dissociation is the product of inhibitory *decoupling* (compartmentalization) of mental processes at three information processing stages: automatic processing (orienting schemas) strategic processing (within modes) and conscious control systems (between modes)[1]. Figure 2.2 illustrates the relationship between the three stages.

Dissociation in the levels model represents a switch from the normal associative information processing involved in Beck's model, to inhibition of this associative processing, producing compartmentalization. This may come (through negative reinforcement, or 'escape from awareness' (Heatherton and Baumeister, 1991)) to serve a 'defensive' process, keeping traumatic information outside of conscious awareness. The impact of a switch to dissociative instead of associative information processing is hypothesized to impact the various levels outlined in Beck's model as follows:

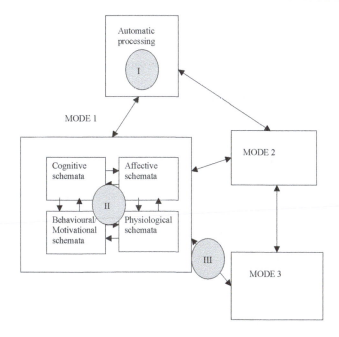

I **Dissociation in response to automatic association with threatening stimulus features** results in failure to further integrate incoming information (DETACHMENT) and 'traumatic' rather than 'normal' memory storage (COMPARTMENTALIZATION). Incomplete dissociation results in **intrusive imagery**: visual, auditory, somatic, olfactory experiences which may have an hallucinatory and 'here and now' quality.

II **Dissociation of links between cognitive, affective, motivational/behavioural, physiological schemata** results in **inaccessibility** (COMPARTMENTALIZATION) of thought/feelings/behaviour or motivation/physiological responses (e.g., flattened affect, conversion symptoms). Incomplete dissociation results in **intrusive** thoughts/feelings/behaviour or motivation/physiological responses (e.g. non-organic pain; behavioural re-enactment of trauma).

III **Dissociation of links between modes** results in identity disturbances (COMPARTMENTALIZATION) ranging from dissociative identity disorder (relatively complete dissociation) through borderline personality disorder to severe mood or state switching (relatively incomplete dissociation).

Figure 2.2 Personality structure and stages of dissociation

Level 1 'Automatic dissociation'

Hypothesized to occur at the level of orienting schemas, and within the limbic system or mid-brain, both during and on recall of a trauma, this level of dissociation results in compartmentalization during and post trauma. Detachment (see below) may occur simultaneously.

The orienting schemas associatively process incoming information from the body or the environment, just until the input is *recognized* as a severe threat. Such recognition is based on stimulus features of the input (colour, smell, sounds, physical sensation, etc), very like Brewin, Dalgleish, and Joseph's (1996) 'situationally accessed memories' (SAMs). Further processing of information at the orienting schema level then stops.

Once the input has been matched with existing information in the orienting schemas, and identified as threatening, information is relayed direct to the amygdala (Kennerley and Kischka this volume) where the fight/flight/freeze response is triggered. Adrenaline, cortisol and other chemicals released as a result may inhibit further processing (encoding) of incoming information and produce symptoms of *detachment* such as spacing out, depersonalization and derealization.[2]

The brain stores information about the different aspects of any event in separate parts of the sensory and association cortices, sounds in the auditory cortex, sights in the visual cortex, etc. Usually the hippocampus would integrate these aspects into a whole experience, but high perceived levels of threat may inhibit hippocampal functioning during and immediately after trauma, so that the experience remains compartmentalized or 'fragmented' (see Huntjens, Dorahy and Van Wees-Cieraad, this volume). Upon efforts to recall the trauma, a similar set of reactions may occur, again preventing integration of the material.

Because threat perception has to be crude, quick and focus on stimulus characteristics of threat, various stimuli come to be classically conditioned to the threat: previously innocent features come to be indicative of threat and can produce *intrusive imagery*. Intrusive imagery is seen as the break through into consciousness of compartmentalized trauma-related material.

> *Mary was raped by a man with blue eyes. She was having dinner with a colleague, who happened to have the same shade of blue eyes. Suddenly she felt severe pelvic pain, the same pain she had felt when she was raped. Because the information about pain was not integrated with other aspects of the experience, she did not 're-live' it, that is, she did not see, hear or smell the rapist.*

It is known that dissociative responses involving detachment and compartmentalization occur not only in response to a traumatic event but also upon recall of the event (Huntjens, Dorahy and Van Wees-Cieraad, this volume). Stimulus characteristics about an event are stored together at the same time. In normal recall processes, the network of stimulus characteristics is recalled as a complete memory (Kennerley and Kischka, this volume). However, dissociative responses inhibit recall of stored information about trauma, either completely or partially (Kennerley and Kischka, this volume). Break-through imagery is triggered as a result of partial dissociation at level 1: only a part of the stored network becomes available, recall of the rest is inhibited. Whenever this happens there is an opportunity for more of the stored network to become available to consciousness, but dissociation at level 1 may prevent the rest of the networked information becoming available. In contexts where there is a trusting and safe relationship, e.g. in therapy or a loving relationship, dissociative responses may cease to be triggered upon recall of traumatic information, allowing more and more of the traumatic memory to enter conscious awareness. The client may not only see, but also hear and feel the trauma, culminating in a 're-living' experience, when the person experiences *all* sensory aspects of the event *as if it is happening again.* Although all sensory aspects of the event are now conscious, the memory is still not stored in a 'time-line' with other memories and personal information, and so it still feels like it is happening 'now'.

> *During a therapy session, Mary was recalling the pelvic pain she felt during the dinner with a colleague. Suddenly she saw the blue eyes of her rapist, felt severe pelvic pain, and a choking sensation in her throat. She viewed the event from above, as if she were looking from the ceiling.*

In this example one might conclude that Mary's condition was deteriorating, and it would be very distressing for the client. However, an understanding of how dissociation reduces and allows conscious experiencing might lead us to formulate that this represents an improvement: traumatic material is becoming available for processing in a non-dissociative way. Mary might be helped by understanding this too, as well as by learning ways to manage the accompanying distress.

Dissociation at Level 2

After processing at the orienting schema level, according to Beck (1996), there is activation of a mode. The mode contains stored information as to how to think, feel, behave and respond physiologically to the situation. Slower 'strategic' processing involves more of the brain cortex and most people are able consciously to observe and report thoughts, feelings etc. For example, Beck's 'lift mode' contained schemas for negative thoughts, the emotion of fear, physiological arousal (fight/flight) and the urge to run away.

Level 2 dissociation renders some of these schemas within a mode inaccessible to consciousness (compartmentalization): the person may be unable to experience any *emotion* about, say, a death.

'Mental blanking' or inability to *think* can be conceptualized as compartmentalization of thoughts or cognitive aspects of an experience. Behavioural schemas within a mode may be compartmentalized, resulting in inability to carry out certain *skills*, such as walking or talking. Such problems may be temporary and only occur in response to triggers reminiscent of the trauma: these triggers may not be apparent to the person suffering, and may be seen as 'malingering' by those around the person because of their transient nature and the fact that there is no organic basis to the symptoms. Physiological compartmentalization may occur, resulting in inability to feel pain, for example. These could be described as level 2 *negative symptoms*.

Because these aspects of experience are compartmentalized, conditioned triggers may produce *intrusive* experiences, activating of schemas at inappropriate times. Thoughts about a trauma might intrude during a birthday party; anger may burst into the awareness of a soldier playing football with his son. Behavioural intrusions may occur: self-harm behaviours sometimes mirror previous abuse. Physiologically, trauma-related symptoms of fatigue, exhaustion, or seizures can occur.

> *A refugee from Afghanistan experienced non-epileptic seizures: his eyes rolled in his head and he became unresponsive to those around. His arms moved backwards as if pinned behind him and his head thrashed side to side as if he was struggling to escape.*

These intrusive level two symptoms could be described as *positive symptoms*.

Dissociation at Level 3

In Beck's 1996 model, modes are integrated into a 'personality'. A specialized set of schemas represent the concept of 'self', 'I' or 'me', the conscious control system. This system contains a sense of identity, choice, values and will. Sometimes a mode is in conflict with conscious values and intentions. The conscious control system can, with practice, over-ride the mode's activation. In the lift example, the conscious control system could over-ride the behavioural urge to flee, and 'reason with' irrational thoughts. At level 3, dissociation produces and maintains *more than one conscious control system*, evolved adaptively, often in childhood, to cope with irresolvable conflicts between the need for nurturing and attachment and the need for self-preservation in the context of an abusing carer or carers (Johnson, 2009).

These modes, which underlie our interpretation of and responses to the physical and social world, may be learned relatively separately in early childhood and later joined together to form an integrated sense of self, a developmental task in itself. This is not a new concept (see for example Putnam, 1997). In level 3 dissociation this integration may occur between some modes only and not others. PTSD symptoms encountered during childhood abuse may be isolated in a few modes within the personality structure. A separate sense of self may develop around these isolated clusters of modes.[3]

Compartmentalization of clusters of *modes* can limit personality damage and allow pseudo-normal attachment to dangerous caregivers.

A compartmentalized cluster of modes with its own conscious control system is known a 'dissociated self-state'. Dissociated self-states may be one source of confused identity and state-switching in borderline personality disorder (BPD). In dissociative identity disorder (DID), self-states are so dissociated that one

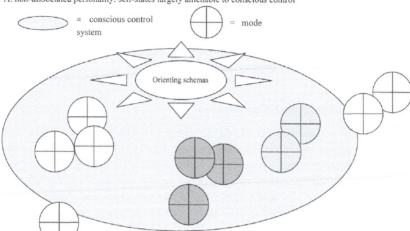

A. non-dissociated personality: self-states largely amenable to conscious control

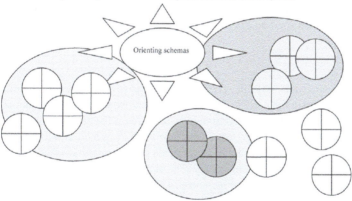

B. dissociated personality: self states within separate conscious control systems

Figure 2.3 Conscious control systems in non-dissociated and dissociated personalities

self-state experiences other self-states as 'not me'. Clients may describe their self-states as 'sharing' their body or as alien, outside the body, or as unwelcome 'invaders' taking over the body. [4]

The Wessex Dissociation Scale (WDS)

Developed to measure levels of dissociation, the WDS has good reliability and validity (Kennedy *et al.*, 2004; Braakmann, Knackstedt, and Schwieger (submitted)). Factor analyzes broadly support levels 1 and 2 dissociation but not level 3. A mixed-method study by Braakmann and colleagues uses the WDS and qualitative interviews with BPD, PTSD and DID clients to clarify level 3 phenomena (Braakmann, personal communication). The WDS produces scores for level 1, 2 and 3 dissociation which can be used in formulation and outcome assessment (see Appendix 2.1).

Assessing amnesia and dissociation

'Psychogenic' amnesia is considered definitive of DID (Steinberg, 1994; DSM IV-TR, 2000) but the information-processing model implies amnesias at each level, with corresponding 'positive' symptoms because dissociation is always incomplete: not all pathways can be permanently inhibited successfully. The clinician should carefully assess the kinds of memory problems presented.

The 'self-memory system' (SMS) theory (Conway, Singer, and Tagini, 2004) is a useful tool to help researchers and clinicians think about memory and dissociation. Autobiographical memory (key memories and beliefs about the self), episodic memory (memories of recent relevant events) and the 'working self' (organizing current experience and 'being in the psychological present') are all important ways that memory interacts with our sense of self. Each of these types of memory can be disturbed by dissociation.

Level 1

Memory *of the trauma* may be fragmented because compartmentalization prevents recall; amnesia for periods of the trauma may exist because detachment has lead to a failure to encode information at all: this information will not be recoverable. The person may have lost consciousness during the trauma resulting in gaps in memory: the clinician should always rule out organic brain damage as a result of injury. Compartmentalization may inhibit recall of aspects of the trauma during treatment, and detachment in response *to the trauma memory* may prevent exposure so that treatment becomes ineffective.

Level 2

Behavioural, physiological, affective or cognitive schemas may be unavailable to consciousness (compartmentalized). The client may say 'I have forgotten how to walk'. These functions are not forgotten in the normal sense, just *unavailable*. The client may become unable to think (cognitive schema unavailable because of dissociation) whilst discussing a trauma, or even during normal conversation (when classically conditioned stimuli may trigger a trauma response). This will interfere with information and emotional processing during therapy, resulting in lack of therapeutic progress and possibly amnesia for parts of the session.

Level 3

Compartmentalized self-states can result in amnesia for recent events, affecting episodic memory, and interrupt personal narrative, affecting autobiographical memory. Self-states with separate conscious control systems may not have access to information processed by other conscious control systems. Symptoms include 'losing' chunks of time, even whole life-periods; 'coming to' suddenly with no knowledge of immediately preceding events; ignorance of appointments or conversations which occurred whilst in a dissociated self-state.

Clinicians and researchers need to be very specific in identifying and assessing these different kinds of amnesias. Amnesia can generally be seen as missing information: the brain has a tendency to complete the 'Gestalt' or whole picture, which can result in the construction of narratives about events which are plausible but may never have actually occurred. Actively imagining a situation increases the likelihood of a memory being created of an event that never happened (Heaps and Nash, 1999). Each time an intrusive image or flashback occurs, the brain may attempt to complete the picture, which will in turn interact with stored memories. Thus deliberate efforts to recall traumatic material can lead to confusion and inaccurate recall.

All memory is, by definition, reconstructed (see Kennerley and Kischka, this volume; Stopa, this volume); memories 'recovered' during therapy are even more vulnerable to distortion because of the 'join the dots' activity of the brain in response to amnesia. Clinicians can validate the personal meaning of these memories whilst not subscribing to the idea that they accurately represent facts.

Diagnoses and dissociation

Table 2.1 organizes diagnostic categories according to a continuum of severity of dissociation. Less severe presentations may involve only levels 1 and 2, for example, Type I ('simple', often single trauma) PTSD. 'Re-living' or exposure treatments (Ehlers and Clark, 2000) are effective and recommended by NICE. Identity disturbance (level 3) characterizes more severe presentations. In BPD, for example, the individual may not have the emotional resilience to manage re-living approaches (Kennerley, 2009). Techniques such as imagery re-scripting (Layden *et al.*, 1993) work with intrusive imagery without risking re-traumatizing the person.

Treating dissociation

Cognitive and Behavioural processes influencing dissociation

Cognitive therapy is underpinned by an understanding and formulation of the cognitive processes maintaining the problem. Clinical formulation of dissociative responding is likely to be part of a wider general formulation of the client's

Table 2.1 Levels of dissociation along with treatment strategies for different mental health presentations

Diagnostic category	Focus of work	Recommended techniques	Structure needed	Level of dissociation	Level of risk
Simple/Type I PTSD (one-off trauma)	Re-process compartmentalized trauma memory Address meaning of event and consequences e.g. shame, guilt, loss	Exposure/'re-living' and Cognitive restructuring (Ehlers & Clark, 2000) Compassionate mind Mindfulness 'Grounding' if detachment-type dissociation present	Usual CBT requirements: basic faith in therapist and treatment Orientation and consent of client Relatively short-term work	lower (1 & 2)	lower
Complex/Type II PTSD (recurrent trauma often during development and at hands of carers) Borderline Personality Disorder with less severe dissociation Depersonalization disorder Conversion/ Somatization disorders e.g. non-organic pain, non-epileptic seizures, loss of physical function Dissociation based psychosis	Develop attachment/ trust Develop self soothing Develop self control Process meaning of traumatic history and consequences Address associated problems/ co-morbidity e.g. self-harm, substance misuse, eating disorder	Dialectical Behaviour Therapy (DBT) approaches: group skills training for emotion regulation and distress tolerance; individual therapy for functional analysis of maladaptive behaviour; dialectical approach to relationship Schema therapy approaches Compassionate mind approaches Use graded approach to trauma, imagery re-scripting, grounding Do not use/allow 're-living' if possible to prevent	DBT structure including : Life goals/values Behavioural targets Motivational work Highly structured sessions Therapist supervision and support Multi-disciplinary team (MDT) setting Risk to self and others management plan	high (1,2 &3)	high
Borderline Personality Disorder with severe dissociation Dissociative Disorder Not Otherwise Specified (DDNOS) Dissociative Fugue Dissociative Identity Disorder (DID)	As for box above, plus Develop awareness of self-states Develop acceptance of self-states Develop control of self states ?Integrate self states	As for box above plus Mapping the system Group/family metaphor: therapist works with 'group' Individual skills training	As above plus Specialist therapist supervision and support Active 'management' of MDT members and other agencies by therapist Risk management prioritized	highest	highest

problems as a whole. Both classical and operant conditioning are important mechanisms which can maintain dissociative responding. Formulation should also consider meta-cognitions (Wells, 2000): the client's beliefs and expectations about dissociation, (e.g. whether it means she is possessed, or mad, whether it can be treated and whether she should be ashamed of it) will affect the therapeutic approach. Exposure is often the 'antidote' to dissociative responding and may be achieved through behavioural procedures and mindfulness/acceptance approaches. However, the clinician needs to balance stabilization, building the client's understanding and coping resources, with gradual exposure to traumatic material without de-stabilizing the client.

Phases of treatment

Linehan (1993), Steele, Van der Hart and Nijenhuis (2005), and others, advocate a 'phased' approach to disorders associated with complex trauma:

1. Developing/tolerating attachment and stabilizing behaviour
2. Re-visiting and re-processing traumatic experiences
3. Re-stabilizing and adapting to normal life.

In Phase 1 work, detailed discussion of the trauma is often impossible for the client, and the therapist should discourage it as much as possible in case further destabilization and compartmentalization should occur. The author's experience is that Phase 2 may be brief: re-processing traumatic experience may occur without detailed re-visiting of trauma, as a result of validation of the client's pain and changing her responses in the here and now. For example, a client who has suffered extensive intra-familial abuse since she was a tiny child does not need to re-live every abusive incident that comes to consciousness during therapy. Often memories are amalgams of many events and the important therapeutic response is to respond with empathy, along with helping the client to process the events in terms of their effects on her life and their meaning to her.

Basic treatment principles

- Use a 'pre-therapy' stage: client and therapist explore proposed treatment and why they want to do it, identify the client's goals/values.
- Manage risk at all times: assess risk to the therapist, others and the client and act for their protection, especially children and vulnerable adults.
- Where possible, begin dissociation work at level 3, to reduce compartmentalization of the personality.
- Attachment usually follows a 'wave pattern' of closeness and distance as approach/avoidance conflicts occur.
- Personality compartmentalization should not be promoted (e.g. by giving new names to dissociated self-states when the client does not). There is

only one client even in DID. If necessary, use terms like 'Angry Mary' and 'Critical Mary', incorporating the client's own name in each description.

- Do not use re-living with complex cases; use graded exposure, mindfulness, imagery re-scripting (Layden *et al.*, 1993), and self-soothing (Linehan, 1993).
- Structure the treatment, perhaps using a DBT-style treatment hierarchy of behaviours to reduce, starting with the riskiest.
- Structure sessions carefully: one third of the session to catch up, review homework/diaries, one third to do new work (e.g. re-scripting; communication between self-states), one third to ensure the client is grounded ready to leave.
- Attend to formulations and reinforcement contingencies within/outside sessions and within the system of care.
- Validate memories, educate the client as to the re-constructive nature of memories, focus on meaning rather than detail.
- Take a 'dialectical' approach; opposite opinions (e.g. between therapist and client) each have validity and we need to reach a synthesis which encompasses both.
- Teach and reinforce the following skills: *Staying in the moment (mindfulness), self awareness, tolerating distress, emotion regulation, relationship skills, concentration skills, memory skills and attention to rather than avoidance of threat.*

Brief case examples

Level one dissociation in an obsessive-compulsive presentation

Sonya, a sculptor, experienced visual hallucinations and ruminations about sexually abusing her baby boy. During time as an inpatient she was observed to be good at caring for her child and there was no evidence that she had ever harmed him. The baby's social worker was concerned about Sonya's self-reported risk and needed to investigate this.

Sonya reported no abuse during childhood but had an often-absent and pre-occupied academic father; her mother abandoned the family when Sonya was eight.

Sonya reported clear visual images of abusing the baby. A new and highly anxious mother, she had intrusive thoughts about being 'sick' and 'dangerous', feeling compelled to check whether she committed abuse by asking for reassurance. She often felt detached from reality and as if she was living in a dream. The WDS showed high dissociation scores at level one, clinically identified as intrusive imagery.

Formulation

The 'junk mail' metaphor for thoughts illustrates how random thoughts arrive endlessly like e-mail, but most of us put most of them into SPAM.

Sonya believed that her mother left because Sonya was 'dangerous' and 'sick': this was resonant with a random sexual impulse and a 'what if I was sexually attracted to my son?' thought. Imagining herself abusing the child was very traumatic, causing her to experience panic symptoms.

In this case, the traumatic event was the imagined scene in Sonya's mind. This posed a high level of threat with consequences of damaging and/or losing her child. This trauma had been compartmentalized, so that it had no context in place or time and was kept out of her awareness as much as possible. She experienced visual hallucinations (level 1) of this imagined event, triggered by handling her child, and could not distinguish whether she had carried out the acts she had seen or not. Seeking reassurance led to temporary relief, a negatively reinforced compulsion. The detachment symptoms made thinking about the problem difficult and may have been negatively reinforced because they allowed escape from the anxiety and rumination which were present when Sonya was not detached.

Treatment

Treatment began by teaching grounding techniques (Kennerley, 1996). Sonya carried a ball of clay she used in her sculpture work, which she stroked and squeezed to remind herself of reality and being here and now. This technique was used during sessions to focus Sonya when she showed or reported signs of detachment, which enabled her to stay in the present.

Sonya's values were explored: why she wanted to be a mother, what being a good mother would look and feel like. At this point it was clear that Sonya had unrealistic expectations of herself and so a '*good enough*' mother concept was suggested and discussed. There were also issues about not having had good enough parenting herself.

Sonya was asked to *imagine* being a good mother, whilst using mindfulness techniques to observe and describe negative thoughts she had, such as 'that will never be me'. She was asked to make a sculpture of a mother and child in a loving and safe relationship, again practising mindful non-judgmental observation of any negative thoughts.

Sonya was asked to imagine that she was the 'good enough' mother in the sculpture, reporting feelings, thoughts, physical state and behaviours she had in this role. This was a very moving and positive experience.

Imagining herself as the child in the duo produced feelings of grief and loss. A compassionate nurturing mother (see Gilbert, this volume) was imagined to occupy the mother's form.

When handling her child, Sonya used these positive images to replace the visual hallucinations: she kept a photo of the sculpture to remind her of them.

This intervention used the power of Sonya's imagination to help recover from the trauma produced by her past experiences and her imagination. She became less detached and more able to focus on her child.

The idea of negative reinforcement was explained, so Sonya understood that she gained short-term relief from receiving reassurance, but this produced longer term worsening of her problems: she stopped asking for reassurance. A rationale for intrusive images was presented, using the junk mail metaphor, which helped normalize her experiences. She rated the likelihood that she had abused her child as 0/10 at this point.

Levels 1 and 2 dissociation in a PTSD presentation

Ahmed, an Indian engineer, had been stabbed in the back by his stepson with a screwdriver. At the time he experienced strong imagery of himself in a wheelchair for the rest of his life, unable to walk again. He recovered well physically, until several years later he met the stepson again. Then he began to experience intrusive images (flashbacks, level 1). Periodically he became unable to walk (level 2), causing him to need a wheelchair. When in a wheelchair Ahmed experienced feelings of helplessness, depression and catastrophic thoughts.

Ahmed showed other symptoms of delayed onset Type I PTSD and this diagnosis seemed to help him understand the problem. However, his wife found it very difficult to see why, if he could walk one day, he would be unable to do so on another day.

Formulation

As well as a wider formulation of the avoidance, re-experiencing and hypervigilance features of PTSD, the information-processing model of dissociation was shared with Ahmed and his wife, to normalize the dissociative phenomena. At level 1, the flashbacks were explained as intrusive imagery from 'split-off' (compartmentalized) traumatic memories. At level 2, loss of gait was formulated as dissociation of the behavioural and physiological schemas within a mode.

Treatment

In the context of a more general treatment approach for PTSD (Ehlers and Clark, 2000), including re-living of the stabbing incident which reduced the level 1 and 2 symptoms, the level 2 dissociation was directly addressed as follows: Ahmed was asked to try to identify trigger stimuli which might precede the wheelchair episodes. These turned out to be times when he felt helpless for some reason (e.g. not being able to pay a bill) and times when he was reminded of the stabbing incident (e.g. using a screwdriver to replace a battery). He was asked to re-create such trigger situations in session, whilst holding on to a picture of himself playing football. He was asked to actively imagine himself playing football alongside the image of the screwdriver.

Ahmed was asked next to sit in his wheelchair and imagine he was now wheel-chair bound. He was asked to actively access the physical feeling of playing football in his legs and reported his legs becoming restless in response to this effort. He requested to get out of the wheelchair but was asked to remain there, holding the sensations in his legs alongside the information about how it felt to be in the wheelchair when he could not move.

In this way, connections were made between the two behavioural and physi-ological sets of experiences, so that the compartmentalization gradually broke down.

Cognitive work was applied to the meaning of the attack for Ahmed, including the shame he had felt when rendered helpless by his stepson and his anger towards the stepson. This anger had not been available to Ahmed's conscious awareness previously.

Since the intervention, Ahmed has not needed to use a wheelchair for several years now, though he does occasionally experience difficulty walking at times of stress: he uses the positive imagery of playing football as well as stress-management techniques to handle these times.

Level 3 dissociation in a DID presentation

Dorothy was a counsellor and mother of four children. At the age of forty she sought help, reporting that she was being haunted by ghostly figures. These were malevolent, with no faces, mocking her and out to get her. She interacted with these figures at the expense of interacting with the real people around her. She described several 'people inside' her, who had conflicting opinions and prefer-ences and interfered with her functioning from day to day. Her scores were very high on all three levels of the WDS.

A risk assessment conducted for Dorothy's children concluded that her husband was caring for them adequately and that Dorothy's behaviour did not put them at significant risk.

A lengthy pre-treatment stage was used to

- clarify Dorothy's goals (to be effective as a mother, wife and counsellor)
- map the system (see below)
- anticipate therapy-interfering behaviours (e.g. 'little Dorothy' would not like to leave the house to come to therapy)
- build commitment

At level 3 the aim is always to *increase self-awareness and self-management.* Working with the self, we aim to promote/develop an over-arching self-schema in four stages:

1   Awareness of all aspects of self
2   Acceptance of all aspects of self

3   Control of all aspects of self
4   Integration of all aspects as one self

1   For Dorothy, awareness was developed by 'mapping the system'. Client and therapist begin to observe and describe different self-states, a step towards developing an over-arching self-awareness. Dorothy's subjective multiple selves were accepted alongside the reality that she was only one person: buttons of different shapes and sizes were used to represent self-states as well as the 'ghosts' and relationships between them.
2   Acceptance was increased by promoting communication and co-operation between self-states and between self-states and therapist. A communication book was started for her to use in different self-states. 'Joint' projects in the real world were planned (cf. teambuilding work) for her to carry out using different self-states together, e.g. meeting her psychiatrist, Dorothy accessed self-states where she could be strong and understanding, to keep an angry self-state under control. She accessed multiple self-states to label the 'ghosts' as 'not-us' and 'not-real' and ignore them.

Traumatic material was accepted and validated, but the therapist worked to steer the content of sessions away from great detail, focusing on validation of the awfulness of the traumas, assigning meaning and exploring consequences.

3   Self-control was gradually achieved by identifying triggers for 'switching' between self-states; pre-planning how to use different self-states to handle chllenges; and developing control of switching. For example, Dorothy chose one CD track to represent each self-state (the music, in Dorothy's words, that this 'person' liked). By choosing to play a given track, Dorothy learned deliberately to activate and de-activate the different self-states.

Integration usually occurs spontaneously as a consequence of removing the need for compartmentalization, in the context of a long-term trusting relationship with the therapist and of increased skills. For some clients, good 'team' functioning may be sufficient. Integration should not be seen as the outcome gold standard.

4   In Dorothy's case, after three years' work, the language she used began to change, first to 'we' as her conscious awareness began to encompass more than one self-state at a time, then to 'I'. When asked about the different 'people' she said, for example, 'little Annie seems to have blended into me!'

Useful metaphors to keep therapists on track include doing 'group or family therapy': imagining one has all the self-states in the room (or even asking them all to be present) and interacting with the 'group' rather than just one self-state at a time. Team-building tasks borrowed from business coaching can be useful to increase co-operation within the 'group'. See Cowdrill (this volume) for a detailed DID case example.

Level 3 work is, of course, not confined to DID: BPD with dissociation and other presentations involving identity disturbance can also indicate level 3 work.

Conclusion

A cognitive model of dissociation is needed to fill a gap in our understanding of widespread, mysterious and difficult-to-treat phenomena within a CBT framework. It has implications for assessment, collaborative formulation with clients, and effective treatment. Failure to address dissociation can lead to failure in treatment approaches. Dissociation should be formulated within the context of the full presentation of the client and treatment approaches chosen with this context in mind. Awareness of classical and operant conditioning as well as meta-cognitions around the experience of dissociation are important in formulating specific problems and patterns in a client's presentation. The model is consistent with other theoretical approaches in the field and can contribute extra insights into cognitive processes underlying presentations such as PTSD and the impact of trauma on the development and sense of self. It is distinct from other theories of dissociation, such as structural dissociation, and these differences offer opportunities for further research.

The field is developing rapidly and we can look forward to much more effective treatments in future. It is important that clinicians and researchers begin to use treatment protocols for mental health problems involving dissociation and evaluate their effectiveness so that we can properly assist those deep in the distress that causes and maintains their problems and so utterly affects their lives.

Appendix 2.1 The Wessex Dissociation Scale (WDS)

This questionnaire asks about experiences that you may have in your daily life. Please indicate, by ticking one of the boxes, how often you have experiences like these. It is important that your answers state how often you have these experiences when you are **not** under the influence of alcohol or drugs.

		Never	Rarely	Sometimes	Often	Very Often	All the time
1	Unwanted images from my past come into my head						
2	I hear voices when no-one has actually said anything						
3	Other people describe meetings that we have had but that I cannot remember						

		Never	Rarely	Sometimes	Often	Very Often	All the time
4	Unwanted memories come into my head						
5	My personality is very different in different situations						
6	My mood can change very rapidly						
7	I have vivid and realistic nightmares						
8	I don't always remember what people have said to me						
9	I feel physical pain, but it does not seem to bother me as much as other people						
10	I smell things that are not actually there						
11	I remember bits of past experiences, but cannot fit them together						
12	I have arguments with myself						
13	I do not seem to be as upset by things as I should be						
14	I act without thinking						
15	I do not really seem to get angry						
16	I just feel numb and empty inside						
17	I notice myself doing things that do not make sense						
18	Sometimes I feel relaxed and sometimes I feel very tense, even though the situation is the same						
19	Even though it makes no sense, I believe that doing certain things can prevent disaster						
20	I have unexplained aches and pains						
21	It feels as if there is more than one of me						

		Never	Rarely	Sometimes	Often	Very Often	All the time
22	Unwanted thoughts come into my head						
23	My mind just goes blank						
24	I feel touched by something that is not actually there						
25	I have big gaps in my memory						
26	I see something that is not actually there						
27	My body does not feel like my own						
28	I cannot control my urges						
29	I feel detached from reality						
30	Chunks of time seem to disappear without my being able to account for them						
31	I sometimes look at myself as though I were another person						
32	Things around me do not seem real						
33	I do not seem to feel anything at all						
34	I taste something that I have not eaten						
35	I find myself unable to think about things however hard I try						
36	I talk to myself as if I was another person						
37	I do not feel physical pain as much as other people						
38	I hear things that are not actually there						
39	I find myself in situations or places with no memory of how I got there						
40	It is absolutely essential that I do some things in a certain way						

Scoring: Never = 0
           Rarely = 1
           Sometimes = 2
           Often = 3
           Very Often = 4
           All the time = 5

Level 1 score = items (1+2+4+7+10+11+22+24+26+34+38)/11

Level 2 score = items (9+13+15+16+17+19+20+23+33+35+37+40)/12

Level 3 score = items
(3+5+6+8+12+14+18+21+25+27+28+29+30+31+32+36+39)/17

Overall score = all items/40

	Clinical Means and SDs	Non-clinical means and SDs
Level 1	1.48	0.72
Level 2	2.06	1
Level 3	2.12	0.88
Overall score	1.9	0.88

Kennedy *et al.*, 2004. Behaviour Therapy and Experimental Psychiatry
Reproduced with permission
For a copy of the scoring and graph template, contact Fiona Kennedy
drkennedy@greenwoodmentors.com
A copy of the scale is available to download from www.routledge.com/9780415687775

Notes

1 *Differences between Beck and Young's shared terms 'schema' and 'modes'.* In Beck's
   model, schemas are defined as *neurological structures* responsible for identifying
   and responding to internal and external events. In Young's work, a schema describes
   the self in relation to the world and others, e.g. 'self-sacrifice'; 'mistrust/abuse'.
   When triggered, a schema can determine the person's responses to events. A man
   rejected by his girlfriend experiences triggering of his 'abandonment' schema and
   makes frantic efforts to get her back, or swears never to get involved with anyone
   ever again.
       For Beck, a 'mode' is a conformation of schemas which constitute the totality of
   an experience: the thoughts, feelings, behaviours and urges and physiological aspects
   of an experience, as in the 'lift phobic' mode in Beck's example. A man might have a
   'being a boyfriend' mode which includes beliefs he isn't good enough as a partner, fear
   of losing the girlfriend, physiological anxiety responses and the urge to stick around
   her at all times. For Beck, the sum of all the modes is the 'personality'.
       Young's concept of modes (e.g., the 'Angry Protector', the 'Frightened Child')
   is more akin to a self-state concept than to Beck's concept of a mode. For further
   comparison of these terms, see Young, Klosko and Weishaar (2006).

2 There is an inhibitory pathway from the pre-frontal cortex to the amygdala (see
   Kennerley and Kischka this volume) which de-activates the amygdala, the centre for
   strong emotion, and may result in emotional numbing or flattened affect.
3 cf. Van der Hart and Steele, this volume, who formulate PTSD in this way.
4 Evidence for compartmentalization (in which information remains available but is
   inaccessible) comes from Huntjens' (2005) work where she used perceptual priming
   (increased likelihood one will see, say, a camouflaged shape, after being shown the
   shape in advance). This effect still operates even when the priming shape is shown to
   DID patients in one self state and another self state (with no memory of being shown
   the priming shape) later views the camouflaged picture. So information is present, but
   not available to conscious awareness.
5 Brown (this volume) provides more detailed cognitive concepts for formulating
   somatoform symptoms.

Chapter 3

Can the foundations of dissociation be found in childhood?

David Pearson

'There are known knowns; there are things we know we know. We also know there are known unknowns; that is to say we know there are some things we do not know. But there are also unknown unknowns – the ones we don't know we don't know.' (Rumsfeldt, 2002).

The former US Secretary for Defense was of course talking about the probability of weapons of mass destruction in Iraq. However this statement sums up rather well the situation regarding the relationship between child experiences and dissociation in later life.

Trauma is not necessary or sufficient to explain all dissociative symptoms but is often linked to disordered attachment (Korzekwa, Dell and Pain, 2009). It is clear that almost all adults who experience problems with dissociation without a history of recent relevant trauma often report childhood histories that are bizarre, containing neglect or abuse. The mechanics of the relationship between negative childhood experiences and later dissociation is very apparent but not always clearly understood. The aim of this chapter is to explore the relationship between child abuse and neglect within a developmental context with later dissociative problems. Only short references will be made to the current state of dissociation in children.

Can dissociation be a part of normal child development?

I will assume that the experience of dissociation lies on a continuum ranging from everyday to pathological, although other chapters look at this position in much more detail, discussing evidence arguing in favour and against it. I will also assume that dissociation is a failure to integrate information as expected, which may at times be defensive in nature. When considering dissociation in children, or the foundations of dissociation in childhood, we need to look at similar experiences that would generally be considered as everyday or even encouraged by adults or parents. The way in which these experiences are considered as abnormal or pathological is to some extent age dependent. Consider Kathy's report after going to a party:

Kathy asked her imaginary friend George whether he enjoyed the party and he said it was really good but he did not like Jean who he felt was showing off. George went on to say that if Jean could not behave better then Kathy should not be friends with her. Kathy thanked George for the conversation, it was good advice and she decided not to be friends with Jean any more, and to stop talking to her. Kathy also thought that it is fortunate that George is here with her to give good advice as she can't always make these decisions and anyway she can sometimes forget what decisions she has made. It's nice being with George as Kathy feels that she is a much more confident person, being able to do more things when she is with him. In fact when Kathy is with George she seems to be a different person, much more confident and able to relate to people better.

If Kathy is seven years old then this report may be seen as 'cute' and may be even viewed as Kathy being creative, encouraged by parents who can often use George to their advantage, particularly at meal times. If, on the other hand, Kathy is 37, depending on the context this could be viewed as a psychotic episode of voice hearing or even intrusive thoughts and memory impairment that she is unable to control. Kathy may be seen as a woman who is unable to recognize that her thoughts are not voices and, depending on our orientation, we as clinicians may be interested in why she cannot integrate her thoughts and reality, perhaps being interested in whether her voices are perceived as being inside or outside of her head. The only thing that changed in these two interpretations of Kathy's report was her age. This raises the question in diagnostic terms as to when 'cute' becomes 'psychotic or dissociative'; is it perhaps on your tenth, fifteenth or eighteenth birthday? This example is of course fabricated, but it opens the doors to the richness of the exploration of childhood experiences and dissociation. Kathy's example demonstrates why there is a need to consider both a non-clinical and clinical view of dissociative experiences in childhood. The division between what is accepted or even encouraged and what is seen as abnormal in childhood is blurred, to say the least.

Dissociation as a childhood disorder

Dissociative disorders are not included in the section of DSM IV-TR (APA, 2000) that describes disorders usually diagnosed in infancy, childhood or adolescence, and dissociation is rarely diagnosed in children (Putnam, 1989). Many dissociative child experiences are considered normal and, as illustrated above, even encouraged by adults. This position has been challenged by evidence that suggests dissociation should be considered a mainstream diagnosis and with recognized treatment. Generally, dissociation in childhood that warrants treatment or therapy is linked to abuse or neglect. This is reflected in research concerning this area where the data are often collected from specialist clinics. These links appear consistent throughout relevant studies. For example, Coons

(1996) found that with a group of patients aged between five and seventeen disso-ciative disorders were related to trauma and developed in complexity as the child got older. Similar findings have been reported by Hornstein and Putnam (1992) who compared adolescents with children eleven years old or younger. Although the complexity of the dissociative problems increased with age, there continued to be good evidence for the diagnosis. Similar evidence was also found when the Children's Perceptual Alteration Scale was used to measure dissociation in children (Rhue, Lynn and Sandberg, 1995). In a group of pre-school children Macfie, Cicchetti and Toth (2001) found similar links to maltreatment, arguing that the pre-school years are an important period for the development of disso-ciation. Pathological levels of dissociation were found by McElroy (1992) when investigating the symptoms of sexually and physically abused children, which may be defensive in nature.

There seems to be some reluctance on the part of parents, carers and clinicians to recognize or diagnose dissociative symptoms in children; they often assume such symptoms are a product of harmless immature imagination. It could also be argued that children are being protected by their parents or carers who are avoiding having damaging psychiatric labels entered into their children's medical notes. As most clinical dissociation in children is linked to abuse, it may also be minimized along with the acceptance (or denial) of abuse by adults. It is also commonly argued that children cannot distinguish between reality and non-reality and one hears terms such as 'they will grow out of it' or 'it is just a vivid imagi-nation'. Thus, these experiences are often seen as socially acceptable behaviours of young children, even though there is evidence of them continuing through into adolescence (Pearson *et al.*, 2001a).

Links with abuse and neglect

This chapter will go on to look at some aspects of child development and the effects that trauma, abuse and neglect can have upon development. It will be argued that damage to normal developmental processes holds the key to the mechanism that links childhood experiences to adult dissociation problems as development continues. As many childhood experiences could be described as dissociative in nature but are rarely seen as clinical problems, this could be seen as an argument for a continuum model with axes ranging from child to adult (age) and also non-clinical to clinical (pathological) (Pearson *et al.*, 2001b; Pearson *et al.*, 2008). It has been argued that children are unable to distinguish between reality and non-reality during their early years, allowing many behaviours and symptoms to be considered features of imagination. However, children's dissociative type experiences can continue well beyond these ages, making the inability to understand reality due to immaturity argument redundant. The example of Kathy earlier in this chapter demonstrated that the same experience can be viewed as clinical or non-clinical according to the age of the person who had the experience. When Kathy was seven years old she was seen as having an imaginary companion, which made her parents smile and think of their daughter as being creative. It is clear that Kathy's seven-year-old experience would not be seen as pathological using DSM categorization (see page 500, DSM IV-TR). But this position may be accepted too readily. Although the diagnostic criteria rule out imaginary companions as symptoms, there has been no research to inform a careful clinical differentiation between imaginary companions and dissociative projections or hallucinatory experiences (Pearson *et al.*, 2001b; Pearson *et al.*, 2008; Silberg, 1998). Indeed, in Jaynes's iconic 1976 text *The Origin of Consciousness in the Breakdown of the Bicameral Mind* he describes experiencing an imaginary companion as 'true hallucination' (p. 396). It is clear that all people have the natural ability to hallucinate in certain circumstances, e.g. when ingesting certain substances, as a response to sleep deprivation or in young children when experiencing high bodily temperatures.

It is often commonly assumed that physical or sexual abuse during childhood are the major links with later adult mental health and dissociation problems. However, it has been established that a wide range of adversities which are often not considered, including poor nutrition, high levels of stress during pregnancy, abandonment, witnessing domestic violence, ineffective or dysfunctional parenting, parental mental health problems, bullying, childhood illness, war trauma and extreme poverty, are also predictors of many forms of an equally wide range of later mental health problems (Read and Bentall, 2012). Most research has concentrated on providing strong links between histories of child abuse and neglect, and dissociation both during childhood and also, mainly, in adulthood. For example, children who are abused are nine times more likely to experience psychosis in later life than non-abused children (Read and Bentall, 2012). Research often considers abuse in categories of sexual or physical without separately considering neglect and other adversities. I would suggest that this bias is due, at least in part, to the majority of research taking place in developed countries where severe poverty is almost unknown. These links warrant more attention and will be covered later in this chapter.

The belief that adult dissociation is primarily linked with child sexual abuse has some support, but is still far from clear. Kisiel and Lyons (2001) assessed 114 adolescents aged from 10 to 18 and found that there was a significant positive relationship between histories of sexual abuse and dissociation, which was not found with physical abuse. Kisiel and Lyons described a unique relationship between sexual abuse and dissociation, also describing dissociation as a critical mediator of psychiatric symptoms. Leverich (2002) found that sexual abuse in childhood was highly associated with the development of dissociative disorders. The argument that child sexual abuse often occurs without physical violence allows the victim to feel partly responsible, creating a more powerful effect and causing confusion in later intimate or sexual relationships (Noll, 2008). Using a group of pre-school children, Macfie, Cicchetti and Toth (2001) found little difference between sexually and physically abused children regarding the levels of dissociation that they experienced. It is possible that the age of these children may have influenced the results, as they were pre-schoolers. Rhue, Lynn and Sandberg (1995) found a higher incidence of dissociation in children suffering physical abuse rather than sexual abuse. Within an adult group of women with bulimia nervosa, neglect and sexual abuse was highly correlated with dissociation (Hartt and Waller, 2002). When a similar study looked at an eating disordered group in Japan, physical abuse was correlated with dissociation, but sexual abuse was not. Using the Wessex Dissociation Scale with adults, Johnston, Dorahy, Courtney, Bayles and O'Kane (2009) found that the schema modes of 'angry impulsive child' and 'abandoned and abused child' uniquely predicted dissociation scores. Over ninety percent of women patients in a Turkish study with 'pseudoseizure-type' disorders could also be diagnosed with a dissociative disorder, with all types of childhood abuse significantly correlated with dissoci-ation, the most significant being emotional followed by physical and then sexual abuse (Ozcetin et al., 2009). Perception of emotional neglect scores correlated with significantly higher dissociation scores for patients with 'psychosomatic' skin diseases compared to non-psychosomatic and healthy controls. These high dissociation scores were mediated by stressful life events (Besiroglu et al., 2009). Evidence can be found to support arguments that sexual or physical abuse are the prominent components of later dissociative problems. Perhaps the data indicate that abuse of all types can be significant, but there may be other factors involved in this equation. Using data from Russian students, Dalenberg and Palesh (2004) found that the best predictor of dissociation was a history of child abuse becoming more symptomatic following recent adult trauma. Although the base-line of dissociation was higher than in previously studied US students, Dalenberg and Palesh were able to exclude the effects of popular media exposure influencing reporting as this was not readily available to the participants due to cultural reasons. Recent negative experiences combined with childhood trauma have also been implicated in the mediation of pseudoseizures (Ozcetin et al., 2009). It has been suggested that different types of dissociation may originate from different types of abuse (Waller et al., 2000) which may explain contradictory results. An unusual example of this notion stems from a study conducted by Devor (1994) which suggested that some cases of transsexualism may be an adaptive extreme dissociative response to severe child abuse. Kessler et al. (2010) found no speci-ficity between childhood adversity and later mental health pathology using the WHO Mental Health Surveys, which used data from 52,000 participants. The role of internalizing and externalizing experiences of maltreatment may differ according to gender (McLaughlin et al., 2010; Kessler et al., 2010) suggesting more factors that may have to be considered. Stovall-McClough and Cloitre (2006) found that *unresolved* abuse in adult females caused a 7.5 fold increase in likelihood of being diagnosed with PTSD, although unresolved loss did not seem to have the same effect. The debate may continue regarding the importance of different types of abuse predisposing to later types of adult dissociation, however the strong general link between abuse and dissociative problems is accepted (see Read and Bentall, 2012 for a short review). After controlling for a history of hallucinations or delusions in first-degree relatives, it was found that people who had been abused as children were nine times more likely than non-abused people to experience pathology level psychosis (Janssen *et al.*, 2004). Table 3.1 illustrates examples of studies that provide such evidence.

It has been suggested that dissociation has a mediating role, that is to say it is a mechanism connecting early experiences and later mental health problems, e.g. Egeland and Susman-Stillman (1996), Waller *et al.* (2000), Kisiel and Lyons (2001), Narang and Contreras (2000). These findings, although consistent, are not inclusive of all experiences. Some children who have negative childhood experiences do not go on to experience adult mental health problems nor report

Table 3.1 Examples of studies linking child abuse with later dissociation problems

Clinical area examples		*Country of origin examples*	
Personality Disorder	Hetzel and McCanne (2005)	Berger *et al.* (1994)	Japan
Pseudo-seizures	Ozcetin *et al.* (2009)	Dalenberg and Palish (2004)	Russia
Post Traumatic Stress Syndrome	Stovall-McClough and Cloitre (2006)	Hartt and Waller (2002)	UK
Dysfunctional schema modes	Johnston *et al.* (2009)	Putnam (1997)	USA
Being a psychiatric patient	Waldinger, Swett, Arlene and Kristen (1994)	Ozcetin *et al.* (2009)	Turkey
Borderline Personality Disorder	Korzekwa, Dell and Pain (2009)	Hirakata (2009)	Canada
Murderers with Dissociative Identity Disorder	Lewis, Yeager, Swica, Pincus and Lewis (1997)	Kessler *et al.* (2010)	21 countries
Kessler *et al.* (2010)	All major mental disorders, using WHO WMHS data		

dissociative problems. This may be due to individual resilience, good quality post-abuse/neglect care or the absence of other negative life events. There is no evidence of a totally inclusive direct relationship between negative child experiences and later mental health problems. Interestingly, neglect may be more powerful than abuse due to its potential to cause organic damage.

When considering dissociation in adults it is common to look only at the history of probable causes and this can overshadow the on-going circular effect. As we have seen, there is a weight of evidence showing a link between earlier abuse and later dissociation. There is also evidence that parents who have dissociation problems are much more likely to abuse and neglect their children, thus creating an inter-generational cycle (Noll, 2008; Egeland and Susman-Stillman, 1996). Narang and Contreras (2000) recognized that dissociation can be a survival mechanism for a child, but can lead to abusive parenting. Mann and Sanders (1994) found links between parental dissociation and parenting inconsistency involving rejection. Their results also indicated a correspondence between father and sons' dissociation scores. Furthermore, Egeland and Susman-Stillman (1996) argue that dissociation accounts for the transmission of maltreatment across generations.

Failure to thrive and attachment disorder

The potentially long-term effects of overt abuse are clearly documented, but the equally damaging effects of neglect and poverty are not always appreciated. This damage can be both organic and psychological. Neglect covers a wide range of physical and psychological experiences including malnutrition, abandonment, emotional neglect and poverty. Poverty has been characterized as 'the cause of causes' by epidemiologists Richard Wilkinson and Kate Pickett in their 2009 book *The Spirit Level*. The most apparent physical characteristic of long-term neglect and severe poverty is failure to thrive. In a nutshell, children who fail to thrive do not follow their expected (pre-determined) growth pattern as measured on growth charts. Failure to thrive falls into two categories:

- Organic: where a child is not growing as well as it should be due to lack of food or due to disease or a syndrome
- Non-organic: where a child is not growing as fast as it should do due to abuse or emotional neglect

Non-organic failure to thrive provides evidence of the potentially devastating impact that experience (e.g. emotional abuse or neglect) can have upon expected organic development (e.g. growth). This concept has been known for over a century, as evidenced by the term 'ceased to thrive' being found in the *Diseases of Infancy and Childhood* by L. Emmett Holt in 1897, with the term 'fail to thrive' appearing in the 10th edition of that classic text (Schwartz, 2000). Although it may be of little interest, when considering dissociation, how tall or short a child is compared with the size it should have been, this position changes when

Attachment Disorder is also considered. It has been recognized over generations that children who fail to thrive also commonly have similar psychological problems to each other. In the late 1960s the psychosocial aspects of failure to thrive became synonymous with maternal deprivation syndrome and earned an entry in the DSM III as 'reactive attachment disorder' (Schwartz, 2000). Reactive attachment disorder is unique in the DSM system as it is applied to infants and recognizes the potential damage that the environment can have on development. Much of the recent evidence was gathered following political changes in Eastern Europe when children from deprived Romanian orphanages were adopted in the West, (see O'Connor and Rutter, 2000). O'Connor and Rutter assessed 165 children aged 6 years who had been adopted from Romania and indexed a distinct set of symptoms and behaviours showing clear evidence for attachment disorder. Attachment disorder covers a wide spectrum of symptoms and is not without its critics. Most of the information for attachment disorder comes from fostering and adoption systems, as most children in these systems have experienced neglect or abuse. Chaffin *et al.*, (2006) noted that the term 'attachment disorder' is increasingly being used to describe a wide range of behaviours of children who are maltreated – particularly those in foster and adoptive families. Attachment disorder recognizes that when a child fails to thrive it is not just that growth is slowed but that the whole of development is damaged. Common failure to thrive and attachment disorder behaviours include: relationship problems, pathological attachments, poor information processing, high levels of anxiety, confused emotions, hyperarousal and maturity confusion. This is not to say that fostering or adoption are damaging, but rather that the children who are fostered or adopted are likely to have suffered severe abuse and neglect previously.

The links to failure to thrive provide evidence that attachment disorder is developmental in origin. This means that development has to be not only taken into account but also suggests that these problems can be long term and carry into adulthood due to developmental processes. Before considering attachment disorder further it would be useful to look at the evidence for the organic effects of abuse, neglect and severe poverty on development. The majority of mental health research is based on adult populations, which are more straightforward than child populations as children change constantly as a part of development. The evidence for failure to thrive is clear and easy to recognize, but less recognizable are neurobiological effects. Only a brief summary of the neurobiological effects are considered here, as there are more extensive reviews in other chapters of this volume. Children who are abused demonstrate similar abnormal, biochemical and structural issues (Benoit, Coolbear and Crawford, 2008). Child maltreatment causes a wide range of neurobiological effects and brain pathology (Korzekwa, Dell and Pain, 2009). Abuse can activate biological stress systems, which contribute to adverse brain development (DeBellis, Spratt and Hooper, 2011). Exploratory work suggested that exposure to stress in infancy can permanently alter an individual's responses to stress (Essex, Klein, Cho and Kalin, 2002). Essex and her colleagues used salivary cortisol levels to suggest that first graders (4.5 years) with high levels of cortisol also had more mental health symptoms. Using longitudinal data, Van der Vegt, Van der End, Huizink, Verhulst and Tiemeier (2010) established a link between cortisol, childhood maltreatment and adult anxiety disorders. In addition, exploratory work suggests that victimization increases dopamine sensitization which is thought to play a role in later psychosis. Poor cognitive functioning has also been established as a result of failure to thrive (Mackner, Starr and Black, 1997) which increases if there is an accumulation of risk factors, e.g. failure to thrive *and* abuse. On a positive note, Corbett and Drewett (2004) conducted a meta-analysis and found that there is evidence that cognitive deficits are recoverable. Caution should be applied here as these data would only apply to cases that have been identified by care or health systems and in turn received a service, thus counteracting the neglect or abuse. Such an example is Boddy, Skuse and Andrews (2003) who found that the negative cognitive effects diminished over time for a malnourished (not abused) group of children but the negative growth effects remained.

To summarize, abuse and neglect can severely damage child development causing changes in growth patterns that are linked to attachment disorder behaviours. There is the potential for a wide range of psychological and organic problems which may be long term and continue into adulthood. Less severe abuse or neglect may not affect growth but still is likely to produce attachment disorder type behaviours. The following vignette demonstrates typical behaviours that this situation can produce:

> *Stacy looks younger than her 10 years of age and often acts much younger at times of stress or excitement, like a 3- or 4-year old. Since she was 12 months old, she has been in a number of foster placements – usually lasting 6 to 12 months. For the last 10 months she has been in her current foster home. Stacy's mother has a history of severe mental health difficulties and a diagnosis of borderline personality disorder, depression and anxiety. She is regularly admitted to the local mental health unit, usually for 3 to 4 weeks at a time, but sometimes longer. Stacy's mother has had numerous partners, most of whom have been aggressive. It is not clear, but it has been suggested that some of mother's partners have abused Stacy. Stacy's foster carers are worried and are not sure that their family can manage to care for her. She appears to attach quickly to people who come to their house, not perceiving danger, but often seems to reject them during their visit, sometimes within a few minutes of their arrival. The foster carers describe this as Stacy appearing to touch, hold hands and seem rather sexual with visitors and strangers. The foster carers find these behaviours difficult to accept, causing them anxiety, and they are worried about the effect on their 9-year-old son. Stacy's foster carers have noticed that Stacy seems to somehow attach the wrong emotions to the wrong events. When the carer's son fell off the slide injuring himself, Stacy could not stop laughing and seemed really happy, but the next day started to cry when she was given a treat. Strangely, at times*

she seems to show no emotions at all. These confused emotions happen a lot at bed-time, when Stacy likes baby stories to be read to her. At school Stacy performs poorly especially if the task involves remembering information. She has few friends and is constantly disruptive during lessons.

Although this is a fictional case it describes common behaviours that foster carers or adoptive parents report. As with Kathy's example earlier in this chapter, the diagnostic implications would change with age and not necessarily with the content of the case. It is remarkable how similar childhood attachment disorder and failure-to-thrive behaviours are to adult diagnoses such as dissociative disorders, borderline personality disorder or psychosis. Barach (1991) suggests that multiple personality disorder is essentially an attachment disorder where dissociation is used as a coping style. Pearson *et al.* (2001b; 2008) suggested that imaginary companions are in fact formed of normal population hallucination mechanisms, which could contain negative content. If we change Stacy's age to say 30, her case would be looked at very differently at the assessment or diagnostic stage. Figure 3.1 demonstrates possible adult interpretations of Kathy and Stacy's behaviours, which often include or occur co-morbidly with dissociation in adults.

Kathy's normal child development	Possible interpretations if Kathy is an adult
Has an imaginary companion to whom she talks to and who talks to her	Hearing voices of a person who is not there Hallucinations, psychosis Dissociative Identity Disorder
Stacy's child behaviours due to attachment disorder and failure to thrive	**Possible interpretations if Stacy is an adult**
Looks younger than she is, acts younger than she is especially at times of high emotion or stress	Immaturity, regression, regression to another self-state, switching between selves
Attachment problems, attaching quickly, touching inappropriately, also rejecting quickly, sexual with strangers, using inappropriate sexuality in interactions	Idealization, devaluation, lack of boundaries, bizarre relationships
Not recognizing/managing emotions, attaching inappropriate emotions to events	Emotional dysregulation, inappropriate affect, lack of empathy, intrusive affect, numbing of affect
Not doing well at school, does not follow instructions well, gets confused easily	Cognitive deficits, confusion often correlated with dissociation (see Kennerley and Kischka, this volume), thought disorder
Hyperarousal, high anxiety, (separation anxiety still evident)	High anxiety, hyperarousal, panic, inability to self-soothe

Figure 3.1 Comparative perception of child vs adult behaviours

It is essential that developmental tasks are achieved in a clear order within set time parameters (often known as 'milestones'). Although the notion of critical periods (i.e. developmental tasks have to happen at a set time otherwise the resultant damage is un-repairable) has little contemporary support, there is considerable support for sensitive periods (i.e. it is more difficult for development to catch up if it has not happened at the expected time). It may be useful to think about this as children being geared up biologically/neurobiologically (Preeda and Gallardo-Pujol, 2011; Van der Vegt *et al.*, 2010), psychologically and socially to develop at speed at pre-destined times (useful to think of as milestones) and in a set order. If these sensitive periods are missed then the child may have difficulty completing the missing tasks at a different time, leading to confused development. A child with confused development may have long-term problems as they are constantly trying to 'catch up' and age-appropriate foundations are not in place. In Stacy's example, she is 10 years old but 'collapses' to 3 or 4 years old at times of stress. This suggests that her developmental tasks are sound and completed at the 3- or 4-year-old level, but that she is now struggling to complete missing 5- to 6-year-old tasks to move her development on. Stacy's sensitive periods are now geared up (biologically, psychologically and social expectations) to complete 10-year-old tasks, not the 5-or 6-year-old tasks that she is currently working at. It is also clear that Stacy has not developed the skills to form safe relationships, not recognizing nor managing her emotions, which makes her vulnerable to further abuse and, in turn, to further damage.

Proposed developmental model

The following model demonstrates how early experiences such as abuse and neglect can result in experiences such as dissociation, that involve a mixture of normal and damaged development. The effects of this mixed development can continue through to adulthood.

Earlier in the chapter the example of normal population hallucinations was introduced. It is often assumed that all hallucinations are signs of pathology, but this notion ignores the data concerning normal population hallucinatory experiences. Approximately 70 per cent of the general adult population reported hallucinatory experiences, with about half of these reporting experiences every day (Posy and Losch, 1983; Barrett and Etheridge, 1992). Pearson *et al.* (2008) found identical results in adolescents aged between 14 and 15 years. Following a study by Feelgood and Rantzen (1994), Pearson *et al.* (2001b) exposed children aged between nine and eleven to ambiguous stimuli which generated hallucinatory experiences in an identical way to adults. These data indicate that there is potentially a continuum between children and adults regarding hallucinatory experiences. Pearson and colleagues suggested that imaginary companions are in fact manifestations of normal population hallucinations that are socially acceptable and also noted that children who experienced imaginary companions also generated more hallucinatory experiences. It is clear that only a tiny percentage of people who experience hallucinations need or request treatment from mental health services. Hallucinations generally become distressing when the content is negative or harmful (Romme *et al.*, 1992; Read and Bentall, 2012) and positive hallucinatory content often makes people feel special. Romme *et al.* (1992) also noted that the content of hallucinations reflected everyday events which were often unresolved. If imaginary companion type experiences are hallucinatory in nature, then it would be expected that these would be negative if the child was in an abusive situation, reflecting everyday experiences. Using Kathy's example earlier in the chapter, George, her imaginary companion, could have had an abusive content to his interaction if Kathy's everyday experiences were abusive. In this way normal developmental experiences would become negative and possibly pathological as the content and function of those experiences changed with neglect, abuse or trauma.

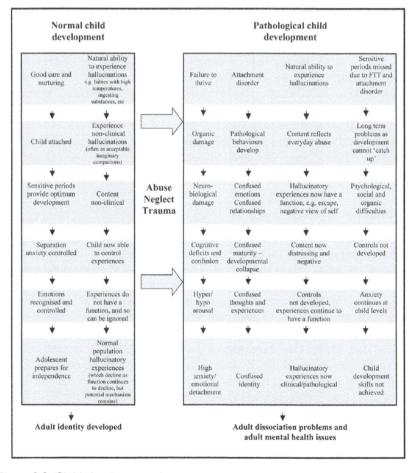

Figure 3.2 Child developmental patterns

Figure 3.2 illustrates how abuse, neglect and trauma can change normal developmental processes to potentially pathological processes. Only a few examples of developmental processes are illustrated and Figure 3.2 is by no means exhaustive. Many of the tasks during development are concerned with gaining control. An example of this is separation anxiety, which keeps a young child safe and close to carers, but becomes unnecessary as a child gets older and separates from constant care. In a similar way emotions are gradually recognized and managed as skills develop. If these skills (milestones) are not acquired then development continues in a confused, inappropriate way and the mechanisms that structure and drive development now drive an abnormal developmental process. Attachment disorder and failure to thrive gives rise to a range of abnormal organic, psychological and social symptoms that can become long-term due to the child's sensitive periods being out of sync with the expected tasks of development. This means that at each stage of development the child is geared up organically, psychologically and socially for an earlier stage of development making progress more difficult. Stacy looked younger than expected for her age, could not recognize nor control her emotions and attached to people inappropriately quickly. This means that Stacy is very vulnerable and may be using sexuality as an inappropriate function in everyday life. Stacy is now more likely to be a victim of abuse and not socially geared up to protect herself. She is learning that being involved in abusive relationships may be the only way that she can exist in society. Stacy is not able to gain the skills necessary to recognize and control dissociative experiences which she needs to rely on as she matures. Using such mechanisms 'symptoms' will be carried to adulthood when they could be re-diagnosed as adult health problems – including dissociation.

Summary

The links between child abuse and later problems with dissociation are irrefutable. Data suggest that a range of child adversities should be included in these links, not just sexual or physical abuse. Neglect is not always considered in this research as it is seen as the province of paediatrics, but it can be equally, if not more, damaging. Child adversity can cause attachment disorder and failure to thrive – both of which damage development causing pathological symptoms. This damage can become long-term due to its timing in relation to a child's sensitive periods. Bad timing can make recovery more difficult. The impact of child maltreatment has been described as the single most preventable cause of mental illness (DeBellis, Spratt and Hooper, 2011) as child adversity accounts for 30 per cent of all mental health disorders worldwide (Kessler *et al.*, 2010).

Chapter 4

The brain and memory

Helen Kennerley
Udo Kischka

One hundred billion neurones keep us alive, shape our personality and generate emotions, perceptions and thoughts which guide our behaviour. Thanks to neuro-imagery its mysteries are being revealed little by little and we can now understand processes which eluded us even a few years ago.

So much of what is now written about dissociation incorporates some mention of neuro-anatomy, memory or emotional processing and this can be challenging if we lack an understanding of 'brain basics'. Therefore, we will outline some fundamental neuropsychological facts and findings which we hope will make the contemporary theory and neurological research regarding dissociation more accessible and interesting. Bear in mind that brain function is complex and there is invariably *much* more to be said, but we will keep it simple so that the neuro-science is as understandable (and therefore useable) as possible. We will just address the basics of brain, memory and emotional processing – neuropsychology on a 'need-to-know' level for the psychotherapist.

Brain basics

In the base of the brain is the *brainstem*, the 'reptilian brain'. The oldest brain structure, responsible for basic survival in terms of evolution, it plays an important role in regulating cardiac and respiratory function, regulating the central nervous system, and is pivotal in maintaining wakefulness. The brainstem is embedded in the *limbic system* (the 'mammalian brain') which evolved to evoke emotional responses at an unconscious level. It is the area of appetites, emotions and urges which are central to active survival. The definition of the limbic system has undergone many revisions in the last decades – the current view is that the parts of the brain involved in emotional processes are the amygdala and the hypothalamus, but also cortical areas (the cingulate cortex, orbito-frontal cortex, and insula).

Overlying the limbic system is the *cortex* – the 'human brain'. In the mid and posterior brain are the specialized:

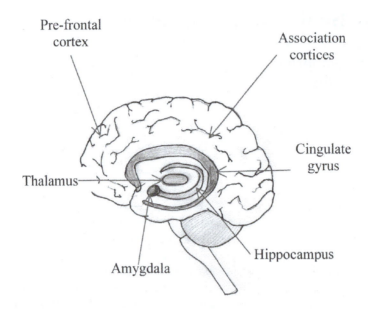

Figure 4.1 The neuro-anatomy of the brain

- *sensory cortices* which process perceived information, and specific areas are identified as the visual, auditory, sensory, gustatory and olfactory cortex.
- *association cortices* store memories and are situated around the sensory cortices. They allow us to compare all incoming information with our memories, enabling us to 'cross-reference' our experiences and put them into context.

At the front (anterior) of the brain are the very sophisticated:

- *frontal lobes,* in particular the *pre-frontal cortex,* which control our actions. They manage the 'executive functions' which are complex and include our ability to initiate goal-directed activities, to plan our actions, to react flexibly and creatively in new situations, to appropriately suppress our impulses including aggressive and sexual urges, to reflect upon our actions and on the effect they have on other people, and to respond to social cues.

The brain is bi–lateral; the left and right sides are clearly differentiated, independent but networked together by the *corpus callosum.* The left hemisphere is the more 'verbal' and analytical one, whereas the right hemisphere is more visual and holistic. Figure 4.1 is a very simple illustration of the brain to help you orientate yourself to its neuro-anatomy.

Memory basics

Forming enduring memory involves three distinct processes:

- Learning (encoding): taking in information, paying attention well enough for a memory trace to be established
- Storage (retention): holding this information in a permanent form
- Recall (retrieval): accessing relevant information

Disruption in any of these mechanisms results in the disruption of memory. Such interference may constitute part of the neurobiological processes underlying the psychological processes of dissociation. Our senses are constantly bombarded by information but only a fraction of this will be noted and held in short-term memory (STM). Here it is retained for a short time (long enough, say, to recall a door code and get into a building), but unless it is of significance it will not be transferred to long-term memory (LTM).

LTM is subdivided into different types and within the literature you will find a, sometimes confusing, range of labels. Here we will try to tease out the terminology to make things clearer with a diagram (Figure 4.2) to help. First is the distinction between *explicit* (or declarative) learning and *implicit* (non-declarative) learning.

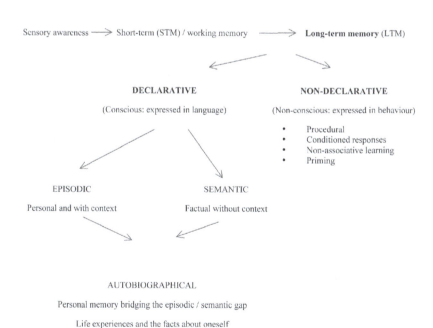

Figure 4.2 A simple overview of memory

Explicit (declarative) memory

Relates to recollections that we are aware of, and that we are able to talk about: remembering our graduation day, or knowing that Paris is the capital of France; recalling a trauma or believing that certain places are dangerous. Distinctions are made within explicit memory, namely:

- Episodic memory: Conscious recollections of personal experiences – episodes in one's life often rich in contextual detail: one's wedding day, visiting the White House with friends, sitting in school learning French vocabulary. These memories vary in their intensity of detail and precision: I might remember vividly sitting with my French books or I might have done this so often that I have a 'one-size-fits-all' recollection of sitting in Madame Beauchamp's classroom – a generic memory of French classes. This is not uncommon in victims of repeated trauma and our patients often find that they cannot distinguish specific episodes of abuse.
- Semantic memory: Nuggets of pure information devoid of context. Knowing what a bridegroom is and what is expected of him, or that the capital of the USA is Washington DC or that café is a French word, for example, but without necessarily remembering how you learnt this.
- Autobiographical: This is a personal memory, or personal narrative, which combines episodic and semantic recollections (Conway, 1996). Remembering your hospital visit last week requires activation of autobiographical-episodic memory, while recalling your date of birth and address calls on autobiographical-semantic memory. It is fundamental to our sense of self as it contains 'self-defining' knowledge (see Stopa in this volume for an elaboration). The quality of autobiographical memory can range from precise to quite vague. Imagine your patient says something upsetting happened last week; you ask her to say more, to give you more detail. She replies:

'I was very upset, quite angry really, because she did it again – my mother – she undermined me in front of my friends. Right there in my own home: mean-spirited remarks. I remember thinking that this was either very careless or downright spiteful and either way it hurt.'

This patient has a good autobiographical memory. Contrast that with the patient who replies:

'It was my mum.'

You gently press for more detail:

'She's just so, so – I don't know – so annoying.'

You ask if there was something in particular that she had done:

'Oh it's always the same with her – putting me down ...'

You try to get a little more detail, asking if she can recall the actual events from last week:

'She came round – she just was putting me down. I can't remember just what she said but she made me feel bad.'

Your second patient has poor autobiographical memory; it's vague. The gist is there but not the detail. This can be challenging for the therapist whose quest is to elicit detail and establish meaning, and possibly frustrating for the patient who can't articulate detail. That is not the only obstacle to therapy, particularly a pragmatic one like cognitive behaviour therapy (CBT), because poor autobiographical memory is linked with poor problem-solving ability (Williams *et al.*, 2007) and this is a significant handicap for any of us and one which must disadvantage psychotherapy patients. Interestingly, poor autobiographical memory is associated with a history of childhood trauma and neglect, seems to be a marker for post traumatic stress disorder (PTSD) and to correlate with borderline personality disorder (BPD) (see Williams *et al.*, 2007 for a review). Williams and colleagues (2007) suggest that traumatized children cope by processing information in a vague way ('mum upsets me') which is less distressing and easier to cope with than considering the specifics ('mum humiliates me in front of others. It's as if I don't matter to her') and then this more vague processing becomes habitual. Just as interesting is the finding that mindfulness meditation training seems to improve the quality of autobiographical memory (Williams, Teasdale, Segal and Soulsby, 2000) and this in turn improves problem-solving abilities.

Implicit (non-declarative) learning

Results in memories expressed by an automatic behavioural or physiological response. We do not necessarily have words to describe them and they often occur unconsciously: our ability to ride a bicycle (a procedural memory), an automatic physiological response to a trigger (a conditioned response), sensitization/ habituation to a dripping tap (non-associative learning), the ease and speed with which we process familiar or anticipated information (priming). In brief, implicit memory describes information processing which occurs outside awareness: recall does not require conscious awareness and it can sometimes take a person by surprise, for example when a conditioned physiological response seems to come out of the blue or a primed response kicks in without apparent warning. If we are fortunate these are pleasant memories, but so often with our patients they are traumatic recollections which seem outside their control.

The brain and memory

Several parts of the brain help us remember. The *pre-frontal cortex* keeps information active for several seconds ('working memory'), enabling us to act on our experiences: we read a telephone number and are able to dial that number a few seconds later. If the information is not rehearsed, or is not personally significant, then it is lost and never encoded. The encoding phase of long term explicit memory involves the *hippocampus* (a structure in each temporal lobe). Our experiences are passed on to the hippocampus, which keeps the information 'alive' over weeks and months, perhaps years. During this period, it deposits pieces of information into their final *storage* places in the separate *association cortices*. A memory is not permanently stored in a single place, but the elements of it are fragmented according to property. For instance, our memory of our wedding day is not all stored within one part of the brain, but the memories of the smell of the burning candles are stored in the olfactory association cortex, the organ music in the auditory association area, the image of the bride in the visual association cortex. The emotional aspects of a memory are stored in a separate structure, the *amygdala* which nests within the temporal lobes.

Whenever we *recall* an earlier memory, the *pre-frontal cortex* retrieves the traces from the different association areas and reconstructs it in the working memory. Memory traces sit like jigsaw puzzle pieces ready to be reassembled when a memory of an event is recollected. This means that (explicit or declarative) memory is reconstructed rather than simply re-played. A common misconception is that everything we experience is mentally recorded and remembering is simply a re-run of a detailed recording. By now you will appreciate this is not so and to expect this of our patients is a mistake – it is just not possible to accurately reproduce an entire scene because:

- *We only note a fraction of our experiences*, and most are not committed to long-term memory. During particularly emotional times our attention becomes focussed and peripheral detail is missed. The phenomenon known as *'weapon focus'* is described by Baddeley (1996) where victims of assault can describe in detail the gun or the knife used in an attack but not the attacker's face – understandably, attention is exclusively focussed on the weapon. We also all have *attention biases* which are coloured by our personal schemata – we notice certain information selectively. On becoming a mother a woman selectively notices the sounds and visual signs of infants; a bird watcher notes wildfowl others would miss; a rape survivor has a heightened awareness of signs of sexual danger (Waller and Smith, 1994). Also, as we said earlier, we only bother to retain information which has *personal relevance* or which we have *repeated* often enough for it to enter long-term storage. If something doesn't seem relevant or interesting we tend not to remember it, and this is why one of the authors still can't operate a camera properly.

- *We forget:* since Ebbinghaus' work in the 1880s we have known of the disappointingly poor performance of declarative (explicit) memory: we simply forget a huge amount of information, even if we try to attend to it. The telephone number which you might have 'committed to memory' probably faded from your recollection some minutes or hours later.

Memory, trauma and dissociation have been linked both theoretically and empirically over the years and assumptions are sometimes made that not being able to recall elements of a traumatic experience must be the result of a dissociative reaction. This might be the case, but McNally (2004), wisely reminds us not to jump to conclusions. He urges us not to confuse everyday forgetfulness with dissociative (sometimes also called 'functional' or 'psychogenic') amnesia – a subconscious selective inability to recall some information. Unwanted memories can actually be excluded from awareness, and researchers have looked at the neural systems involved in this dissociative amnesia. Memory repression in dissociative amnesia is associated with an altered pattern of neural activity, namely increased pre-frontal activation (particularly dorsolateral areas) which inhibits the activity of the hippocampus and thus disrupts recall (Anderson *et al.*, 2004; Kikuchi *et al.*, 2010).

Post-trauma, traumatic memories are less integrated with autobiographical memory in those with PTSD than in those who are free of the symptoms (Kleim, Wallott and Ehlers, 2008). Thus post-trauma memory problems should not be assumed to reflect post-traumatic amnesia for the trauma as the memories might simply not yet be fully processed. In addition, McNally (2004) urges us to guard against mistaking the following for dissociative amnesia:

- *Everyday forgetfulness:* no-one can encode and retain all experiences. We simply forget things.
- *Incomplete encoding:* not all we experience will be noted and the heightened stress which accompanies trauma interferes with memory such that much information is not encoded.
- *Organic amnesia:* insult to the brain can impair recollections of an event.
- *Non-disclosure:* some people will simply choose not to disclose their trauma.
- *Childhood amnesia:* autobiographical memory is very poor in pre-school children and it is quite normal not to be able to remember events, traumatic or otherwise.
- *Not thinking about something for a long time:* can make material harder to access. This is very different from not being able to recall a traumatic event.

Recollection is reconstructive not reproductive

Each time we recall something we piece together a memory, rather like putting together a jigsaw puzzle made of memory fragments from different parts of the brain (*association cortices and amygdala*) where they have been stored according to function. Recalling a walk through the park last year one would draw on memory fragments from the visual cortex, the olfactory cortex and so on, reconstructing the memory. This process does render memory 'unstable' and subject to distortion, which perhaps helps us appreciate the benign origins of false memories. A fabulous resource for those of you who want to know more about memory processes is Baddeley's: *Your memory: a user's guide* (1996). In it he recounts experiments illustrating how memory can be manipulated by careful choice of words. Students watching a video of a traffic accident saw a green car drive past, but they were asked about a *blue* car and they tended to recall a blue or bluish-green one. Students who had watched a different traffic accident were asked to estimate the speed of cars as they 'contacted' each other, and they tended to 'remember' a slower speed than if the term 'smashed' was used in the question. So, declarative (explicit) memory can be disrupted and distorted, and because of this the British Psychological Society (2000) has produced very useful guidelines for working with probable survivors of childhood trauma. These reflect the findings of the 1995 British Psychological Society working party which was commissioned to look at the status of recovered memories. This expert body concluded that there was good evidence that memory, especially for detail, can be distorted, although the panel also noted that this is rarely a major problem in real life as the gist of memory tends to be reliable. In other words, when I go to rent a DVD I can recognize a film and can often recall that I enjoyed it, or that it was funny, or that I never want to see it again, but when pressed for details I might well be vague about the minutiae of the plot or even the precise ending. Our recollection of detail is not very reliable even though our recall of the general event can be.

Of course, a memory which is of particular concern to trauma therapists is the flashback. In the past it was suggested that flashbacks were literally 'frozen memories' and therefore reflected an accurate account but, as McNally (2003) notes, flashbacks are declarative memories and as such, are reconstructed with each recollection, thus they are vulnerable to confabulation. A major clinical conclusion here is that we need to be extremely careful in our enquiries about the content of traumatic memories (and recollection in general) and that there are clearly advantages to using good Socratic methods (enquiry that allows the patient to 'discover' information they already know, without suggesting or adding to it) so as not to lead patients in their recall of events, or indeed their post-hoc interpretations.

Explicit (declarative) memory requires good functioning of the hippocampus for laying down and retrieving memories. The hippocampus provides context for STM (what/how/where/when), the amygdala contributes emotional content and the pre-frontal cortex directs the hippocampus to compare memories, cross-reference and check information – if there is no need for emotional arousal the hippocampus can shut down production of the stress agents in the brain. During the stress response, memories which are unrelated to the stressor tend to be blocked. Stress agents increase glutamate activity which speeds up the flow of information to the hippocampus and the dynamic at the synapses enhances learning. The hippocampus is particularly cortisol-sensitive and, up to a point, increased levels of cortisol 'beef up' neurones in the hippocampus and these cells become dedicated to the emotionally charged memory. However, while some cortisol helps 'wire in' memory, too much suppresses this process and is actually toxic to the hippocampus so that we do not form memories, nor can we easily retrieve old ones. Thus, chronic stress which results in elevated levels of cortisol makes it hard to learn new material and blocks access to existing memories.

Implicit (non-declarative) memory, which includes conditioning, does not involve the hippocampus, but rather the amygdala, basal ganglia and cerebellum. As therapists, we need to consider the role of non-verbal learning (which is often achieved through experiential methods) to help us work at this non-declarative level. This is particularly important when you consider that there are direct pathways from the amygdala to the dorsolateral PFC, but not the other way. In short, the amygdala can send the message: 'be afraid, be very afraid' but the dorsolateral PFC is not very effective when it responds with: 'it's ok, it's safe, no worry.' You have probably encountered patients who say, ' I *know* it but I just don't *feel* it yet.' This 'head-heart gap' is linked with our neuro-anatomy and is perfectly understandable, but it does mean that we need to ensure that our therapy combines both cognitive *and* behavioural learning opportunities.

Emotional processing basics

In evolutionary terms, the limbic system might be 'primitive' but it is active, constantly feeding information to the highly developed cortex which surrounds it (see Figure 4.1). Deep within the limbic system sits the *thalamus,* the sensory gate-keeper, directing sensory input to the appropriate *sensory cortex* (images to the visual cortex, sounds to the auditory cortex, etc.) for detailed analysis. Simultaneously, the thalamus sends sensory input to the *amygdala* which determines whether the new information has emotional significance.

The response pathway to the amygdala, within the limbic system (Route 1), has been dubbed the 'quick and dirty' route (LeDoux, 1998) because of its speed and lack of fine processing. The amygdala enables us to draw a 'quick and dirty' conclusion, unconsciously, about incoming stimuli: 'friend or foe', 'safety or danger', etc. It is particularly sensitive to threat, responding by triggering bodily reactions (neuronal and hormonal) including the release of adrenaline and noradrenaline. These contribute to preparing the body to respond with flight, fight, freeze or appease.

If you see what could be a spider (and you fear spiders), or if you hear what could be your child's cry of distress, or if you touch something which seems repulsive, your amygdala sends out strong alert signals enabling you to deal with the situation quickly. This happens rapidly and unconsciously; we react to danger rather than reflect on it (LeDoux, 1998) which can be life-saving. The amygdala also activates what is known as the hypothalamus-pituitary-adrenal (HPA) axis, an efficient sequence of hormonal activations, the end result of which is the release of cortisol into the bloodstream. Cortisol, along with the adrenaline, prepares us for action. As this happens, the thalamus simultaneously relays a message to the sensory cortices (Route 2) which are 'data banks' of information which can provide a 'second opinion' a fraction of a second after the amygdala has initiated an emotional response. Knowledge stored in the sensory cortices puts the emotional response into context; information about time, place, previous experiences, etc. enable us to make realistic judgments of a situation. We might confirm or disconfirm our initial emotional response, and continue an appropriate defensive move or modify an inappropriate response. For example, a mother hears a baby's cry of distress – the amygdala is sensitive to the possible emotional significance of this and sends neural and hormonal messages which ready her mind and body for action. She is alert and ready to protect her child *in an instant*. However, information held in the sensory cortices is also mobilized and puts the experience in context – her child is in a nursery right now; she is on a busy street where it is common to hear an infant's cry and so on. The initial response is reviewed and the mother 'sees the bigger picture'. She can then relax, knowing it is not her child crying.

The *pre-frontal cortex* also has a key role in seamless emotional processing:

- the medial pre-frontal cortex (MPFC) allows us to recognize and experience the emotion
- the orbito-frontal cortex (OFC) helps us modulate and control it
- the dorsolateral pre-frontal cortex (DPFC) enables us to plan and problem solve as necessary

If the mother had been at home with her toddler and baby and had, indeed, heard her own infant's cry, she would have recognized that she felt anxiety (MPFC), and would have kept it under control (OFC) sufficiently to ensure that she first made safe her toddler before checking on the baby (DPFC).

This account of emotional processing is summarized in Figure 4.3.

Areas in the PFC appear to have a further and crucial function: in the event of over-arousal in the limbic system it can become highly active and suppress emotional responses (Hopper, Frewin, and Lanius, 2007). Thus, high emotional arousal can be rapidly followed by activation of the PFC which very effectively dampens down the amygdala and thus the intense affect it generates. There is a good chance that we have all had the experience of becoming emotionally numb in the face of shock and it can be highly adaptive: it keeps us calm while we check that everyone in a car accident is ok; it enables us to get home to a safe place before becoming overwhelmed with emotions. Clearly one can have too much of a good thing and sometimes this response is exaggerated so that people experience unhelpful emotional numbing, such as depersonalization and derealization.

Responses evoked by smells are particularly interesting. In addition to the pathways through the thalamus, olfactory information is also directly sent into the

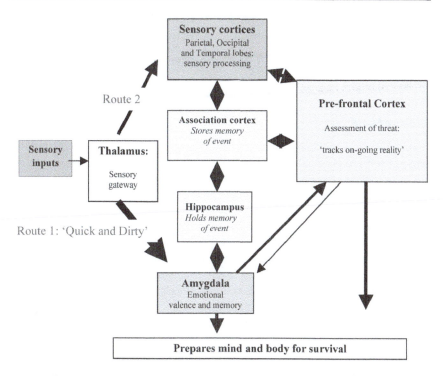

Figure 4.3 An overview of emotional processing

amygdala within the limbic system. Thus, an olfactory stimulus is very rapidly processed and this explains why smell so readily triggers powerful emotional responses. Because of this, olfactory responses are easily conditioned, and are particularly resistant to de-conditioning (Kirk-Smith, Van Toller and Dodd, 1983). Thus, even after some time a particular after-shave or food can evoke a moment of re-living, just as the smell of petrol can persistently trigger traumatic flashbacks in the road traffic accident survivor.

In reading about information and emotional processing you might come across the intriguing terms:

- 'data-driven' or 'bottom-up' processing
- 'schema-driven' or 'top-down' processing

Data-driven processing refers to interpretation of sensory data, using this information as 'basic building blocks' without the distortions or modifications of pre-existing expectation. In contrast, schema-driven processing is guided by the expectations captured in our schemata which enables us to anticipate and 'read between the lines', to go beyond the basic data. This means that we can process information very rapidly and it generally stands us in very good stead. Problems arise when our schemata lead us to 'read between the lines' in a distorted way, seeing danger or rejection in benign situations, for example, a distortion not uncommon in those who have been subject to abuse or neglect.

Sense of self

Given that so many manifestations of dissociative disorders involve shifts in sense of self (de-personalization, DID, for example) it is worthwhile considering the neurological status of the self. Stuss and Alexander (2000) quite clearly tell us: '... the most important role of the frontal lobes may be for affective responsiveness, social and personality development, and self-awareness ...' (p. 289) and it has been shown that dysfunction of the pre-frontal cortex (which we have seen is crucial to autobiographical memory) is associated with an impaired ability to maintain a sense of past, present and future self, to achieve an awareness of our historical context. It has also been established that the PFC, the orbito-frontal cortex (OFC) in particular, is most closely associated with personality (Cummings, 1993). The OFC develops from infancy, predominantly in response to nurturing, does not start to mature until toddlerhood and its development is severely disrupted by emotional neglect (Chugani *et al.*, 2001). In theory, a compromised OFC might not be able to integrate a stable and comprehensive sense of self, thus rendering a person vulnerable to depersonalization disorder or even DID. This has indeed been proposed by Forrest (2001) who hypothesized that the experience-dependent maturation of the OFC in early abusive environments may result in a pattern of conflicting subsets of self-representations because, when the integrity of the individual was threatened, the OFC inhibited integration into a unified self. For example, an abused child might form a distressing self-representation of being 'contaminated' but the OFC does not adequately integrate this into her 'bigger' sense of self. In the short term the child might gain relief, but ultimately might experience problems. Representations of the self are explored in more depth in Stopa's chapter (this volume), so, if you find this subject gripping we would suggest you read her views, too.

One final point concerning self is that it is generally accepted that there are two temporally distinct forms of self-reference: extended and momentary. The former refers to an enduring sense of self with experiences linking across time, while the latter indicates acute self-reference focused on the present (in Stopa's chapter she neatly refers to this as the 'current on-line self'). Farb *et al.* (2007) studied these two aspects of self-awareness in a non-clinical population and brain scans showed particular activity in the MPFC but, more interestingly, a distinct neural dissociation between the two forms of self-awareness. Although they are usually integrated, they can be dissociated through attention training. This might begin to shed further light on the distressing states of depersonalization disorder and dissociative identity disorder.

The brain under stress

Our account thus far has described the impact of acute threat, but many patients suffer repeated or chronic trauma, in adulthood or in childhood or in both. This has been long since shown to take its toll on the size and functioning of the hippocampus – chronic stress diminishes it and the processing of memories suffers (LeDoux, 1998). This is probably linked with the high levels of adrenaline and cortisol which are produced during trauma and stress and the usually homeostatic hypothalamus-pituitary-adrenal circuit failing to regulate cortisol (see Frodl and O'Keane, in press). The net result is over-stimulation of the amygdala and diminished activity (and possibly volume) in the hippocampus. Not only does this have a significant effect on memory functioning, but reduced hippocampal function has been associated with a vulnerability to developing PTSD (Gilbertson *et al.*, 2002). As we have seen, the PFC can moderate the amygdala, however, stress induces increased levels of catecholamines (namely, noradrenaline and dopamine) which can 'turn off' the PFC so that the amygdala can rage unabated (Figure 4.4).

In childhood the central nervous system is, in parts, immature and thus particularly sensitive to the impact of stress: myelinated areas of the brain seem to be especially sensitive to stress (see De Bellis, Spratt and Hooper 2011, for a review). A consistent finding is that survivors of developmental trauma have smaller brain volume, which correlates positively with the severity of the trauma. De Bellis *et al.*, (1999) discovered links between childhood trauma and diminished intracranial volume and a smaller corpus callosum. Of particular note is the finding that earlier onset and longer duration of abuse correlated with smaller intracranial volume, and these structural changes were in turn associated with: intrusive symptoms, avoidance, hyper-arousal and dissociation, which, of course, we see in PTSD. Survivors of childhood trauma also show an enhanced neurobiological sensitivity to [perceived] threat, which means that they may be in a chronic state of 'Red Alert', a state which perhaps relates to the 'heightened startle response' of PTSD. It is known that children with insecure attachments release more cortisol in response to stress (Essex *et al.*, 2002), which we have seen could compromise the volume and functioning of the hippocampus, although there is yet little evidence to support this (De Bellis *et al.*, 2011).

Figure 4.4 The impact of stress on the amygdala

There is, however, evidence of disruption in the development of the amygdala and the pre-frontal areas of brain which are so very important in regulating emotion. Within the PFC, the OFC is key in experiencing empathy and processing emotions as well as integrating environmental information with inner states. A compromised OFC can thus undermine mood moderation, development of relationships and the ability to integrate emotionally relevant experiences: all very relevant to a patient in therapy.

In addition to the structural changes that can result from childhood abuse and neglect, neuro-transmitter production is affected by chronic stress (see Heim and Nemeroff, 2009, for a review) and in particular, serotonin levels are reduced. Amongst other things, this is important in the regulation of the pre-frontal cortex, the amygdala and the hippocampus, all key players in emotional experience and regulation. Thus, repeated and/or early trauma might significantly compromise the neurological system that processes emotional experiences and perhaps dissociative responses to strong emotional reactions become the default. This is explored further in the next chapter.

On a happier note – our brains retain quite an encouraging degree of plasticity and this is especially so in the PFC and hippocampus.

Summary

We humans have evolved with an extraordinary capacity to orchestrate material so that we respond and remember and survive. Only under unusual conditions, such as extreme stress, does the system sometimes falter. Understanding the mechanism of the functioning and the dysfunctioning of the brain can inform our understanding of both the strengths and the needs of our patients.

Chapter 5

The brain, neuropsychology and dissociation

Helen Kennerley
Udo Kischka

In the past decade, at least in the world of cognitive therapy, there has been an increasing interest in brain function, and both observation and conjecture about neurological correlates of dissociation have contributed to our understanding of the neuropsychology of dissociation. This understanding has been incorporated into several widely used psychological models of flashbacks (e.g. Ehlers and Clark, 2000; Brewin, 2001b) and other dissociative phenomena such as derealization (Baker, Hunter, Lawrence and David, 2007).

An interesting thing about research and theory that incorporates neurological findings is that if we are familiar with some neurological basics, we can generally appraise the quality of the work quite well. However if we are 'neuro-naïve' we tend to be bowled over by the neuroscience, accept the conclusions and rate the quality of the work quite highly (Weisberg, Keil, Goodstein, Rawson, and Gray, 2008). Here we aim to provide enough information for you to be critical of dissociation-and-the-brain literature by presenting relevant and contemporary neurological models and findings as simply as possible whilst ensuring that the information is sound. So, we will:

- consider the neuro-anatomy, neuro-chemistry and neuro-psychology of dissociation and its relevance to psychotherapy, particularly to cognitive-behavioural therapy,
- explore the impact of psychological trauma and neglect (acute and chronic) on the developing brain and on the adult brain,
- look at neuro-biological and psychological explanations for different presentations of dissociation associated with trauma and neglect,
- outline the neuro-biology of traumatic memories which can present in the form of flashbacks and other unwanted intrusions, in relation to PTSD and other psychological disorders.

Towards the end of the chapter we will look at how an increased understanding of the brain processes underlying dissociative experiences can inform our clinical formulations, clinical practice and the management of dissociation-related problems.

Neuro-psychological understandings of dissociation

If you read the previous chapter, you will be familiar with brain and memory 'basics' – now we need to consider how this fits with neuro-psychological research on dissociation.

Our starting point echoes the common neuro-psychological distinction between *compartmentalization* and *detachment* which has been made elsewhere in this book. By now you are probably familiar with the idea that compart-mentalization involves an inability to access all relevant information and is manifest in flashbacks and hyperarousal but also in psychogenic amnesias. Detachment is distinguished by alterations in consciousness – feelings of unreality, numbing of emotions. Over the years this distinction has been generally borne out by neurological research, for example using brain scanning techniques. Hopper, Frewen and Lanius (2007) distinguish 'pathological over–engagement' (i.e. re-experiencing) and 'pathological under-engagement' (which is similar to detachment). The former correlates with more limbic activity and the latter with more frontal activity. Schauer and Elbert (2010), also postulate two distinct types of dissociation – that with dominant sympathetic nervous activation (which triggers the fight/flight response) and that with dominant parasympathetic nervous activation (which promotes a drop in arousal and numbing of emotions). They also propose that there is progression from sympathetic to parasympathetic dominance – that the fear response initially primes us for action but in some cases this progresses to a state of emotional 'shut down'.

Compartmentalization

Traumatic memory, hyperarousal and PTSD

The most systematic research has been in the field of post-traumatic stress disorder (PTSD: DSM IV-TR, APA, 2000) with a particular emphasis on traumatic flashbacks. Flashbacks are so often referred to in the dissociation literature that they merit some elaboration here. It is worth remembering that traumatic flashbacks can be linked with 'Type I' or 'Type II' trauma (that is, acute, unexpected trauma versus chronic and anticipated trauma – a useful distinction made by Terr in 1991) whether or not the sufferer has a diagnosis of PTSD.

The term 'flashback' describes an involuntary and vivid waking recollection of an emotionally meaningful experience, or parts of the experience – the recollection is often so vivid that people say it's as if they are 're-living' it (Frankel, 1994). Sometimes the memory is predominantly visual, sometimes auditory, sometimes visceral or olfactory (Ehlers, *et al.* 2002); sometimes it lingers for a moment, sometimes it persists for minutes or more. In short, there is a wide variation in flashback experiences, but Sam's experience is not uncommon:

Amazingly, Sam arrived at work on time – though she'd not slept well. She'd been so 'hyper' throughout the night, and the thoughts – the memories – just kept racing in her head. Even now, she felt the adrenaline and it was not just the face she kept recalling but the same emotions would well up as though she were experiencing it all over again. There were moments when she felt as though she was reliving it. On the tube, a stranger's after-shave brought it all back in an instant. It was as if she could not control what was happening in her mind and body ...

What do you imagine she's 'reliving'– recalling so vividly? Well it might surprise you to learn that she fell in love the night before and this powerful affective experience etched itself on her amygdala and now it keeps coming back to haunt her in a pleasurable way. The thing is, flashbacks are not necessarily traumatic in content – they are emotionally powerful, vivid recollections and the emotion can be positive. In fact, there is evidence that even in those with a diagnosis of PTSD, the majority of flashbacks is not traumatic (McNally, 2003). It's just that we tend not to dwell on our lovely flashbacks because they don't upset us. As a result, as we will see later, they are rapidly transformed into 'regular' memories, which do not keep returning with the intensity and freshness of a flashback.

All flashbacks are 'dissociative', in that they represent a disruption in the usually integrated functions of consciousness, memory or perception. However the term 'dissociative flashback' has been rather misleadingly used specifically to describe more intense flashbacks, often of longer duration where the sufferer is overtly re-experiencing a traumatic episode. It might be more useful to use the term 'prolonged flashback' to describe the more protracted episode and 'brief flashback' to denote those of short duration and to use the term 'multi-sensory' to describe those which are rich in sensory detail as opposed to those which comprise just one or two sensory elements. This is not to suggest that the 'brief' or the less sensory-loaded flashbacks are less distressing.

Accounts given by survivors of Type I trauma (a single or short duration trauma) indicate that their traumatic flashbacks tend to involve intense visual imagery, accompanied by panic symptoms, and are associated with dream disturbances. These occur most often in PTSD patients who score highly on a measure of general imagery ability (McNally, 1999). Flashbacks precipitated in laboratory conditions have led to interesting observations (Rainey *et al.*, 1987) such as:

- flashbacks precede panic, rather than being triggered by panic
- they generally begin gradually, increasing in severity over several minutes
- they seldom replicate actual traumatic experiences, but rather related confabulations

The latter is consistent with the fact that memory is reconstructive and not reproductive (see the previous chapter for more on memory basics) and as McNally (2003) says: '... [flashbacks only] produce the illusion of reliving the trauma' (p. 117). In writing about PTSD, Grey (2009) reminds us to be aware of both *veridical* intrusions (which replicate an event reasonably accurately) and *non-veridical* memories (which refer to events which are confabulated in some way). That is to say, we need to be open to the possibility that recollection is not accurate and accept and work with that. Arntz and Weertman (1999) wisely asserted that in helping sufferers of intrusive images from childhood, our aim:

'... *is not to discover the (repressed) 'true facts' but to change the meaning of schematic representations that have roots in childhood ... the therapist must be aware of the (re)constructive processes of memory and restrain from suggesting any historical 'facts'...'* (pp. 716–7).

They are reminding us that memory is vulnerable to distortion and we need not to set too much store by the accuracy of detail, and that we should take care in asking questions so that they are not leading.

So what causes the flashback to persist? The most popular neurological theory is that the hippocampus (which is central to memory formation and retrieval and acts as a 'go-between' for the cortices and the amygdala) does not function well at very high or low levels of arousal (hyper- and hypo-arousal). This is why we tend to perform badly in exams or driving tests if we are too anxious or too relaxed: we cannot bring to mind crucial information because our memory is impaired. Studies have shown that cortisol and adrenaline modulate the ability of the hippocampus to store and retrieve information and to cross-reference current experience with past events (Frodl and O'Keane, in press). In the case of high arousal the hippocampus is inhibited and if we are in danger this is no bad thing – we sense threat, and thanks to the effective link between the thalamus and amygdala, we prepare for survival with no interfering peripheral thoughts, as the hippocampus 'goes offline' and we rapidly become ready for action. As le Doux (1998) puts it, we react to danger rather than reflect on it because detailed reviewing of the situation could cost us valuable time and cognitive resources.

Figure 5.1 illustrates this – those of you who have read the preceding chapter will recognize the information-processing model from that chapter, but now you see it altered by extreme levels of arousal.

The amygdala takes centre stage and hippocampal activity is reduced. This process is further enhanced because cortisol and adrenaline increase amygdala activity while also suppressing the hippocampus. Transmission of information between the amygdala in the limbic system and the cortices is impaired, as is memory formation and recollection. Flashbacks occur when a recollection in effect 'tricks' our brain into believing that an event is immediate and the amygdala kicks off just as we described above. In the case of a traumatic flashback, this means that the fresh, emotionally loaded memory of a trauma is not initially 'contextualized', it is not catalogued for time and place and outcome because the hippocampus cannot provide the link between the data-rich cortices and the emotionally laden amygdala (remember – it's gone 'off-line') nor can it contribute the recent memory for events which it holds. Generally this is not a problem as the level of arousal that the memory provokes diminishes over time

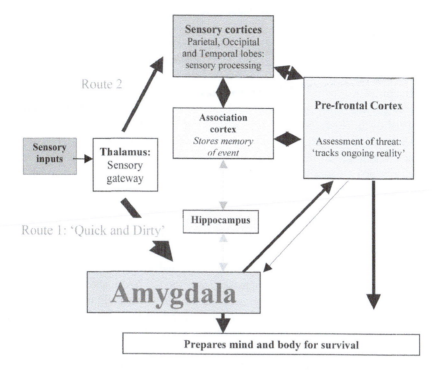

Figure 5.1 Information processing under stress

and the hippocampus comes back 'on-line' and does its job. The memory is then contextualized – properly catalogued so that when it is recalled, it might still be emotionally arousing but it is clearly a memory and there is no sense of re-living. This is the natural history of a flashback: this is what happened to Sam and in her case was rather disappointing to her as she lost the intensity of recollection which gave her so much pleasure.

Our patients experience no such pleasure and those with problem flashbacks find that the intensity of the memories does not diminish over time. This is because, when the memory is recalled, the recollection itself is so hyper-arousing that the hippocampus functions ineffectively. Then there is no 'cross-referencing' and updating of information and the powerful emotional response remains out of context – hence the 'sense of current threat' and of 'reliving' an event, even in the absence of danger. As we noted earlier – the sense of reliving does not mean that the event is being accurately replicated, but it feels like that to the sufferer.

Flashbacks associated with Type I trauma PTSD are well documented and psychological models have been devised to understand them (Foa and Kozak, 1986; Brewin, Dalgleish and Joseph, 1996; Ehlers and Clark, 2000) and treatment approaches have evolved from these models and have been evaluated (Foa and Kozak, 1986; Resick and Schnicke, 1992; Ehlers and Clark, 2000). In 1986 Foa and her colleagues presented an habituation model of PTSD with an associated exposure-based treatment. By the mid-nineties Brewin *et al.* (1996) proposed the more neuro-cognitively complex 'dual representation' model of PTSD which postulated that trauma-related memory is subject to two levels of information processing. One level contained narrative traumatic memory and reflected the operation of a 'verbally accessible memory' (VAM) where trauma memory was integrated with other autobiographical memories. These memories were contextualized with regard to time and perspective, and they could be deliberately retrieved. The second level reflected 'situationally accessible memory' (SAM) which was triggered involuntarily by situational, non-verbal reminders of trauma (e.g. a cabled sweater triggers a rape victim's memory of her experience because the rapist wore a similar garment). Brewin *et al.* suggested that VAMs and SAMs usually integrate, via the hippocampus, to form contextualized memories. When you recall a distressing occasion you will also remember that it happened some time ago and, although you might feel something of the emotion from that time, it is not overwhelming and it does not feel like actual reliving. However, flashbacks maintain a powerful sense of 'here and now' and an intense emotional charge because, according to the dual representation model, VAM and SAM have not integrated. SAM is triggered and without the contextualizing information from VAM, the memory is vivid and immediate. This psychological model fits perfectly with the neurobiological model described in Figure 5.1 and with Kennedy's psychological model of dissociation (see Kennedy's chapter in this book) if we consider SAM representing first level processing and VAM second level processing. More recently, Brewin and colleagues (2010) have elaborated their model and developed a 'neural systems model of healthy memory and imagery' which embraces more neurological pathways and which can be applied to a range of psychological problems in addition to PTSD, problems such as depression and other anxiety disorders. They now refer to the two patterns of information processing as C-reps (abstract, flexible and contextualized representations) and S-reps (inflexible, sensory bound representations) but continue to stress the need for functional interaction between the neural systems supporting S-reps and C-reps via visuo-spatial working memory, which involves the pre-frontal cortex (PFC). In short, the information and emotional processing model which they propose again sits well with the current neuro-biological theory and research findings, and the authors very usefully consider the treatment implications for psychological therapy.

Other pioneers in the psychological field of trauma are Ehlers and Clark who, in 2000, proposed a cognitive model of PTSD. Although predominantly cognitive-behavioural in its description of PTSD intrusions and problem behaviours, this empirically grounded model encompasses an understanding of the neuro-psychological processes which maintain flashbacks via a disturbance of autobiographical memory which is characterized by poor elaboration and contextualization, strong associative memory and strong perceptual priming.

The psychological treatment of Type I trauma flashbacks reflects these neuropsychological understandings and typically involves some form of exposure to the flashback combined with cognitive reinterpretation which helps to contextualize, or 'up-date', the memory. The most systematically evaluated intervention is probably Ehlers and Clark's 'reliving' paradigm (2000) whereby a patient recounts the traumatic event as if it is happening, whilst introducing orientating and contextualizing information to 'update' the recollection – in particular the most distressing aspects (sometimes called the 'hot spots'). The updates involve not only contextualizing the memory in terms of a more comprehensive recollection of the trauma (e.g. the patient did all they could to survive), a real timeframe (i.e. it happened in the past) and its outcome (e.g. the patient survived, perhaps even good things happened) but the intrusion is also reviewed in the light of what the patient knows now.

Alicia believed that she was responsible for being raped and this belief contributed to the hyper-arousal which sustained her flashback. However, she was able use cognitive restructuring (see glossary) to realize that the rapist took an active decision to assault her, threatened her with violence and that she actually responded as best she could, given that she feared for her life. Thus during reliving she was able to appreciate that her options had been limited, that the trauma was in the past and she was not about to be killed, and also that she was not to blame.

These sorts of realizations decrease arousal and allow the hippocampus to come 'back on-line' and what was a dissociated recollection becomes an integrated memory. This seems to be the key to the psychological management of flash-backs – holding the memory whilst effecting sufficient de-arousal to enable the hippocampus to do its work. Foa's exposure paradigm achieved this through habituation, while some patients achieve it purely through psycho-education which reassures them that they are not crazy and that there is hope. Clearly, there might be many ways to manage flashbacks and our formulation and a good under-standing of patient resources will guide treatment decisions.

Cognitive and/or behavioural interventions are not the only way to achieve de-arousal and integration. There is a growing body of research that supports the pharmacological treatment of flashbacks. For some time now the SSRIs (selective serotonin reuptake inhibitors) and other anti-depressant medications have been investigated and they have shown limited results (see Bisson, 2007 for a review), but more recently, 'Ecstasy' or MDMA (3, 4-Methylenedioxymethlyamphetamine) has become the focus of research (Mithoefer, Wagner, Mithoefer, Jerome, and Doblin, 2010). In their study, assisted de-arousal during relieving is achieved pharmacologically. The process is simple – the impact of the medications (de-arousal) enables the hippocampus to remain active and so intrusions are more readily contextualized. This might have really significant implications for helping those whose PTSD is resistant to psychotherapy alone and the Mithoefer study has already inspired the first UK clinical trials. However the research is in its early stages and we might have some time to wait before we can get Ecstasy on prescription.

Flashbacks associated with Type II trauma (chronic trauma, often occurring during childhood and affecting personality, attachment patterns and development, see Pearson, this volume) have also been described (for example in Layden, Newman, Freeman and Morse, 1993) but not as systematically and thoroughly as their Type I trauma counterparts. Layden and colleagues noted that flashbacks resulting from developmental trauma might be represented not verbally and visually but more kinetically, as this would be a child's most salient sensory modality. Thus it is often helpful if therapists check out body imagery flashbacks and not just visual imagery. You might remember that we noted in the previous chapter that the older the flashback, the more likely it is to have become distorted over time and that pre-school children have very poor autobiographical and narrative recollection. Thus, developmental trauma flashbacks are less likely to be veridical. There are guidelines for helping Type II trauma patients integrate fragmented recollections and manage unwanted intrusions (Layden et al., 1993; Arntz and Van Genderen, 2009), but there have been no randomized controlled trials (RCTs) and few case series which simply target Type II trauma flashback management. However, imagery rescripting (see glossary) has been used successfully to manage childhood trauma intrusions in women with BPD who were engaged in a RCT of Schema Therapy (Giessen-Bloo et al., 2006).

It is tempting to assume that Type II trauma flashbacks will be amenable to the re-living strategies developed for managing Type I trauma flashbacks. This might be so, given that the neurological mechanism of a flashback is essentially the same for both. However, we now know that chronic trauma can compromise the development of those parts of the brain involved in regulating emotions and behaviour, so reliving could possibly overwhelm the survivor of chronic trauma. Therefore, the more graded re-scripting approaches of Layden et al. (1993) and Arntz and Van Genderen (2009), which involve periods of preparation and stepped practice, might be more tolerable. In fact, a period of learning to manage emotions and deal with interpersonal stresses (a 'stabilization' period) prior to intrusion-focussed work has been shown to be optimal for those who have PTSD in the context of developmental trauma (Cloitre et al., 2010).

Hypnosis and conversion disorders

Hypnotic states have been described as states of focussed attention that allow dissociation of sensations such that we can attend precisely to particular thoughts or events and to marshal resources in unusual ways (Kosslyn et al., 2000). However, hypnosis presents us with a complicated neurological picture. Studies have shown varied associations of areas of brain activity and hypnotic states – for example the brainstem, thalamus, anterior cingulate cortex, cortical areas – but few clear patterns of activity (Rainville et al., 2002). Rainville et *al.* did, however, find that hypnotic *relaxation* seems to involve an increase in occipital regional cerebral blood flow (rCBF) and a decrease in cortical arousal, while increases in *mental absorption* during hypnosis were associated with rCBF increases in a distributed network of cortical and subcortical structures described as the brain's 'attentional system'. All this might then be consistent with findings that different manifestations of dissociation are reflected by different activity, and the diverse brain responses linked with hypnosis might simply parallel the wide range of neurobiological responses of dissociation itself: hypnosis can induce different types of altered consciousness and this manifests in different brain patterns.

Conversion disorders – still often referred to as hysterical sensori-motor syndromes – describe a form of compartmentalization in which a person has blindness, paralysis, or other nervous system symptoms that cannot be explained by medical evaluation. These have recently been reviewed (and linked with hypnosis) by Bell, Oakley, Halligan and Deeley (2011) and here we can see more clear patterns of brain activity. The authors concluded that early processing in primary sensory and motor cortices remains functionally intact in patients with conversion disorder, so we can see that the capability is there. Whether clinically diagnosed or simulated using hypnosis, impairment seemed to stem from task-related inhibition involving high-level processes. Thus the potential to see, move and so on exists but is not realized because of inhibition by the PFC. Again we see the potential for the PFC to promote dissociation. Here we have only been able to touch on conversion disorders, but Brown, in his chapter in this book, does explore the concept more extensively and considers interventions based on our neuropsychological understandings.

Detachment

Detachment incorporates depersonalization and derealization, 'spacing out' and other feelings of unreality. There is little disturbance to sense of identity insofar as the person still recognizes him or herself. Hopper and colleagues (2007) noted that although dissociative experiences can take the form of high emotional arousal or 'pathological over-engagement' as in flashbacks, another kind of disso-ciation takes the form of 'pathological under-engagement' or detachment, and these presentations show quite distinct neurological patterns.

Several brain mechanisms are likely to be involved in detachment, but a main player is the PFC. Stein and Simeon (2009) succinctly summarize the likely neurological process of detachment. They suggest that depersonalization may occur when there is a dysfunction of the cortical sensory association areas that normally match incoming sensory information with corresponding stored memories (see Figure 5.1). The resulting mis-match can underpin the sense of detachment. More specifically, they propose that in some people, there is an *over-activity* of the PFC which in turn *over-inhibits* limbic system structures such as the amygdala and the insula. This can have 'knock on' effects, including:

- autonomic nervous system 'blunting', with decreased heart rate and reduced galvanic skin response in patients with high dissociation.
- dysfunctional hypothalamic-pituitary-adrenal (HPA) axis activity, so patients with Depersonalization Disorder (chronic depersonalization) may have elevated cortisol levels at baseline, but an attenuated cortisol response to stress.
- dysregulation of certain neurotransmitters, such as glutamate and serotonin. It is of note that LSD and psilocybin, which act on serotonin receptors, cause depersonalization states.

In short, PFC activation can suppress the activity of the limbic system and quell strong emotions so that the detached person is overtly unreactive to stress despite the brain being very stressed. The detached person is on red alert but unreactive.

Fran heard what the doctor said and, strangely, felt nothing. She realized the shocking implications of the diagnosis, but felt detached and a little unreal. She drifted through the rest of the day feeling calm – and yet emotional in an intellectual way. She was able to get on with her work. Her colleagues would have had no idea that she was stressed.

This is a highly functional response when we need to keep our calm in a difficult situation. Cordelia Fine (2007) nicely describes detachment as 'the ace your brain keeps up its sleeve for when the chips are down' (p. 45). Fran was able to continue to function and many of us will be familiar with this helpful reaction. However, when detachment is an exaggerated, prolonged or inappropriate response it can cause dissociative problems. Fine (2007) reminds us that '…when the brain turns down the volume on the emotions, your sense of self begins to slip away', (p. 50): patients can suffer a profound lack of sense of who they are and a life that is distressingly unreal.

Baker *et al.* (2007) have proposed that patients with problems of depersonalization and derealization, who experience chronic detachment, have an 'over sensitive emotion-suppressing mechanism' (p. 30) which relates to the pre-frontal cortex. Such patients often report having 'lost their sense of self', which fits well with the neurological findings that our sense of self and personality seem to reside in the pre-frontal cortex. Baker *et al.* (2007) describe a cognitive-behavioural model of depersonalization and feelings of unreality (DPAFU) which again is predominantly cognitive-behavioural, but the authors note the central role of a hyper-reaction to emotions and sensations that results in an under-activity of the limbic system which triggers the problem state. Hunter's chapter in this book describes the model and the associated intervention in detail.

So, when we review what is happening in the brain we see that detachment and compartmentalization essentially involves different parts of the brain (although we do have to respect that the brain is rather more complicated than this!) Hopper's concept of 'over-engagement' seems to involve predominant activity of the limbic system, while 'under-engagement' involves activity of the pre-frontal areas of the brain – areas associated with mood moderation and emotional suppression. We begin to see how it makes sense that patients' presentations of 'dissociation' can look so different – they are neurologically different.

A word about self-injurious behaviours

Those of you who work with patients who self-harm without suicidal intent will probably have noted a link between self-injury and dissociation. Patients tend to self-harm either in order to escape from painful experiences or in order to combat feelings of 'nothingness' by creating a powerful response (see Klonsky, 2007, for a review). The key to managing self-harming behaviours is to understand why they are compelling. An appreciation of the role of dissociative processes helps us to see why self-injury might be so difficult to resist. You might hear things like:

> *'The stress is too much – my head feels as though it will explode, I can't think straight, I hate myself and then I cut and the tension slips away ...'*

> *'I can't sit still, can't get my head straight – but when I scratch and keep scratching I get calm.'*

> *'I reach the point where I feel so numb I feel dead. Then I don't care what I feel as long as I feel something. When I burn myself I'm alive – in pain but alive.'*

The main function of self-injurious behaviours (SIBs) seems to be emotional regulation, but in addition many patients feel that it's 'right' that they should be punished and the SIB sits comfortably with that. So what happens during an episode of SIB – what so efficiently achieves the patient's goals? In an old, but still excellent paper, Suyemoto (1998) explores the psychological meanings of self-harm and recognizes that a single act can simultaneously fulfil many functions (elation, distraction and punishment, for example). This helps us appreciate the absolutely compelling quality of SIBs, but what is happening at a physical level to explain the compulsion?

It has long been established that endogenous opioids (also called endorphins and encephalins) are natural anaesthetics that can also produce sedation and euphoria. We know that they are endogenous opiates because their effects are blocked by naloxone, a narcotic antagonist. They are predominantly, but not exclusively, produced in the brain in response to physical trauma, but they can ease both physical and psychological pain (see Sher and Stanley, 2008 for a review). They act quickly and can be stimulated via self-injury without the need to access drugs or alcohol, so is it any wonder that patients turn to cutting and burning? Endorphins can also be activated by certain drugs, food and alcohol and this might explain a compulsion to over-eat or misuse drugs and alcohol in order to achieve a dissociated state. As one of our patients reports: 'I eat myself into oblivion'. It is also worth noting that bleeding during self-injury will almost certainly trigger a drop in blood-pressure which will ease tension. In fact, it has been suggested by Shauer and Elbert (2010) that self-injury initiates dissociation (detachment) by inducing a drop in blood pressure and heart rate coupled with emotional shut down via parasympathetic nervous system activation. This happens quickly and effectively and can bring a great sense of relief.

It does appear that self-injurious behaviour is reinforced by its consequences (operant conditioning) – in the short term it achieves the desired effects and so it is compelling.

How does understanding neuropsychology guide treatment?

Along with other psychotherapies, CBT is driven by a patient's formulation. As therapists we strive to achieve an understanding of the patterns which make sense of the patient's problems, and an appreciation of the neurological underpinnings of psychology can really inform our conceptualizations.

But it is not just of benefit to clinicians; it is very often therapeutic for our patients. So many come to clinics believing that they are going crazy – indeed some have been given this impression within the services that support them. We can immediately reassure patients that there are understandable reasons for their absent episodes or for their flashbacks, for their hyper-arousal or their urge to self-harm. The brain is doing what it's set up to do in order to manage traumatic experiences and memories, and to keep us safe and help us regulate affect – it's just doing this too well. It is over-responding or responding too readily. Therapists can de-stigmatize the experience, offer hope and then help patients harness the advantages of their stress response, to bring it back in line so that it works for them and not against them.

Given what we know about the impact of repeated trauma, especially on the immature brain, we need to remember that our patient's capacity to tolerate and manage emotion may be compromised if they were victims of developmental and/or chronic trauma or neglect. That is not to say that therapists should collude in avoidance of addressing problem memories, but that this should be staged according to patient resources and resilience. As previously mentioned, in a recent randomized controlled trial of PTSD patients who had suffered childhood trauma, Cloitre *et al.* (2010) established that optimal treatment involved developing their ability to manage emotional states and to develop interpersonal skills prior to directly addressing problem intrusions. A preliminary period of teaching stabilization skills was necessary for best outcome, a finding which is echoed in the Van der Hart chapter in this book.

Understanding the processes of memory can remind us not to set too much store by the veracity of memory, particularly remote memories which may have become distorted over time. We need to encourage patients not to become too fixed on remembering details as they run the risk of confabulating if they try too hard. Where there is memory deficit or vagueness perhaps we should focus on the *meaning* that the event (however ill recalled) has for the patient, rather than striving for details of recollection. We also need to be careful not to pathologize forgetting in patients with trauma histories, as sometimes they have simply forgotten or never stored information.

As we have seen, there are a few cognitive-behavioural, empirically established models of dissociative disorders to guide our therapy. Clearly if a patient fits a proven model then the treatment protocol should guide the patient's treatment (with the cautions set out above). However, many of our patients' presentations will not fit a model and then we must rely on our ability to generate a meaningful idiosyncratic formulation to guide our work, a conceptualization which can usefully be informed by our neurobiological understanding of dissociation.

Summary

There remains much to be discovered concerning the neurobiology of disso-ciation, but that which we already know can enrich our clinical practice. This knowledge can underpin meaningful formulations which, in turn, help patients appreciate the origin of their problems without stigmatization and fear. It also prompts us to use reasonable caution in our practice so that we maintain a realistic scepticism concerning remote memories and do not overestimate our patients' emotional robustness.

Chapter 6

Imagery and dissociation

Lusia Stopa

Introduction

> *John was driving home from work. He was approaching the traffic lights at a cross road when he saw an ambulance with flashing lights coming from his left. He stopped to let the ambulance through and, as he glanced in his rear-view mirror, saw a van approaching at high speed. At that moment he knew he was going to be hit and he was terrified. Next, he found himself looking down at the scene; he saw his own car and the van that had crashed into him. He saw the driver of the van slumped forward at the wheel and people moving below. They looked small and were 'scurrying around like ants'. All sound was muffled and John felt detached from the chaos. John thought he had died and left his body.*

John's experience of acute dissociation at the moment of impact in a road traffic accident nicely illustrates mental imagery in dissociation. John thought he was going to die; his dissociation depended on his ability to form a mental image of the scene from a different perspective. John was not actually hovering above the scene watching it and yet he 'saw' the collision, and could provide a detailed description, 'as if' he was looking down at it from a completely different vantage point. The perceptual experience was not limited to visual imagery as John described sounds being muffled whereas, in reality, the collision was extremely loud. His dissociation was an automatic protective response that distanced him from a terrifying experience. However, it was maladaptive in the long run because John could not make sense of what happened – he thought he had died and yet simultaneously, he knew he was still alive. The incompatibility of these two views was reinforced by his continuing experience of dissociation during the flashbacks that he experienced long after the accident.

Dissociation is not a unitary phenomenon. The term describes a spectrum ranging from non-pathological experiences, such as day-dreaming, through to severe pathological states such as dissociative identity disorder (see, for example, Ross, Joshi, and Curie, 1990). The consensus view is that in dissociative states, individuals fail to integrate thoughts, feelings and experiences into their on-going stream of consciousness (Bernstein and Putnam, 1986). Explicit examination of the role of imagery in explanations of dissociation is rare, despite imagery's acknowledged importance in the aetiology and maintenance of many clinical disorders (Stopa, 2009). The absence of imagery from current theoretical accounts of dissociation may be due to the emphasis on *process* rather than *content*, which is exemplified by Spiegel's (1997) statement that dissociative disorders are 'a disturbance in the organization or structure of mental contents rather than in the contents themselves' (p. 225). In this chapter, I will argue that a full understanding of dissociation requires attention to both process and content, and that understanding the role of mental imagery is fundamental to a better understanding of dissociation and its treatment.

A mental image is an internally generated percept that can occur in any sensory modality. This chapter is organized around three key questions.

- Is imagery important at all points along the dissociative spectrum?
- Does imagery function in the same way along different points of the dissociative spectrum, or does it vary according to the type and severity of the dissociative experience?
- How can the links between imagery, memory and the self inform our understanding of dissociative experiences?

I will start at the milder end of the dissociative spectrum and consider day-dreaming and fantasy proneness, followed by an examination of imagery, autobiographical memory, and dissociation in trauma. I will then briefly consider different conceptualizations of dissociation before moving further along the continuum to examine motor imagery in somatoform disorder. The final part of the chapter will examine the role of imagery in the most extreme dissociative experiences, such as dissociative identity disorder, in which personality itself becomes fragmented.

Day-dreaming and fantasy proneness

Day-dreaming is often thought of as a 'normal', non-pathological form of dissociation, and is frequently used in clinical practice to explain the concept of dissociation to patients. Day-dreaming is characterized by turning attention towards an internal mental landscape that is frequently populated by mental images of desired future events. People who are day-dreaming may appear to be 'lost in thought' or 'dreaming' and this detachment from awareness of present reality is a characteristic feature of dissociation. Mental imagery is a core feature of day-dreaming; indeed it could be seen as a defining part of it. There are a number of traits linked to day-dreaming such as fantasy proneness, anticipation of future events, mind-wandering, absorption, creativity, and flow. Vannucci and Mazzoni (2006) argue that there is a robust relationship between individuals' tendencies to dissociate (sometimes described as trait dissociation) and their absorption in fantasy and imagination. Indeed, they point out that that mental imagery is so pervasive in these experiences that dissociation in the normal population may be related to a specific cognitive style based on the use of mental images. Interestingly, given this relationship, studies of non-clinical populations have so far failed to find an association between dissociation and vividness of mental imagery (Vannucci and Mazzoni, 2006).

Day-dreaming and fantasy proneness are generally seen as non-pathological. Wilson and Barber (1983) found that around four per cent of the population spent a significant proportion of their time in the world of imagination and fantasy [as much as fifty per cent of waking time for some individuals (Csikszentmihalyi, 1987)]. Their imaginative activity was generally adaptive, and they functioned well in the world. However, not all day-dreaming is benign. Day-dreaming that is used to avoid, escape, or that is a way of coping with extremely aversive experiences, has been called 'maladaptive day-dreaming' and has been defined as 'extensive fantasy activity that replaces human interaction and/or interferes with academic, interpersonal, or vocational functioning' (Somer, 2002; p. 199). One suggestion is that 'healthy' day-dreaming involves using day-dreams to enhance good feelings about the self, whereas negative or maladaptive day-dreaming involves interpreting day-dreams as signs of personal inadequacy (e.g. Gold and Minor, 1983). This binary distinction may be too simplistic. In a small-scale research study (four out of six patients met the criteria for maladaptive day-dreaming), Somer (2002) suggested maladaptive day-dreaming incorporates a range of themes that include both escape from aversive experiences, and the creation of safe and/or ideal worlds/selves.

All of Somer's (2002) participants reported the onset of maladaptive day-dreaming as a way to cope with distressing childhood experiences. Indeed, dissociation is commonly accepted as a protective defence against overwhelming affect – either in direct response to a traumatic event or when a memory is activated (e.g. during a flashback in PTSD). During dissociation, positive imagery can be used as an aid to avoid/escape aversive experiences. Spiegel (1997), for example, cites a patient with dissociative identity disorder who reported that when she was being sexually assaulted as a child, she would go 'to a mountain meadow full of wild flowers' (p. 227). Other trauma victims describe the experience of floating above their bodies, watching themselves, and feeling detached from what is actually happening. Like John, this defence mechanism, in which the individual is able to 'watch' from an observer perspective, is fundamentally dependent on mental imagery.

Many day-dreams are brief and transient; however, they can comprise of detailed and lengthy periods of fantasizing. Schupak and Rosenthal (2009) report a single case-study of a 36-year-old woman who had spent substantial periods of her day involved in elaborate day-dreams since her earliest memories. Even though her day-dreaming had not interfered with academic or vocational success, she experienced significant distress because of her determination to conceal the amount of time she spent day-dreaming from her family and friends, which left her feeling exhausted and demoralized. Schupak and Rosenthal questioned the degree to which her day-dreaming was under volitional control and speculated whether it constituted a type of obsessional-compulsive behaviour.

Day-dreaming is often future oriented and may represent wish-fulfilment, but, as Somer's (2002) study showed, other themes focus on the past, including a rewriting of more desired outcomes. One important function of imagery is the integration of past experiences in order to construct simulations of future events. Brewin, Gregory, Lipton, and Burgess (2010) illustrate this point with reference to the links between intrusive images and intrusive memories in a range of clinical disorders. They point to the similar content of future-oriented images and intrusive memories, and highlight shared properties such as vividness, persistence and uncontrollability. Brewin *et al.* draw attention to Schacter, Addis, and Buckner's (2007) suggestion that similar neural architecture underpins thinking about both past and future. John's case illustrates how the past intrudes into the present and then, in turn, influences the future. One of his principal intrusive images was seeing himself above the scene of the accident. This observer-perspective image (i.e. looking at the self from the outside), provided the link between his experience of acute dissociation during the accident and his memory of that experience. His inability to make sense of two radically different versions of reality – the experience of 'having died and left his body' and the knowledge that he was still alive – produced high levels of distress, an elevated perception of threat in the future, rumination, and behavioural avoidance that prevented him from getting on with his life. The complex relationship between past, present, and future is further amplified when individuals are dealing with the aftermath of multiple traumas.

Imagery, and dissociation in traumatic memory

The relationship between PTSD and dissociation is explored in detail in other chapters and therefore I have only touched on some of the ways in which imagery, dissociation, and trauma are linked. Mental imagery is an inescapable part of the re-experiencing of trauma memories across a range of sensory modalities, and dissociation can contribute to, or exacerbate this process. Intrusive memories can be 'veridical' or 'non-veridical' (Grey, 2009) Veridical memories represent relatively accurate recall of an event (e.g. seeing a car approaching and experiencing the subsequent collision). Non-veridical intrusive memories refer to images of events that did not actually occur; for example, memories that represent what the individual feared might have happened (e.g. seeing oneself dead) or, in the case of multiple trauma, composite images that link parts of many different experiences (e.g. a blend of different combat experiences).

Dissociation influences the formation of memories in different ways. In John's case, peritraumatic dissociation depended on the formation of an image of the scene that was viewed from above, and his intrusive memories and flashbacks repeatedly recalled that moment after the accident. Therefore, mental imagery was involved both in the *experience* of dissociation, and also in the *memory* of the trauma. However, dissociation can influence the way in which memory is registered because it disrupts the normal memory encoding processes leading to a fragmentation of the experience when the memory is recalled. This is illustrated in Megan's case. Megan was abducted and held for several hours, and although she had not been physically harmed, she was constantly threatened with a knife. She was understandably terrified and experienced periods of dissociation throughout the whole trauma. Her intrusive memories of the traumatic experience had a fragmented, dreamlike quality that she could not make sense of, punctuated by moments of intense terror.

Trauma memories are one type of autobiographical memory. Imagery is fundamental to autobiographical memory, which is in its turn an integral component of the individual's sense of self. Autobiographical memory contains the individual's knowledge store that is built up through experience, and includes a category of memories called 'self-defining' (see, for example, Singer and Salovey, 1993). Self-defining memories are memories of personal events that have particular significance for the individual's identity. Such memories can be positive or negative: trauma memories are one particular class of self-defining memories because traumatic experiences often mark a significant rupture in the individual's sense of self. Individuals often make comments such as, 'I'm not the person I was before the accident', which indicate this rupture. Karen's case illustrates this link between imagery, memory and self.

> *Karen was in her late twenties. She had recently been promoted and had got married. She had an accident on her bicycle while riding home from work. As well as the flashbacks of being thrown off her bicycle and lying on the ground, Karen had two very clear images of herself. One was of a functioning, competent self and the other was of herself as a much younger child who was unhappy and felt unloved and uncared for. She commented early in therapy that "I feel as if my old self has died and I can never be the same person again". During the first session of imaginal reliving, Karen described feeling utterly alone and helpless.*

Karen had experienced a very difficult relationship with her mother in childhood and prior to the accident she believed that she had become a much stronger person. She was proud of what she had achieved and thought she had left the old self behind. Activation of the image of her younger self was highly distressing and sometimes triggered mild dissociative experiences, such as feeling unreal and 'floaty', which further intensified her sense of alienation from her 'competent self'. We conducted a dialogue between these two conflicting self-images in treatment to help Karen understand why the images of her younger self had been activated – feeling vulnerable, alone and helpless both in the accident and in hospital afterwards – and to allow her to connect and integrate the two self-representations. One notable effect was that during the subsequent reliving, Karen immediately retrieved memories of people who had helped her at the time of the accident. She also stopped dissociating.

Memory is not a direct replay of past experiences; instead it is always a reconstructive process (Bartlett, 1932). Individuals retrieve information relating to a memory, which is then combined to produce the 'recollective experience' – a combination of information about the event, sensory images and a subjective feeling of remembering. This means that people can have false memories; they can remember something that did not in fact occur. This is relevant to the extremely contentious issue of 'recovered' memories of early childhood abuse. Some ingenious experimental work suggests that both imagery and dissociation may shed light on the mechanisms that could underpin why some people might remember events that did not occur, although this is by no means intended to suggest that all recovered memories are false. Indeed, the study of dissociation more generally has helped us to understand why and how memories can be split off from conscious awareness and then retrieved at a later date.

Imagery and dissociation may both contribute to the creation of false memories. Hyman and Pentland (1996) asked parents of participants to complete a childhood events questionnaire, which contained ten categories of events. In subsequent interviews, participants described between two and five 'true' events (parent-supplied) and one 'false' event (experimenter-supplied). Participants in a guided-imagery condition created more false events, and recovered more memories of previously unavailable true events than participants in a control condition where they simply thought about the event for one minute. Hyman and Pentland suggest that high trait dissociation may increase the tendency to accept false memories as real because it disrupts the normal integration of consciousness and makes it more difficult for individuals reliably to monitor the source of information.

Heaps and Nash (1999) also suggest that trait dissociation has an important role in creation of false memories. They found that trait dissociation was one of two predictors of the imagination inflation effect (the experimental finding that adults are more likely to judge a childhood event as having actually happened if they create mental images rather than just thinking about it: Garry, Manning, Loftus, and Sherman, 1996). They argue that trait dissociation disrupts episodic memories, and therefore individuals who regularly dissociate may be more susceptible to imagination inflation because they are used to accepting memories as 'real' on the basis of less information than low trait-dissociation individuals who are less likely to experience disruptions in the encoding of memories and therefore have a fuller and more accurate record of the original memory. Hyman and Pentland (1996) go beyond the creation of the false memory to suggest that findings such as theirs and Heaps and Nash's raise questions not only about the malleability of autobiographical memory, but also about self-concept itself – a point that is highly salient when we discuss imagery and dissociative identity disorder later in the chapter.

Conceptualizing and understanding dissociation

So far I have relied on the idea of dissociation existing on a continuum. Holmes *et al.* (2005) challenge this idea and argue for a distinction between two qualitatively different sets of experiences, which they label detachment and compartmentalization. Detachment refers to the experience of feeling in some way separated from normal day to day consciousness or sense of self and includes experiences such as flashbacks, depersonalization and derealization, as well as more extreme manifestations such as out-of-body experiences. By comparison, compartmentalization encompasses dissociative amnesia and symptoms that are characteristic of conversion disorders such as unexplained paralysis, sensory loss, seizures etc. Holmes *et al.* argue that this qualitative distinction between detachment and compartmentalization is a more accurate way to conceptualize dissociation, fits better with the evidence, and is more useful both clinically and theoretically than the idea of a continuum.

These two contrasting conceptualizations are not necessarily mutually exclusive, as there may be a continuum of types and severity of dissociation within each of the two categorical distinctions. Continua remain at the heart of two recent models of dissociation (Van der Hart, Van der Kolk, and Boon,1996; Kennedy *et al.*, 2004). Both models suggest that there are three stages of dissociation. In Van der Hart *et al.*'s model, primary, secondary, and tertiary dissociation refer to processing the trauma in parts (e.g. sensory fragments are not integrated into the trauma narrative), peritraumatic dissociation, and splitting of the personality respectively. Kennedy *et al.*'s model draws on the concept of modes of processing that are defined as sets of schemas responsible for encoding cognitive, affective, behavioural and physiological information. In normal circumstances switching between modes and integrating information across modes is unconscious and automatic. In the model, dissociation can occur at the initial stage (one) of processing when incoming information is registered (e.g. dissociating at the time of the trauma, day-dreaming), it can occur *within* a mode (stage two) where there is a failure to integrate different types of information (e.g. failure to integrate different parts of a trauma memory), or it can occur *between* modes (stage three) when information is encapsulated within one mode and not available for another (e.g. dissociative amnesia, dissociative identity disorder).

Interestingly, none of these conceptualizations or models of dissociation explicitly addresses the role of imagery at any of the different stages of dissociation. Failure to specify and delineate the role of imagery means that we can have, at best, only a partial explanation of dissociation.

Imagery and somatoform dissociation

In the next part of this chapter, I will concentrate first on somatoform dissociation and then on the group of dissociative disorders that includes dissociative identity disorder. Nijenhuis (2000) distinguishes between 'psychological' and 'somatoform' dissociation. Psychological dissociation encompasses experiences that primarily involve psychological variables, such as amnesia, depersonalization, derealization and alterations to identity. Somatoform dissociation describes primarily bodily symptoms, which can include things such as sensory anaesthesia, and perceptual disturbances, but also encompasses unexplained pain and aberrant motor symptoms. Sławek, Wichowicz, Cubała, Soltan, Palasik, Wilczewska, and Fiszer (2010), for example, describe the case of a 42-year-old woman who had developed axial myoclonus (sudden, involuntary muscle jerks) nine months earlier. She was admitted to hospital for investigations, which were all normal, but during the period she was in hospital she started to have epileptic seizures. Investigation of these again failed to find any underlying abnormalities and she was diagnosed with conversion disorder (one of the group of somatoform disorders according to DSM IV-TR: American Psychiatric Association, 2000). Nijenhuis points out that although this distinction between psychological and somatoform dissociation is phenomenologically useful, it does not imply differences in causation. The two types of dissociative symptoms can overlap and may simply be different expressions of the same underlying cause.

The concept of somatoform dissociation is rooted in the traditions of nineteenth-century French psychiatry, with its detailed examination of hysteria by people such as Briquet (1859) and Janet (e.g. 1889, 1893). It is beyond the scope of this chapter to do justice to this extensive history beyond acknowledging the key figures (chapter one provides a detailed history of dissociative disorders). Here, I am concerned with focusing specifically on the role of imagery.

Somatoform dissociation is one of the few areas in the dissociative literature where imagery has been explicitly studied, albeit from the narrow perspective of motor imagery. This limited literature focuses almost exclusively on motor paralysis in the absence of any neurological pathology (most patients studied have a diagnosis of conversion disorder or conversion paralysis). The rationale for examining motor imagery is that real and imagined movements are both controlled within the same neurocognitive systems (Maruff and Velakoulis, 2000) and that in some neurological syndromes (e.g. Parkinson's) there are difficulties with the formation of motor images as well as with actual physical movement (Dominey, Decety, Brouselle, Chazot, and Jeannerod, 1995). Roelofs et al. (2001) point out that little is known about whether patients with pseudo-neurological symptoms (another term for conversion or somatoform symptoms) also have difficulties with motor imagery.

In one study, Liepert, Hassa, Tüscher, and Schmidt (2011) measured motor evoked potentials (MEPs) while a group of patients with psychogenic paralysis of a lower limb either imagined flexing their ankles or watched another person perform ankle flexions. Compared to healthy controls, the patient group showed reduced MEPs when imagining their own movements, whereas healthy controls showed an increase. Furthermore, patients did not differ from controls when watching another person. Liepert et al. argue that this may be due to inhibition and suggest that there are therapeutic possibilities in asking patients to imagine other people's movements.

Another path of enquiry is comparing real and imagined motor movements in patients with psychogenic paralysis. A series of studies by de Lange, Roelofs and colleagues (de Lange, Roelofs, and Toni, 2007; Roelofs, Van Galen, Kesjers, and Hoogduin, 2002; Roelofs, Näring, Keijsers, Hoogduin, Van Galen, and Maris, 2001) investigated the neural control of action in patients with paralyzes of various limbs and compared both real and imagined action, as well as the impact of explicit (verbal instructions) and implicit cues. For example, Roelofs *et al.* (2001) compared mental motor imagery in six patients with conversion paralysis and six healthy controls and found that the patient group was significantly slower than the non-patient group on mental rotation tasks and that their motor imagery was more affected when they created images of the affected limbs than when they focused on non-affected limbs. They explain these, and other related results, as a general slowing of the whole intentional movement system in the patients with paralysis.

The study of motor imagery as a way to explore somatoform dissociation is promising, but is at a very early stage. None of the studies described above looks at spontaneous mental imagery. There is one single case study that suggests this may be a fruitful line of enquiry. Cassell and Dubey (2007) used the Rorschach test to assess a surgical patient who developed chronic pelvic pain following successful treatment for bowel cancer. The patient apparently denied any fears of undetected tumours, but described an image of his pelvis being attacked by bugs. The study of imagery in chronic pain suggests that patients often have extremely vivid and graphic images of the parts of their bodies experiencing pain (Gillanders, Potter, and Morris, 2012). It is reasonable, therefore, to suppose that pain arising in the context of somatoform dissociation may also be accompanied by mental imagery and that this imagery may play a role in maintaining the symptom. What we do not know is whether the absence of sensation, such as in psychogenic paralysis, is also accompanied by mental images of the relevant body part.

Imagery and the dissociative disorders

The term 'dissociative disorders' includes dissociative amnesia, dissociative fugue, dissociative identity disorder, depersonalization disorder, and dissociative disorders not otherwise specified (DSM IV-TR, APA, 2000). This collection of disorders represents the most extreme end of the dissociative spectrum, where the failure to integrate the normal functions of consciousness that is characteristic of dissociation in general includes a failure to integrate self and memory. This is perhaps best illustrated by dissociative identity disorder (DID), which is defined by DSM IV-TR as 'the presence of two or more distinct identities or personality states (each with its own relatively enduring patterns of perceiving, relating to, and thinking about the environment and self', p. 529). At least two of these identities must take control of the person's behaviour and there is extensive inability to recall personal information. According to the guidelines issued by the International Society for the study of dissociation (ISSD, 2005), DID affects between one and three per cent of the population.

The ISSD (2005) review of aetiological models of DID highlights the assumption that DID arises from a failure in the normal developmental functions of self-integration, which occurs because overwhelming stress or trauma and disrupted attachment relationships in childhood block the normal developmental path. The central importance of self and memory in DID and other severe dissociative states suggests that our understanding might benefit from the clear account of the complex relationship between self and memory provided by Conway and Pleydell-Pearce's (2000) self-memory model (SMS). I will briefly outline the key points of the model and then discuss how it can applied to DID.

The revised SMS (Conway, Singer, and Tagini, 2004) consists of three key components:

- long-term self
- episodic memory system
- working self

The long-term self comprises the autobiographical knowledge base and the conceptual self. Autobiographical memory represents the knowledge store built up throughout the individual's life experience, whereas conceptual knowledge refers to more abstract semantic knowledge about the self ('I am a good/bad person') and awareness of personality traits (impatient, extravert, lively). The episodic memory system contains the record of recent events and encodes aspects of experiences such as sensory and perceptual details, as well as cognitive and

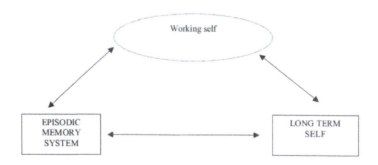

Figure 6.1 The structure of the self-memory system
   Reprinted with permission from 'The Self and Autobiographical Memory: Correspondence and Coherence' by M. A. Conway, J. A. Singer, and A. Tagini (2004) Social Cognition 22(5), p. 494, New York: Guilford Press.

affective information. Conway *et al.* (2004) link the episodic memory system to the pursuit of goal achievement and argue that episodic memories are only retained if they become linked to important information in the long term. The working self represents the individual's current 'on-line' self, which is made up of a subset of the long-term self together with relevant material from episodic memory. The functions of the working self are to allow flexible responding to current situational demands so that the individual can achieve his or her goals, and the organization of current experience, or the '*psychological* present' (p. 502).

How can the SMS model help us to understand DID? Take Mary, for example, a young woman at university, who also expressed herself as 'Tina'. In this frame of mind she would sometimes send abusive text messages to friends. Mary got very upset when her friends complained about these messages and denied sending them. She defended herself, saying she would never do such a thing and claimed that someone must be taking her phone and trying to cause trouble. Mary was not aware of 'Tina' but did report losing time and blackouts that she was very worried about. However, when she was in the mind-set of 'Tina' she was fully aware of both Tina and Mary because sometimes her messages would tell the recipient 'not to tell Mary'.

What is the best way to conceptualize these two different identities – Mary and Tina? Do they represent two different 'working selves' that are not integrated into a coherent long-term self? Alternatively, do they represent an actual splitting of the long-term self? If the latter, does each different long-term self have its own discrete autobiographical memory store and create different working selves to meet specific external demands? Images are potentially important here because, as well as being a fundamental component of autobiographical memories, images can represent the current working self and the long-term self (Stopa, 2009).

So, in order to understand how an individual maintains separate identities, we need to consider three inter-related components: imagery, memory and the self (or selves). These relationships could operate in a number of ways. First, images might represent different senses of self, and may help to organize the information/memories relevant to that state. Second, autobiographical memory is replete with sensory images. Presumably these images are in some way separated into coherent clusters that link groups of memories to particular senses of selves. However, it may be difficult to compartmentalize the long-term self effectively so as to prevent intrusions from one group of memories and linked self-knowledge from intruding on another. This may then lead to intrusions from a set of memories belonging to one sense of self bleeding into those of another, causing identity confusion and a sense of unreality as the individual at that moment has no recollection and no context for interpreting these intrusions.

It is too early to make specific therapeutic recommendations on the basis of the ideas outlined above. However, given the importance of imagery to other disorders, it would not be remiss for clinicians to start assessing imagery – both in relation to selves and memory and to include imagery in their aetiological and maintenance formulations.

Conclusion

The aim of this chapter is to consider the role of imagery in dissociation. By way of conclusion, it may be useful to return to the three questions around which the chapter is structured. The review of different points along the putative dissociation spectrum, while necessarily selective, suggests that imagery does occur at all points along the spectrum. The role and function of imagery does, however, appear to have some differences. At the mild end of the spectrum, day-dreaming can have a purely positive and enjoyable function of imagining oneself achieving desired outcomes. However, as discussed earlier in the chapter, day-dreaming can also have the function of escape and protection, a function that becomes increasingly important as we move to the more severe end of the spectrum. It is possible that images may aid the failure of integration that is a fundamental part of dissociation in disorders such as DID by representing distinct selves that are linked to specific groups of autobiographical memories. However, this suggestion is purely speculative at the moment. Finally, I would like to argue for the inclusion of normal models of the relationship between self and memory in models of dissociative disorders, and for the role of imagery to be explicitly examined and incorporated in order for us to gain a fuller understanding of dissociation as a whole. Better understanding will in turn lead to improved treatments and benefit those individuals whose lives have been damaged by trauma and adversity and who suffer from dissociation in all its manifestations.

Chapter 7

Dissociation and memory fragmentation

Rafaële J. C. Huntjens
Martin J. Dorahy
Rineke van Wees-Cieraad

The characteristic nature of trauma memory and its link to other autobiographical memories (i.e. the memories of events from one's life) are considered to play a key role in the development and maintenance of posttraumatic psychopathology. Ehlers and Clark (2000) metaphorically describe trauma memory as like a cupboard in which many things have been thrown in quickly and in a disorganized fashion. Such memory produces different, and at times opposing, symptoms: things may fall out at unpredictable times (i.e. involuntarily triggered intrusive memories), and an item cannot be found when needed (i.e. the experience of dissociative amnesia, where people are unable to voluntarily recall aspects of the event). Trauma survivors also report not having a detailed, coherent memory of the experienced event that can be translated into a cohesive narrative. Rather, the memory is disorganized and incoherent, consisting of 'items' scattered around in the 'cupboard' as well as some that are missing, hampering the construction of a clear, coherent narrative. This inability to voluntarily retrieve and describe trauma memory in an organized, coherent fashion is called fragmentation (e.g. Van der Kolk and Fisler, 1995). Several excellent reviews focus on the association between memory fragmentation and posttraumatic symptoms in the context of post traumatic stress disorder (PTSD) (O'Kearney and Perrott, 2006; Zoellner and Bittenger, 2004, see also Brewin, 2007).

Here we focus on the association between fragmentation and dissociative experiences because these experiences are considered to play a pivotal role in the origin and maintenance of fragmented memories. Subsequently, we discuss some mechanisms by which dissociation may influence the structure and content of the trauma memory. A more general review of memory processes involved in dissociation can be found in Dorahy and Huntjens (2007).

Fragmentation and peritraumatic dissociation

While some people describe their thinking during a traumatic event as extraordinarily clear and say they kept analyzing the situation, others report confusion and overwhelming sensory impressions (Clark and Ehlers, 2005). These latter individuals report experiencing alterations of perception during the traumatic event, such as time slowing, reduction in awareness of one's surroundings, out-of-body experiences, altered pain perception, emotional numbing, and experiencing the event as if unreal (Zoellner and Bittenger, 2004). These experiences are labeled peritraumatic dissociation. Such reactions to a traumatic stressor are common. For example, in a study of pregnancy loss, 70 per cent reported symptoms of peritraumatic dissociation (Engelhard, Van den Hout, Kindt, Arntz, and Schouten, 2003). Cardeña and Spiegel (1993) reported that 47 per cent of earthquake survivors experienced their attention narrowing, 40 per cent felt that their surroundings were unreal, and 23 per cent experienced emotional numbing. In a meta-analysis Ozer, Best, Lipsey, and Weiss (2003) found peritraumatic dissociation to be the strongest predictor of later PTSD, among prior trauma, prior psychological adjustment, family history of psychopathology, perceived life threat during the trauma and post trauma social support, (see also Lensvelt-Mulders *et al.*, 2008).

One of the critical mechanisms underlying the relationship between peritraumatic dissociation and later posttraumatic symptom development may be impaired encoding of the traumatic event in memory (Holmes and Bourne, 2008; Holmes, Brewin and Hennessy, 2004). In non-traumatic situations, the memory of an autobiographical event contains both specific information about the event itself and contextual information (Clark and Ehlers, 2005). For example, a young woman may remember walking through the local park with her baby in the pram last Wednesday. In a traumatic situation, however, the series of experiences that is encoded into memory is considered to be incoherent in terms of spatial and temporal details. For example, a woman may remember being attacked in the park, but not her attacker's appearance, where she was attacked, nor how long the attack lasted and the sequence of events within the attack episode maybe unclear to her. Also, temporal integration problems may arise within the context of previous and subsequent experiences that day. So the woman has no sense of the attack occurring after she sat on a bench or before she spoke to her husband. Finally, she may experience difficulties in elaboration (i.e. providing meaning to the event) and her memory of the attack is not assimilated, that is, integrated with further autobiographical memories (e.g. other memories of walks in the park). Many different terms, definitions and operationalizations have been used in the study of trauma memory fragmentation. In this chapter, we use the term *coherence* to refer to the embedding of the central spatial and temporal elements of the event in memory. We reserve the term *integration* to refer to the embedding of the event within the temporal context of immediate previous and subsequent autobiographical experiences. Fragmentation is characterized by reduced coherence and a lack of integration.

Memory coherence and temporal integration

In assessing memory fragmentation, some studies have analyzed trauma narratives for indications of fragmentation in the structure or content. Others have included self-report measures, in which participants rate their own sense of memory fragmentation. Additionally, objective fragmentation tasks have been developed in the laboratory.

Memory coherence in traumatized individuals

The structure of trauma narratives has been operationalized in terms of number of words used and reading ease of the narrative, hypothesizing that fragmentation in high dissociators would be evidenced by shorter and more difficult-to-read trauma narratives (Halligan, Michael, Clark, and Ehlers, 2003; Harvey and Bryant, 1999; Zoellner, Alvarez-Conrad and Foa, 2002). The evidence for this hypothesis so far is inconclusive. This may be because these indexes are rather nonspecific with regard to the disordered temporal and spatial elements of trauma narratives.

Harvey and Bryant (1999) used an alternative measure when they compared motor vehicle accident survivors who either developed or did not develop Acute Stress Disorder (ASD). Participants provided a narrative within 12 days of the accident, and completed a measure for ASD severity. Participants described the traumatic event in the present tense, as vividly and in as much detail as possible, including the surroundings, their activities, feelings, and their thoughts during the event. The narratives were analyzed for fragmentation or confusion within the utterance (e.g. 'I think I sat there for five minutes wondering what I should do'), disjointedness (e.g. 'asked the doctor knows a few things we got everything came back to me'), and repetition of an utterance (e.g. 'finally the ambulance arrived finally the ambulance arrived'). They found more fragmentation in narratives of people with ASD (see also Zoellner *et al.*, 2002; Jones, Harvey, and Brewin, 2007). Moreover, meeting the ASD dissociation criteria and meeting the avoidance criteria (as assessed with the Acute Stress Disorder Interview) showed more fragmentation (Bryant, Harvey, Dang and Sackville, 1998).

Halligan and colleagues (2003) assessed victims of physical or sexual assault who had been assaulted more than three months previously. Peritraumatic dissociation was assessed using the State Dissociation Questionnaire (SDQ; Murray, Ehlers, and Mayou, 2002). Memory coherence was assessed using indices comparable to Harvey and Bryant (1999). Also, an observer gave a global rating of coherence after reading each narrative. A subjective self-report scale of coherence was used where participants reported deficits in intentional recall (e.g. 'I cannot get what happened during the assault straight in my mind'). Retrospectively assessed peritraumatic dissociation correlated significantly with all measures. Thus, this study found that narrative analysis, observer ratings and self-report by survivors all showed a relationship between peritraumatic dissociation and narrative fragmentation.

Murray, Ehlers, and Mayou (2002) used both observer and self-report ratings of narrative fragmentation in inpatients with physical injuries and in outpatients seeking accident and emergency services following road traffic accidents. Unlike Halligan *et al.*'s (2003) findings, no correlation was found between peritraumatic dissociation and observer ratings. However, self-reported memory fragmentation did correlate significantly with peritraumatic dissociation in the outpatient group, but not the inpatient group. In this study, only self-report was related to dissociation and only in the outpatient group.

Engelhard *et al.* (2003) asked women four weeks after pregnancy loss how much their memory of the event consisted of 'fragmented pieces as opposed to a whole entity'. Dissociation at the time of the pregnancy loss was assessed with the Peritraumatic Dissociative Experiences Questionnaire (PDEQ; Marmar, Weiss, and Metzler, 1997). The measures correlated significantly but the effect was small. In this study a weak relationship between memory fragmentation and dissociation was found.

Rubin and colleagues (2004) asked veterans diagnosed with PTSD to indicate whether 1) the memory was 'in pieces with missing bits' and 2) whether the memory came to them 'as a coherent story or episode and not as an isolated fact, observation, or scene'. The first question was significantly correlated with PTSD avoidance symptoms, as indexed by the Davidson Trauma Scale (DTS; Davidson *et al.*, 1997), and (pre-trauma) trait dissociation, as indexed by the Dissociative Experiences Scale (DES; Bernstein and Putnam, 1986; Carlson and Putnam, 1993). The first question was not correlated with other PTSD symptoms, while ratings for the second question were not significantly related to any PTSD symptom cluster or dissociation measure.

In summary, the studies conducted with traumatized individuals show that those with higher dissociation (mostly peritraumatic dissociation during the event), typically show greater memory incoherence. Their stories of the traumatic event are not well ordered in terms of space and time, but are disjointed and seem to be 'in bits'. This is especially evident in, though not limited to, self reports of memory coherence problems.

Memory coherence in analogue studies

While studies focusing on the natural occurrence of traumatic events have the advantage of studying more directly the phenomenon to be explained, their disadvantage is that a number of other variables may influence the results. This means that the exact cause or causes of a study's finding is obscured. Among potential other explanatory variables are pre-trauma cognitive functioning, attentional functioning during the traumatic event, and the amount of previous retrieval of the trauma memory (Zoellner and Bittenger, 2004). Also, they differ widely in the elapsed time between the traumatic event and the subsequent study. These factors are better controlled in analogue studies, which are studies that attempt to replicate or simulate, under controlled conditions, a situation that occurs in real life. Kindt and Van den Hout (2003), (see also Kindt, Van den Hout and Buck, 2005) showed an extremely aversive film to a student sample whose memory fragmentation was objectively measured by a memory task assessing the sequence of events in the film four hours after it was watched. Participants saw clips from the film and were asked to indicate the original order in which the clips were shown during the film. As an index of subjective memory fragmentation, participants rated how much their memories felt like a 'snap-shot.' 'Peritraumatic dissociation' (i.e. state dissociation while watching the aversive film) was assessed with an adapted version of the PDEQ. Participants who tended to dissociate more during the film did not perform worse at ordering the clips correctly, as was expected, but did rate their memory for the film as more fragmentary. Thus dissociation at the time of watching the film was associated with participants' sense of having fragmented memory, but not with actual fragmented memory.

Using a comparable task in patients with depersonalization disorder, however, Giesbrecht, Merckelbach, Van Oorsouw and Simeon (2010), did find objective memory fragmentation (poorer performance on ordering clips) in addition to subjective (self-rated) fragmentation. So memory fragmentation was seen in the performance of a clinical group but not a student group. Giesbrecht and colleagues used a memory task which might have been more difficult than Kindt et al.'s, as their task consisted of ordering more clips which were shown for a shorter period. The different results may also be due to other methodological issues (e.g. the use of different scoring methods), so more standardized research is needed which includes this kind of objective fragmentation measure in analogue and clinical studies.

Embedding with the broader autobiographical knowledge base (assimilation)

To our knowledge, the only study so far considering the embedding of trauma memories in the broader autobiographical knowledge base was by Kleim, Wallott and Ehlers (2008), with assault survivors with and without PTSD. They hypothesized that, if assault memories were less well assimilated into the context of other life experiences, recalling the assault would slow down retrieval of other autobiographical memories. They used the speed with which participants could provide autobiographical information while remembering 1) the assault and 2) the worst moment of another negative life event, as an index of assimilation. Autobiographical information questions asked, for example, about their last birthday or holiday, or the name of their primary school. In line with the prediction of reduced memory assimilation, the PTSD group took longer to retrieve autobiographical memories when exposed to the assault memory script compared to the control group. The PTSD group also took longer to retrieve other personal memories when recalling the assault than when recalling an unrelated negative memory. Importantly, dissociation while listening to the scripts (assessed with the SDQ) was positively related to a lack of memory assimilation.

In summary, the slower recall of other personal (autobiographical) memories when a trauma memory is uppermost in mind, suggests that trauma memories are not well integrated with the rest of the personal memory store.

What are the mechanisms relating peritraumatic dissociation and memory fragmentation?

Several authors have argued that dissociation allows traumatic memories to be separated from awareness in order to minimize distress. The trauma memories (or some sensory and affective components) somehow become dissociated from the ordinary memory system and the memory as a whole (or some components of it) is inaccessible for conscious retrieval (Janet, 1907; Spiegel, Koopman, Cardeña and Classen, 1996; Terr, 1991; Van der Hart, Bolt, and Van der Kolk, 2005). However, most theories lack a specification of the mechanisms involved in the dissociative processing of trauma memories.

Data-driven versus conceptually-driven processing

The cognitive model of PTSD developed by Ehlers and Clark (2000) provides greater specificity. They argue that the trauma memory is characterized by data-driven (i.e. perceptual) encoding (i.e. processing the sensory impressions and perceptual details) and lacks conceptual processing (i.e. processing the meaning of the situation in an organized way and placing it into context). An emergency service worker with PTSD remembers vividly and involuntarily the smell and sight of blood, but has little awareness of the sequence of events or length of time he was there. Evidence for the link between dissociation and data-driven encoding comes from priming studies. People shown a picture of, say, a camel, will react faster to that picture when seeing it for a second time compared to a picture they have not seen before: 'priming' is this faster reaction to a previously experienced stimulus. Participants with high trait dissociation showed relatively stronger perceptual priming compared to participants with low trait dissociation (Michael and Ehlers, 2007). State dissociation during encoding has been found to be a predictor of perceptual priming (e.g. Michael and Ehlers, 2007; Lyttle, Dorahy, Hanna and Huntjens, 2010). When a terrorist victim is exposed to a list of words including 'bomb' and 'comb' while experiencing dissociation, they will be more likely to complete the word fragment 'bo__' with 'bomb' than 'co__' with 'comb.' Dissociation may facilitate perceptual memory processing for threat stimuli compared to neutral stimuli. The word associated with the attack ('bomb') is closer to the 'front' of the victim's mind than an unassociated word ('comb'). In short, dissociation *enhances* perceptual processing and *impairs* conceptual processing. This suggests that those who experience dissociation while processing a distressing event are more likely to limit processing to perceptual representations (visual, auditory, bodily sensations, olfactory). In therapy, patients may experience imagery rather than ascribing meaning: the woman attacked in the park may see the attacker's face/hear his voice rather than make sense of the attack.

Perceptual processing has been linked to memory fragmentation. Halligan *et al.* (2003) assessed self-reported perceptual processing during an assault (e.g.

'It was just like a stream of unconnected impressions following each other') and found significant correlations with several narrative fragmentation measures (see also Murray *et al.*, 2002). Halligan, Clark, and Ehlers (2002) assessed the type of cognitive processing (perceptual versus conceptual) that participants reported during previously experienced stressful life events. They divided participants reporting a tendency to use data-driven processing from those reporting conceptual processing. They then showed both groups a trauma film as an analogue stressor. To measure memory fragmentation, they used a self-report scale (e.g. 'I cannot get what happened during the videotape straight in my mind'). They also asked the participants to describe everything they could recall from the film. They noted what proportion of events from the film were recalled in the correct order, to obtain a more objective measure of 'memory coherence'. The data-driven group reported more analogue PTSD symptoms in the week following the film. On fragmentation measures, the data-driven group scored twice as high as the conceptually-driven group on the self-report scale but did not differ on the order measure. So increased data-driven encoding was related to memory fragmentation, but this pertains only to self-reported memory fragmentation. When a more objective measure of memory fragmentation was used, no association was found.

In summary, the empirical evidence so far is consistent in pointing out data-driven processing as a central mechanism resulting in memory fragmentation. Dissociation during encoding facilitates fragmentation. Yet, the research thus far has been confined to subjectively experienced memory fragmentation.

Self-referential processing

A second possible mechanism explaining the link between peritraumatic dissociation and memory fragmentation is the lack of 'self-referential' processing (i.e. relating the events experienced to the self) during the traumatic event. Clinically, this is evident in statements like, 'I know this happened to me, but it doesn't feel like it did, it doesn't seem real.' Ehlers and Clark (2000) proposed that an inability to establish a self-referential perspective during the trauma, involving processing the experiences with respect to oneself and relating them to other autobiographical information, impedes the assimilation of memories into the autobiographical memory base. Disrupted self-referential processing of traumatic experiences has been understood as a central aspect of dissociation, and referred to by some authors as a lack of personification (Van der Hart, Nijenhuis and Steele, 2006). Interestingly, Halligan *et al.* (2003) included a measure of self-referential processing, assessing the extent to which participants perceived the event as happening to someone else and the extent to which they felt the experience was incorporated with other autobiographical information relating to the self ('I felt as if it was happening to someone else'). Lack of self-referential processing was significantly associated with all fragmentation measures.

Methodological considerations

Most, but not all, *self-report* and *experimenter-rated* measures show a positive relation between memory fragmentation and dissociation. Yet, the evidence is inconclusive for the more *objective* measures (i.e. ordering of film clips) included in experimental studies. Several factors may account for the inconsistent results.

- There may be an effect of study procedures. For example, in some studies, participants are probed for more details while describing the traumatic event. This procedure may counteract the habitual avoidance strategy of not voluntarily retrieving specific (emotional) details of the traumatic memory.
- While some studies have determined the level of peritraumatic dissociation within days after the traumatic event, most have measured peritraumatic dissociation well after the event. The association between fragmentation and peritraumatic dissociation may be magnified when the person is suffering PTSD, dissociative or other symptoms (their view of the event itself may be biased by their current suffering).
- Self-report measures of memory fragmentation are widely used. The extent to which cognitive processing can be inferred from introspections is doubtful. Self-report measures reflect a *metamemory judgment* about the participant's memory functioning. This also may be strongly influenced by current symptoms.
- Confounding factors such as pre-trauma lower verbal intelligence, general cognitive ability, and articulation difficulties (Zoellner and Bittenger, 2004) have typically not been controlled. Lower intelligence has been found to explain differences in the reading level of written trauma narratives in students with and without PTSD (Gray and Lombardo, 2001).
- Traumatic brain injury may have the same effects on coherence as those that are ascribed to dissociative pathology (Jones *et al.*, 2007).
- Distress or avoidance during recall may make accounts incoherent in the absence of actual memory problems (Halligan *et al.*, 2003; Van Minnen, Wessel, Dijkstra and Roelofs, 2002).

Future studies of trauma memory should consider the organization of the traumatic event within experiences preceding and following it in voluntary recall, so that the 'hot spot' (most traumatic part) is not examined in isolation (e.g. Michael and Ehlers, 2007). As knowledge based on *past* negative experiences may influence *current* reactions to trauma, studies should look at the interplay of trauma memories and other relevant memory representations laid down in the autobiographical knowledge base.

Persistent dissociation

Peritraumatic dissociation has been described as dissociation experienced either during or immediately after a distressing event. Bryant, Friedman, Spiegel, Ursano and Strain (2011) have argued that the time frame in this definition is ambiguous, and that dissociation occurring 1) during or 2) after the event may produce different outcomes. They argue that dissociative reactions during the event may be a normal and transient reaction to stress, and may even serve a protective function, as reduced awareness of the experience may limit encoding of the distressing event. Persistent dissociation, occurring immediately after the trauma and lingering, may impede retrieval of traumatic memories and their associated affect, thus limiting emotional processing and elaboration. Persistent dissociation may thus be implicated in the development and maintenance of posttraumatic disorders. Murray *et al.* (2002) found that persistent dissociation (measured four weeks after a road traffic accident) was a stronger predictor of chronic PTSD than peritraumatic dissociation. The authors concluded that their pattern of results suggests that although initial dissociation may put people at risk for PTSD, many are able to compensate by post-event processing, and only those who continue to dissociate may be at risk of persistent problems (see Briere, Scott and Weathers, 2005; Panasetis and Bryant, 2003).

Halligan and colleagues (2003) interviewed participants within three months of being assaulted and again six months later. They tested whether persistent dissociation explains the severity of chronic PTSD symptoms at six months over and above peritraumatic cognitive processing. The results indicated that the factors predicting PTSD were negative appraisals of intrusive memories and related thoughts (e.g. 'If I cannot control my thoughts about the assault, something terrible will happen'), persistent dissociation and memory fragmentation, but not peritraumatic dissociation.

Current empirical findings suggest that dissociation may contribute to posttraumatic symptom development via a pathway that combines peritraumatic and persistent dissociation, and their impact on trauma memory processing. Putting the literature together allows the development of a model that might guide sensitive hypothesis testing (see Figure 7.1). Peritraumatic dissociation may increase perceptual, and reduce self-referential, encoding of a distressing event. These processes underpin memory fragmentation in the form of reduced coherence and insufficient integration, resulting in posttraumatic symptoms. In most cases, dissociation does not persist. However, in cases where dissociation persists in the days or weeks following the trauma, an alternative pathway to post trauma symptoms consists of hampered voluntary retrieval of the trauma memory, resulting in a lack of elaboration (i.e. providing meaning) and assimilation of the trauma memory in the autobiographical knowledge base. Both pathways may exist in isolation, but the persistent dissociation pathway may also influence the relationship between the impaired encoding processes and post trauma symptoms by hampering the retrieval of already fragmented memories, further increasing the risk for later posttraumatic symptoms.

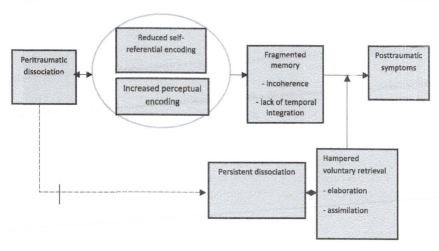

Figure 7.1 Cognitive model of fragmentation

Future studies

Only one study (Engelhard *et al.*, 2003) attempted to investigate the hypothesized relationship between peritraumatic dissociation, memory fragmentation, and posttraumatic symptoms. The results of this study indicated that the relationship between peritraumatic dissociation (at four weeks) and acute PTSD symptoms (determined at the same time), but not chronic PTSD (at four months), was driven by self-ratings of memory fragmentation (together with thought suppression of pregnancy loss). Following the model outlined above, prospective studies are needed which consider the mechanisms linking dissociation, memory fragmentation and later psychopathology. These studies should include measures of peritraumatic and persistent dissociation and a range of posttraumatic symptoms. Also, measures of possible mechanisms (e.g. data-driven/perceptual processing and lack of self-reference) should be included.

Such studies could extend the timeline of dissociative response measurement and examine predictors of dissociation. For example, Engelhard *et al.*'s (2003) follow-up study found that peritraumatic dissociation was predicted by prior poor control of emotions, dissociative tendencies, and lower levels of education. Such longitudinal studies incorporating multiple related factors may shed light on the causal and maintaining factors of posttraumatic symptomatology. The model we offer above is a foundational starting point for further exploration.

There is also a strong need to define more clearly the dissociative phenomena hypothesized to influence trauma memory encoding and retrieval. The concept of dissociation is complex and includes a range of different phenomena which may have different psychological and structural underpinnings. Unraveling which aspects are central in the development of fragmented memory is an important goal. In the PTSD field, some efforts have been made to define the dissociative phenomena that most strongly predict chronic PTSD (e.g. Bryant *et al.*, 2011). Halligan and colleagues (2003) found emotional numbing, confusion and altered time sense to show the closest relationship with chronic PTSD. Brooks and colleagues (2009) found two distinct factors in a factor analysis of the Peritraumatic Dissociative Experiences Questionnaire, one referring to alterations in attention, and the other to altered perceptions of self or one's surroundings. Only the latter was associated with acute stress reactions. Determining the posttraumatic outcomes of dissociation as manifest in detachment-type experiences (e.g. derealization) versus compartmentalization-type experiences (e.g. amnesia) is also important (e.g. Allen, Console and Lewis, 1999; Holmes *et al.*, 2005; Steele, Dorahy, Van der Hart and Nijenhuis, 2009).

Treatment

At the beginning of this chapter we used Ehlers and Clark's (2000) analogy of traumatic memory as a cupboard into which many things have been thrown quickly and in a disorganized fashion. In order to close the door of the cupboard, all the things inside have to be organized. This entails looking at items and putting them into place. Once this is done, the door can be shut with the contents ordered and accessible when needed.

To facilitate this, most cognitive theories of PTSD agree that elaboration and assimilation of the trauma memory is a necessary component for recovery (Brewin *et al.*, 1996, 2010). Adaptive resolution involves

- creation of a coherent narrative or story with a clear beginning, middle and end (increased coherence)
- development of conceptual associations or meaningful links between the different elements of the memory (increased coherence)
- development of associations with existing non-trauma-related autobiographical information (increased assimilation) (Ehlers, Hackmann and Michael, 2004)

The mixing up of different periods in the timeline of an individual's life can be problematic with respect to the future, as this can greatly hinder the ability to plan and to set goals. If the trauma is seen as a time-limited terrible experience in the past, it does not necessarily have threatening implications for their future (Clark and Ehlers, 2005).

The elaboration and assimilation of the trauma memory can be accomplished by

- repeatedly reliving the event in exposure therapy

In addition, some form of

- cognitive restructuring may be helpful, altering the trauma memory by incorporating new information and changing negative assumptions about recalling the trauma

The retrieval of the aversive trauma memory may be inhibited by the formation of new memories created through therapy (Brewin and Holmes, 2003). In clinical practice, highly dissociative patients are often excluded from exposure treatment, as dissociation is considered to hamper adequate fear activation, so trauma memory structures are not adequately activated and exposure therapy fails. However, this notion may need a more nuanced and sophisticated rethink. Recently, Hagenaars, Van Minnen, and Hoogduin (2010) assessed the impact of dissociation on the efficacy of prolonged exposure treatment for PTSD. Pre-treatment levels of dissociative and depressive symptoms were similar in dropouts and completers, and patients with high levels of dissociation pre-treatment showed similar improvement compared to patients with low levels. Interestingly, not only did dissociation not hamper effective exposure treatment, but symptoms of depersonalization, numbing and depression declined as a result of exposure therapy. The results thus implied that patients presenting with dissociative symptoms may profit similarly from exposure treatment as do patients with minimal dissociative symptoms.

We still need to determine what factors influence whether a PTSD patient with dissociation will a) benefit from exposure directly or b) require affect regulation strategies (e.g. grounding) to help them stay with the fear during exposure. Patients with DSM IV-TR dissociative disorders such as dissociative identity disorder are sensitive to affective arousal (Cloitre *et al.*, 2010; Herman, 2011; Kluft, 2007) and may need affect regulation work before exposure. Dealing with dissociation is central to therapy: as outlined in the model above, it is hypothesized to impede conceptual processing and maintain memory fragmentation. Without addressing dissociation, the therapist and client may not succeed in resolving these effects of trauma.

Chapter 8

The eating disorders and dissociation

Victoria A. Mountford

Clinicians have long observed the phenomenon of dissociation in eating disorders (ED) (Vanderlinden, Vandereycken, Van Dyck and Vertommen, 1993; Everill, Waller and Macdonald, 1995), particularly related to specific ED behaviours (e.g. binge-eating). This chapter summarizes dissociation research in the ED, and links it to clinical practice.

Research findings

Dissociation and eating disorders

Women with ED demonstrate significantly higher levels of dissociative psychopathology than nonclinical controls (e.g. Everill *et al.*, 1995; La Mela, Maglietta, Castellini, Amoroso and Lucarelli, 2010) and 12–20 per cent experience symptoms fulfilling criteria for a dissociative disorder (Dalle Grave *et al.*, 1996; Vanderlinden *et al.*, 1993). Vanderlinden and colleagues (1993) found significantly higher levels of identity confusion, loss of control, absorption and amnesia in ED participants (Dissociation Questionnaire; DIS-Q; Vanderlinden, Van Dyck, Vertommen and Vanderecyken, 1992). ED inpatients also show high levels of dissociation (DIS-Q scores; Vanderlinden *et al.*, 1992), with almost 20 per cent indicating severe dissociative symptoms compared to 3 per cent of controls (Dalle Grave, Rigamonti, Todisco and Oliosi, 1996).

Diagnosis is less useful in determining dissociation than the presence or absence of bulimic behaviours. Waller, Babbs, Wright, Potterton, Meyer, *et al.* (2003) found patients with restrictive anorexia nervosa (AN) were no different from healthy controls on measures of psychological and somatoform dissociation. Those with bulimia nervosa (BN) or AN binge-purge subtype present with higher levels of dissociative experiences than those with other EDs (Dalle Grave *et al.*, 1996). Everill *et al.* (1995) hypothesized that this is because restriction alone is a slow-acting behaviour, which therefore fails to provide the same sense of immediate relief from unwanted emotional states as bingeing does. An elaboration of that idea is that the more compulsive behaviours observed in restrictive EDs serve the similar function of reducing distress awareness, eliminating the need for dissociation, supported by the finding that, in a mixed diagnosis clinical group, dissociation negatively correlated with compulsive personality patterns (Kennedy, Clarke, Stopa, Bell, Rouse, Ainsworth et al., 2004).

Specific links exist between binge-eating and dissociation (e.g. La Mela et al., 2010; McShane and Zirkel, 2008). Frequency of binge-eating is associated with identity confusion, loss of control, but not absorption (DIS-Q; La Mela et al., 2010). Using retrospective self-report methodology Lyubomirsky et al. (2001) found women with BN reported more dazed feelings during and after a binge than preceding a binge – in others words, the likelihood of these feelings increased as the binge progressed. Moreover, in an experience sampling study, significant levels of dissociation were present, but only during the actual binge-purge cycle (McShane and Zirkel, 2008). A clear pattern, in which levels of dissociation were highest during and just after the binge – but before the purge – emerged (McShane and Zirkel, 2008). However, contrary to the bingeing-dissociation hypothesis, there is little evidence of dissociation in patients with binge-eating disorder (Dalle Grave et al, 1996; Waller, Ohanian, Meyer, Everill and Rouse, 2001). One explanation may be the lower rates of sexual abuse in this group (Tobin and Griffing, 1996), suggesting a different pathway to binge-eating – possibly hunger-driven – in operation. An alternative possibility is that the true link is between purging and dissociation (each related to trauma – Tobin and Griffing, 1996), and that binge-eating only appears to be relevant because of its association with purging behaviours. Links have been shown between disso-ciation and laxative and alcohol abuse (Waller et al., 2001).

Nijenhuis, Spinhoven, Van Dyck, Van der Hart and Vanderlinden (1996) elaborated the concept of dissociation, distinguishing its psychological and somatoform components. Psychological dissociation (measured by the DES and DIS-Q) represents a disruption in cognitive or emotional processes (e.g. absorption, amnesia, depersonalization, derealization). In contrast, somatoform dissociation represents disruption to the normal integration of physiological, kinaesthetic and sensory processes (measured by the Somatoform Dissociation Questionnaire; SDQ-20, Nijenhuis et al., 1996). Symptoms may be positive (e.g. pain, loss of motor control, alteration of senses) or negative (e.g. anaesthesia). Somatoform dissociation may be associated with childhood trauma involving physical contact or trauma, whilst psychological dissociation may be associated with a wider range of non-contact trauma. Whilst both are present within the EDs, it is suggested that somatoform – rather than psychological – dissociation might be the key element in relationships with ED attitudes and behaviours (e.g. Fuller-Tyskiewicz and Mussap, 2008; Waller et al., 2003). For example, the presence of specific purging behaviours (laxative and diuretic misuse and diet pills) (Waller et al., 2003) and binge-eating (Fuller-Tyskiewicz and Mussap, 2008) were linked to higher levels of somatoform, but not psychological, dissociation.

This distinction is of interest given developments in the conceptualization of dissociation as two qualitatively different phenomena – 'compartmentalization' and 'detachment' (Holmes, Brown, Mansell, Fearon, Hunter, Frasquilho and Oakley,

2005; Spitzer, Barnow, Freyberger and Grabe; 2006). Compartmentalization is a partial or even complete failure to deliberately control processes or actions that would normally be amenable to such control. It incorporates dissociative amnesia, unexplained neurological symptoms characteristic of conversion disorder and somatoform dissociation. Conversely, detachment – the subjective experience of an altered state of consciousness – may equate to the above description of psychological dissociation.

Dissociation and body image

Interest in the relationship between dissociation and body image has been limited. The research that does exist has shown links between body dissatisfaction and dissociation in female college students (Valdiserri and Kihlstrom, 1995) and patients with ED (Beato, Cano and Belmonte, 2003). Negative body attitudes were the best predictors of dissociative symptoms at treatment follow-up in inpatients (Vanderlinden, Vandereycken and Probst, 1995), and such attitudes seemed to be strongly related to severity of abuse (in particular, childhood sexual abuse). Negative body experiences might mediate the link between abuse and development of ED and dissociative symptoms (Vanderlinden, Vandereycken and Claes, 2007). In patients with a history of sexual trauma, the desire to be underweight might reflect a wish to be unattractive or to punish the body. Given these putative links, therapists should be aware of the possibility of triggering dissociation while treating body image.

An alternative hypothesis is that the relationship between dissociation and disordered eating is due to dissociative disruptions to body image (Fuller-Tyszkiewicz and Mussap, 2008). Somatoform dissociation might undermine the normal integration of appearance-related information, leading to body image vulnerability – manifesting as internalization of the thin-ideal, increased body comparison attitudes and behaviours and/or body dissatisfaction – and instability (Mussap and Salton, 2006), in turn driving disordered eating. Consistent with this is the finding that body dissatisfaction and comparison mediates the relationship between somatoform dissociation and binge-eating in college students (Fuller-Tyszkiewicz and Mussap, 2008).

Dissociation and trauma in the eating disorders

Well-established associations exist between a reported history of childhood sexual, physical or emotional abuse and the development of ED (e.g. Johnson, Cohen, Kasen and Brook, 2002; Smolak and Murnen, 2002) and dissociation (e.g. Dorahy and Van der Hart, 2007), leading many to propose a three-way relationship with dissociation mediating the relationship between early abuse and later eating pathology. A critical caveat is that some individuals may not recall or be consciously aware of some traumatic episodes (Briere and Armstrong, 2007; Dalle Grave *et al.*, 1996), affecting our understanding of the correlation between trauma and other phenomena, such as eating.

Root and Fallon (1989) conceptualized BN as a post-trauma response and others have supported the notion that eating pathology may be a survival mechanism to escape the psychologically distressing experience of trauma by avoiding or suppressing memories (Dalle Grave *et al.*, 1996; Holzer, Uppala, Wonderlich, Crosby and Simonich, 2008; Vanderlinden *et al.*, 1993). Higher levels of dissociation have been found in ED patients who experienced trauma, particularly incest and sexual abuse (Brown, Russell, Thornton and Dunn, 1999; Dalle Grave *et al.*, 1996; Vanderlinden *et al.*, 1993).

Another perspective is to see such links as reflecting an association between disorganized attachment style and dissociative experiences (see Chapter 4). Experiencing disorganization (e.g. frightening or unpredictable parental behaviour) (Briere and Armstrong, 2007; Cassidy and Mohr, 2001) in infancy may lead to a vulnerability to dissociative states, which can be triggered by later traumatic experiences (Liotti, 1999a, 1999b). Such theories have parallels with the construct of an invalidating childhood environment (Linehan, 1993b), hypothesized to lead to difficulties in distress tolerance and subsequent maladaptive attempts to avoid or manage such emotional states (Mountford, Corstorphine, Tomlinson and Waller, 2007), including dissociation (Waller, Corstorphine and Mountford, 2007).

In summary, the research shows that dissociation is associated with ED and is more frequent and severe among individuals with bulimic psychopathology. It can manifest in psychological or somatic forms and is a plausible candidate as a mediating factor between abuse and the development of an eating disorder – for some individuals. However, that link is not a simple one, as dissociation is also present in a subset of people with ED who do not report abusive experiences.

Understanding dissociation within the eating disorders

Models of dissociation

First, in the *'escape from awareness' model*, Heatherton and Baumeister (1991) suggest that people who binge-eat are likely to hold unusually high standards, relating specifically to body image or more generally to success, achievement, virtue and popularity. Individuals compare themselves against their stringent criteria, deeming themselves inadequate, leading to low self-esteem, blaming, anxiety and depression. To escape such feelings, attention is switched from the abstract (self-evaluation) to the level of physical surroundings or stimulus (i.e. food), removing awareness of faults and inadequacies. This shift also removes inhibitions, increasing the likelihood of binge-eating without consideration of longer-term consequences, such as weight gain or guilt (La Mela *et al.*, 2010). The 'escape from awareness' model suggests that dissociative experiences precede bulimic behaviours (McManus, 1995) and appears comparable to compartmentalization.

Julia's binge episodes often followed contact with her younger sister, whom she perceived as prettier, popular and more successful. She would get caught in cycles of increasing self-criticism. As she got home, she would feel as if on autopilot (switch to lower level, concrete processing). She would binge immediately, losing track of time and what she had eaten. She would only become aware of the consequences some time later, triggering further self-disgust and guilt.

Some evidence supports the 'escape from awareness' model. Subliminal abandonment threats lead to enhanced state dissociation (measured by the DES-II) in women with BN but not controls (Hallings-Pott, Waller, Watson and Scragg, 2005), compatible with the hypothesis that state dissociation is the immediate response to threats to oneself (e.g. self-criticism, perceived failure) and that such dissociation will precede binge-eating. A study of the temporal sequencing of affect, dissociation and binge-eating (Engelberg, Steiger, Gauvin and Wonderlich, 2007) found both negative affect and dissociation increased the likelihood of a binge.

Second, the 'blocking' model suggests dissociation is the *result* of using bulimic behaviour, given that bingeing and purging can 'anaesthetize' or block negative emotional states, such as anger and loneliness (e.g. Lacey, 1986; Root and Fallon, 1989). Instead, the focus is on food, weight, eating and purging, and the self-disgust that follows purging. However, the distraction from thoughts and feelings is only temporary, and a binge-purge cycle emerges. In contrast to the 'escape from awareness' model, it is posited that binge-eating precedes the dissociative state. This model may be comparable to detachment and authors (La Mela *et al.*, 2010; McManus, 1995; Meyer, Waller and Waters, 1998) have equated the binge experience, in which patients often describe themselves as numb or 'spaced out', and the concept of dissociation, often characterized by amnesia, derealization, depersonalization and absorption.

The 'escape from awareness' and the 'blocking' models are not incompatible and McManus and Waller (1995) hypothesized that the onset of bingeing might best be accounted for by the escape from awareness model, while the blocking model explains the continuation of the behaviour. This shift from one model to another might account for the way in which women with BN are more likely to report dissociative states as the binge progresses, suggesting that dissociation both triggers and maintains binge-eating (Lyubomirsky *et al.*, 2001).

Julia reported a binge could last a whole evening. She would binge, purge, and then binge again. Over the course of the evening her focus would shift from the initial distress triggered by negative self-evaluation and comparison to her sister, to intolerable states of self-disgust and hopelessness at her actions.

In considering ED patients with a history of emotional abuse and invalidation, Waller, Corstorphine and Mountford (2007) describe two distinct presentations; *chaotic-dissociative* – linked with impulsive-bulimic presentations – and *detached-alexithymic*, linked with compulsive-restrictive presentations. A chaotic-dissociative style is associated with experiences of emotions as overwhelming and terrifying, leading to the triggering of a dissociative state, either intra-psychically or driven by an impulsive blocking behaviour (Root and Fallon, 1989), whereas individuals with a detached-alexithymic style present as emotionally 'cut-off', unable to reflect on their emotional experiences. Individuals may oscillate between the two; particularly those with binge-purge AN. Pathological traits of dissociation were highly associated with alexithymia in non-ED female psychiatric patients (Grabe, Rainermann, Spitzer, Gänsicker and Freyberger, 2000).

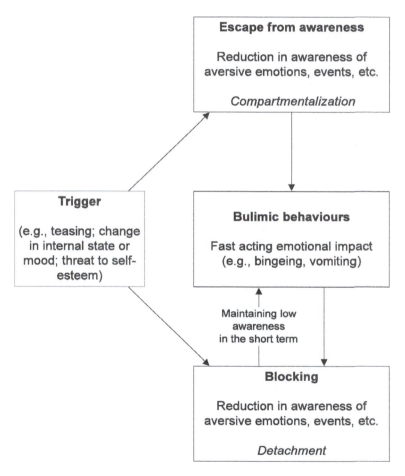

Figure 8.1 Possible interaction of escape from awareness and blocking models

A further element of the dissociation-eating pathology link is body dissatisfaction (Fuller-Tyszkiewicz and Mussap, 2008; Mussap and Salton, 2006). Somatoform dissociation can lead to instability and vulnerability of body image, due to disruption of normal processing of appearance-relevant information and self-awareness. In a society that emphasizes the thin-ideal, such disruptions can lead to body dissatisfaction and subsequent disordered eating. This hypothesis is not incompatible with those above, however, validation with an ED sample is required (Fuller-Tyszkiewicz and Mussap, 2008).

Links to co-morbid conditions

EDs may present in individuals with co-morbid diagnoses with high levels of dissociation (e.g. BPD, Sansone, Levitt and Sansone, 2005; PTSD, Brewerton, 2007). Dissociative episodes may be more strongly associated with the non-ED diagnoses or may act as a mediator between such diagnoses and disordered eating. PTSD was a significant and powerful mediator of the relationship between sexual trauma and disordered eating; leading Holzer *et al.* (2008) to suggest that traumatized individuals who develop PTSD may be more likely to develop an ED, in an attempt to regulate the underlying aversive emotional states. Links have been demonstrated between self-harm and dissociation in women with EDs (Demitrack, Putnam, Brewerton, Brandt and Gold, 1990; Paul, Shroeter, Dahme and Nutzinger, 2002) – particularly those who experienced sexual abuse before the age of 15 (Claes and Vandereycken, 2007). Dissociation may be a mechanism to manage traumatic memories and in turn, self-injurious behaviours may bring the individual 'back to reality' following dissociation (Claes and Vandereycken, 2007).

In my clinical experience, there may also be psychosomatic disturbances, for example, unexplained seizures or physical pain. Medical investigations are fruitless, and the phenomena diminish as the individual recovers.

Neurological bases

The contribution of neuropsychology and neurobiology in understanding the ED has been increasingly recognized (e.g. Kaye, Frank, Bailer and Henry, 2005; Tchanturia, Campbell, Morris and Treasure, 2005) and it is likely that there are links with the neuropsychology of dissociation. A full discussion is beyond the scope of this chapter but readers are referred to Southgate, Tchanturia and Treasure (2005) for a review.

Summary

To integrate the above models, a theoretical model explaining dissociation in the ED is hypothesized. A complex interplay exists between biological factors (e.g. genetics, biological changes, innate hypnotizability, brain circuitry) and environmental factors (e.g. childhood or adulthood trauma, an invalidating childhood environment) which will increase vulnerability to pathology. One pathway to dissociation may be independent of eating pathology and via a co-morbid disorder. Alternatively, dissociation may occur though somatoform disruptions and/or the need to escape from self-awareness. As the eating pathology develops, interactions occur between specific triggers, bulimic and restrictive behaviours and the physiology (i.e. bingeing driven by restriction). Such behaviours are reinforced by the subsequent reduction in emotions via fast or slow-acting mechanisms. See the figure below.

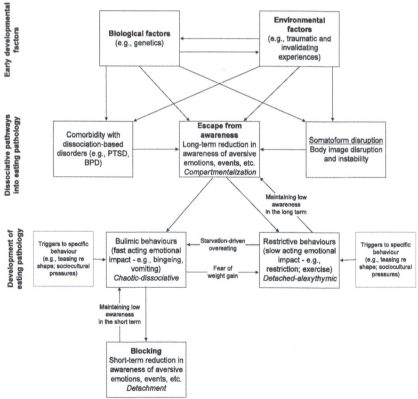

Figure 8.2 Hypothesized model of dissociation and eating pathology

Clinical implications

Understanding how dissociation might be causally linked to some ED behaviours and how it might impede therapy has emphasized the need to address dissociation in treatment (e.g. La Mela *et al.*, 2010; Vanderlinden *et al.*, 2007).

Assessment

Assessment can be complex, due in part to our incomplete understanding of dissociation (Briere and Armstrong, 2007). Many patients will be unfamiliar with the concept of dissociation but aware of, and frightened by, its manifestations. Therefore, it needs to be explained as a normal process (see below). You need to be aware of the associations between ED psychopathology, dissociation, self-harm, co-morbidity (e.g. alcohol or substance misuse, BPD, PTSD) and trauma. The presence of one should prompt enquiries regarding all because individuals may be unaware of the significance of these links or reluctant to raise distressing experiences, such as abuse. Asking about levels of dissociation before, during and after binge-eating and encouraging patients to monitor emotional states and levels of dissociation will inform your formulation.

In some cases, dissociation may occur during the therapy session. Some signs of dissociation are easily noticed (e.g. flashbacks), whilst others are more subtle and require sharper observation (e.g. momentary absences or vagueness). Asking 'It seemed like something just happened there – can you tell me about it?' can lead to a clearer understanding of when else this happens for the individual and what it means to them.

Measures (e.g. DIS-Q, DES) can assess dissociative symptomatology. In more extreme cases (e.g. dissociative identity disorder), a semi-structured interview is recommended.

Top tips – recommended questions to assess dissociation

- Do you ever feel cut off from the world or unreal, as if you're looking at the world through a pane of glass, or trapped in a bubble? (Derealization)
- Do you ever feel that you are out of your body, for example, it is as if you are watching yourself in a film or from elsewhere in the room? (Depersonalization)
- Do you ever find that there are segments of time that you do not remember, for example, not knowing how you got somewhere or other people insisting that you had had a specific conversation? (Amnesia)
- In the case of trauma; do you ever experience the original event as if it were happening in the here and now all over again? (Flashbacks/ absorption)
- *During* the trauma, did you feel that you were out of your body, for example, as if you were watching yourself in a film or from elsewhere in the room? (Peritraumatic dissociation)

Explaining dissociation

Terms such as 'flashback' or 'spacing out' are likely to elicit immediate recognition from clients who experience such states. For many, the recognition and acknowledgement can be reassuring and validating. Some will see a dissociated state with relief, acknowledging the role in managing intolerable emotional states, while others find it frightening. Explaining that dissociation exists on a continuum from the everyday (e.g. going into 'autopilot' during an emergency; feeling numb after a bereavement) to more extreme presentations (e.g. amnesia; flashbacks), and that it can be experienced as beneficial/adaptive to severely distressing/disabling depending on the context, can reduce anxiety. In the case of a post-traumatic reaction, dissociative detachment can be explained as having its origins as a normal 'survival mechanism'. When an individual is unable physically to escape a traumatic situation, the mind enables 'escape' through cutting-off and detaching from the experience. Although this response tends to diminish over time, in some it develops into a pervasive, and dysfunctional, coping style, triggered by a range of stimuli or perceived threats (often of less severity than the initial trauma).

Formulation

Incorporating co-morbid difficulties within a formulation is established within ED work (e.g. Waller, Cordery, Corstorphine, Hinrichsen, Lawson, Mountford and Russell, 2007). Considering the underlying mechanisms that explain both dissociation and the disordered eating can help patient and therapist understand the presentation.

> *Nadia, a 19-year-old girl with BN, described how binge-eating blocked everything out in stressful situations. Her head was screaming and 'if I binge, it will block it all out'. As she started to binge, she felt a sense of relief; her emotions were numbed and she felt safe again.*

Nadia described how she got extremely angry or anxious very quickly. Her formulation emphasized her difficulty in managing intense emotional states and the function of bingeing in blocking such states. Nadia also experienced derealization, and self-harmed. All three features share the function of enabling Nadia to cut off or manage her extreme emotions. Which one was triggered depended on factors including intensity of emotional state, hunger levels or availability of self-harm equipment or binge foods. Further, self-harm had two functions – to enable dissociation or to ground self following dissociation, and thus followed derealization or bingeing.

Nadia: Cross-sectional formulation

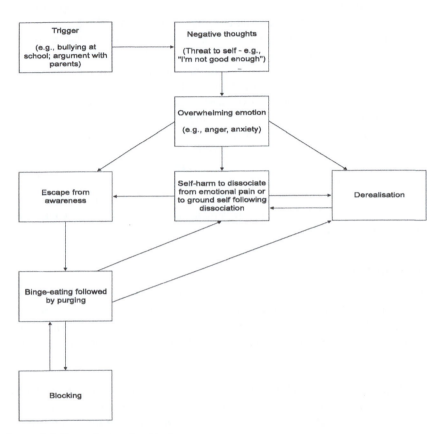

Figure 8.3 Formulation for Nadia

Addressing dissociation in treatment

Preliminary factors

Recognition of the protective role of dissociation highlights the need for a careful, planned treatment strategy, emphasized by the association between dissociation and self-harm (Brown *et al.*, 1999). There should be awareness of factors that might trigger an increase in distress or dissociation (e.g. disclosure of abuse, significant anniversaries, body image work, therapist's tone of voice). Decisions regarding the risks and benefits of addressing dissociation should be made collaboratively with the patient, bearing in mind their capacity to tolerate distress at that point and the potential increase in risk if a protective strategy is removed.

Impact of dissociation on other elements of treatment

Dissociation may impact on the broader therapy (e.g. homework not completed, poor memory for skills, presenting in an unpredictable manner). Practical steps such as recording sessions, jointly making notes for the patient to review and developing flashcards with prompts for new skills might offer simple solutions to those with poor memory. Exploration of reasons for difficulties in completing homework (e.g. forgetfulness, fear it will trigger painful memories or dissociation) can enable therapist and patient to generate solutions such as proceeding at a gentler pace or practising first in session. For patients who present in an unpredictable manner or with repeated crises, together you can consider the impact on therapy and how such difficulties manifest in real life. Thereafter, an agreement to set and keep to an agenda may better contain the individual.

Therapeutic approaches

The presence of dissociation does not make redundant the use of current recognized treatments for EDs (e.g. Fairburn, 2008; Waller *et al.*, 2007). A number of CBT-based therapies show promise in addressing dissociation, some of which have been adapted for EDs, including dialectical behaviour therapy (DBT; Hill, Craighead and Safer, 2011; Kroger, Schweiger, Sipos, Kliem, Arnold, Schunert and Reinecker, 2010; Linehan, 1993b), cognitive emotional behavioural therapy (Corstorphine, 2006), and schema-focused cognitive behavioural therapy (Waller, Kennerley and Ohanian, 2007; Young, Klosko and Weishaar, 2003).

If dissociation is not addressed, it is possible that the ED behaviours being targeted may simply be replaced by other behaviours or an increase in dissociative tendencies (Everill and Waller, 1995). The Emotion Regulation and Distress Tolerance modules of DBT (Linehan, 1993b) can help clients to manage overwhelming emotions through learning how to identify and label emotions, understand the functions of emotions and develop skills to manage intolerable emotions without acting impulsively. Given that bingeing can occur when levels of dissociation are high, a key goal of therapy is to help patients tolerate negative self-awareness (i.e. thoughts of inferiority or failure) without having to escape into a dissociative state (Engelberg *et al.*, 2007; La Mela *et al.*, 2010). As the dissociative symptoms become better controlled, it is possible to address the ED (Waller *et al.*, 2007).

Strategies to manage dissociation

A priority is to develop immediate strategies to manage dissociation, particularly if they increase the risk of harm to self or others. Once triggers have been identified, patients can learn to respond in more adaptive ways. In the case of ED patients, specific foods, or situations involving food or the body (e.g. physical contact or body-directed attention) are sometimes reminders of the original trauma, triggering dissociation.

Grounding is a powerful strategy to help patients reorient to reality. It encourages patients to shift their attention away from the internal world to connect with external reality by focusing in great detail on the environment around them (refocusing) or to take themselves to an alternative 'place in mind' where they are able to be calmer. A number of different techniques exist (Kennerley, 1996, 2000; Najavits, 2002) and a useful patient guide is in Kennerley (2000). Grounding requires practice to work effectively, particularly in times of high arousal. Clinicians should check to ensure such techniques are used as coping strategies and not safety behaviours. If a patient dissociates frequently within sessions, therapist and patient can agree a grounding statement, such as 'Nadia, this is your therapist, Vicki. It is Tuesday and you are at the London Hospital. You are safe here'. If working with an inpatient who experiences dissociation, all staff should be aware of the agreed grounding strategy (see Charlotte, below). With the patient's permission, you may consider involving family or carers, for example, educating them about dissociation and grounding strategies so they can support their loved one.

Graded exposure to triggers, particularly food triggers or body talk or contact is important. Where possible, this may be done in-vivo initially, as the patient builds up confidence to try by herself. If the trigger is an interpersonal situation, then cognitive restructuring and role-play can help the individual reappraise the threat and practice appropriate ways to reassert herself or express her discomfort.

Nadia often felt attacked and that she had to 'fight her way out of the corner'. Thought diaries demonstrated that she distorted any small criticism into an extreme attack (to the level at which she was bullied). Handling such scenarios better reduced the extreme emotional response.

For those patients whose dissociation is linked to traumatic episodes, imagery rescripting (e.g. Arntz and Weertman, 1999; Hackmann, 2011) may enable the trauma to be processed at a verbal rather than automatic level. As the information becomes incorporated in this way, flashbacks and other dissociative phenomena reduce.

Nadia's treatment

At the beginning of treatment, it was evident that although Nadia was aware of both 'spacing out' and feeling disconnected, she did not know about dissociation. First, Nadia was educated about her experiences, including consideration of how and why such a process may have emerged. Nadia commented how the formulation assisted her in understanding her difficulties, which she and her family had been confused by. Next, Nadia monitored her mood states, dissociation, bingeing and self-harm to identify triggers and patterns. She noted that she was vulnerable when she felt attacked or criticized. In fact, Nadia discovered that keeping the diary helped significantly in managing her emotional state and she began to use this as a strategy to prevent dissociation. She experimented with different grounding techniques before settling on a smooth pebble from her favourite beach. She increased her positive activities, in particular artwork and writing her blog. A mindfulness meditation exercise was carried out at the end of every session and Nadia practiced this during the week. Nadia also had a list of alternative behaviours she could use. Finally, noting that perceived attack was a powerful trigger, we worked to enable Nadia to evaluate interpersonal situations more accurately and respond more effectively. Treatment targeted at the cognitions and behaviours associated with BN continued alongside. At the end of treatment, Nadia noted that she was less vulnerable to emotional instability and had not binged, self-harmed or experienced a dissociative state for some time.

Body image

In particular, care should be exercised using body image work with those with a history of sexual trauma, as it may trigger dissociation.

Charlotte had been raped one evening on her way home from work. She had also witnessed and experienced significant physical violence whilst growing up. She had disclosed the rape during individual therapy but had said little more about it. After she started the body image group, Charlotte experienced increasingly intense and frequent flashbacks to the rape. Her individual therapist worked with her to explain the processes underlying the flashbacks and to plan with Charlotte how best to manage these (for example, Charlotte reported that being supported by female rather than male staff and repeated grounding of where she was and who the staff member was, to be most helpful). Charlotte continued to attend the group where facilitators remained alert to early signs of dissociation, attempting to use grounding techniques where possible. If a flashback followed, facilitators supported Charlotte to leave the group, as planned. To minimize the risk of negative reinforcement through providing an escape route from a potentially distressing group, such events were always discussed afterwards with Charlotte. In fact, there was only one occasion where the level of dissociation required Charlotte to leave the group. Finally, with Charlotte's permission, the facilitators helped others in the group to understand what was happening.

Top tips – Treatment

- Educate the patient and normalize the experience of dissociation for them
- Before embarking on treatment, assess risk, and tailor interventions accordingly
- Be aware of ways in which dissociation may interfere with therapy and prepare grounding strategies

- Use diaries to identify and monitor aversive emotional states which may be linked to dissociation or binge-eating episodes and work to increase tolerance of such states without dissociation
- If possible, work in-vivo with dissociation as it occurs during sessions
- On an inpatient unit, ensure all team members are aware of the presence and nature of dissociative pathology and how to manage this for each individual

Summary

Dissociation is overrepresented within individuals with EDs, in particular those with bulimic psychopathology. Physiological processes are core within EDs and research has highlighted the significance of somatoform over psychological dissociation. For some, but not all, there appears to be a three-way relationship, linking early trauma – often sexual in nature – with dissociation and the development of eating pathology and disturbed body image. A number of models – some more developed than others – have been proposed to understand such processes, and it is likely that no single model will suffice.

Consensus exists (e.g. La Mela *et al.*, 2010; Vanderlinden *et al.*, 2007) regarding the importance of addressing dissociation in treatment to optimize outcome and certainly, the presence of dissociation may add to an already challenging therapeutic presentation. However, techniques and interventions for dissociative symptomatology can be integrated alongside more standardized ED treatments.

A review of the literature highlights the need for further research into potential links between body image and dissociation, including testing of the body image instability hypothesis. Further consideration of the mechanisms of dissociation in those who do not binge or purge is also essential.

Chapter 9

The role of dissociation in psychosis

Implications for clinical practice

Katherine Newman-Taylor
Suzanne Sambrook[1]

Cognitive theory and therapy for psychosis have developed dramatically over the last two decades. We now have psychological models to guide our understanding and interventions with people living with voices, paranoia and other psychotic experiences. Moreover, the National Institute for Clinical Excellence (2009) recommends cognitive behavioural therapy and family interventions for people with a diagnosis of schizophrenia.

Clinically, we know that people with psychosis often describe fragmented experiences, may 'tune out' when talking about distressing events or struggle to describe particular memories with coherence and clarity. Yet, with notable exceptions (e.g. Kilcommons and Morrison, 2005; Moskowitz, Read, Farrelly, Rudegeair and Williams, 2009; Moskowitz, Schäfer and Dorahy, 2009; Schäfer, Harfst, Aderhold, Briken, Lehmann *et al.*, 2006; Vogel, Spitzer, Kuwert, Moller, Freyberger *et al.*, 2009), there has been little examination of the links between dissociation and psychosis. Ross (2007b) argues that this gap in the literature is due to historical and erroneous distinctions between environmental versus genetic aetiology, neurotic versus psychotic symptomatology, and psychotherapeutic versus medical interventions as treatments of choice for dissociation and psychosis respectively. Given the empirical links between trauma and distressing psychosis, and the role of dissociation in the relationship between traumatic events and psychopathology, it is now necessary to look more closely at the role of dissociation in this group.

This chapter will consider the role of dissociation in distressing psychosis, within a cognitive behavioural framework. It will be shown that there is good theoretical reason to expect dissociation to be a key process in the development and maintenance of distress in psychosis for some people, but that this is largely ignored in the clinical and research literature.

It is important to understand these relationships in order to work effectively in clinical practice. Broadly speaking, cognitive behavioural interventions for people with psychosis aim to support people to live well with voice hearing and other intrusive experiences, and provide an opportunity to re-evaluate key cognitions (such as paranoid beliefs and self-appraisals) in order to alleviate distress. By contrast, trauma-based interventions, including those for dissociation, aim to facilitate the integration of fragmented experience and self-representations, and thereby reduce the occurrence or severity of distressing intrusions. It is unclear, therefore, how we should work with individuals with psychosis, in the event that the person's history and presentation indicate complex responses to traumatic experience, or indeed what the aim of such interventions should be.

In this chapter, we will argue that we need to pay attention to possible dissociative processes involved in distressing psychosis; we need to consider dissociation in our assessment, formulation and interventions if we are to work effectively in therapy.

Definitions

Historically, it is of interest that early descriptions of psychosis make explicit reference to dissociative processes. Kraepelin (1919) noted fragmentation of internal experiences in his accounts of 'dementia praecox', which Bleuler (1950) went on to rename 'schizophrenia' (meaning 'split mind disorder'), arguing that the 'splitting of psychic functions' was central to the diagnosis (see Moskowitz *et al.*, 2009).

Today our diagnostic categories define psychosis in quite different terms. The DSM IV-TR definition of psychosis as delusions, hallucinations, disorganized speech and grossly disorganized or catatonic behaviour (American Psychiatric Association, 2000) reflects the experiences typically associated with a diagnosis of schizophrenia, yet is simpler and more flexible than previous versions. Dissociation is defined as 'a disruption in the usually integrated functions of consciousness, memory, identity or perception of the environment' (p. 811). Until recently, the dissociation literature was dominated by psychoanalytic and psycho-dynamic accounts. This has presented a problem for clinicians adopting other approaches. The model proposed by Kennedy and colleagues (Kennedy, Clarke, Stopa, Bell, Rouse *et al.*, 2004; Kennedy this volume) is welcome as it enables us to think about dissociation in cognitive-behavioural and learning-theory terms. This model starts from the assumption that dissociation functions to reduce awareness of intolerable information and may occur in a number of ways. Based on Beck's (1996) theory of personality as represented by a collection of 'modes' (sets of schemas for encoding and responding to affective, cognitive, behavioural and bodily information), the model proposes that dissociation can occur at three levels during the processing of threatening information. *Automatic dissociation* involves the decoupling of orienting schemas due to classically conditioned associations with threat stimuli, and may result in sensory intrusions such as flashbacks and nightmares. The automatic processing of orienting schemas takes place without conscious effort or volition (Beck and Clark, 1997), and dissociation at this level is likely to be preconscious. By contrast, processing of schemas within modes tends to be strategic (Beck and Clark, 1997), and *within-mode dissociation* of the usually integrated experiences of emotions, thoughts, behaviours and bodily sensations may result in the involuntary accessing of material when not wanted (e.g. streams of intrusive thoughts) or an inability to access material when wanted (e.g. flattened affect or an inability to think). Dissociation at these two levels of processing is characteristic of Acute Stress Disorder and PTSD. The third stage, *between mode dissociation*, involves the decoupling of links between modes and leads to the state-switching typically associated with borderline personality difficulties, complex PTSD and the much debated diagnosis of dissociative identity disorder.

The epidemiological literature clearly indicates an overlap between dissociation and psychosis. This is evident in studies of co-morbidity (e.g. Butler, Mueser, Sprock and Braff, 1996; Hamner, 1997; Hamner, Frueh, Ulmer and Arana, 1999; McGorry, Chanen, McCarthy, Van Riel, McKenzie *et al.*, 1991; Mueser, Trumbetta, Rosenberg, Vivader, Goodman *et al.*, 1998) and correlations between measures of dissociation and psychoticism (e.g. Allen and Coyne, 1995; Allen, Coyne and Console, 1997).

So how are we to make sense of this empirical relationship between dissociation and psychosis? Adopting a psychiatric approach, some have responded by suggesting that this apparent overlap is due to misdiagnosis (see Moskowitz *et al.*, 2009). Others have proposed new diagnostic categories for 'dissociative psychosis' (Sar and Ozturk, 2009), 'dissociative hallucinosis' (Nurcombe, Scott and Jessop, 2009) or a dissociative subtype of schizophrenia (Ross, 2009).

Within a cognitive behavioural framework, we are interested in understanding the processes that may link dissociation and distressing psychosis. As dissociation is typically associated with trauma, it is first useful to consider the evidence linking trauma, dissociation and psychosis.

Trauma, dissociation and psychosis

The relationship between trauma and psychosis remains controversial. Data from the British National Survey of Psychiatric Epidemiology indicates that early experiences of victimization (such as sexual abuse and bullying) are more common in people with psychosis than those with other mental health problems or none (Bebbington, Bhugra, Brugha, Farrell, Lewis, *et al.*, 2004). There is now good evidence that people with distressing psychosis, particularly hallucinations, report high rates of childhood interpersonal trauma and neglect (see Larkin and Read, 2008; Morgan and Fisher, 2007; Read, Goodman, Morrison, Ross and Aderhold, 2004; Read, Van Os, Morrison and Ross, 2005, for reviews), yet methodological problems limit the conclusions that can be drawn about the nature of this relationship (Bendall, Jackson, Hulbert and McGorry, 2008). Mueser and colleagues found that this association extends beyond childhood to high rates of traumatic events over the lifetime for people with psychosis (Mueser *et al.*, 1998). At the same time, there is evidence that dissociation may mediate the relationship between trauma and psychopathology (e.g. Becker-Lausen, Sanders and Chinsky, 1995). Despite a growing recognition that psychosis is linked to trauma for many people, the psychological processes involved in this relationship remain largely untested (perhaps understandably, given ethical and methodological difficulties), and the specific role of dissociation has received little attention. The work of Moskowitz, Read and colleagues (Moskowitz, *et al.*, 2009) is an important exception. In addition, Steel and colleagues' examination of 'contextual integration' (Steel, Hemsley and Pickering, 2002; Steel, Fowler and Holmes, 2005), and McGlashan, Birchwood and others' work on 'sealing over' in psychosis (Drayton, Birchwood and Trower, 1998; McGlashan, 1987; Tait, Birchwood and Trower, 2003) may be conceptually and functionally linked to dissociation.

Moskowitz and Read argue that psychotic experiences may be 'traumatic in origin and dissociative in kind' (Moskowitz, Read *et al.*, 2009). These authors suggest that for many people, psychosis develops following early interpersonal trauma, and that this trajectory is mediated by dissociative processes. The empirical links between trauma and psychosis are indeed strongest for hallucinations (see above). Drawing parallels with voices heard in dissociative presentations, it is suggested that some auditory hallucinations associated with a diagnosis of schizophrenia may constitute unprocessed trauma memories. Despite diagnostic expectations that auditory hallucinations in schizophrenia and dissociative presentations differ in content, duration and location, the evidence (albeit modest) does not support these distinctions, and voices in both groups are often hostile, comment on the person, and are heard inside or outside the head. Similarly, it is argued that sensory hallucinations in other modalities may be intrusions of unprocessed traumatic material best characterized as flashbacks.

The psychotic experiences of disorganized or catatonic behaviour, and disorganized speech or thought disorder, may also involve dissociation for some people. These behaviours are likely to be judged bizarre if the clinician (and possibly the person him or herself) is unaware of relevant historical context. If linked to past trauma, the same behaviours may be understood as fight, flight or freeze responses triggered by flashbacks, and attract a trauma related diagnosis such as PTSD.

Finally, Moskowitz *et al.* (2009) consider the role of dissociation in delusion formation. The clinical cognitive models broadly agree that delusions are causal inferences developed to explain affective, perceptual and cognitive anomalies, such as thoughts heard as voices and heightened affect (see below). To the extent that these anomalies are dissociative, the related delusions are the person's ways of making sense of experiences derived from dissociative processes.

Preliminary evidence supports a relationship between early neglect or abuse and dissociation in people with a diagnosis of schizophrenia (though this does not fully account for correlations between early trauma and current distress) (Schafer, Harfst, Aderhold, Briken, Lehman *et al.*, 2006; Vogel, Spitzer, Kuwert, Moller, Freyberger *et al.*, 2009), as well as the role of dissociation in response to trauma, with depersonalization a significant predictor of hallucinatory experience in people with schizophrenia spectrum disorders (Kilcommons and Morrison, 2005). Within the limitations of the current empirical evidence, Moskowitz *et al.*

(2009) conclude that psychosis, particularly hallucinatory experience, is likely to be dissociative in nature. Although there is some support for the hypotheses that hearing voices (e.g. Honig, Romme, Ensink, Escher, Pennings *et al.*, 1998), disorganized behaviour and speech (e.g. Allen, Coyne and Console, 1997) and delusions (through their explanatory function) may involve dissociative processes, a more systematic examination of these relationships is now needed (Moskowitz *et al.*, 2009).

Steel and colleagues propose an information processing account of intrusions (Steel *et al.*, 2002; Steel *et al.*, 2005). Usually, incoming sensory information is processed and stored in a temporal and spatial context which results in our ability to recall memories voluntarily and in relation to other events (following Broadbent, 1977); Steel *et al.* (2005) refer to this as effective 'contextual integration'. Drawing on cognitive theories of PTSD (Brewin, 2001a; Ehlers and Clark, 2000) and psychosis (Hemsley, 1994), it is argued that traumatic events (or vivid recall) disrupt contextual integration of incoming material at moments of intense distress in both presentations. Clinically these are known as 'hotspots' in cognitive behavioural interventions for PTSD, and are typically associated with heightened affect and catastrophic appraisals (e.g. 'I'm going to die') (Ehlers and Clark, 2000). People with psychosis may be vulnerable to poor contextual integration (following Hemsley, 1994; Jones, Hemsley and Gray, 1991) and so have a lower threshold for ineffective processing of distressing material. That is, people with psychosis may be routinely storing information in a way that is unstable and can easily be triggered as intrusions. The person's vulnerability to poor contextual integration interacts with personally relevant traumatic experience to contribute to the frequency and nature of trauma-related intrusions, which may in turn be appraised as indicative of current threat (Steel *et al.*, 2005).

This account is supported by studies of association assumed to be suggestive of weakened contextual integration in both clinical (Jones *et al.*, 1991) and non-clinical groups (Steel *et al.*, 2002), and now requires direct investigation (Fowler *et al.*, 2006; Steel *et al.*, 2005). The authors rightly caution against simple and reductionist causal models, but do recommend that we attend to possible links between trauma and psychosis, and the emotional and psychosis specific information processing that may be contributing to the maintenance of distress for these individuals.

The process of 'sealing over' has also been examined in people with distressing psychosis, and bears conceptual similarities with both contextual integration and dissociation. Many people with psychosis adopt a 'sealing over recovery style', characterized by cognitive and behavioural avoidance of painful experiences linked to their psychosis, sometimes to the extent of being unable to access these memories (Drayton, Birchwood and Trower, 1998; McGlashan, 1987; Tait, Birchwood and Trower, 2003). People who seal over, in contrast to those who are able to integrate their experiences, report less intrusions and greater avoidance (Jackson, Smith, Birchwood, Trower, Reid *et al.*, 2004), and may have poorer outcomes in terms of mood and social functioning (McGlashan, 1987; Thompson,

McGorry and Harrigan, 2003). It has been suggested that people seal over due to poor personal resilience in adapting to psychosis, and there is some evidence that this is indeed associated with problematic interpersonal childhood experience, insecure adult attachment and problematic self-evaluations (Drayton *et al.*, 1998; Tait, Birchwood and Trower, 2004).

Taken together, these accounts suggest that many people with psychosis are likely to have experienced considerable interpersonal trauma in childhood and adulthood, and be vulnerable to disrupted processing of distressing information. This in turn may result in trauma-related intrusions appraised as currently threatening in the context of schema-level beliefs associated with disrupted early attachments. It is tempting to assume direct links between the concepts of contextual integration, sealing over and dissociation, particularly given a common function of avoidance (whether implicit or explicitly stated). We would suggest caution here. The accounts are not straight-forwardly comparable (not least because the descriptions of contextual integration and sealing over operate at information processing and clinical levels of explanation respectively) and have yielded some apparently contradictory findings to date. For example, while schizotypy (personality traits associated with the symptoms of schizophrenia in non-clinical populations) is associated with dissociative traits (again, of people in non-clinical groups) (Merckelbach, Rassin and Muris, 2000; Startup,1999), there is some evidence that it is schizotypy rather than dissociative traits that predicts impaired contextual integration and trauma symptoms (Steel, Mahmood and Holmes, 2008). It is also of note that people who seal over may report *less* rather than more intrusions (Jackson *et al.*, 2004), contrary to what might be predicted if we equated sealing over with dissociation. With clear working definitions (Startup, 1999; Merckelbach *et al.*, 2000), examination of the relationships between contextual integration, sealing over and dissociation may prove fruitful to our understanding of these pathways to distressing psychosis.

In summary, we are suggesting that dissociation may be part of a pathway to distressing psychosis. This would be consistent with a hypothesis that hallucinatory experience in psychosis may occur at both automatic and within mode levels of information processing. For some people, sensory hallucinations linked to past trauma may constitute direct re-experiencing of memory fragments at the automatic level, disrupting processing of orienting schemas. Brief auditory fragments recalled directly from past experience also occur through this process, for example the voice of a bullying school peer reiterating taunts that were made at the time of the abuse (see also Fowler *et al.*, 2006). More complex voices that comment on the person or talk to each other are unlikely to be accounted for in this way, but may involve within-mode dissociation in which the person's own thoughts and beliefs are heard as others' voices and attributed to an external source. This would be consistent with the suggestion that indirect associations between early and psychotic experience may emerge through the development of core beliefs about the self (e.g. as bad, flawed and vulnerable) and/or others (e.g. as powerful and dangerous) and associated affect (Birchwood, 2003; Fowler *et al.*, 2006; Morrison, 2001). Such core beliefs may contribute to the later development of extreme ideas and moment-to-moment streams of thought categorized as delusional. Similarly, core beliefs are likely to influence appraisals of voices as malevolent, omnipotent and shaming, and corresponding evaluations of the self as subordinated, shamed and inferior (Birchwood and Chadwick, 1997; Birchwood, Meaden, Trower, Gilbert and Plaistow, 2000; Birchwood, Gilbert, Gilbert, Trower, Meaden *et al.*, 2004).

This line of reasoning also raises questions about the so called 'negative symptoms' of psychosis, and whether the absence of components of experience (for example, emotional flattening) may be due to within-mode dissociation for some (Fowler *et al.*, 2006).

These possibilities are largely speculative. Furthermore, it is likely that links between early experience, dissociative information processing and psychosis are many and complex, and that dissociation is just one of a number of pathways contributing to distressing psychosis. Nevertheless, it is important to consider whether and how dissociation is involved in the development and maintenance of psychosis in our clinical work. Given our training in cognitive behavioural therapy, we base our therapeutic work on the clinical cognitive models of psychosis. These models guide our understanding of the person's subjective experience, the psychological processes likely to be involved in their distress, and linked implications for therapy. It is valuable, therefore, to consider what these models tell us about dissociative processes in psychosis.

Dissociative processes in psychosis; what do the clinical cognitive models tell us?

The clinical cognitive models agree that affective, cognitive and perceptual anomalies can lead to psychosis in vulnerable individuals. In a seminal paper, Garety and others (Garety, Kuipers, Fowler, Freeman and Bebbington, 2001) propose that triggers such as stressful life events or substance misuse can disrupt basic cognitive processes (Garety and Hemsley, 1994). This results in unstructured sensory input intruding into consciousness as unintended material from memory (Hemsley, 1993) or in problems monitoring intentions and actions which may then be experienced as alien (Frith, 1992). The resulting anomalous experiences can include heightened perception, thoughts experienced as voices, and causal linking of separate events. In the context of intense emotion and linked information processing, these anomalies are likely to be perceived as originating externally and potentially threatening. The person seeks a causal explanation for his or her experiences, which may be non-psychotic (e.g. 'my mind is playing tricks on me – these are my own thoughts and fears') or psychotic (e.g. 'my neighbours are trying to poison me') if external and personally significant.

A number of models have been developed that aim to map the affective, cognitive and behavioural processes involved in the development and maintenance of distress in psychosis (e.g. Chadwick, 2006; Freeman and Garety, 2004; Gumley and Schwannauer, 2006; Morrison, 2001; Nelson, 2005). To varying degrees, these models recognize the likely impact of serious interpersonal experience including abuse and disruption of early attachments (Gumley and Schwannauer, 2006), victimization in child or adulthood (e.g. Freeman and Garety, 2004), and periods of psychosis and hospitalization as potentially traumatic events in themselves (e.g. Gumley and Schwannauer, 2006). These formative experiences may lead to humiliation, loss and entrapment (Gumley and Schwannauer, 2006); 'interpersonal sensitivity' – the felt sense of being a 'soft target', incorporating beliefs about personal inadequacy, inferiority, and heightened self-consciousness (Freeman and Garety, 2004); as well as distress linked to 'culturally unacceptable' appraisals of intrusions (Morrison, 2001) or the development of problematic core beliefs about self and others (e.g. Chadwick, 2006; Garety *et al.*, 2001; Morrison, 2001; Nelson, 2005).

In line with the work of Garety and colleagues, and with a clear debt to the growing body of literature supporting a continuum model in which psychotic experiences are recognized in both clinical and non-clinical populations (e.g. Claridge, 1990; Combs and Penn, 2004; Johns, Cannon, Singleton, Murray, Farrell *et al.*, 2004; Johns and Van Os, 2001; Romme and Escher, 2006), the clinical cognitive models assume that it is not the experience of voices, paranoia or other unusual ideas that is necessarily problematic, but the crystallization of causal explanations that are distressing and behaviourally disturbing, and then maintained by confirmatory and disconfirmatory processes typical of depression and anxiety presentations (see also Bentall, 2003). We do not yet routinely include assessment of dissociative processes when using these models.

Despite both clinical and theoretical reasons for assuming that dissociation may play a role in the development and maintenance of psychosis, these processes have not yet been explicitly incorporated into the clinical cognitive models to prompt practitioners routinely to consider dissociation in our work. As the proposed accounts of dissociation in psychosis are still to be confirmed empirically this is understandable, but likely to contribute to our continued failure to attend to these processes in clinical practice.

Research and clinical implications

The current research is flawed by a lack of any systematic investigation of the role of dissociation in psychosis. Given the relationship between trauma and psychosis, and the links between trauma, dissociation and psychopathology, the role of dissociation in psychosis now requires attention. We recommend that this starts with an operational definition of dissociation in psychosis, including the function and specific affective, cognitive and behavioural processes involved. The cognitive model of dissociation (Kennedy *et al.*, 2004) provides one possible framework to examine the extent to which different levels of dissociation are implicated in the development and maintenance of distressing psychosis. If it is found that dissociation does indeed contribute to these problems, the challenge will be to consider how best to address these processes in the context of current or enduring vulnerability to psychosis.

Given the literature to date, it would be sensible to consider dissociation in our clinical work. If a person's distress or disability associated with psychotic experience is maintained, at least in part, by dissociation, a failure to recognize these processes is likely to impair treatment. We suggest that psychological assessment routinely (and of course sensitively) ask about past interpersonal trauma (see Read, 2006) and check for any current dissociation (through clinical interview and/or standardized measures). This information can then be incorporated into an individualized formulation where there is evidence that this links to the psychosis. Triggers for automatic dissociation might be systematically identified and named. Within-mode dissociation may also be helpfully represented by linked assumptions (for example 'feelings are dangerous – if I have these feelings then I'll be overwhelmed, so I must avoid them at all costs'). This is not to suggest that such beliefs would necessarily be held in conscious awareness, but that verbal representation may be valuable in facilitating therapeutic change. Formulation may be based on one of the range of clinical cognitive models in the literature. The model of paranoia that we tend to use is presented here to illustrate how dissociation may be incorporated into clinical formulation.

In line with other researchers and clinicians (e.g. Smith, Steel, Rollinson, Freeman, Hardy *et al.*, 2006), we suggest that therapeutic work targeting dissociative processes does not use interventions likely to cause high levels of emotion in people with psychosis, as this may trigger or exacerbate psychotic experience and information processing (Fowler *et al.*, 2006). Grounding (e.g. using verbal or sensory prompts to bring the person's attention to the present) and other distress tolerance skills (Kennerley, 1996; Linehan, 1993) can be useful in early therapeutic work. Indeed, some people may require these skills before attending to detailed formulation, where even very general conversations about current and past experience cue dissociation, and without which the person is unable to process any further therapeutic information.

The process of extended formulation is also likely to be valuable in supporting individuals to make sense of current psychosis in the light of attachment patterns and interpersonal learning history. This may include any tendency to process information in certain ways (e.g. by avoiding information or jumping to conclusions). In this way, the formulation process may facilitate contextualization of material not previously integrated (Fowler *et al.*, 2006). It may be that formulation letters (a narrative description of the development and maintenance of the person's problems, as well as the possibilities offered by therapy) prove to be particularly beneficial in developing a coherent and contextualized narrative for and with the person, linking past and current experience in the context of a compassionate and unthreatening relationship (see Chadwick, 2006; Gumley and Schwannauer, 2006).

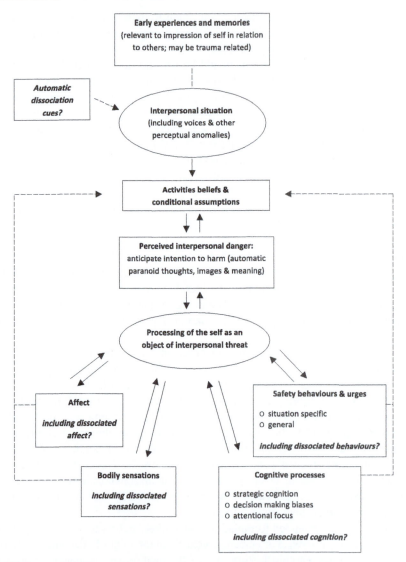

Figure 9.1 A cognitive model of the maintenance of paranoia.
  Following Newman Taylor, K. and Stopa, L. (2013). The Fear of Others: A Pilot
       Study of Social Anxiety Processes in Paranoia. Behavioural and
                 Cognitive Psychotherapy, *41, pp 66–88.*

Clinical example

Pete is in his 40s and has been in a secure mental health rehabilitation hospital
for several years. He has a diagnosis of paranoid schizophrenia and was

viewed as 'untreatable' due to repeatedly poor outcomes following a range of interventions.

Pete reported frequent auditory hallucinations which were generally malevolent and critical. He described delusional beliefs that he had a special sensitivity to the supernatural and would be kidnapped by members of a religious sect if he went out. He managed his fears primarily with avoidance – isolating himself by staying in his room much of the time and avoiding social contact. Pete had been offered cognitive behavioural interventions routinely available on the unit. CBT formulations had mapped the links between psychotic experiences, related appraisals, and the affective, cognitive and behavioural processes hypothesized to be maintaining his distress. Over the years he had engaged in various interventions focused on alleviating his distress through addressing avoidance, safety behaviours and unhelpful appraisals of self and others. These included group CBT focusing on anxiety and auditory hallucinations, supported behavioural exposure, and individual CBT to address his paranoia.

Pete's notes indicate that he had not benefitted from these treatments in terms of alleviation of psychotic experiences, linked distress or risk. The records also suggest that he found it difficult to concentrate when talking to others and would become 'lost' in conversation, apparently forgetting the topic of discussion and needing to check what had been said. He would later have no memory of the conversation. Pete was offered group interventions when they became available as part of the unit programme because he was always keen to be involved in therapeutic activities. However, both subjective and objective measures indicated little benefit beyond brief engagement with the staff team and others on the unit.

Following a review of Pete's care, further psychological assessment was completed, including a detailed interview about his early learning history. Pete had experienced several traumatic episodes in his past. He found these very difficult to talk about, which may explain why these were not explored earlier in his admission. He recalled extremely critical and harsh early parenting that was likely to have influenced his attachment style and thus his ability to manage both internal experience and interpersonal relationships. Pete described strong beliefs from an early age that he was fundamentally bad and that whatever he did would be both wrong and punished. As a young adult, he joined an extreme religious sect where he learnt that 'those who fall by the wayside go to hell'. He left the sect under circumstances which he declined to discuss; any reference to this part of his life provoked extreme anxiety and Pete would become distant and uncommunicative. Immediately prior to his admission, he was involved in a stabbing incident in which the victim later died. This confirmed for Pete that he was 'damned'.

It became clear that Pete's difficulties included both psychotic and traumatic psychological processes, and specifically dissociation. In order to assess this further, he completed a measure of dissociation (the Wessex Dissociation Scale; Kennedy *et al.*, 2004) which yielded scores at the clinical level for all three forms of dissociation[2] (automatic function = 1.6; within-mode = 1.8; between-mode = 1.5). A reformulation was developed to name Pete's early interpersonal threat experiences, represent his formative learning in terms of core beliefs and underlying assumptions, and identify the role of dissociation in the maintenance of his distressing psychosis.

It was hypothesized that Pete had developed a classically conditioned response (automatic dissociation) to threat-related material that triggered sensory intrusions

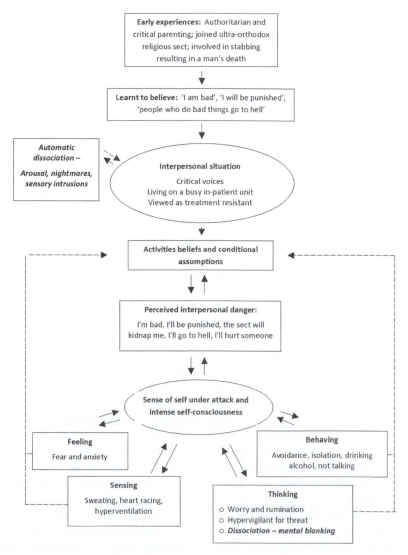

Figure 9.2 Reformulation for Pete

into conscious awareness. In addition, it was hypothesized that he had adopted a sealing over or avoidant response style to distressing early and psychotic experience (McGlashan, 1987; Drayton *et al.*, 1998) in which conscious links with original traumatic events had become attenuated and at times lost completely. This may be conceptualized as within-mode dissociation with Pete's inability to think about certain material as the dissociated element. This experience of 'blanking out' could account for Pete's inability to benefit from previous interventions; the material had been processed as threatening and triggered dissociative responses which in turn prevented effective processing of potentially therapeutic information.

The treatment plan was then adapted to prioritize dissociation using low arousal strategies (Kennerley, 1996; Linehan, 1993). Pete was taught grounding and other distress tolerance techniques. With practice, these enabled him to experience threatening thoughts, feelings and sensations without recourse to dissociation. The process of formulation itself was valuable in helping Pete recognize how both trauma- and psychosis-related processes interacted to prevent processing of new information, thereby maintaining his distress and social disability. Once he was able to manage the dissociation, he began to contextualize past memories and re-evaluate key self and other appraisals through discussion and behavioural experimentation, in line with a more typical CBT approach to psychosis. The Clinical Outcomes in Routine Evaluation (CORE; Mellor-Clark, Barkham, Connell, and Evans, 1999) indicated significant changes in all subscales. Importantly, psychological intervention took place in the context of a whole-unit approach to Pete's recovery. The interventions targeting his dissociation and psychosis allowed Pete to take part in the wider unit programme which was focused on his re-integration with the local community. Over time, he started to go on unescorted leave, hold conversations without losing the thread,

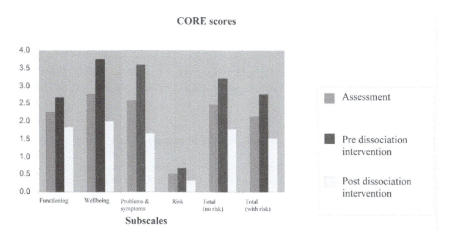

Figure 9.3 CORE scores for Pete

and become more independent in practical skills (e.g. cooking and self-care). The staff noted that he engaged in more daily activities and without previously observed levels of anxiety. Subjectively, Pete reported feeling less distressed, more able to make sense of his past, and able to manage psychotic experiences day to day. After a period of consolidation, Pete was successfully referred to a non-secure community placement.

As a case study, we need to take care not to generalize from these ideas and interventions without further examination of the role of dissociation in psychosis. Nevertheless, it is our clinical judgement that the incorporation of both traumatic and psychotic processes into the cognitive behavioural formulation was essential in this therapy.

Summary and conclusion

Distinctions between dissociation and psychosis in terms of aetiology, symptomatology and indicated treatments are no longer helpful (Ross, 2007b). The empirical links between trauma and psychosis are compelling and likely to involve complex psychological pathways. Dissociation may be a key process in the development and maintenance of distress in psychosis for some people. This now needs to be the subject of a systematic research endeavour.

If we are to work effectively with individuals with psychosis, we need to pay more attention to possible dissociative processes in our assessment, formulation and interventions. For some people, voices, delusions and other psychotic experiences may be the consequence of multifaceted yet understandable responses to traumatic experience. The development of low-arousal interventions that address these processes in the context of ongoing psychosis presents a significant challenge.

The assertion made by Moskowitz, Read and colleagues (2009), that psychosis is essentially dissociative in nature, is a bold and provocative contention. The task for clinicians is to recognize early trauma where this is relevant, name dissociative processes maintaining distressing voices, delusions and disorganized behaviour, and address these therapeutically. More widely, we have to face up to the societal and political challenges raised by the prevalence of early abuse and neglect in our society, and the serious impact this can have on our mental health.

Notes

1 The authors would like to thank Craig Steel for his comments on an earlier draft of this chapter.
2 Automatic function clinical mean = 1.5, SD = 0.8; within-mode clinical mean = 2.1, SD = 0.9; between-mode clinical mean = 2.1, SD = 0.9 (Kennedy *et al.*, 2004).

Chapter 10

Dissociation and somatoform disorders

Richard J. Brown

Since the creation of the Dissociative Disorders category in the third edition of the *Diagnostic and Statistical Manual* (American Psychiatric Association (APA), 1980), dissociation has typically been identified with symptoms such as amnesia, identity disturbance, or alterations in awareness such as depersonalization and derealization. In contrast, the earliest psychological models of dissociation encompassed a much wider range of phenomena, including a host of physical symptoms such as convulsions, paralyzes, sensory disturbances, pain and gastro-intestinal problems for which no medical cause could be found. Recent years have seen a resurgence of interest in the role of dissociation in these complaints, which are now classified within the somatoform disorders section of the fourth edition of the *Diagnostic and Statistical Manual*, text revision edition (DSM IV-TR) (APA, 2000). This chapter summarizes research and theory concerning disso-ciation in somatoform disorders,[1] focusing on a recent approach (the Integrative Cognitive Model; (ICM)) which identifies dissociative compartmentalization as a core process in many such complaints, particularly functional neurological symptoms.[2] The implications of this model for the assessment, formulation and treatment of these conditions are then outlined.

In this chapter, I use the terms 'somatoform disorder', 'somatoform symptoms', 'functional symptoms' and 'medically unexplained symptoms' interchangeably to refer to enduring and potentially debilitating physical symptoms for which no medical explanation can be found. I use the terms 'dissociative disorder' and 'dissociative symptoms' to refer to the phenomena described within the DSM IV-TR dissociative disorders.

How relevant is dissociation when treating somatoform disorders?

Numerous scholars have argued that the dissociation concept is relevant to under-standing somatoform disorders, although theory far exceeds evidence in this area. Typically, the main arguments for justifying this association are that

- somatoform and dissociative symptoms frequently co-occur; and

- a history of trauma is reported by many patients with somatoform disorders, which is taken to mean that these are post-traumatic, and therefore dissociative, phenomena (Brown, Cardeña, Nijenhuis, Sar and Van der Hart, 2007; Bowman, 2006; Nijenhuis, 2004; Kuyk *et al.*, 1996).

Findings pertaining to these arguments are much more mixed than generally thought and methodological and conceptual problems abound (Brown, 2005; Sharpe and Faye, 2006; Brown *et al.*, 2007; Giesbrecht, Lynn, Lilienfield and Merckelbach, 2008; Brown and Lewis-Fernández, 2011). There are certainly many patients who have both somatoform and dissociative symptoms but such overlap is not found in all cases. Similarly, the available evidence suggests that trauma is neither necessary nor sufficient to explain somatoform illness, despite being implicated in a proportion of cases. It is understandable, therefore, why someone might question the relevance of dissociation for understanding and treating somatoform disorders. One of my main goals in this chapter is to show that the dissociation concept is relevant to somatoform phenomena, regardless of whether a history of trauma or co-morbid symptoms is present.

There are already well-established and reasonably effective cognitive behavioural treatments for many somatoform disorders, which make little or no reference to dissociation as an explanatory concept (for reviews see Kroenke and Swindle, 2000; Looper and Kirmayer, 2002; Kroenke, 2007). It is debatable whether incorporating the dissociation concept into these treatments would add to their efficacy. As such, this chapter focuses mainly on the treatment of functional neurological symptoms, where there is a lack of evidence-based treatments (Ruddy and House, 2005) and where the dissociation concept has more face validity. Nevertheless, I will introduce ideas that may be useful when established treatments for other somatoform disorders have proved unsuccessful.

Defining dissociation

In previous work we have sought to improve on current psychiatric definitions of dissociation by distinguishing between two qualitatively different types of dissociative phenomenon (Holmes, Brown, Mansell, Fearon, Hunter, Frasquilho and Oakley, 2005; Brown, 2006a). We have defined *detachment* as an altered state of consciousness characterized by a sense of separation from aspects of everyday experience, which encompasses most instances of depersonalization and derealization (including 'peri-traumatic' dissociation), out-of-body experiences and emotional numbing. Such symptoms may be reported by patients with somatoform disorders and may even be misdiagnosed as medically unexplained symptoms (e.g. derealization being labelled as a functional symptom or non-epileptic attack when encountered in a neurology service); however, they are not somatoform phenomena in their own right (Brown, 2002b). In contrast, we have defined *compartmentalization* as a potentially reversible deficit in the ability to control processes or actions that would normally be amenable to such control, but in which the apparently disrupted functions continue to operate (Holmes *et al.*, 2005; Brown, 2006a). This definition encompasses a range of phenomena, including psychoform symptoms such as amnesia, flashbacks, pseudohallucinations and identity alteration, and somatoform symptoms such as convulsions, sensory loss, paralysis, gait disturbance and so on. It is the category of dissociative compartmentalization that we are concerned with here.

The concept of compartmentalization is well illustrated by a study on amnesia in patients with epilepsy or psychogenic non-epileptic seizures (PNES; Kuyk, Spinhoven and Van Dyck, 1999). Patients in each group were hypnotized and given suggestions to recall what happened during a seizure for which they had previously displayed profound amnesia. While none of the epilepsy group recovered memories using this procedure, 17 out of 20 PNES patients were able to retrieve information that was subsequently corroborated by independent observers. Evidently, the amnesia displayed by these patients resulted from a reversible retrieval deficit that left stored information inaccessible or 'compartmentalized' within the cognitive system.

Compartmentalization is also evident in patients with subjective sensory loss who display intact perceptual processing in the affected modality (so-called 'implicit perception'), which has been demonstrated in functional anaesthesia, deafness and blindness (for a summary and references see Kihlstrom, 1992). Evidence of preserved motor ability in patients with functional weakness (e.g. Sonoo, 2004) demonstrates a similar phenomenon in that group. Put simply, these patients exhibit a lack of integration between how they experience their neurological functioning and objective evidence concerning that functioning. In this sense, functional neurological symptoms are dissociative by definition, irrespective of whether they are precipitated by traumatic events or accompanied by other dissociative problems.

Mechanisms of compartmentalization: The Integrative Cognitive Model

Having clarified our definitions in this way, we are in a position to consider how dissociation (i.e. compartmentalization) works and how it can be treated. My approach has been to model how subjective experience and volitional control are generated by the cognitive system, and then apply this to cases where experience and control seem to break down, such as functional symptoms. As the Integrative Cognitive Model (ICM) is described in detail elsewhere (Brown, 2002a, 2004, 2006a; Brown and Oakley, 2004), only the most general principles are outlined here.

Consciousness as an interpretation of the environment

Consider the familiar thought experiment about how someone might experience an ambiguous night time noise, which is often used clinically to illustrate that how we feel depends on how we interpret events. In this case, there are many possible interpretations of such a noise, including an intruder entering the building, a member of the household returning after a night out, the house 'settling', an effect of the wind and so on, each of which is likely to lead to a different emotional experience. Traditional CBT theory suggests that a key factor in determining which interpretation is selected is the person's beliefs and assumptions about themselves, others and the world, derived from their past experiences. Someone who has been burgled, for example, or who has experienced a lifetime of poor treatment at the hands of others, may be more likely to interpret the ambiguous noise as an intruder – and thereby experience anxiety – than someone without such a history.

Such examples illustrate that how we interpret and feel about the world depends on information stored in memory. A central tenet of the ICM model is that information in memory also plays a major role in shaping what we actually experience (i.e. the contents of awareness) and not just how we interpret those experiences. Consider, for example, the placebo effect, in which a patient's symptoms improve following a sham medical procedure (e.g. saline injection) that is presented as having restorative properties. Here, the sham procedure generates an idea in memory (i.e. an expectation) that not only shapes how the patient interprets their symptoms but how they actually experience their body. The ICM attempts to systematize these ideas within a detailed account of how memory in the cognitive system influences the contents of conscious awareness. By this view, sensory input (e.g. an ambiguous noise) triggers a spread of activation within knowledge systems, generating a number of possible hypotheses about that input based on prior experience. A primary attentional system (PAS) then combines the most active hypothesis with the corresponding sensory data to create a working model or 'primary representation' (i.e. 'best-guess' interpretation) of the environment (cf. Marcel, 1983). The ICM assumes that this is an effortless and pre-conscious process that forms the basic contents of experience, which are associated with an intuitive, pre-reflective form of awareness. Once generated, primary representations can be subjected to further processing via a secondary attentional system (SAS), involving effortful processes associated with self-awareness.

Behavioural control

According to the ICM, the contents of consciousness serve as triggering input for behavioural control processes. Following Norman and Shallice (1986), the model assumes that most behaviour is controlled by a hierarchical network of cognition and action programs, which are automatically activated by primary representations and triggered when their activation threshold is reached. Minimal input from the SAS is required for this process, allowing for rapid and efficient behavioural control in routine situations. The SAS can, however, intervene in this process by increasing or decreasing the activation levels of relevant programs as necessary, allowing for appropriate control in novel situations and those where habitual responses are inappropriate.

This distinction between behaviour triggered automatically by primary representations and behaviour controlled by the SAS is apparent when we learn a complex skill such as driving a car. When we first learn to drive, the task is novel and requires extensive SAS input as we think about what we're doing and consciously perform actions at the appropriate times. As the task becomes more routine, however, and we develop memory programs that represent how to drive, the need for SAS involvement decreases and the task becomes more effortless. The task eventually becomes so automatic that we are able to dedicate SAS resources to other complex tasks (e.g. talking) whilst driving; if a novel situation (e.g. an accident in the road ahead) were to arise, however, then our conversation would cease as SAS resources are diverted back to controlling the primary task.

Rogue representations and functional symptoms

According to this model, what we experience and do are determined by numerous factors, only some of which are under conscious control. Particularly crucial are the activation levels and thresholds of mental representations (i.e. schemata) stored within the system, including the representations that determine how sensory information is interpreted, and the representations that are responsible for guiding thought and action. In normal circumstances, the activation levels and thresholds of these representations are such that they only control perception, cognition and behaviour in situations where they are appropriate. In some cases, however, the activation levels/thresholds of representations may be such that they are selected inappropriately, leading to perceptual disturbances, unwanted behaviour and other compartmentalization phenomena. Enduring problems arise when these 'rogue representations' are chronically over-active (as in continuous symptoms) or prone to episodic over-activation in particular circumstances (as in PNES and other intermittent symptoms). Factors that may contribute to this process are described below.

In this account, therefore, compartmentalization results from any chronically active mental representation that is at odds with information coming from the senses. The precise nature of the problem depends on the underlying rogue representation. Pain, for example, could result from the over-activation of perceptual memories from a previous pain experience, blindness from the automatic selection of a procedural representation inhibiting visual processing and unintentional movements from the activation of inappropriate motor programs. As these processes occur automatically and pre-reflectively, the resulting experiences and behaviours are perceived as subjectively 'real' and outside the individual's volitional control. In each case, the symptom arises relatively late in the processing chain, meaning that earlier processing that is inconsistent with the rogue representation is still represented in the cognitive system and can influence other aspects of cognition, emotion and action. This compartmentalized processing is the source of the implicit perceptual, memorial and motor phenomena described above.

Clinical implications of the model

Relation to existing cognitive behavioural treatment for functional neurological symptoms

Although there are no empirically established psychological treatments for functional neurological symptoms (Ruddy and House, 2005, 2009), some of the most promising data are for a cognitive behavioural intervention for PNES in which dissociation is a key concept (Goldstein, Deale, Mitchell-O'Malley, Toone and Mellers, 2004; Goldstein, Chalder, Chigwedere, Khondoker, Moriarty, Toone and Mellers, 2010). This intervention is based on a modified fear-avoidance model, which assumes that many PNES arise when the brain temporarily 'switches off' (i.e. dissociates) as a way of coping with intense fear (Goldstein *et al.*, 2004, 2010). The treatment is similar to those for health anxiety and other somatoform disorders (e.g. Warwick and Salkovskis, 1990; Brown, 2006a), aiming to reduce anxiety by targeting maladaptive appraisals, preoccupation with possible disease causes, avoidance of feared situations, social reinforcement, excessive reassurance seeking and other abnormal illness behaviours. The main difference between this and other treatments for somatoform disorders is in the socialization phase, when patients are given a dissociative explanation of their symptoms and a number of everyday examples (e.g. not hearing one's name being called whilst absorbed in a good book) to illustrate this. No attempt to distinguish between different types of dissociation is made, however.

There are important theoretical differences between the ICM and the model described by Goldstein and colleagues. For example, the ICM rejects the assumption that dissociative complaints always arise as a defensive response to acute anxiety. Although this may be relevant in many cases, 30–50 per cent of PNES patients are unable to identify an obvious emotional trigger for their attacks (Selkirk, Duncan, Oto and Pelosi, 2008). It is also unclear whether an acute response to anxiety could explain functional symptoms that are less episodic in nature (e.g. continuous paralysis). The ICM accommodates this by assuming that functional symptoms result from normal mental processes that can go awry for various reasons, including (but not limited to) acute anxiety. In this way, it is able to account for symptoms that occur in the apparent absence of trauma, 'unconscious' emotion, anxiety and psychosocial stress, whilst being able to accommodate these things where necessary. The concept of rogue representations also allows the model to explain features that are not well accounted for by other approaches, such as the seizure-like motor activity in many PNES, 'glove anaesthesia' in patients with functional sensory loss, symptoms that mimic those encountered in others and so on. Like every theory in this area, however, the model remains speculative at present and any treatment based on it is necessarily experimental. Nevertheless, it does offer a new way of approaching a set of problems that many clinicians find confusing and difficult to treat.[3]

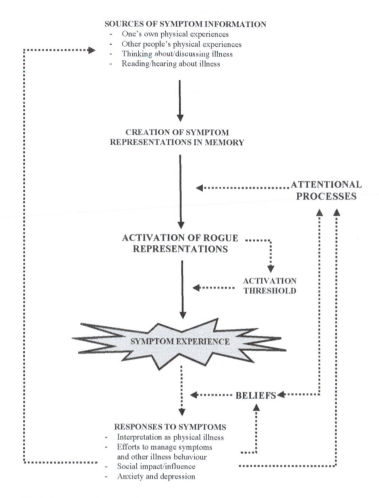

Figure 10.1 Proposed steps (bold arrows) in the creation of functional symptoms and factors moderating this process (dashed arrows).

Implications of the model for assessment and formulation

According to the ICM, assessment and formulation should seek to identify the origins of the rogue representations underlying symptoms and the factors that are influencing their activation (Figure 10.1).

Origins of rogue representations

In some cases, the source of the rogue representation may be less important than what is keeping it chronically active, although the treatment will probably have more face validity for the patient if there is a plausible explanation for symptom onset. In others, understanding the origins of a symptom representation may be a crucial part of treatment (e.g. when it relates to an unprocessed traumatic event). Probably the main source of symptom representations is firsthand experience of illness or injury (Stone, Carson, Aditya, Prescott, Zaubi, Warlow and Sharpe, 2009) or other physical states (e.g. autonomic arousal, normal variations). The model assumes, however, that they are acquired whenever and wherever symptoms are encountered. Thus, witnessing symptoms in others, reading about possible medication side effects, hearing about disease in the media etc. are all sufficient to generate some kind of mental representation of the corresponding symptoms.

Case 1 (Andrew): Description of case and formulation of symptom origins.

Andrew has recently been diagnosed with PNES. His original attack occurred on a night out when he tried cannabis for the first time. Following this, Andrew had a period of attacks resembling faints, which developed seizure-like motor features over the next few months. More recently, his attacks have been preceded by what he describes as 'an aura' characterized by lightheadedness and 'feeling weird'. Andrew describes having been quite alarmed by his first attack, particularly after reading about epilepsy whilst researching possible causes on the Internet. Having initially been concerned about physical illness, he has been increasingly worried about his mental health since receiving the diagnosis of PNES. He has also been castigating himself for experimenting with cannabis, which he thinks may have caused brain damage, mental illness or both. Aside from worry and anxiety about the attacks, there are no other apparent psychiatric problems and there is no evidence of past trauma or abuse. Discussion with Andrew's GP reveals that his initial attack was most likely a benign faint related to cannabis use and dehydration, but that no medical cause for his subsequent attacks had been found, despite extensive investigation.

The rogue representations underlying Andrew's PNES are likely to have a number of sources, including the experience of his initial faint, observers' descriptions of this and subsequent episodes, and his ensuing research about epilepsy and other possible causes (Figure 10.2). These representations appear to be embedded in a wider network of representations, including unhelpful beliefs about his physical (e.g. 'I have brain damage') and mental health (e.g. 'PNES is a psychological condition ... I must be going mad!'), which increase the perceived threat value of his attacks.

Factors contributing to the activation of rogue representations

The model assumes that the main source of representational activation is from the primary and secondary attentional systems. There are numerous overlapping sources of attentional activation and not all will be relevant in every case; they include:

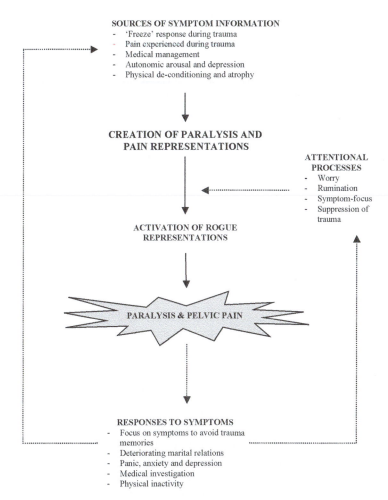

SOURCES OF SYMPTOM INFORMATION
- 'Freeze' response during trauma
- Pain experienced during trauma
- Medical management
- Autonomic arousal and depression
- Physical de-conditioning and atrophy

CREATION OF PARALYSIS AND PAIN REPRESENTATIONS

ATTENTIONAL PROCESSES
- Worry
- Rumination
- Symptom-focus
- Suppression of trauma

ACTIVATION OF ROGUE REPRESENTATIONS

PARALYSIS & PELVIC PAIN

RESPONSES TO SYMPTOMS
- Focus on symptoms to avoid trauma memories
- Deteriorating marital relations
- Panic, anxiety and depression
- Medical investigation
- Physical inactivity

Figure 10.2 Formulation of Andrew's difficulties from the perspective of the ICM.

- worrying and ruminating about symptoms
- anticipating, checking for or otherwise being 'on the lookout' for symptoms (i.e. hypervigilance)
- mental avoidance/suppression of somatic experience
- high-level attentional dysfunction (e.g. problems with disengaging attention), such as that resulting from chronic stress/arousal, head injury, congenital brain dysfunction, substance misuse, perseverative cognition etc.
- liberal perceptual decision-making criteria (i.e. a bias towards sensory signals being interpreted as present)
- sensory filtering problems that make it hard to distinguish relevant from irrelevant bodily sensations

- over-emphasis on conscious, deliberate processing in perception, cognition and action, including 'over-control' of behaviours/cognitive processes that are normally performed automatically

These attentional processes may be pre-existing or may arise in response to symptom experience. Other aspects of the individual's response to symptoms can also contribute to the activation of rogue representations, including:

- interpreting symptoms as evidence of physical disease
- emotional consequences such as anxiety and depression
- medical or other help/reassurance-seeking, which expose the individual to further illness information and appraisals
- avoidance, which maintains unhelpful illness beliefs and limits opportunities for more adaptive representations to be activated
- positive reinforcement of symptoms (e.g. receiving attention from others)
- negative reinforcement of symptoms (e.g. being removed from a potentially distressing situation)
- the reactions of other people and the impact that symptoms have on them

The individual's beliefs (e.g. about symptoms/illness and how to manage them; metacognitive beliefs about worry) clearly influence, and are influenced by, these processes.

Case 1 (Andrew): Formulation of symptom maintenance

The activation of the rogue representations underlying Andrew's symptoms are likely to have been maintained by Andrew's exposure to repeated medical investigation, his worry and rumination, and his hypervigilance for signs of an impending attack (e.g. his self-diagnosed 'auras', which are probably normal variations or symptoms of autonomic arousal). Encountering such signs may then push the rogue representations over their activation threshold, resulting in a non-epileptic seizure. This then 'confirms' Andrew's worst fears that he has a serious physical or psychological problem, further cementing his preoccupation and illness beliefs.

Implications of the model for engagement and socialization

The emphasis on routine mental processes in the ICM offers an emotionally neutral way of socializing patients to a psychological account of their difficulties. A useful way of explaining the model to patients is by referring to everyday examples that illustrate how experience is often inconsistent with what is 'really' happening in the world, and the automatic nature of most behaviour. Examples of the former include placebo and nocebo effects,[4] 'phantom vibration syndrome' (mistakenly believing that one's mobile telephone is vibrating; e.g. Rothberg, Arora, Hermann, Kleppel, Marie and Visintainer, 2010), phantom limbs, and numerous somatic and other illusions (e.g. Hayward, 2008). Examples of automatic behaviour include action slips and other habitual phenomena,[5] skill acquisition[6] and hypnotic/suggested behaviours.[7] Likening functional symptoms to these phenomena may help convey a psychological model without implying that the patient is 'mad', feigning or even stressed. The purpose of formulation is then to understand what has caused an essentially 'normal' phenomenon to become a problem for that individual.

Case 1 (Andrew): Socialization to the model

Socializing Andrew to an account of his PNES based on the ICM challenges his belief that he has a serious physical or psychological condition and provides a plausible alternative explanation that views his attacks as inconvenient, but essentially meaningless, events. This provides a platform for reducing Andrew's symptom preoccupation.

Implications of the model for treatment

From this perspective, the goals of treatment are

- to remove factors that are contributing to the chronic activation of rogue representations
- to increase the activation of more adaptive mental representations

The model is agnostic as far as the most appropriate methods of achieving these aims are concerned, with many of the techniques recommended by other models having potential in this regard (e.g. Goldstein *et al.*, 2004; Howlett and Reuber, 2009).

From a CBT perspective, standard cognitive restructuring and behavioural reattribution methods, worry/rumination postponement, detached mindfulness, distraction, sensory grounding, activity scheduling, exposure, attention training, relaxation, mindfulness meditation, problem-solving and so on may all have a role depending on what is maintaining symptoms. Similarly, imagery techniques,[8] direct suggestion (hypnotic or otherwise), physiotherapy, graded exercise, neuro-rehabilitation etc. may be useful methods for activating healthier mental representations.

Case 1 (Andrew): Treatment

Andrew's symptom preoccupation can be targeted through techniques such as worry postponement and detached mindfulness, by agreeing to ban further infor-mation-seeking about epilepsy, and by agreeing appropriate limits on medical help-seeking. His hypervigilance can be further targeted using distraction and external attention re-focusing, particularly when he encounters seizure warnings. If necessary, appropriate verbal and behavioural reattribution techniques may be used to counter residual illness beliefs, or maladaptive metacognitions concerning the dangers or benefits of worry and rumination (Wells, 2000).

Application of the model to cases where symptoms may be serving a psychological function

Psychodynamic models suggest that functional symptoms often serve a psychological function, such as allowing the individual to express distress whilst avoiding painful traumatic memories. Although the ICM demonstrates that it is possible to explain somatoform phenomena without assuming that symptoms serve a psychological function, the following case example illustrates the potential value of accommodating this idea within the ICM framework.

Case 2: Kelly

Kelly has an 18-month history of bilateral functional paralysis and pelvic pain that began a fortnight after walking, scared but unhurt, from a minor car accident. She has also experienced panic attacks, nightmares and depression since the accident, and spends a lot of time worrying about her health. Her pelvic pain has meant that Kelly and her husband have not had successful sexual intercourse since the accident, leading to problems in their relationship. During the assessment, it emerges that Kelly's nightmares concern a rape that she experienced twenty years ago, which she has never spoken about and which she dealt with by keeping busy and 'trying to think about other things'. Kelly provides few details of the rape other than it was physically very painful and that she had been 'frozen with terror' for much of it. It becomes apparent that any attempts to talk about the rape invariably lead to a discussion of Kelly's physical symptoms and her worries about these.

Possible formulation

It appears that the acute anxiety experienced by Kelly during her car accident has brought back memories of her rape, triggering an episode of delayed-onset PTSD. Kelly's description suggests that the rogue representations underlying her paralysis and pelvic pain are probably sensory fragments originating in the rape, and that her functional symptoms may be akin to continuous somatic flashbacks to that event (Figure 10.3). Kelly's avoidance of trauma reminders then maintains the activation of these representations by preventing emotional processing of the trauma. It is possible that Kelly's preoccupation with her health may be one method that she uses to suppress trauma memories (whilst also being an understandable consequence of the symptoms themselves), which negatively reinforces illness and further fuels the activation of rogue representations. Negative reinforcement may also be contributing to Kelly's pelvic pain, which has had the effect of limiting sexual contact with her husband and thereby removing a significant

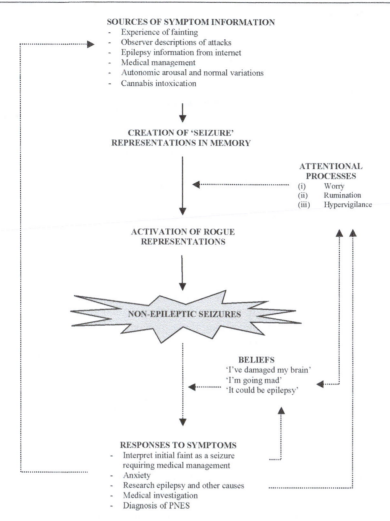

Figure 10.3 Formulation of Kelly's difficulties from the perspective of the ICM.

trauma reminder, albeit with adverse consequences for her mood and marital relationship. Finally, long periods of inactivity resulting from Kelly's paralysis are likely to have had adverse physical consequences (e.g. muscle atrophy), providing a further source of rogue representations and illness preoccupation.

Possible treatment

Although Kelly's difficulties are closely related to her traumatic past, directly confronting her with this is likely to provoke intense anxiety and further avoidance, possibly in the form of increased symptom preoccupation. Using the ICM, however, an initial formulation that makes no reference to trauma could be provided as a way of socializing Kelly to a psychological model of her difficulties. Having established a therapeutic relationship, guided discovery could then be used to help Kelly recognize the likely origin of her symptoms and how they might be addressed through trauma-focused therapy. Cognitive (e.g. Ehlers and Clark, 2000) and/or metacognitive therapy (e.g. Wells and Sembi, 2004) for trauma may then be applied, with the emphasis on minimizing worry, rumination and cognitive avoidance in the latter having particular potential. If appropriate, Kelly might also be encouraged to discuss her trauma with her husband, with a view to repairing some of the damage to their relationship and further facilitating emotional processing. Physiotherapy may be a useful adjunct to psychological treatment in this case, both to improve the physical strength of Kelly's legs and to activate healthier mental representations.

Conclusions

In this chapter I have argued that dissociative compartmentalization is a central feature of functional neurological symptoms and described an integrative model of the cognitive mechanisms underlying these phenomena. I have outlined some of the implications of this model and illustrated how it might be used to understand and treat patients with functional symptoms, whether trauma and primary gain are present or not. Although the emphasis has been on functional neurological symptoms, the second case example demonstrates how the ICM might be used to understand chronic pelvic pain and other somatoform phenomena that have proved resistant to treatment.

Notes

1   Nijenhuis (2004) uses the terms 'psychoform' and 'somatoform' dissociation to refer to the phenomena classified within the Dissociative and Somatoform Disorder categories of DSM IV-TR respectively.
2   Many such symptoms are classified as conversion disorders within the DSM IV-TR somatoform disorders and dissociative (conversion) disorders in ICD-10 (World Health Organization (WHO), 1992), although full diagnostic criteria are often not met because psychosocial precipitants are either absent or not considered (Brown and Lewis-Fernández, 2011). This chapter pertains to all functional neurological symptoms regardless of whether full conversion disorder criteria are met.
3   For the sake of brevity, this chapter does not consider aspects of treatment (e.g. appropriate communication of an unequivocal diagnosis) that are relevant whatever model is used.
4   The negative counterpart to the placebo effect, in which physical symptoms are reported following a sham medical procedure that is presented as having symptom-inducing properties.
5   Examples include driving to one's old house following a move; writing the wrong date at the start of a new year; reaching for a cigarette having recently given up etc. Such phenomena illustrate how automatic behaviours can be both inconsistent with

our intentions and difficult to resist, making them particularly useful for detoxifying functional symptoms.

6   As in the above example of learning how to drive.

7   The defining characteristic being the perceived involuntariness that accompanies the suggested action. There are numerous examples including Chevreul's pendulum, arm levitation, 'magnetic' hands etc. (see British Psychological Society, 2001). Suggestion has also been used with susceptible individuals to create phenomena that mimic functional neurological symptoms (e.g. temporary paralysis, sensory loss, pseudon-eglect) and it seems likely that common processes are involved (Brown and Oakley, 2004; Bell, Oakley, Halligan and Deeley, 2011). It has also been claimed that people with functional neurological symptoms are highly suggestible, although the evidence is equivocal (Brown and Lewis-Fernández, 2011). Similarly, the apparent promise of hypnosis as an adjunct to treating functional symptoms remains to be converted into solid empirical findings (Ruddy and House, 2005/2009).

8   For example, a paralyzed patient may be encouraged to identify and mentally recreate vivid memories of a time when they were able to use their legs (e.g., playing football).

Chapter 11

Dissociative experiences in patients with borderline personality disorder

Vegard Øksendal Haaland
Nils Inge Landrø

This chapter examines dissociative experiences in patients with borderline personality disorder (BPD). The chapter will present knowledge about the prevalence, aetiology and correlates of dissociative experiences in BPD. The relationship between BPD and the dissociative disorders will be discussed. The chapter will also present findings regarding the neurobiology of dissociative experiences as well as clinical implications of dissociation in BPD.

The core features of BPD are disturbed relational abilities, fear of abandonment, affective dysregulation, and lack of behavioural control. In addition, several studies have shown increased levels of dissociation. The occurrence of 'transient, stress-related severe dissociative symptoms or paranoid ideation' is one of the criteria defining the disorder, a criterion that was added to the *Diagnostic and Statistical Manual of Mental Disorders* of the American Psychiatric Association (APA) in the 1994 edition (DSM-IV). This criterion, which is met in around 75 per cent of patients with BPD, shows excellent specificity. Thus, dissociative symptoms are highly specific for differentiating patients with BPD from other diagnostic groups, with the exception of the dissociative disorders. According to the DSM IV-TR (APA, 2000) dissociation can be defined as a 'breakdown in the usually integrated functions of consciousness, memory, perception of self or the environment, or sensory/motor behaviour' (p. 811).

Childhood sexual abuse, as well as inconsistent treatment in childhood, tends to dominate discussions of the aetiology of dissociation in BPD. The frequency of dissociative experiences in BPD ranges from low to moderate and severe dissociation. However, most studies of dissociation in BPD are confounded by failures to identify individuals with co-morbid dissociative disorders. Thus the high numbers of patients with moderate and severe dissociation may depend on different factors and it remains unclear whether the dissociative symptoms in BPD are driven by mechanisms and aetiological factors that are exclusive to BPD or common with the dissociative disorders.

According to the DSM IV-TR, dissociative symptoms in patients with BPD are in particular associated with stress-related situations. This connection has also been demonstrated experimentally in a recent study that found higher levels of cortisol in BPD patients with high levels of dissociation. This finding may indicate that dissociative symptomatology is a marker of heightened biological vulnerability to stress in BPD.

Dissociation has been associated with inwardly directed aggression such as self-harming behaviour and suicide attempts. Patients with BPD and severe dissociative symptoms also show more severe symptoms of co-morbid disorders such as depression, anxiety, PTSD, and alcohol abuse. They also make more frequent use of the mental health system. Recent research has increasingly tended to focus on the relationship between cognition and dissociation. While studies of the neuropsychological functioning of patients with BPD generally have revealed various results, a consistent finding is reduced executive functioning compared to non-clinical controls. A study focusing on the association between dissociation and cognition in this patient group identified dissociation to be a potential influential moderator. A subgroup of patients with BPD and pathological dissociation was found to have lower IQ scores and reduced executive functioning, working memory and verbal long-term memory. Dissociative symptoms have also been related to difficulties in recalling specific autobiographical memories. Emotional learning has been found to be slower during dissociative states. Since psychotherapeutic treatment requires information processing abilities in general from the client, and in particular might focus on reprocessing of emotional memories and relearning of emotional reactions, these findings might have potentially large clinical relevance.

Borderline personality disorder

BPD is a severe and prevalent disorder, affecting about 1–2 per cent of the population (Lenzenweger, Lane, Loranger, and Kessler, 2007; Torgersen, Kringlen, and Cramer, 2001). In mental health clinical groups about 10 per cent of outpatients and 20 per cent of inpatients are affected (Lieb, Zanarini, Schmahl, Linehan, and Bohus, 2004). BPD is characterized by a pervasive pattern of severe affective instability, impulse control dysfunction, instability in self-image and interpersonal relations and cognitive disturbances (APA, 2000; Lieb et al., 2004; Siever and Davis, 1991; Skodol, Siever, et al., 2002). About three quarters of the patients show self-harming behaviour (Clarkin, Widiger, Frances, Hurt and Gilmore, 1983).

A complicating factor in the research on BPD and in the treatment of patients with BPD is high co-morbidity with other mental disorders. The most common co-morbid disorders include affective disorders, anxiety disorders (including PTSD), substance related disorders, eating disorders and other personality disorders (Skodol, Gunderson et al., 2002). As we will see later on in this chapter, our knowledge about co-morbid DSM IV-TR dissociative disorders in BPD is limited.

The severity of the disorder, and the co-morbidity, is reflected in a high mortality rate due to impulsive behaviour or suicide. The suicide rate is about 10 per cent, which is comparable to other severe mental disorders like schizophrenia and bipolar disorder (APA, 2000). BPD is also associated with a high consumption of health care services, and thus high costs to society (Ansell, Sanislow, McGlashan and Grilo, 2007; Jerschke, Meixner, Richter and Bohus, 1998).

Dissociation in BPD

The current conception of the BPD diagnosis, as it is defined in the DSM IV-TR, is primarily influenced by Gunderson and Singers' article 'Defining Borderline Patients' (Gunderson and Singer, 1975). Besides outlining most of the current diagnostic criteria, they also pointed out that patients with BPD frequently display disturbed states of consciousness (dissociation), which they described as 'peculiar ego states'. Commonly these states were referred to as 'borderline states' to differentiate them from the personality based features (i.e. traits). Gunderson and Singer also emphasize that these states are seen as responses to changes in affectivity, such as anxiety, depression and rage, and as prepsychotic experiences. Thus dissociative experiences triggered by emotional distress were recognized as a central feature of the borderline condition. However, in 1980, when the disorder was first included in the DSM-III, these 'peculiar' experiences were not covered in any criteria.

In the revised fourth edition of DSM a new criterion was added (criterion 9) describing these states as 'transient, stress-related paranoid ideation or severe dissociative symptoms' (APA, 2000, p. 710). This criterion, occurring in approximately 75 per cent of patients with BPD, has been shown to have very good specificity and can therefore serve to separate patients with BPD from patients with other mental disorders (Skodol, Gunderson *et al.*, 2002). According to the DSM IV-TR, dissociative symptoms in patients with BPD are in particular associated with situations with high levels of stress (APA, 2000). This association has also been demonstrated experimentally (Stiglmayr *et al.*, 2008; Stiglmayr, Shapiro, Stieglitz, Limberger and Bohus, 2001). Stiglmayr and co-writers (Stiglmayr *et al.*, 2008) found dissociative experiences in patients with BPD to be related to everyday stress. In this study, participants rated subjective stress and dissociative experiences every hour. Dissociation scores were found to be higher in patients with BPD than in clinical and non-clinical controls during low, medium and high levels of stress. Thus, patients with BPD show stress-related increases in dissociative experiences as well as a general heightened level of dissociation, compared to non-clinical controls.

Several studies have shown elevated levels of dissociation in patients with BPD compared to non-clinical controls as well as to patient groups with other personality disorders or other mental disorders (Brodsky, Cloitre and Dulit, 1995; Herman, Perry and Van der Kolk, 1989; Jones *et al.*, 1999; Zanarini, Ruser, Frankenburg and Hennen, 2000; Zweig-Frank, Paris and Guzder, 1994). Typically dissociation was measured through self-report questionnaires like the Dissociative Experiences Scale (Bernstein and Putnam, 1986). Zanarini and colleagues (Zanarini, Ruser, Frankenburg and Hennen, 2000) studied 290 inpatients with BPD and found that about one third reported normal DES scores (0–10). More than 40 per cent reported moderate scores, and thus significant dissociative symptoms (11–29). Severe dissociative symptoms scores (≥ 30) were found in about one quarter of the participants.

The validity of these findings has been disputed because most of the studies on dissociation in BPD fail to take into account diagnosis of any co-morbid dissociative disorders (Sar and Ross, 2006). Thus Korzekwa and co-writers (Korzekwa, Dell and Pain, 2009) argue that reports of dissociation in BPD may be accounted for by three different phenomena: 1) over-reporting, 2) dissociation driven by mechanisms that are specific to BPD, and 3) dissociation driven by mechanisms specific to the dissociative disorders (DDs). Ross (2007a) argues that the ninth criteria in the DSM does not account for the complexity or the frequency of the dissociative experiences in BPD. Furthermore, it does not provide adequate rules for deciding when the dissociative experiences are severe enough to warrant a separate dissociative disorder diagnosis (Ross, 2007a). The relationship between the dissociative disorders and BPD is discussed later in this chapter.

Aetiology of dissociation in BPD

Developmental psychopathology is the study of mental disorders with a developmental perspective. The focus might be on the life course of a disorder or more narrowly on the developmental aspects of the occurrence of the disorder. Few longitudinal studies with a developmental psychopathological perspective are devoted to theories about the aetiology of BPD. The same can be said for the aetiology of most mental disorders. Thus, most of the proposed aetiological factors stem from retrospective reports, correlational designs and, in some cases, genetic studies. Our knowledge about gene-environment interaction, possible epigenetic processes, and eventual causal influence of organic, biological or environmental factors is also limited. Even our correlational knowledge is confounded with the possible influence of BPD features on the retrospective reports. It is not unlikely that the development of a disorder like BPD, and the symptoms associated with the disorder will have an influence on how a person recalls and reports their life-story. Accordingly, we have little knowledge about causation, and some knowledge about co-occurrence. The same can be said for our knowledge about the aetiology of the dissociative phenomena in BPD.

One of the factors that, it is suggested, plays a significant role in the development of BPD as well as in the development of dissociative symptoms is childhood abuse and neglect. Patients with BPD usually report higher rates of abuse (including sexual abuse) and neglect than do patients with other personality disorders (Battle *et al.*, 2004; Zanarini, Ruser, Frankenburg, Hennen and Gunderson, 2000). Dissociation scores in adulthood have been found to correlate with childhood abuse and may be the most important predisposing factor for some patients with BPD (Ross-Gower, Waller, Tyson and Elliott, 1998; Shearer, 1994; Van den Bosch, Verheul, Langeland and Van den Brink, 2003). The dissociative phenomena can be seen as adaptive reactions to trauma experiences (Goodman and Yehuda, 2002). In childhood the dissociative response to traumatic events might have had a protective function i.e. if the experiences were too difficult to process and integrate. This factor cannot, however, explain the development of dissociation in all patients (Goodman and Yehuda, 2002; Shearer, 1994; Van den Bosch *et al.*, 2003; Zanarini, Ruser, Frankenburg and Hennen, 2000).

Several other factors have been found to correlate with adult dissociative experiences, and are thought potentially to mediate these symptoms. These include genetic factors, severe maternal dysfunction, being witness to violence, inconsistent treatment by caregiver, adult sexual assault, fearful attachment style in adulthood (i.e. 'bad me, bad other'), and substance abuse (Shearer, 1994; Simeon, Nelson, Elias, Greenberg and Hollander, 2003; Van den Bosch *et al.*, 2003; Zanarini, Ruser, Frankenburg, Hennen and Gunderson, 2000). Van den Bosch and co-writers (Van den Bosch *et al.*, 2003) point out that patients who also abuse substances may confuse phenomena experienced under substance intoxication with dissociative experiences when filling out self-report questionnaires. Individuals with cognitive dysfunctions, like memory difficulties or difficulties with executive functioning, may have a greater probability for developing dissociation as an adaptive strategy (Judd, 2005).

Grosjean and Tsai (2007) suggest that cognitive dysfunctions and symptoms such as dissociation in patients with BPD may be a result of dysregulation of the N-methyl-D-aspartate (NMDA) neurotransmission, a part of the glutamatergic system. NMDA is central in neuroplasticity and cognitive functioning, and studies suggest that it may be central to the development of various mental disorders. The NMDA dysregulation may be a result of a combination of biological vulnerability and lack of environmental stimulation or chronic stress in the early years of childhood, a critical period for the development of the glutamatergic system. Chronic stress leads to levels of the stress hormone cortisol and glutamate that may be toxic, and can lead to brain organic changes, including poor synaptic density and reduced volume, in structures such as the frontal cortex, hippocampus and the anterior cingulate cortex. These changes may lead to increased sensitivity for stress, cognitive difficulties, mentalization deficits and heightened probability for dissociation.

BPD and the dissociative disorders

As previously described, the relationship between BPD and the dissociative disorders is not fully understood. The diagnostic criterion does not give adequate guidelines as to when the dissociative phenomena are severe enough to warrant a separate dissociative diagnosis. Studies have focused on the co-morbidity of BPD and dissociative disorders. It has been reported that 53 per cent of patients with BPD also fulfilled the criteria for a DSM IV-TR dissociative disorder (11 per cent Dissociative Identity Disorder (DID)) (Conklin and Westen, 2005). Ross (2007a) found that 59 per cent of those with BPD had a DSM IV-TR dissociative disorder (18 per cent DID), whereas Sar and co-writers found DSM IV-TR dissociative disorders in 73 per cent of their participants with BPD (Sar, Akyuz, Kugu, Ozturk and Ertem-Vehid, 2006) and Korzekwa and co-writers found DSM IV-TR dissociative disorders in 76 per cent of their participants (Korzekwa, Dell, Links, Thabane and Fougere, 2009). Thus between one half and three quarters of patients with BPD seem to also fulfill the criteria for one of the dissociative disorders. In the other direction Sar, Yargic and Tutkun (1996) identified BPD in 31 per cent of patients with DID, Ellason, Ross and Fuchs (1996) in 56 per cent of patients with DID, Dell (1998) found BPD in 53 per cent, whereas in the study by Ross *et al.* (1990), 64 per cent were diagnosed with BPD. Thus between one and two thirds of people diagnosed with DID also have a co-morbid diagnosis of BPD.

The association between the disorders is scarcely researched. This is most likely due to limited knowledge about the co-morbidity between the disorders as well as their common historical roots (Sar *et al.*, 2006). Sar and co-writers point out that BPD and the dissociative disorders both have their historical roots in the concept of hysteria and that these roots may have been overlooked in modern research due to the elimination of the concept of hysteria from the diagnostic and the psychiatric terminology (see also Kennedy and Kennerley this volume).

Given the presumed association of BPD and of dissociative disorders with childhood trauma experiences, it has been suggested that they may be a single disorder (Benner and Joscelyne, 1984; Chu and Dill, 1990). Sar and co-writers, however, found that although the co-morbidity was high between BPD and the dissociative disorders, the two categories were related to different types of childhood trauma. While the dissociative disorders were found to be related to emotional neglect, BPD was associated with childhood emotional and sexual abuse, physical neglect, and total childhood trauma severity. The fact that no interaction was found between the diagnoses with respect to any of the trauma categories supports the thesis that they are separate diagnoses (Sar *et al.*, 2006).

Correlates of dissociation in BPD

The level of dissociative symptoms in patients with BPD has been found to be positively correlated with other symptoms characteristic for the disorder, including self-harming behaviour and behavioural dysregulation (Brodsky *et al.*, 1995; Shearer, 1994).

Patients with BPD who report high levels of dissociative symptoms also have higher levels of self-reported childhood physical and sexual abuse as well as adult sexual assault (Brodsky *et al.*, 1995; Shearer, 1994).

Self-harm has been found to be the most powerful predictor of dissociation in BPD, even in studies in which childhood abuse was controlled for (Brodsky *et al.*, 1995). However, even when BPD and childhood abuse are controlled for, there seems to exist an independent association between dissociation and self-harm (Zlotnick, Mattia and Zimmerman, 1999).

Dissociation is also associated with higher levels of symptoms of co-morbid disorders like posttraumatic symptoms (Shearer, 1994), alcohol abuse (Shearer, 1994), and depressive symptoms (Brodsky *et al.*, 1995). One study suggests that higher levels of general psychiatric symptomatology in patients with BPD, as compared to other personality disorders, may be mediated by higher levels of dissociative symptoms (Wildgoose, Waller, Clarke and Reid, 2000). Thus dissociative symptoms may be characteristic of a more severe subgroup of patients with BPD. In this light it is not surprising that dissociation in BPD is also associated with lower adaptive functioning and higher consumption of psychiatric treatment (Brodsky *et al.*, 1995; Shearer, 1994).

BPD is also associated with cognitive dysfunctions, where reduced executive and memory functioning is the most robust finding (Fertuck, Lenzenweger, Clarkin, Hoermann and Stanley, 2006; Haaland, Esperaas and Landrø, 2009) including impairments in decision making and planning (Bazanis *et al.*, 2002; Haaland and Landrø, 2007). The association between cognitive functioning and dissociative symptoms has been the subject of few studies. In one study dissociative symptoms were associated with difficulties in recalling specific autobiographic memories (Jones *et al.*, 1999).

In one of our own studies (Haaland and Landrø, 2009) patients with BPD and pathological dissociation (measured with the pathological dissociation taxon of the DES) were found to have reduced executive functioning, working memory, and long-term verbal memory performance compared to patients with BPD without pathological dissociation. With regard to attention and long-term non-verbal memory, no differences were found between the two groups. Compared to a non-clinical group, patients with BPD with pathological dissociation showed reduced performance on every cognitive domain including attention, working memory, long-term visual and auditory memory, and executive functioning. Patients with BPD without pathological dissociation showed only reduced executive functioning. Thus, pathological dissociation might be a clinical variable that differentiates patients with BPD with regard to cognitive functioning. The two groups also differed with respect to general intellectual abilities, with the group with pathological dissociation scoring more than one standard deviation below the group without pathological dissociation. This is a crucial finding that, along with the results regarding the other cognitive domains, allows for several hypotheses. Firstly, one could argue that reduced cognitive abilities enhance the probability of pathological dissociation. This would be in line with Judd's (2005) theory that individuals with cognitive dysfunctions may have greater probability for developing dissociation as an adaptive strategy. Secondly, one could hypothesize that there is a common factor of reduced cognitive abilities and pathological dissociation; it could be a question of traumatic experiences that, at a certain stage, would affect neurobiological development. Thirdly, it is of course possible that the pathological dissociative phenomena per se cause reduced test performance, i.e. pathological dissociation during test uptake conflicts with the tasks solved. Nonetheless, pathological dissociation and reduced working memory, executive functions, long-term verbal memory performance, and IQ seem to be co-occurring in patients with BPD.

Ebner-Priemer and colleagues (Ebner-Priemer *et al.*, 2009) studied the influence of dissociative states on emotional learning processes in patients with BPD using a paradigm with a classical condition task, where a neutral stimulus was paired with an aversive sound. They found that patients with BPD who experienced high levels of dissociative symptoms during the learning phase did not show any conditioned response to the neutral stimuli that had been paired with an aversive sound. Patients with low levels of dissociative symptoms and non-clinical controls did show conditioned responses. The differences were found on a physiological measure (skin conductance) as well as in self-report measures. This study indicates that dissociative symptoms may alter emotional learning processes in patients with BPD, a finding with potential clinical relevance, which will be discussed later in the chapter.

Neurobiology of BPD and dissociation

Dysfunctions in the neural systems for affect regulation, behaviour regulation, and social cognition, are assumed to account for the neurobiological foundations of BPD (Corrigan, Davidson and Heard, 2000; Herpertz, Kunert, Schwenger and Sass, 1999; Linehan, 1993). According to this theory, emotional vulnerability develops as a result of emotional hyperarousal, of high sensitivity with respect to emotional stimuli, and of high emotional intensity. Difficulties with the regulation of emotional responses lead to marked and fast changes in emotional states and predispose for various forms of impulsive self-destructive and impulsive aggressive behaviour. Impulsivity is used as a maladaptive mechanism to lighten intense, unbearable negative emotions (Herpertz, Sass and Favazza, 1997; Linehan, 1993). Dual brain pathology is assumed to account for some of the characteristic features. Both frontal and limbic circuits are proposed to be affected; more specifically the anterior cingulate cortex, the orbitofrontal and dorsolateral prefrontal cortex (PFC), hippocampus, and amygdala seem to be involved (Bohus, Schmahl and Lieb, 2004; Schmahl and Bremner, 2006). Reduced volumes, as compared to non-clinical controls, have been demonstrated in the amygdala and hippocampus as well as in the PFC and the anterior cingulate cortex (Bohus *et al.*, 2004). Several studies have found hyper-reactivity of the amygdala in response to emotional stimuli. It is assumed that a lack of inhibition of the amygdala through the PFC is a central mechanism of the disorder (Schmahl and Bremner, 2006). This mechanism is, however, probably not specific for BPD as it also has been suggested as underlying major depression (Siegle, Thompson, Carter, Steinhauer and Thase, 2007).

Through diffusion tensor MRI (DTI) the neural circuits connecting different parts of the brain with each other can be imaged and measured. In a DTI-study with women with BPD and co-morbid attention deficit hyper-activity disorder (ADHD), without PTSD or major depression, Rüsch *et al.*, (2007) found that dysfunctional affect regulation, anger–hostility, dissociative symptoms and general psychopathology were associated with reduced strength of the connections within the orbitofrontal cortex and between the orbitofrontal cortex and the basal ganglia and limbic areas. In this study the dissociative symptoms were less significantly associated with the strength of the connections than the other symptoms were. The authors suggest that this finding reflects that more extended neural networks are involved in dissociative symptoms including temporal and parietal, as well as occipital areas.

A MRI-study of 30 women with BPD and a history of severe childhood abuse, and 25 non-clinical controls, explored the volume of different parts of the parietal cortex (Irle, Lange, Weniger and Sachsse, 2007). Most of the patients in this study had co-morbid dissociative disorders that, in most cases, manifested itself as depersonalization disorder. A reduced volume of the precuneus compared to non-clinical controls was found. A subsample of 17 patients revealed reduced resting glucose metabolism as measured by PET scan in the same area (Lange, Kracht, Herholz, Sachsse and Irle, 2005). The precuneus is hypothesized to be responsible for continuous collection and processing of information about our internal and external situation. It is thus associated with episodic memory, reflections upon self, as well as aspects of consciousness (Cavanna and Trimble, 2006). It is therefore related to our continuous and integrated self-perception in relation to our environment (Gusnard, Raichle and Raichle, 2001). These findings might be associated with the disturbed sense of self as well as some of the relational difficulties in BPD.

Patients with BPD have also been found to have higher pain threshold than non-clinical controls, a finding that was associated with severity of dissociative symptoms (Ludäscher et al., 2007). Patients with BPD also have reduced activity in the precuneus when exposed to pain (Schmahl et al., 2006). Symptoms of depersonalization however were found to be associated with a larger volume of the right precuneus in women with BPD (Irle et al., 2007). It is suggested that the precuneus is activated through normal conscious states as well as through pathological conscious states such as dissociation (Irle et al., 2007).

Enhanced startle responses (measured by electromyogram) have been found in patients with BPD (Ebner-Priemer et al., 2005). Startle responses are primarily amygdala-driven, and the enhanced responses are thought to reflect amygdala hypersensitivity, or lack of prefrontal inhibition of the amygdala response. Patients with high state dissociation during testing showed lower startle response than patients with low state dissociation. Dissociative states may block enhanced amygdala response. The dissociative symptoms seen in BPD might therefore serve as a regulatory mechanism that prevents the typical BPD startle response, a function with possible clinical implications.

The ninth criterion for BPD in DSM IV-TR, 'transient, stress-related severe dissociative symptoms or paranoid ideation' (APA, 2000, p. 710) states the connection between dissociative symptoms and stress. Dissociative symptoms as measured with the DES have been found to be associated with stress hormone systems such as the hypothalamic-pituitary-adrenal (HPA) and the noradrenergic systems. A pilot study demonstrated that patients with BPD and high dissociation have greater cortisol responses to stress than patients who were low in dissociation (Simeon, Knutelska, Smith, Baker and Hollander, 2007). The authors conclude that dissociative symptoms in BPD may be associated with greater reactivity to stress in the HPA axis and the noradrenergic system, as well as with a lower noradrenergic baseline level. The lower noradrenergic baseline level may be seen as a result of autonomic nervous system blunting, a hypothesized biological marker of dissociative states (Simeon *et al.*, 2007). This finding may indicate that dissociative symptomatology is a marker of (or an effect of) heightened biological vulnerability to stress in BPD.

Clinical consequences of dissociation in BPD

As a previous section of the chapter has shown, patients with BPD who also experience pathological levels of dissociative symptoms are more frequently in need of mental health care. However, few studies have explored the clinical consequences of dissociative symptoms in BPD. This is particularly true with regard to the effect of dissociation on treatment outcome. The introductory parts of this chapter presented findings that theoretically could reveal something about the potential effect of dissociation on outcome. For instance, dissociative symptoms in BPD are associated with higher severity of other BPD symptoms such as self-harming behaviour and impulsivity. This finding alone may imply a more worrying prognosis, as may the notion that patients scoring high on dissociation show more severe symptoms of co-morbid disorders. A special therapeutic challenge presents itself in patients with BPD and co-morbid dissociative disorders. As Ross argues, these patients are probably in need of special treatment protocols or at least special adaptations of the treatment protocols developed for BPD (Ross, 2007a). In concluding this chapter, we will however limit our focus to the aspects of dissociation itself that may alter the effect of treatment interventions.

The primary clinical intervention for BPD is psychotherapy. Several specialized psychotherapeutic treatments have been developed during the last twenty years. Today the prognosis for BPD is considered to be good in a 10 years perspective (Zanarini, Frankenburg, Hennen, Reich and Silk, 2006).

Among the several aspects of dissociation in BPD that may have an impact on the psychotherapeutic process we must emphasize that the phenomenon of dissociation in itself implies changes in basic information processing functions. The DSM IV-TR definition: a 'breakdown in the usually integrated functions of consciousness, memory, perception of self or the environment, or sensory/motor behavior' (APA, 2000, p. 811) emphasizes these changes. When dissociative states occur during psychotherapy one can assume that the effect of the psychotherapeutic techniques will be reduced. This is certainly true in cases where the dissociative phenomena are not discovered and thus disregarded in the therapy. In

BPD, dissociative states are thought to occur as a response to stress. The psycho-therapeutic process will in most (or all) cases involve some levels of stress, so that the setting in itself may provoke dissociative responses. The level of stress and the responses thereto should be monitored by the therapist during therapy, and stress-regulating interventions should be part of the treatment. One example of such interventions is the use of mindfulness, acceptance, and emotion regulation skills in dialectical behavioural therapy (DBT) (Linehan, 1993). Mindfulness, as well as the focus on acceptance, increases the capability to tolerate emotions and distressing internal states, while the emotion regulation skills involve learning to identify and label, as well as changing, emotions. Bohus and co-writers found that when patients developed affect regulation and distress tolerance abilities as part of an inpatient DBT, they also reported a reduction in dissociative experiences (Bohus *et al.*, 2000).

We have also seen that pathological dissociation is associated with reduced cognitive functioning on several cognitive domains. Regardless of whether this reduced cognitive function is a result of dissociation, a reason for dissociation, or dependent on a third variable that covariates with dissociation, the reduced cognitive functioning will most likely have an influence on the effect of psycho-therapeutic treatment. Patients with cognitive deficits might have difficulties remembering appointments or problems planning ahead to make sure they show up to an appointment. In the sessions, working memory difficulties may alter the communication and the information processing. Between sessions memory difficulties might make transferral of experiences from therapy to real life and vice versa difficult. Such problems might also reflect deficits associated with the ability to switch flexibly between mental sets. Furthermore, specific problems to inhibit irrelevant information could be associated with emotional dysregulation. In general, a systematic assessment of basic neuropsychological functions might be a useful tool to individualize the therapeutic strategy.

As described earlier in the chapter, findings also indicate that dissociative states disturb emotional learning. Ebner-Priemer and co-writers (Ebner-Priemer *et al.*, 2009) argue that even though their study only focused on the acquisition of new associations, the findings would probably also imply the same difficulties with extinction, due to the amygdala's involvement in both processes. As psychothera-peutic treatment of BPD to a great extent involves affect-related learning (e.g. affect tolerance, affect modulation and affect recognition) the therapist should be aware of the occurrence of dissociative states during therapy. On the one hand the focus on emotions might trigger dissociative responses, on the other hand dissociative states might prevent the patient from learning new emotional skills in therapy.

As Ebner-Priemer and co-writers (2005) suggest, dissociative states may serve as a regulatory mechanism. The therapist should be aware of the possible role of dissociative symptoms in reducing other BPD features. Theoretically, treatment that specifically targets the dissociative symptoms alone might have a negative impact on other symptoms like self-harm, substance abuse, impulsivity, or affect instability. In therapy the focus should therefore also be on general skills, such as emotion regulation and distress tolerance because such skills might serve to reduce the basis for several clusters of symptoms.

Some studies have included dissociative symptoms as a predictor for outcome or as an outcome variable. One study showed no differences between the subgroup of patients with BPD and high dissociation, and low dissociation on relative improvement on general psychiatric pathology after dialectical behavioural therapy (DBT) in an in-patient setting (Braakmann et al., 2007). With regard to the dissociative symptoms the largest relative reduction was found in the group with high dissociators. It is most likely that this was influenced by the fact that DBT and the therapeutic setting were directed toward dissociative symptoms. A recent study found that high levels of dissociative symptoms in patients with BPD was associated with poor improvement on general psychopathology after a three-month in-patient DBT intervention (Kleindienst et al., 2011). A reason for the different findings in these two studies may be that Kleindienst et al. included the possible confounding baseline symptom severity as a covariate, arguing that high levels of general symptomatology also implies larger possibilities for improvement.

Zanarini and co-writers followed a group of patients with BPD over a ten-year period in a naturalistic setting with mostly unspecific treatment (Zanarini, Frankenburg, Jager-Hyman, Reich and Fitzmaurice, 2008). Dissociative experiences were measured at baseline and every two years of the study with the DES. They found that, for the whole group, the overall severity of dissociation decreased over these ten years. More than 90 per cent of patients who were high on dissociation at baseline showed remission at one or more points during the ten years. Remission continued during the follow-up time for about two thirds of these patients. Thus, even with no specific treatment, most patients with BPD get better with regard to their dissociative symptoms, and it is likely that the improvement will occur more quickly with specific treatment addressing these symptoms.

In conclusion, high levels of dissociative symptoms in BPD are associated with higher severity of other aspects of the disorder, including co-morbidity and cognitive dysfunction, factors that may have implications for treatment response and choice of therapeutic interventions. Aspects of dissociation may interfere with therapy and thus imply a reduced effect. Although dissociation is assumed to be stress related in BPD and, as such, state dependent, higher levels of general dissociation are also reported in BPD. Psychotherapeutic intervention should take both aspects of dissociation in BPD into account. The assessment of dissociative symptoms is therefore vital, both in the planning stages and in the execution of treatment. Dissociative responses in the therapeutic setting should, in particular, be monitored.

Chapter 12

Understanding and treating depersonalization disorder

Elaine C. M. Hunter

'I feel light-headed and things around me seem strange and unfamiliar. My arms sometimes feel like they don't belong to me and I often have the sensation of being very tall or small. I experience life as though it is projected onto a screen and not actually happening to me. I've odd physical sensations too, such as creeping, nervy feelings in my face and the experience of being divided into two. My head feels like it is crammed with cotton wool and my hearing strangely muffled, like listening to sound under water. Distances are exaggerated, as if looking down the wrong end of a telescope. Incessant, probing thoughts continue to bring the existence of everything, including myself, into question. I feel fragmented and disjointed, with an overwhelming impulse to strip meaning from all things. My increasing detachment is accompanied by a kind of all-pervading numbness, making it hard to connect with other people and the real world.' Carole, 2011.

This client's account vividly captures the distressing, and disabling, experience of depersonalization disorder (DPD) – part of the spectrum of dissociative disorders – and gives a flavour of the challenge of working with people with DPD. To guide your work, this chapter starts with a brief overview of the phenomenology, epidemiology and theories of DPD, followed by a focus on its treatment, with a CBT model and a case example illustrating the process of therapy.

Understanding depersonalization disorder

The syndrome of depersonalization disorder

The defining characteristic of depersonalization disorder (DPD) is a sense of unreality and detachment. The syndrome comprises two related conditions: depersonalization and derealization. With depersonalization, these feelings of unreality are primarily focused on the person's internal world (e.g. their sense of themselves, memories, sensory experiences), whereas in derealization the sense of unreality is focused on the external world. Depersonalization and derealization can occur on a continuum, from individuals simply reporting transient experiences lasting only a few seconds, to chronic, clinically significant DPD (*Diagnostic and Statistical Manual of Mental Disorders* (DSM IV-TR) APA, 2000; *Classification of Mental and Behavioural Disorders* (ICD-10) WHO, 1992).

In depersonalization, people often describe their experiences as if they are living in a dream or viewing life from behind glass. Even their own voice, reflection or parts of their body may seem strange and unfamiliar. They may feel emotionally numb, as if nothing really matters anymore, and sometimes lack of empathy for others. There may be physical numbness in some or nearly all of the body and/or a sense of weightlessness.

In derealization, familiar places can appear artificial as though replaced by a stage set, other people may seem like actors, and objects can appear flat, two dimensional or not solid.

In addition to the core symptoms of unreality and detachment, other cognitive and perceptual symptoms are commonly reported, such as finding it hard to concentrate or take in new information, alongside sensory distortions such as alterations in perspective, sizes of objects, colours or sounds. These experiences are not delusional or hallucinatory, since the person retains insight that these are subjective phenomena rather than objective reality. For classic descriptions of the phenomenology of depersonalization disorder see Mayer-Gross (1935) and Akner (1954a). Given that the symptoms of depersonalization and derealisation commonly co-occur, the term depersonalisation disorder will be used to describe both throughout this chapter, for simplification. A list of the range of the core symptoms of DPD is presented in Table 12.1.

The Epidemiology of depersonalization disorder

The symptoms of depersonalization disorder are the same as those experienced in transient episodes of depersonalization and/or derealization, except that in DPD the symptoms are chronic, cause significant distress and result in functional impairment (Shorvon, Hill, Burkitt and Halstead, 1946; Ackner, 1954a, 1954b).

Experiences of DPD symptoms are surprisingly common in both non-clinical and clinical populations (Hunter, Sierra and David, 2004). In non-clinical samples, the lifetime incidence of brief periods of DPD symptoms has been estimated at between 34 and 70 per cent, particularly under conditions of fatigue or trauma (Noyes and Kletti, 1977; Sedman, 1966; Shilony and Grossman, 1993) or when under the influence of recreational drugs such as 'ecstasy' or cannabis (Mathew, Wilson, Humphreys, Lowe and Weithe, 1993; McGuire, Cope and Fahy, 1994; Medford, Baker, Hunter, Sierra, Lawrence *et al.*, 2003). Prevalence rates for current, chronic and clinically significant DPD in randomized community surveys vary from 1–2 per cent in the UK (Bebbington, Hurry, Tennant, Sturt and Wing, 1981; Bebbington, Marsden and Brewin, 1997; Lee, Kwok, Hunter, Richards and David, 2012), 1.9 per cent in Germany (Michal, Beutel, Jordan, Zimmermann, Wolters *et al.*, 2007) and 2.4 per cent in North America (Ross, 1991).

Table 12.1 Symptoms of depersonalization disorder

Affective

Feelings of unreality
Dream-like state
Sense of detachment
Emotional numbing (for positive and negative affect)
Lack of empathy
Sense of isolation
Lack of motivation
Loss of a sense of the consequences of one's behaviour
Anxiety
Depression

Physiological / Perceptual

Partial or total physiological numbness
Feelings of weightlessness
Lack of a sense of physical boundaries to the body
Sensory impairments (e.g. taste, touch, colour, sound)
Visual distortions (e.g. microscopia/macroscopia, altered sense of distance/ perspective, external world appearing two-dimensional, objects do not appear solid)
Loss of a sense of recognition of one's own reflection and voice
Changed perception of time
Dizziness

Cognitive

Impaired concentration
Mind 'emptiness'
'Racing' thoughts
Memory impairments
Impaired visual imagery
Difficulty in processing new information

Higher prevalence rates of symptoms of DPD are commonly reported in clinical samples (Hunter *et al.*, 2004). Epidemiological surveys have reported symptoms of DPD in 30 per cent of war veterans with PTSD (Davidson, Kudler, Saunders and Smith, 1990), 60 per cent of patients with unipolar depression (Noyes, Hoenk, Kuperman and Slymen, 1977) and 83 per cent of patients with panic disorder (Cox, Swinson, Endler and Norton, 1994). Moreover, there is a high incidence of co-morbidity of DPD symptoms with anxiety disorders, such as panic (Cassano, Petracca, Perugi, Toni, Tundo *et al.*, 1989; Segui, Maruez, Garcia, Canet, Salvador-Carulla *et al.*, 2000), 'free-floating anxiety' (Roth, 1960), generalized anxiety disorder (Simeon, Gross, Guralnik, Stein, Schmeidler *et al.*, 1997), post-traumatic stress disorder (Bremner, Krystal, Putnam, Southwick, Marmar *et al.*, 1998), obsessive compulsive disorder (Roth, 1960; Sedman and Reed, 1963; Shorvon, Hill, Burkitt and Halstead, 1946; Simeon *et al.*, 1997) and hypochondriasis (Shorvon *et al.*, 1946). DPD symptoms are also reported in patients with depression (Ackner, 1954a and b; Mayer-Gross, 1935; Roth, 1960, Sedman and Reed, 1963) and other dissociative disorders (Ross, Miller, Reagor, Bjornson, Fraser *et al.*, 1990a; Steinberg, Rounsaville and Cicchetti, 1990), There is also a significant co-morbidity with Axis II personality disorders (DSM IV-TR, APA, 2000), particularly borderline, avoidant and obsessive-compulsive (Simeon, Guralnik, Schmeidler, Sirof and Knutelska, 2003), although all personality disorders are represented. However, the symptoms of DPD can also occur as a primary disorder in the absence of other conditions.

The course and nature of depersonalization disorder

Several case series of DPD from specialist clinics in the UK and US have been useful in outlining the nature and course of the disorder (Baker, Hunter, Lawrence, Medford, Sierra *et al.*, 2003; Simeon *et al.*, 1997; Simeon, Knutelska, Nelson and Guralnik, 2003). These have found that roughly equal numbers of men and women experience DPD and the mean age of onset for DPD in these studies ranged from 16 to 23 years. DPD usually includes symptoms of both depersonalization and derealization. Baker *et al.* (2003) reported 73 per cent of patients experienced both symptoms, 21 per cent experienced depersonalisation only and 6 per cent had symptoms of only derealization. In most cases, the DPD was chronic and persistent in severity. Typically, three differing patterns of onset are described.

• Sudden onset of severe symptoms that then remain chronic – the most common pattern;
• Episodic, with episodes becoming longer and more severe until the DPD is pervasive and unremitting;
• In a minority of cases the person may report having always had some level of DPD since childhood.

In terms of *precipitating factors*, the onset of DPD is frequently preceded by a period of psychological stress. Other common precursors for DPD include acute intoxication or withdrawal from alcohol and/or a variety of drugs, especially 'ecstasy' (McGuire *et al.*, 1994), marijuana (Moran, 1986) and hallucinogens such as LSD (Waltzer, 1972). Depression is also cited as a precipitating factor, with Mayer-Gross (1935) reporting 50 per cent of those with DPD describing the onset of their depersonalization during the course of an episode of depression. Moreover, Ackner (1954b) and Sedman (1972) suggested there may be a 'depressive depersonalization' syndrome. Several authors have noted an association between panic and the initial onset of DPD (Mayer-Gross, 1935; Roth, 1960; Shorvon *et al.*, 1946). Mayer-Gross (1935) reported that in 39 per cent of his patients the symptoms of DPD 'appear suddenly without any warning ... a patient sitting quietly reading by the fireside is overwhelmed by it in full blast together with an acute anxiety attack' (p. 116). Shorvon *et al.* (1946) found that 92 per cent of the 66 cases of DPD they studied reported symptoms starting in a similar manner. Finally, in a minority of cases no precipitating factor can be elicited (Simeon and Hollander, 1993). This may be due to the onset of symptoms occurring following, rather than during, a period of extreme stress (Shorvon *et al.*, 1946).

An anonymized case study, James, illustrates the pattern of DPD and the CBT treatment protocol throughout this chapter.

James was a 27 year old, single, advertising executive who came to therapy for help with his DPD. In terms of his personal history, he had a loving family background with his parents and three siblings but described himself as an anxious, 'clingy' child. When James was young his mother and father had a difficult period in their marriage and he remembered hearing arguments and seeing his mother crying. He described his father as somewhat authoritarian and his mother as a worrier. He did well at school and was popular until in his mid-teens when he had a year of bullying. During this period he felt outcast from his peers and became withdrawn, until he stood up to one of the bullies and the situation improved.

His first experience of DPD had been at University when he tried recreational drugs. On one occasion, when smoking cannabis, he suddenly had a profound and terrifying sense that the whole world was a lie and that everything seemed fake and unreal. Although this feeling faded away, over the next few weeks he was in constant fear of this happening again and experienced occasional waves of DPD again where he felt as though he was living in a dream. These experiences would be accompanied by panic attacks. He was terrified that he was developing schizophrenia and was too frightened to tell anyone. At home during the Christmas holiday, his experiences intensified, he felt distant from his family, became depressed and at one point wished he would die. When he returned to college he disclosed his problems to his tutor who was able to reassure him that this was not schizophrenia, which helped him, as did getting back into a routine at college. After University, he worked in various advertising jobs and the DPD seemed to fade more into the background, although he always feared it would return and could still experience brief symptoms when under stress.

In the year before coming to therapy he had a difficult period when both a long-term relationship ended and he had a period of unemployment. This had left him low in mood. Recently, his luck had improved and he had been offered a new job but he was on a temporary contract, the job was very demanding and he felt he needed to prove himself. He found himself working long hours, drinking copious amounts of coffee and getting increasingly stressed and anxious. Then a few weeks ago his DPD had suddenly returned 'as fresh as ever' and now he was experiencing the symptoms hourly over the course of the day, although only for a few minutes at a time. He had decided to seek help with this before it took hold again.

Theories of depersonalization disorder

A psychophysiological theory of DPD (Sierra and Berrios, 1998) suggests that extreme anxiety may trigger changes to the functioning of specific neurochemicals and/or brain regions involved in the control and expression of emotional responses (see also Kennerley and Kischka, this volume). Psychoanalytic theories have suggested that DPD is a 'defence mechanism' to protect the ego from internally generated psychodynamic conflicts (Horney, 1951; Schilder, 1939; Torch, 1987), and more recent psychodynamic theories suggest that dissociative responses, such as DPD, protect the person from the psychological impact of adverse experiences such as childhood emotional abuse (see Simeon and Abugel, 2006 for a review). However, these theories, which are based on DPD acting as a mechanism to reduce anxiety, fail to explain how although those with DPD may feel a sense of emotional disconnection, they do not report a reduction in subjective anxiety. Indeed, although emotional numbness and a sense of unreality may serve an adaptive function in the short-term response to threat and/or anxiety, paradoxically, the lack of emotional response and the unpleasant experiences of DPD appear to generate a great deal of fear and distress in those with chronic symptoms. Therefore, if DPD is a short-term defence against overwhelming anxiety, as these models suggest, its persistence becomes a problem in the longer term.

Given the links between severe, repeated childhood trauma (such as physical or sexual abuse) and the development of dissociative disorders (such as dissociative amnesia and dissociative identity disorder) which have been well documented in the research literature (see Bremner, 2010 for a review), similar associations between severe childhood trauma and DPD were predicted. However, although an early small-scale study appeared to indicate that those with DPD might have had more childhood trauma than a non-clinical comparison group (Simeon *et al.*, 1997), further analyzes with larger samples have found that only childhood emotional abuse or emotional neglect has been significantly associated with subsequent depersonalization (Simeon, Guralnik, Schmeidler, Sirof and Knutelska, 2001; Simeon and Abugel, 2006; Michal *et al.*, 2007). An alternative aetiology of DPD is suggested by a longitudinal study of a large sample (N=3,275) of people followed up since birth (Lee *et al.*, 2012). This found that objective ratings of anxiety in children at age 13 by their teachers was found to be a significant predictor of adult DPD. These studies suggest that there may be a different aetiology for DPD compared to other types of dissociative disorders, and that the origins of DPD may lie in more subtle forms of childhood adversity and childhood anxiety, or that later experiences are more important than childhood experiences.

A CBT model of DPD

The strong associations between DPD and anxiety disorders, especially panic, in the literature outlined above suggested that anxiety (perhaps as a consequence of childhood emotional abuse/adversity or later precipitants) may be key in both the aetiology and/or onset of DPD experiences. This led to the development of a different model of DPD (Hunter, Phillips, Chalder, Sierra and David 2003: see Figure 12.1) that is similar to misappraisal CBT models of anxiety disorders, particularly panic (Clark, 1986) and health anxiety (Warwick and Salkovskis, 1990).

As epidemiological surveys have highlighted, transient symptoms of DPD are common and usually benign. In the CBT model of DPD, the central process that maintains these normally transient experiences is the catastrophic misinterpretation of the DPD phenomena as more threatening than they really are. These misinterpretations are characterized as catastrophic appraisals of the meaning and consequences of recently experienced symptoms and are linked to catastrophic attributions as to their cause, indicating a generalized tendency which predisposes to the occurrence of specific catastrophic appraisals (Salkovskis, 1996; Salkovskis, Warwick and Deale, 2003). The CBT model of DPD proposes that the symptoms of DPD can be triggered by a range of affective and situational events. The attributions ascribed to these symptoms influence whether a vicious cycle is instigated or not. If the person attributes 'normalizing' attributions to the transient symptoms, the latter will be viewed as benign and are likely to be ignored. However, if the person ascribes a catastrophic attribution to the usually transient symptom, such as them being indicative of madness, loss of control, becoming

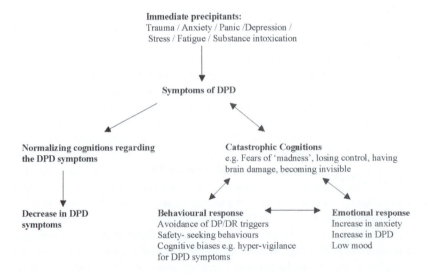

Figure 12.1 Adapted from Cognitive-behavioural model of depersonalization disorder, Hunter et al., 2003

invisible and/or brain disease, this may create a vicious cycle. These catastrophic cognitions are likely to lead to an increase in anxiety which exacerbates and perpetuates the symptoms of DPD. Moreover, similar to cognitive models of anxiety disorders, the person is also likely to develop a range of behaviours and cognitive biases that fuel a maintenance cycle. In DPD these may include:

- Avoidance of certain situations which have triggered the DPD;
- Behaviours which the person believes might prevent the feared outcome but which are ultimately unhelpful (i.e. 'safety seeking behaviours');
- Cognitive or attentional biases, such as an increase in symptom monitoring, leading to an increased likelihood in the perception of symptoms and a reduced threshold for the perception of threat.

In this way the CBT model can provide a way of understanding how the common, transient symptoms of DPD can develop into the chronic condition of DPD, as well as providing a coherent framework and rationale for treatment.

The treatment of DPD

DPD treatment studies

Despite the relatively high rates of reporting of DPD symptoms, there has been little in the way of treatment protocols for this distressing condition. Early published literature on psychological treatments is confined mainly to single case studies. Those reporting successful outcomes have employed psychoanalytical techniques (Ballard, Mohan and Handy, 1992; Torch, 1987), family therapy (Cattell and Cattell, 1974), behavioural methods (Blue, 1979) and imaginal exposure using tapes of grossly exaggerated narratives of previous DPD episodes (Sookman and Solyom, 1978). There was one larger series of 54 patients treated with undefined 'psychotherapy', which had somewhat mixed results (Ackner, 1954b). From these studies, the prevailing view was that generally DPD had a poor prognosis for psychotherapeutic intervention and this seems to have significantly limited research into treatments, as little work was conducted in this area until recently.

The CBT model of DPD enabled a treatment protocol to be developed and an open study with 21 patients with DPD conducted (Hunter, Baker, Phillips, Sierra and David, 2005). Significant improvements in patient-defined measures of DPD severity as well as standardized measures of dissociation, depression, anxiety and general functioning were found post-treatment and at six-month follow-up. Moreover, there were significant reductions in clinician ratings on the Present State Examination (Wing, Cooper and Sartorius, 1974), and 29 per cent of participants no longer met criteria for DPD at the end of therapy. These initial results suggest that CBT for DPD may have some efficacy, although there is clearly scope for further improvements. This might include offering CBT earlier in the development of the DPD (the mean duration of DPD in participants in the open study at the time of starting CBT was 14 years), as well as conducting further research to determine which specific interventions within a course of CBT are the most effective at reducing symptoms.

CBT for DPD

Assessment

Many clients have difficulty in describing their DPD, as many of the symptoms are existential in nature or of perceptual anomalies. It is therefore helpful for clinicians to go through a checklist of possible DPD symptoms within the context of a clinical interview (for example those listed in Table 12.1), as well as asking clients to complete standardized measures of DPD and other dissociative experiences (a battery of useful assessment measures is listed in the Appendix). Not only will this enable the clinician to get a clearer picture of the range, and severity, of their client's symptoms, but will also help to educate the client in understanding the wide scope of experiences that fall within the spectrum of DPD. Many clients report how reassuring it is for their often bewildering array of symptoms to be explained within the syndrome of DPD. However, it is important to stress that the assessment of DPD and other types of dissociative phenomenon should be part of a thorough, wide-ranging assessment so that these experiences can be understood within the broader context of the individual's history and current presentation. Included in the assessment phase, a brief period (e.g. up to a fortnight) of diary keeping, assessing fluctuations in DPD severity and associated factors, is useful. Information from this diary can help test the commonly held belief that symptom levels do not fluctuate, and can be used to analyze what factors alleviate and exacerbate their DPD. Manipulations of these factors can be used to increase clients' sense of control.

In our first session, our case study James told me about the onset and pattern of his DPD to date. An assessment of his current symptoms was carried out through clinical interview, and standard questionnaire measures of DPD were taken as well as of mood and anxiety. His goals were to gain an understanding of his DPD and to be able to manage it so that he could cope at work. He also wanted to be able to feel less anxious and worried generally. James agreed to complete a diary before the next session, where he recorded the severity of his DPD on a scale of 0 to 10 during the day and what he was doing at the time.

In our next session we were able to look at his diary to analyze what factors were associated with increases and decreases in his DPD. James was able to highlight that stressful social situations, being hung-over from too much alcohol and worrying about work all led to a significant increase in his DPD symptoms. He also realized how much of the time he spent anticipating the symptoms. What had helped during the week was reducing his coffee intake and re-starting the meditation he used to do. We discussed together what further steps he could take to enhance his coping by increasing the factors which helped, and decreasing those factors that made his DPD worse. In these early sessions, I gave James information about how common DPD experiences were. He was very surprised about this as he had not talked about it with anyone else apart from his college tutor, for fear of what others would think.

Formulation

An individualized formulation, developed collaboratively with the client, is the foundation of effective CBT (Kuyken, Padesky and Dudley, 2009), and the CBT model for DPD in Figure 12.1 can be used as a basis to inform this idiosyncratic conceptualization. Drawing out the CBT model together in sessions, using the client's own words and experiences, helps the client understand how their thoughts, emotions and behavioural responses are potentially exacerbating and maintaining their difficulties. Given that this shared, idiosyncratic formulation with its individualized maintaining cycles will guide all future interventions, it is worth spending time on it in therapy. In order to be effective, the formulation needs to capture the key elements that are keeping the problem going. When drawing this out together, start by using information from the client's diary to list the situations that trigger an increase in their DPD symptoms. Ask the client what specific symptoms they notice first about their DPD worsening. Getting the client to describe these as vividly as possible will help them to remember better the associated cognitions and emotions. Next, ask the client if, *at the time when they experience an increase in DPD symptoms*, they have any negative, or worrying, thoughts, and write these down verbatim. Then ask the client how these thoughts make them feel (to identify their emotions), and finally ask about what they do at this point, to ascertain their behavioural response. At each stage in this process, keep asking for more examples until the client is unable to provide any new information. However, if the client is merely using synonyms for the same emotion or behaviour (e.g. feeling frightened, scared, anxious), then agree on one way to describe it so the shared conceptualization doesn't become unnecessarily complex and wordy. Ideally, the client will be able to complete the conceptualization using their own examples, perhaps with the help of some guided discovery, but if they get stuck or miss out something that you believe is important, then the therapist can offer some examples or suggestions, so long as this is done in a gentle and neutral manner. Give the client a copy of what you have drawn up in the session to take home and ask them to add to it if they notice or remember anything else. Once you have agreed that it is as complete as possible, then it is useful to type it up and each keep a copy. Referring to these in your later sessions will help to maintain a focus on what needs to be addressed in therapy. An example of an individualized, CBT model of DPD that was developed in collaboration with James is illustrated in Figure 12.2.

James found creating his individualized CBT formulation one of the most helpful parts of therapy. The process helped him see how his thoughts and

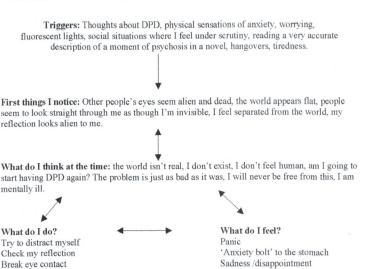

Triggers: Thoughts about DPD, physical sensations of anxiety, worrying, fluorescent lights, social situations where I feel under scrutiny, reading a very accurate description of a moment of psychosis in a novel, hangovers, tiredness.

First things I notice: Other people's eyes seem alien and dead, the world appears flat, people seem to look straight through me as though I'm invisible, I feel separated from the world, my reflection looks alien to me.

What do I think at the time: the world isn't real, I don't exist, I don't feel human, am I going to start having DPD again? The problem is just as bad as it was, I will never be free from this, I am mentally ill.

What do I do?
Try to distract myself
Check my reflection
Break eye contact
Finish the conversation sooner

What do I feel?
Panic
'Anxiety bolt' to the stomach
Sadness /disappointment
Hopelessness
Emotional tiredness

Figure 12.2 James' Cognitive-Behavioural model of Depersonalization Disorder

responses to the DPD symptoms were exacerbating the problem and that the problem could be beaten. He said 'my DPD is not the issue; it is my response to it that is driving it and has been keeping it going all this time'. James recognized that his DPD was driven by his anxiety ('my anxiety is the demon') and that by discussing his DPD, rather than avoiding it, he was losing his fear of it.

Interventions

Although there may be specific differences in the content of thoughts and behaviours in DPD from other disorders, standard CBT techniques such as cognitive restructuring of unhelpful thoughts, setting up behavioural experiments and encouraging clients back into situations which they have been avoiding, can all be successfully utilized when working with DPD (see Westbrook, Kennerley and Kirk (2011) for a useful guide to general CBT skills). Given the strong associations between DPD and anxiety, basic anxiety reduction interventions will also be of help. However, given the unusual nature of the symptoms, the wide array of these and the fears about what DPD symptoms might indicate, it is important to include other interventions that are specifically helpful with DPD. These include:

- Psycho-education and normalizing. Most people with DPD will not be aware of how common these symptoms are and how people can recover from these problems. Giving information about this can help alleviate much of their anxiety. Many of those who have had CBT will cite this as one of the most helpful interventions in their treatment.

- Teaching in the use of grounding strategies. These are useful early in therapy and include techniques such as focussing on environmental stimuli or using grounding words, objects or imagery to help the person remain focussed in the here and now (see Kennerley, 1996; Baker, Hunter, Lawrence and David, 2007 for more details). These strategies are particularly useful for those who have intermittent episodes of DPD, as well as for those with chronic DPD who can use grounding strategies at times when their DPD is most severe. It is best if clients practise these regularly to become skilled in their use so that they are more effective when needed, and it is important to check regularly that grounding skills are being used as coping strategies and not cognitive avoidance strategies.
- Many clients will have become hyper-vigilant for DPD symptoms, but this symptom monitoring is likely to lead to an increase in both the perception, and perceived severity, of symptoms. The first step to intervening with this is by helping the client understand how this pattern might be contributing to the maintenance of their problem. This can be achieved with some simple, quick experiments in session where the client compares what happens when they focus intently on their DPD for a couple of minutes, versus how the perception of the severity of their DPD reduces when they concentrate on another task (such as a few minutes of mental arithmetic). This will illustrate that if they can shift attention away from their DPD symptoms onto the external environment that this will be helpful (Hunter, Salkovskis and David, under review). This can be enhanced further through the instruction and practice of techniques such as attention training (Wells, 1990; Wells, White and Carter, 1997) or task concentration training (Bogels, Mulkens and De Jong, 1997).
- Behavioural experiments can be set up to reality-test any negative predictions from unhelpful cognitions associated with the DPD. These might include going into certain situations that have been avoided because the person predicts these will intensify their symptoms (e.g. crowded places) or testing out a belief that other people can notice their DPD.
- Thought-record techniques can be used to look at the evidence for, and against, any catastrophic thoughts about DPD symptoms. For example James, our case example, was able systematically to look at what made him believe his thoughts such as 'the world is not real'. Doing this helped him to realize that it was only the symptoms of DPD that made him think this. On the other hand, he was able to generate a long list of counter-evidence for this thought. In writing down this counter-evidence, he was able to use these statements later on when he felt the symptoms of DPD starting again so that he could challenge such thoughts before his symptoms worsened.
- Finally, practising techniques that help with reducing rumination may be important to include in the package of therapy (e.g. Nolen-Hoeksema, 2000). These might include examining the pros and cons of rumination, listing active distraction strategies that can be utilized when the person notices they are ruminating, or using mindfulness techniques (e.g. Baer, 2003; Kabat-Zinn, 2003).

For more details on the CBT approach to DPD, the self-help book, *Overcoming Depersonalization and Feelings of Unreality* (Baker *et al.*, 2007) gives a comprehensive programme of interventions which are useful for those experiencing DPD symptoms, as well as for interested clinicians.

In subsequent sessions with James, we used a thought-record worksheet to list the evidence for, and against, each of the thoughts he had when his DPD was triggered. James was able to generate some excellent counter arguments during our sessions and continued to use these at home for DPD-related thoughts, and subsequently for anxiety-related thoughts. As our sessions progressed, James reported fewer episodes of DPD and, when these did happen, he was able to either just let the sensations pass without anxiety, or to deal with them using a thought record. In our later sessions, we looked at some other related issues. He decided to reduce his alcohol intake and we worked on improving his self esteem. At this point, he was no longer experiencing DPD regularly and felt that the breakthroughs in therapy had a major impact on his understanding of the phenomena. He described how he was able to cope with symptoms by thinking of them like having a headache – a bit of a pain and unpleasant – but something that would pass in time and therefore not something to engage with or worry about. After 15 sessions, James felt that he had achieved his goals and we ended our sessions.

Summary

Depersonalization and derealization are related conditions where, respectively, one's sense of self, or the outside world, appears unreal and unfamiliar. These experiences are common transient phenomena but they can develop into the chronic condition of depersonalization disorder (DPD). Although excellent descriptions of the phenomenology of DPD have been published for around a century, little has been developed in the way of treatment of this distressing condition. A recent CBT model of DPD, derived from anxiety disorder models, has helped in understanding how transient symptoms may develop into a chronic condition, and provides a framework for treatment. This approach appears to be efficacious, although larger scale trials are needed to evaluate this further.

Appendix 12.1 Assessment battery for DPD

Assessment of:	Type	Name of Measure	Author(s), date	Brief description
Depersonalization/ Derealization/ DPD	Self-report questionnaire	Cambridge Depersonalization Scale (CDS)	Sierra and Berrios, 2000	29-item scale measuring the severity of trait Depersonalization/ Derealization / DPD symptoms over the past 6-month period
DPD – formal diagnosis	Semi-structured clinical interview	DPD section of the Structured Clinical Interviews for DSM-IV for Dissociative disorders Revised (SCID-D)	Steinberg, 1994	Questions relating to criteria for Depersonalization/ Derealization/ DPD. Participant's answers can be classified into 'Mild' Depersonalization/ Derealization (with each episode lasting from a few seconds to a few minutes); 'Intermittent' Depersonalization/ Derealization (i.e. infrequent episodes, where symptoms last from minutes to weeks); and DPD where episodes are persistent or recurrent and the symptoms are chronic and can be of several years duration.
General dissociation, including Depersonalization/ Derealization subscale	Self-report questionnaire	Dissociative Experiences Scale (DES)	Bernstein and Putnam, 1986	28 items of dissociative phenomena, each rated as a percentage experienced in everyday life. The Depersonalization/ Derealization/DR subscale score is comprised of the mean score of 6 items (7, 11, 12, 13, 16 and 28)

Chapter 13

Unravelling the mystery of dissociative identity disorder

A case example and therapist's journey

Vivia A. Cowdrill

> *'[Tim remembers being] … five years old … Mom stays at home and Dad has a sales job … Dad also drinks … When Dad comes home drunk and angry … Tim [faces the] rage of a man in his late thirties. He does not have the physical defences, but he can make himself 'go away'. While Dad yells, Tim sits quietly. Then, when the fear becomes too much to handle, he projects himself into a corner of the room and another boy, Matthew, takes the father's abuse. Later, when it begins to feel safe again, Tim re-joins his body.'* (Bray-Haddock, 2001, p. 28).

It is common for clients with histories of severe and chronic trauma to make conscious and subconscious attempts to deny, forget, minimize and avoid painful childhood experiences. Dissociative symptoms are one of many psychological problems related to childhood trauma (Chu, 2011). There are a number of emerging theoretical accounts of these symptoms and implications for treatment, several described elsewhere in this book. Here I focus on the complexity of working with someone with dissociative identity disorder (DID), the risks and apparent contradictions involved and the impact this can have on the therapist. As Allen (2002) documented, 'Working intensively with severely traumatised clients is a highly stressful occupation' (p. 373). Expert supervision is essential. In this chapter I describe my work with Ruth (an anonymized client).

Dissociative identity disorder (DID)

The diagnostic criteria for DID are as follows:

- The presence of two or more distinct identities or personality states (each with its own relatively enduring pattern of perceiving, relating to, and thinking about the environment and self).
- At least two of these identities or personality states recurrently take control of the person's behaviour.
- Inability to recall important personal information that is too extensive to be explained by ordinary forgetfulness.
- The disturbance is not due to the direct physiological effects of a substance

(e.g. blackouts or chaotic behaviour during alcohol intoxication) or a general medical condition (e.g. complex partial seizures). Note: in children, the symptoms are not attributable to imaginary playmates or other fantasy play. (*Diagnostic and Statistical Manual of Mental Disorders, Fourth Edition, Text Revision* (DSM IV-TR), American Psychiatric Association, 2000, p. 259).

The diagnosis of DID has a controversial history (Fahy, 1988; Piper, 1994; Merskey, 1995). Symptoms are often dramatic, and critics suggest it is the 'fascinated therapist that creates the disorder through suggestion and reinforcement of behaviour consistent with the diagnosis' (Allen, 2002, p. 189). Cormier and Thelen (1998) found that cognitive-behavioural therapists were particularly skeptical about DID. When I first met Ruth, the notion of DID was far from my mind.

Ruth's referral

Ruth's contact with the Community Mental Health Team (CMHT) was at the age of 44. Her path to working with me was not straightforward. Child and Social Services had intervened and provided support for Ruth and two of her sons for several years, when Ruth sedated one son with her antidepressant medication. At this point, a psychiatrist concluded she had no mental illness but was stressed due to her marriage breakdown and the demands of childcare. The Child Protection Team (CPT) became involved because her deteriorating mental health had an impact on her parenting. Ruth reported to her GP that she had urges to sexually abuse her youngest son. A psychodynamic psychotherapist assessed Ruth as having severe character difficulties, fragmented memories about being abused as a child and PTSD symptoms. He considered Ruth too vulnerable for psychodynamic therapy and referred her to the CMHT for further assessment and support, with ongoing liaison with the CPT.

As Consultant Clinical Psychologist for the CMHT, I planned to identify her primary symptoms and the factors maintaining them. This would be shared with the CMHT to inform a risk assessment, management and treatment plan.

Assessment

Ruth appeared nervous during our meetings. She was worried and preoccupied with thoughts she could not control. She had difficulty articulating her problems and spoke in a stilted and vague manner.

First assessment phase

Ruth's background

Ruth is seventh of eight children, the only girl. She described a traumatic childhood of sexual abuse by her step-father, brothers and 'invited guests'.

She blamed her mother for orchestrating the abuse, speaking of her as a bully. Throughout her life she had had times when she was out of touch with reality and experiencing voices, though these were always transitory. Recent deterioration of her mental health seemed to have been triggered by the first contact from her mother in 20 years. She angered Ruth by forbidding her to speak to the authorities about recent allegations of sexual abuse involving one of her brothers.

Current situation

Ruth had four sons, two adults living away, two at home. She had difficulties managing the twelve year old; the nine year old, Jack, had a learning disability. Ruth said she loved her children and had no intention of harming them. She had a volatile relationship with her ex-husband.

Current problems

As well as sedating and reporting an urge to abuse her youngest son, Ruth made her ex-husband a cake with laxatives 'to teach him a lesson' and sprayed his food with flea spray, and he subsequently required hospital treatment. She expressed remorse, stating that she had not realized the possible consequences. She was also confused as to whether some events had occurred or not.

Ruth had intrusive images, e.g. of her mother putting her hands around her throat, the sound of a baby crying and also of someone undoing a zip, and 'voices' in her head. She had fragmented memories, e.g. of 'hurting a baby and making its head bleed'. She was unable to make sense of these experiences.

Ruth self-harmed by cutting her arms and legs. She had sleep problems and nightmares. She would go to bed to cope with depression but there she was plagued with flashbacks. She wanted to get rid of her memories.

Initial conclusions and therapy plan

Ruth was clearly a traumatized woman with poor impulse control which led to serious consequences for herself and others. She exhibited many aspects of borderline personality disorder (BPD, DSM IV-TR, APA, 2000), with emotional control difficulties and limited coping skills. Although distressed, Ruth accepted that I had a duty to share information about risk and harm to others with the CMHT and CPT as part of the ongoing risk assessment.

Dialectical Behavioural Therapy (DBT), (Linehan, 1993) is recommended by the National Institute for Clinical Excellence for patients/persons with BPD who self harm. With this in mind, I offered further sessions to assess whether Ruth's presentation met the diagnostic criteria for BPD, and her willingness to engage in therapy.

Second assessment phase

My plans to use DBT were confounded by the following information that was gained during sessions. Ruth told me she had taken Jack to hospital and needed to be punished for doing this. Someone called Hazel had been shouting because going to the hospital had frightened Little Ruth. I was confused. Who was Hazel and who was Little Ruth? Ruth said Hazel would often shout at her from inside her head, when Little Ruth was in danger. I wondered whether this presentation was consistent with DID, with different identities or personality states taking over. These inner characters can be construed as dissociated self-states (see Kennedy, this volume) and are from here on referred to as self-states. For clarity, from this point on the name 'Ruth' will be reserved for one self-state, which is only part of the client's whole personality. The client as a whole person will be referred to as 'the client'.[1]

My assessment of this client's problems continued for several months. The more information I collected the more confusing the clinical picture became, causing me to question my judgement as a therapist. The following are some of the high risk behaviours reported by the client during this second assessment phase.

- *Keeping her son away from school.* The CPT raised concerns about Jack, who was not attending school. The client said she kept Jack home so Little Ruth would have a playmate.
- *Killing her cat.* The client reported that Little Ruth self-state became frightened by the family cat, so the Hazel self-state gave 'instructions' to the client to either kill the cat or self-harm by cutting her legs and drinking the blood. The client killed the cat.
- *Targeting a vulnerable female.* Other self-states were reported: 'Valerie – Mother' and 'Marie – Grandmother.' Whilst in these self-states the client seemed to feel powerful and in control and was involved in targeting, exploiting and threatening to kill an adolescent with a learning disability.
- *Befriending a paedophile.* Whilst in another self-state, which the client called 'Craig', she befriended a sex offender whom she believed was sexually interested in children. The client reassured me she would rather hurt herself than any child, but clearly she was not in control whilst in another self-state. This information was passed on to the CMHT and CPT. The CPT suspected that Jack was in danger of being abused, either by the client herself or by the sex offender. As part of the CMHT risk assessment, I attended meetings with the child-protection team.
- *Threatening a member of the public.* A man in a car caught the client's eye and smiled. This seemed to trigger dissociation into the self-state Hazel. In this self state she got out of her own car and threatened to hit him. Her words were 'who did he think he was smiling at? He was clearly after something and he wasn't going to get it.' Luckily, the traffic moved on and the man drove away.

In the self-state Ruth the client reported 'seeing' these things happening but felt powerless to do anything about them. She pleaded with me to get rid of Hazel and the others in her life. She told me that Little Ruth would often show her things she did not want to see and she wanted it all to stop.

In response to the above information, a forensic psychiatrist was consulted. He recommended the client could safely be monitored, assessed and managed in the community by the CMHT.

Psychometric assessments

To assess dissociation the Wessex Dissociation Scale (WDS: Kennedy *et al.*, 2004; Kennedy this volume), and the Dissociative Experiences Scale were used (DES II: Carlson and Putnam, 2003). The Millon Multiaxial Clinical Inventory (MCMI–III: Millon, 2006) measured mental health symptoms and personality problems. The WDS measures three levels of dissociation: automatic dissociation, within-mode dissociation and between-mode dissociation. The client scored 4.1 on automatic dissociation (clinical mean (CX) for this level is 1.5, standard deviation (SD) 0.8), 3.6 on within-mode dissociation (CX 2.1, SD 0.9) and 4.2 on between-mode dissociation (CX 2.1, SD 0.9).These very high scores indicate severe dissociation at all three levels. The client's DES score was 42. DES scores above 30 indicate high levels of dissociative pathology consistent with DID. MCMI-III scores were above the cut off point of 85 on schizoid, avoidant, depressive, passive-aggressive, schizotypal and borderline personality problems, and on symptoms of anxiety, dysthymia (chronic depression), PTSD, thought disorder and major depression. The results suggested the client had severe dissociative symptoms including a fragmented personality structure, with a number of personality disorders and mental health problems.

Is this DID?

Before embarking on therapy for DID the person's presentation must meet the criteria (Chu, 2011). Using the DSM IV-TR criteria for DID (APA, 2000) these were my conclusions:

- *The presence of two or more distinct identities or personality states (each with its own relatively enduring pattern of perceiving, relating to, and thinking about the environment and self).* Several different dissociated self-states had been reported.
- *At least two of these identities or personality states recurrently take control of the person's behavior.* Judging by the reported incidents above, and the client's experience of being powerless to prevent them, it did seem that these self-states recurrently took control of her behaviour.
- *Inability to recall important personal information that is too extensive to be explained by ordinary forgetfulness.* At certain times the client was able

to recognize different aspects of herself, and at others seemed partially or totally amnesic of them. She had extensive gaps in her knowledge of recent and long-past events, and was often confused about whether an event had happened or not.

• *The disturbance is not due to the direct physiological effects of a substance (e.g. blackouts or chaotic behavior during alcohol intoxication) or a general medical condition (e.g. complex partial seizures).* The client did not abuse substances or alcohol and had no known medical conditions that could explain her presentation.

Although often frightened of life, the client was able to socialise and maintain friendships. She had held jobs in the past and was often caring and empathic towards others. Yet there were puzzling and high-risk sides to her character. She experienced sudden changes in her state of consciousness, sense of identity, behaviour, thoughts, feelings and perception of reality to such an extent that these functions did not operate congruently.

The client's presentation met the criteria for DID. I now planned to undertake treatment on this basis.

Case conceptualization

Kennedy *et al.*'s (2004) model of dissociation provided a theoretical basis to conceptualize the client's presentation (see Kennedy, this volume). Severe trauma at the hands of caregivers had led to dissociation at all three levels: level 1 intrusive imagery including voices and flashbacks, level 2 including compulsive behaviours and mental blanking, level 3 fragmented personality structure. She had developed self-states which were dissociated from each other and did not have a shared conscious awareness. Each self-state had developed a separate conscious awareness, including a set of memories and knowledge not always shared with other self-states, so that the client experienced an internal world populated with different 'people' to whom she gave different names. This understanding was shared with the client, who found it helped to make some sense of her confusing world.

Mapping the system

The literature suggests that when working with DID the therapist should map the system of personalities (self-states) (Fine, 1992; Allen, 2002), but this was fraught with episodes of dissociative blanking, vagueness, and state switching, producing jumbled and disjointed information, and the client often appearing to talk to herself. Relaxation training helped her to calm herself and give a more coherent account. Each self-state had a name that we used in therapy, and I helped the client understand her personality structure by drawing a diagram (Figure 13.1).

The client: multiple selves

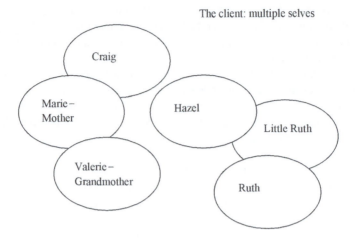

Usual personality structure: one self

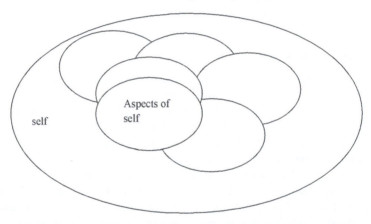

Figure 13.1 Diagram of the client's self-states compared with usual personality structure

The hypothesized functions and the characteristic schemas (thoughts, feelings, behaviours and physiological responses) of each of the different self-states are described in Table 13.1.

The existence of dissociated self-states created an experience of inner conflict.

Formulating levels of dissociation

Using Kennedy *et al.*'s (2004) model, we formulated the client's problems. Below are examples of how dissociation operated at different information-processing levels in the client's case.

Table 13.1 Hypothesized schemas and functions for Ruth's self-states

Self-state	Schemas	Function
Ruth	Anxiety, fear Caretaking behaviour Wanting to get rid of or control other self-states Self-harm behaviour	Communicating with the outside world Seeking help Caring for her children
Little Ruth	Subjective experience of being four years old Trauma-related sensations (sights, sounds, smells, taste, touch) Seeks out adults for protection and care Capacity for laughter, playfulness and spontaneity	Containing terror and distress Child-like attachment to children (Jack) and adults
Hazel	Hypervigilance for threat Anger and rage Aggressive behaviour Harming people and animals Confident, sociable, outgoing, seductive, engaging behaviour	Protecting against perceived threat Communicating with authority Seeking adult attachment
Valerie – Mother	Believes 'children and weak people are too stupid for anything to bother them' Manipulative and brutal behaviour Absence of empathy and pity Feeling powerful and in control	Meeting need for control in relationships
Marie – Grandmother	Critical, blaming, judgemental thoughts Behavioural urges to punish other self-states for imperfection	Reducing vulnerability by ensuring everything is perfect
Craig	Sexual interest in children	Meeting need for power in sexual relationships

Between-mode dissociation (level 3)

Dissociated self-states, hypothesized to be the result of between-mode (level 3) dissociation (Kennedy *et al.*, 2004; Kennedy, this volume), produce a variety of symptoms including sudden switching from one self-state to another.

On one occasion, a social worker visited the client's home. The discussion moved to the (threatening) topic of her children's safety. The client went into the kitchen to make tea, but switched to the Hazel self-state in response to threat. The

Hazel self-state was sociable and 'seductive' and so the client appeared to be a 'different person' to the social worker when she emerged from the kitchen.

At level 3 dissociated self-states also facilitated emotional avoidance. For example, when experiencing intrusive visual images of blood on a baby's body, the client said 'why does Little Ruth keep showing me upsetting pictures?' Subjectively, she was being shown images by another person inside her. This protected her from the idea that related things may lie within her own past experience. Criminal and cruel actions were observed as being carried out by other inner 'people': this was a mechanism for emotional avoidance of responsibility or remorse for these actions. This may have facilitated the client's ability to carry out these actions.

Within-mode dissociation (level 2)

An example of level 2 dissociation was when the client experienced a compulsion to cut herself and *drink the blood*. Much later, during therapy, the client recounted that she thought drinking blood was something an abuser had made her do as a child. This was formulated as activation of a dissociated behavioural schema (see Figure 13.2).

Automatic processing (level 1)

At this level, schemas responsible for pattern recognition (orienting schemas) process incoming information from outside or inside the body just until they are

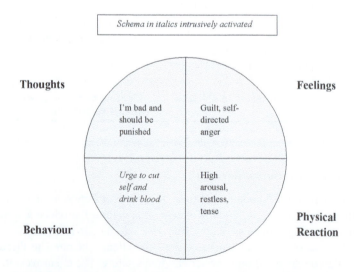

Figure 13.2 Within-mode dissociation: de-coupling of schemas within a mode

recognized as threatening, after which associative processing switches to disso-ciative processing (Kennedy, this volume). This results in fragmented storage of traumatic information. The client claimed that she heard the sound of a zip when lying in bed at night. This may have represented a fragmented memory (Huntjens *et al.*, this volume), an auditory image (hallucination) formulated as the result of level one dissociation. The act of lying in bed seemed to trigger this intrusion.

Orienting schemas and levels of dissociation

Within the model, orienting (pattern-recognition) schemas, operating outside of conscious awareness, interpret information as threatening based on previous learning (classical conditioning). In this way they can trigger dissociation at all three levels: in the incident when she threatened the smiling driver, the client's orienting schemas recognized his blue eye-colour as associated with threat, and the (level 3) switch to the Hazel self-state was triggered in response. In the level 2 example above, the orienting schemas matched the feeling of guilt to being punished and drinking blood, even thought the client herself had no conscious awareness of the connection, triggering (level 2) intrusive activation of a de-coupled behavioural schema.

Sharing simplified formulations helped the client understand how she had come to be as she was and also offer hope of a way forward.

Treating DID

Therapeutic considerations

> '*The implicit and mistaken assumption made by many people is that the alter personalities are separate people. This is a serious conceptual error that will lead to therapeutic error. Alter personalities are not separate people!*'
>
> Putnam, 1992, p. 96.

The client's subjective experience was that 'inside people' controlled her, but the reality was that she was one person. I aimed to validate her internal reality without promoting fragmentation, whilst helping her achieve control over all aspects of herself to reduce high-risk behaviours.

Linehan (1993), Steele, Van der Hart and Nijenhuis (2005) and others, advocate a 'phased' approach to disorders associated with complex trauma (Van der Hart and Steele, this volume). The first phase emphasizes safety, stabilization and skills training (Chu, 2011; Cloitre, Cohen and Koener, 2006; Herman, 1992b; Linehan, 1993). DBT (Linehan, 1993; Koerner, 2012) is a first-phase treatment and provides a structure for working with treatment–resistant presentations (Linehan, Bohus and Lynch, 2007), although it has not been adapted for DID.

DBT aims to increase behavioural control of 'target behaviours' and increase adaptive behaviours (skills). The client's therapy used DBT techniques including skills training, contingency management and the identification of a hierarchy of high-risk behaviours which we aimed to reduce.

Kennedy *et al.*, (2004) suggest work with dissociation should start at level 3, working with the aim to increase self-awareness and self-management. The aim is to promote or develop an over-arching self-schema in four stages:

1   Awareness of all aspects of the self (mapping the system)
2   Acceptance of all aspects of the self
3   Control of all aspects of the self
4   Integration of all aspects as one self

The client's therapy would target control. Integration was not an aim of this first phase.

The 'dialectical' part of DBT involves accepting opposite views of reality, seeking a synthesis between them. To validate the client's internal (multiple selves) reality whilst not promoting fragmentation, I adopted a 'group therapy' approach (Kennedy *et al.*, 2004 and this volume). That is, I imagined I was working with an internal team of people, taking the role of consultant to the team. The goal was to create cooperation between all of the self-states, increasing acceptance, effective functioning and self-control. I used techniques such as calling 'meetings' of all self-states and team-building techniques such as assigning team problem-solving tasks and real-world assignments.

Therapy

Pre-treatment

In the DBT pre-treatment phase, client and therapist decide whether to undertake treatment and prepare to work together. During this phase the client's goals are clarified (the 'why' of the treatment) and a hierarchy of behaviours to reduce is drawn up (the 'how' of the treatment). Commitment to the process is built up and this phase ends with the signing of a contract. In DID, this phase is often protracted, since the client needs to commit to change in each different self-state, so that in effect much work is done in this pre-treatment phase.

For almost a year we mapped the client's internal world. The following six months were spent clarifying her goals and values along with the other pre-treatment tasks. Her goals were to reduce risks to herself and others, to be a better mother and be able to establish loving relationships. Also, to be free of the distressing hallucinations she perceived as being shown to her by Little Ruth. Having goals is an essential element in working with treatment-resistant presentations, as commitment to therapy often wavers (Linehan, 1993).

In order to commit to being her therapist I needed to feel safe and asked for assurances that I would not be harmed whatever self-state she was in. I spelled out in the contract that should I ever be harmed the therapy would end. Therapy could not start without gaining commitment to work whilst in each of her self-states. It is not unusual for people with DID to have strong internal conflicts (Van der Hart, Nijenhuis and Steele, 2006) but internal cooperation was necessary for therapy to be of benefit. I suggested she keep a 'communication book' (Kennedy *et al.*, 2004) where she could capture her thoughts in various self-states. This often got lost and pages were thrown away: fears of losing power, control and sense of identity were common themes in the book. The book finally contained contributions from the client in all of her self-states.

We drew up a hierarchy of behaviours to reduce (target behaviours). The client learned she would have to commit to learning new skills to use instead of existing maladaptive behaviours. Also she would be expected to keep a diary and use telephone coaching between sessions to manage crises.

Eighteen months after our first meeting, after validating the client's concerns, and using commitment techniques such as pros and cons lists and behavioural shaping, the client signed the therapy contract in each self-state. I also signed.

Therapy

Therapy sessions were divided between teaching new skills to regulate emotion and reduce dissociation, and functional analysis of problem behaviours (Figure 13.3). Care was taken to validate the emotions associated with each self-state, even the abusive ones, whilst teaching that there are other ways of managing emotions. Whenever possible I worked with the whole 'group' of self-states rather than interacting with the client in a single self-state. This was done by using metaphors such as 'I want everyone to think about this'. The client came up with the metaphor of her(selves) as a Russian doll 'but some of us are hurt and bandaged up so we don't fit inside the others anymore'.

Skills acquisition

In standard DBT, skills are taught in a group setting. In the client's case the 'group' was an internal group. Internal conflict about change was expressed through some self-states in the 'group' ridiculing the process of learning new skills. The group was reminded about the contract. DBT skills include mindfulness, interpersonal skills, emotion regulation and distress tolerance. To address severe dissociation, the client needed additional and adapted skills, including:

- 'Inner safety': using imagery enabled the creation of places of peace and security for each self-state. For example, Little Ruth had a playroom full of toys.

- Grounding skills (Kennerley, 1996) were used to enable the client to stay in the present particularly when experiencing flashbacks.
- Control over switching between states was taught by, among other methods, inviting the client to deliberately access self-states using the Russian doll metaphor. The client purchased a Russian doll. She allocated one self-state to each doll. When she picked up a given doll she deliberately entered that self-state. By picking up different dolls she began to develop control over which self-state she entered, instead of being subject to automatically triggered self-state switching.
- Mindfulness skills were adapted because the client was avoidant of observing her inner emotions. Initially we focussed on externally using exercises such as observing a candle flame. Later we moved on to noticing her breath. Finally to non-judgmental observation of different emotions.
- Imagery re-scripting (Layden, Newman, Freeman and Byers-Morse, 1993) was used to alter the imagery of distressing flashbacks by imagining empowering outcomes to replace horrific images.

Skills generalization

The client had access to session recordings and undertook behavioural assignments between sessions, helping her develop her skills in different contexts outside the therapy setting. I provided telephone coaching to help her use her skills during crises, and a CMHT crisis phone line covered the night.

Reducing target behaviours

- High risk behaviours

All of the high risk behaviours mentioned above were listed. Functional (chain) analysis was used to examine each specific instance of a listed behaviour. Figure 13.3 and the following are examples:

> *The client's husband made a derogatory remark, she did not know what to say and wanted to hide. She felt angry, ashamed and anxious. She heard Hazel's voice saying she was pathetic allowing him to talk like that. She switched to Little Ruth, self-blaming and wanting to appease, then to enraged Hazel, when she put her medication into his teacup. She then felt calm.*

We highlighted the mix of emotions and then rage, the thoughts (Hazel's voice) which facilitated aggression and the relief as an immediate consequence (negative reinforcement). But we noticed also that in the long term this act had negative consequences for everyone. The client recognized being assertive would be more effective. To achieve assertiveness we would need to:

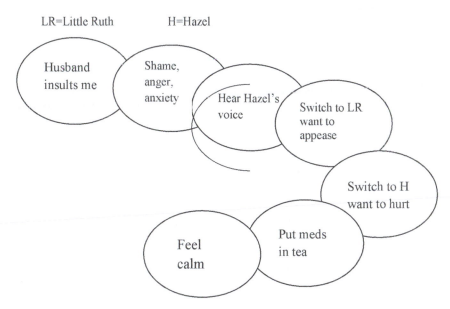

LR=Little Ruth   H=Hazel

Figure 13.3 Chain analysis of poisoning behaviour

- use mindfulness and emotion regulation skills
- address problem cognitions
- develop interpersonal effectiveness skills

We used the communication book to conduct 'discussions' addressing her concerns and resources in each self-state. In the self-state Ruth she was willing to learn skills, though reluctant when in the self-state Hazel. In the self-state Hazel she 'looked through the eyes of' (Boon *et al.*, 2011) self-state Ruth during teaching sessions, to learn emotion regulation and interpersonal effectiveness skills. The client undertook homework to use the new skills with a friend.

Therapy interfering behaviours (TIBs)

TIBs included incessantly talking; changing topic; not completing homework; not using crisis services; not learning new skills and not doing homework. We addressed the TIB of not learning new skills: the client heard voices mocking the usefulness of skills, which limited her progress. I helped the client call an 'inner group meeting' (Boon *et al.*, 2011; Kennedy, this volume) to problem-solve this. Not doing homework was also addressed in this way. It became clear that the client avoided tasks which were emotionally evocative. I needed to pay attention to how emotional a homework task was likely to be, and we needed to develop the client's emotion regulation skills.

Ending therapy

Our work came to an end after three years of therapy when the client moved out of the area. We eventually developed a good therapeutic alliance: the client also engaged with members of the CMHT. Her mood swings had reduced, according to her diary, and she was able to manage high levels of emotional arousal using newly learned skills and without suicidal thoughts or actions. Her relationship with her children had improved and she was able to provide care for them even when she was distressed or stressed. Self-harming behaviours had reduced in frequency from two to three times a week to once in three months; there had been no reported episodes of self-harm to others and only one threat to self-harm during the last six months. The Child Protection Team in her new area continued to monitor her son's safety but their assessment was that the risk of abuse had reduced. It was reported that contact with the sex offender had ceased.

We agreed she had made good progress towards achieving control over her behaviour and so towards her goals of being a good mother and potential partner, although there was still much work to do. She still did not perceive the more abusive self-states Grandmother, Valerie and Craig as parts of herself, though she was able to resist behavioural impulses when in these states. She had come to accept the self-state Hazel as representing a protective and assertive part of herself, without the need to be violent.

The client was assigned a new therapist with a brief to continue work to maintain behavioural control and reduction of risk.

Top tips and summary

My experience of working with this client may differ from that of other clinicians. Research and theory around therapy of DID is limited, and we must always tailor our interventions to the individual.

In the early stages, I was often bewildered after our sessions. Identifying DID was in itself a major stage of the work. The *Structured Clinical Interview for the Diagnosis of DSM IV-TR Dissociative Disorders* (SCID-D R) (Steinberg, 1994) could have further aided my decision making.

Kennedy *et al.*'s (2004) model of dissociation and the WDS gave a framework to formulate and explain dissociation to the client. DBT was adapted to provide a structure for therapy. The learning from this case is summarized below:

- Be prepared for a journey of discovery and ride the roller coaster of uncertainty and confusion.
- Map self-states: find the relevant thoughts, feelings, physiology and behaviour, together with the hypothesized function of each self-state. Remember that other self-states may exist, but do not encourage fragmentation.
- Obtain a written commitment to therapy from the client in all self-states. The pre-therapy stage took several months, but was itself therapeutic and a vehicle for building alliance.

- Find an expert supervisor. Supervision enabled formulation of dissociative symptoms to make sense of the client's confusing and dangerous presentation and helped find effective ways of working.
- Validate all aspects of the individual, including feelings such as strong anger and fear. Be aware that switching self-states often serves an emotional coping function, such as emotional avoidance.
- Work at level 3 (between-mode dissociation). Adopting a team metaphor where the therapist was a consultant to the 'team within' worked well. Working with individual self-states could have promoted fragmentation and exhausted the therapist.
- Prioritize working to reduce risks. DBT structure and skills teaching, along with specific dissociation-reducing work, such as creating an imaginary place of safety and developing grounding skills, gave the client hope that she was capable of change.
- Use a communication book, diaries and recording sessions to enable clients to gain an overview of self-states, contributing towards achieving behavioural control.
- Share information with relevant agencies such as the police, CPT and CMHT.

Allen (2002) writes 'we can hardly help our clients by throwing up our hands in despair *(or embarrassment)*' (p. 161). When working with DID or other complicated presentations involving dissociation, it is all too easy to do this. As therapists we have to do our best to use our knowledge and skills to understand our clients' inner worlds and then be flexible and creative in providing effective therapy.

Although this work has been rewarding, it is not for the fainthearted; treating severely traumatized clients is difficult. Nevertheless, as therapists we need to maintain the hope that, for every client, having a life worth living is possible.

Acknowledgements

The author appreciates Tessa Maguire, Helen Moreton, Katherine Newman-Taylor and Tom Richardson for their valuable and insightful feedback on earlier drafts of this chapter.

Notes

1 The client originally gave her name as Ruth and this is how she is referred to when describing the whole person in this chapter. However, it should be noted that one of the client's dissociated self-states is also named Ruth and in this context is only one aspect of the whole person, the self state in which the client initially communicated with the therapist.

Chapter 14

An evolutionary and compassion-focused approach to dissociation

Paul Gilbert

Compassion focused therapy (CFT) is a multimodal, integrative approach to psychological difficulties. It integrates Western scientific and evolution informed understanding of psychological processes and therapeutic interventions with Eastern insights into the causes of 'suffering' and its alleviation. In this chapter 'suffering' refers to dissociation, a heterogeneous group of experiences relating to a particular kind of 'awareness' (Dell and O'Neil, 2009). There are two major forms: *detachment*, with feelings of depersonalization and derealization associated with feelings of being 'unreal', 'spaced out' and *compartmentalization* which relates to what can and cannot be acknowledged in consciousness, integrated or connected, so that certain types of 'information', memories or emotions exist almost in separate 'places' and cannot be brought together (Holmes *et al.*, 2005).

New brain, old brain

CFT begins with an evolutionary focus on thinking about the evolutionary pressures that shaped the brain, the functions that have evolved (Buss, 2003; Dunbar and Barrett, 2007), the processing systems designed to enact those functions (Panksepp, 2007) and how these might be involved in dissociation (Gilbert, 1989, 1992, 2009a; McGuire and Troisi, 1998).

Humans share basic motivations with other animals, such as feeding and avoiding dangers, fighting and defending, and specific *social* motives such as seeking sexual and affiliative relationships, mating, reproducing, caring for offspring and group belonging. There are emotions guiding such motives (e.g. anxiety, anger, joy, lust) signalling when they are achieved and when threatened, blocked or lost (Panksepp, 2007, 2010). However, humans differ from other animals in that our ancestors evolved an extra, new type of brain, which has capacities for thinking, reasoning, imagining, ruminating, planning and anticipating.

This brain evolved in a piecemeal fashion and to function optimally it needs to *integrate information* with multiple levels of processing. Consequently, one of its key functions is integrating systems, giving rise to certain kinds of intelligence, especially social intelligence for empathy and theory of mind. Suddendorf and

Whitten (2001) have pointed out that a mind with these abilities is a *collating mind* with the ability to bring together (to assemble and integrate) processing systems, doing different jobs, for some common goal. Of all the processes important to the understanding of dissociation, the one that most clinicians agree on is the problem of how a person *integrates information*. A simple example is the complex, multiple tasks of body and attention control in driving a car in heavy traffic and maybe talking to a friend at the same time! No other animal could remotely match that degree of multiple attention regulation and cognitive, integrative complexity. Stress and rumination can cause overload and then integrative functions break down, risking lapses in concentration, forgetfulness and errors of judgement. The smooth flow of multiple actions (as in driving) can be lost.

The frontal cortex is especially important for insightful awareness and capacities for integration (Goldberg, 2002). It enables us to have a sense of self so that we can be aware of what we are doing and the consequences of our actions; what is going through our minds or the emotions we are experiencing; making judgements and having dialogues about that awareness, e.g. I can feel good or bad about my thoughts and feelings. Not only can we think about our own thoughts and feelings but we can think about the thoughts and feelings of other people too. This gives rise to complex empathy and theory-of-mind skills, linked to what has been called *mentalizing* (Allen, Fonagy and Bateman, 2008). Mentalizing requires us to make inferences about a variety of potential mental states and requires different types of processing. In a study of the neural mechanisms involved in ambiguous social situations, Jenkins and Mitchell (2010) have shown that mentalizing involves integration of a number of complex processing systems, especially in the frontal cortex.

If one becomes over aroused or preoccupied, the ability to integrate breaks down and one may enter states of shock and numbness. Shock states (e.g. hearing of someone you love being killed in a car accident) have some similarity with detachment: people talk about being 'spaced out', feeling unreal as if in a dream or paralyzed. Interactions of old brain systems (basic motivational and emotional systems to guide actions), with new brain systems (enabling thinking about the consequences of one's actions) break down.

Integration is also key to memory and how the past influences the present. For example, we have different memory systems (e.g. body memory, time and event memory) which are coded in different ways, in different brain systems and do not always integrate well together (Brewin, 2003, 2006). For example, at a party you have a beer that makes you sick and a couple of days later you may smell beer and feel nausea triggered just by the smell (body amygdala-based memory). But your hippocampal memory tells you *what, when and why* you are feeling and that you had a bad pint of beer at the party. Otherwise, suddenly feeling nauseous would be perplexing. In some cases of trauma this is exactly what happens. People experience emotion-body memories triggered by subtle cues but can't make sense of them unless their time and event memory systems are working (Brewin, 2003, 2006).

When we have an intrusion or flashback memory, we can react defensively to our own internal experiences. The meaning we give to sensory experience is important in determining reactions to sensory changes linked to experiences of dissociation (Ogden, Minton and Pain, 2006). But conditioning may also determine our reactions to the triggering of emotions and memories. Ferster (1973) suggested that when children are punished for showing anger, they experience anxiety and distress over the punishment. Over time, cues that normally generate the experience of anger are conditioned to anxiety and distress almost to the point that the person can't actually process anger without becoming intensely anxious. Conditioning models provide an automatic, out of voluntary control, approach to emotion processing which may be useful in considering compartmentalization dissociative phenomenology (Gilbert, 1992).

A mind built around inner conflicts

In 1992, Coon opened an introductory psychology text with this graphic depiction:

> *'You are a universe, a collection of worlds within worlds. Your brain is possibly the most complicated and amazing device in existence. Through its action you are capable of music, art, science, and war. Your potential for love and compassion coexists with your potential for aggression, hatred ....murder.'*

(p. 1).

We are made up of different possibilities for the creation of meaning and generating brain patterns and states of mind. The problem comes when these different systems begin to seriously conflict with each other and that conflict in itself generates arousal (Gilbert, 2000). Conflicting parts of the mind can actually start to create 'sub-personalities' (Carter, 2008). It is then the conflict between them, and the degree of cognitive dissonance, that can inhibit integration and is probably a source of the dissociation.

Gilbert (1989, 2005, 2007) linked the concept of archetypal with more standard motivational concepts and referred to them as social mentalities. A social mentality orientates us to certain social roles, responds to specific social signals and allows for dynamic interacting sequences of behaviour which are mutually influential. For example, the way our attention, ways of reasoning, behaviours and feelings are integrated and organized when we are motivated to form a sexual relationship is quite different from forming (say) an aggressive relationship with a disliked person, or caring for a loved child. So social mentalities organize and pattern a wide range of psychological processes and can turn on and off specific systems. In order for us to behave aggressively, even cruelly, we have to turn off our capacities for sympathy and empathic connection. There have been many suggestions about how and why we 'dissociate' from the pain we can cause (Kelman and Hamilton, 1989; Zimbardo, 2008). Gilbert (1989) suggested that sometimes social mentalities become closed off from other influences or regulators, particularly when one type of motivation system becomes highly dominant. A tragic example is, of course, intergroup violence and war and the way war creates terrible cruelties, especially when our behaviour becomes 'dissociated' from our moral values (Bateson, Thompson, Seuferling, Whitney and Strongman, 1999). Gilbert (1989) used an example given by Epstein (1982) on reflections by rapists.

> *'Both rapists said they felt badly about what they have done ... They said that in their normal state of mind they could not comprehend how they could brutalise another human being, but they knew they would do it again if they were in the same emotional state of frustration and anger that preceded the rapes.'*
>
> (p. 204).

> *'When asked if a more severe penalty for rape would have deterred him, one of the rapists said that consideration of punishment would have made no difference because when he was in the state that led him to rape, nothing could stop him. He pointed out that after the rape he wept and despised himself for having brutalised another human being but, before the rape, concern for the victim and even his own welfare never occurred to him.'*
>
> (p. 241).

Another example of how we operate in different mental states and social contexts and are then shocked and horrified about our behaviour, is post traumatic stress disorder (PTSD) in returning troops. With the changing social context of home, threat is reduced and capacities for empathic thinking and previous sense of self re-emerge, giving rise to problems of guilt and confusion: 'how could I have done that?' (Hendin and Haas, 1991; Henning and Frueh, 1997). One positive example is the extraordinary self-sacrifice that can occur when others are under threat, where one simply puts aside any concerns with personal safety to help others. After heroic acts people commonly say that thoughts of their own safety never occurred to them and may even be surprised at their courage (Oliner and Oliner, 1986).

We see from these examples that forms of dissociation, which involve compartmentalization and conflict, may be typical of the way the mind works, especially when it comes to threat and motivational conflicts (Carter 2008; Liotti and Gumley, 2008). Dalenberg and Paulson (2009) use the concept of how we can become *absorbed* in one state of mind or motivation system, which then blocks out others. If we are to move the world to a more compassionate place then understanding how we understand 'normal' and 'pathological' forms of dissociation is essential (Dalenberg and Paulson, 2009). One of the most important signatures of dissociation, as a clinical phenomenon, is internal conflict between different systems that cannot then be integrated. Although the new brain, especially the frontal cortex, is important for enabling us to integrate different processing systems, it is still something of a shock to recognize just how 'multiple' and conflicted we are.

Summary

Human evolution has made us especially susceptible to dissociation because we have a complex mind that is highly dependent upon how information is integrated between new and old brain systems and between different motivational systems. It is surprising that we are not dissociated most of the time! It turns out that evolution has also created contexts where integration of information occurs at a higher rate especially in the context of relative safeness and affiliative relationships. Affiliative relationships regulate threat and arousal and make explorative, integrative functioning possible. This is why dissociation is commonly associated with trauma and failures in the affiliative process.

Three types of emotional function and their integration.

Over a number of years basic emotion research and neuroscience has shown that there are at least three types of emotion processing systems that have different evolved functions and different neurophysiologies that co-regulate each other in different ways (Depue and Morrone-Strupinsky, 2005; LeDoux, 1998). These three interacting systems are depicted in Figure 14.1.

- *Threat and self-protection focused systems* – detect, processes and respond to threats. Threat-based emotions e.g. anger, anxiety, disgust, and defensive behaviours, e.g. fight, flight, submission, freeze etc.
- *Drive, seeking and acquisition-focused systems* – detect and pay attention to advantageous resources (e.g. food, sex, alliances) and provide energy (activation) for seeking out and acquiring resources, e.g. pleasure, joy, and excitement in pursuing them.
- *Contentment, soothing and affiliative-focused systems* – enable openness of attention when individuals are no longer threat focused or focused on seeking specific resources (are satisfied), e.g. contentment, quiescence, sense of well-being. Over evolutionary time this system of calming has been adapted for many functions of attachment and affiliative behaviour.

Figure 14.1 Three Types of Affect Regulation System
From Gilbert, (2009) The Compassionate Mind, *reprinted with permission from*
Constable & Robinson Ltd

Motives and emotions do not always follow each other: one can spend years working to pass exams to develop a career and earn money. So there may be times when one is not excited but rather tired and anxious but one keeps studying anyway. Also we can engage in all kinds of defensive behaviours even if we are not anxious in that moment.

Threat self-protection systems.

Anxiety, anger and disgust are all threat-protection-based emotions. These emotions are underpinned with specific neurophysiological systems and can be rapidly activated (LeDoux, 1998). Threat emotions are central to dissociative states (Dell and O'Neil, 2009; Van der Hart, Steele and Nijenhuis, 2006), and they can turn off positive emotions (in spotting the lion one must lose interest in lunch or sex!) Threat emotions can interfere with reflective thinking and abilities to mentalize, which are key functions helping to reduce dissociation (Allen *et al.*, 2008; Liotti and Gilbert, 2011). Some of the defences of the threat system can be troublesome when they are triggered automatically, e.g. climbing out of the fourth floor of a burning house can cause us to go into a paralysis of fear that inhibits escape down the drain pipe. The evolution, organization and impact of threat-based processing systems on our capacities for integration have been the focus of a number of therapeutic approaches to dissociation (Nijenhuis and Boer, 2009; Van der Hart *et al.*, 2006).

Conflicts as threats

Understanding conflicts in our processing systems and how they get resolved is key to understanding dissociation. Inability to discriminate and respond to cues signalling incompatible responses (approach-avoid), has been linked to high threat and disorganized states of mind. Pavlov first noted serious disturbance in dogs (agitation and disorganized behaviour) who could not distinguish stimuli that predicted food from those predicting no food (Gray, 1979). Many later experiments have since explored conflicts where an animal has more and more difficulty in discriminating what to do, e.g. to approach or avoid; to act or not act. These conflicts, which produce arousal and fear and also some rather bizarre behaviours, became known as experimental neurosis (Lindell, 1947).

Conflicts of emotions.

Threat emotions can themselves conflict. Dixon (1998) reviewed the evidence that animals can show emotional and behavioural orientations for fight (anger) and flight (fear) responses at the same time. Humans too can experience different and conflicting threat emotions to the same situation. If our boss criticizes us, we may feel angry and resentful, anxious, but also tearful because we feel exhausted and wanted praise. We have to try to manage these to self-regulate and present a particular self-image – with poise – not easy!

Working with conflicts

Those prone to certain types of dissociation struggle to appreciate that we can have a variety of different emotions in response to the same event, and these emotions can conflict. Different emotions come with their own thinking patterns, physiological states, action tendencies, and emotional memories. One way of helping patients become aware of conflicts within the threat system is guided discovery, explaining that we have different parts of ourselves that can think and feel different things.

> *Imagine you have had a difficult argument with somebody you like. Bring that to mind (pause). See it in your mind. Now first only focus your attention on that part of you that felt angry. We will explore other parts shortly. We can call this 'the angry part' or 'the angry self'. Focus on what angry part thinks – write it down or spend time mentalizing the angry part.*

Writing down information might offer some distance. When the therapist feels that the essence of angry thinking has been elicited, they switch to exploring body experience.

> *Now when anger arises, where do you feel it in your body? And if the anger was to build, where would it go?*

Once the person has explored and considered the bodily feeling of anger we move to the behaviours and action tendencies of anger.

> *Feeling the anger in your body, what would your anger want to do – without constraint, it can just act itself – what would it want to do?*

The feelings and awareness of aggressive actions can be alarming and so normalizing and grounding can help. And of course this is guided discovery and should not overwhelm the person – so go gently. To help people see that each emotion has its own *stream of memories*, you can ask about those memories that come to mind when we just allow ourselves to be in (say) 'angry self'. These may be of the client's own anger, or the anger of others towards them or of anger they have witnessed.

The therapist can then invite a pause and gentle relaxation and then invite exploration of the part that felt anxious in the argument, going though the same guided discovery questions. Then on to the sad self or indeed any other part of the self that might be useful to explore. This exercise helps people recognize that different parts of the self experience different thoughts, feelings, action tendencies and memories.

Next, it is important to take time to stand back and explore conflicts: what does your angry self think about your anxious self; what does anxious self think about angry self? Commonly angry self is angry with, or contemptuous of anxious self, very critical, whilst anxious self is frightened of angry self. Also to recognize different memories associated with parts of the self. Clients can be avoidant of sad self, feeling that if they engage they may become lost in it.

The key point is that threat emotions can be in conflict. Another way to help clarify this is by asking clients to move around in different chairs, exploring angry self or anxious self (almost playfully to start with) so they get the idea that multiple parts of self are normal but problematic when they conflict (see Gilbert, 2012 for a more detailed outline). Becoming a specific part of self on purpose, with deliberate mindfulness to the part, also allows individuals to start mentalizing about emotions and the conflict of emotions.

The final part of the exercise is crucial. Having taught the client how to engage with a compassionate self (Gilbert 2009a, 2010; see below), you can invite them to sit in the compassionate chair, take up the compassion posture and facial expressions, engage in the breathing exercise, and bring to mind compassionate thoughts and memories. When compassionate feelings are activated, look at the arguments with which we started the exercise. This usually enables the person to see the argument in a different way and even start to mentalize and think about why the other person may have been arguing. One then invites the compassionate self to think about the other aspects of self such as angry self, anxious self, sad self. Typically clients begin to see that these parts of themselves are understandable and that there is a way in which they can be thought about in the context of the compassionate self. The therapist then focuses on the fact that clients have this internal wisdom themselves, as a strength and resource. If they learn to pay attention to compassionate self they can develop it and it can be there when they need it – especially for dealing with internal and external conflicts.

Understanding these *multiple domains* of responding and the conflicts between them, and holding them in a single frame of reference that we could call *the self or self-organizing system,* is a psychological feat. This can break down under stress. In extreme cases people may shut down specific affect systems because they are overwhelming, and create a fragmented or even different sense of self (Carter, 2008). So in an argument people might be aware of anger but not their sadness, or be aware of anxiety but not their anger.

Positive Emotions

Working with the threat system alone may not be enough to help regulate it because there are certain types of *positive emotion* that have fundamental, threat regulating properties (Depue and Morrone-Strupinsky, 2005). Understanding the importance of the interaction between positive and negative affect-regulation systems is central to a range of different affect-regulation theories (Kring and Sloan, 2010). Key to this, however, is the recognition that there are two very different types of positive emotion. One is linked to drive, excitement and achievement (dopaminergic), but the other is associated with contentment, safeness, soothing, affiliation and a sense of wellbeing (Depue and Morrone-Strupinsky, 2005) and linked to endorphins (Dunbar, 2010) and oxytocin (MacDonald and MacDonald, 2010). The rest of this chapter will focus on the evolution, functions and role of affiliative-based emotions in the regulation of threat and in particular its capacity for integrating threatening information.

Attachment and the affiliative emotions

Species that do not have an attachment system produce hundreds or thousands of offspring, few of which survive. Parental investment and live birth began to evolve around 120 million years or so ago (Geary, 2000). This gave rise to the internal mechanisms of the attachment system (Bowlby, 1969; Mikulincer and Shaver, 2007). With the advent of attachment, fewer offspring are born but they have a higher survival rate. Attachment caring limits exposure to threat and the presence of the parent signals safeness which typically allows either rest or *playful exploration* (Panksepp, 2007). In these states the brain is able to learn (exploration exposes them to many stimuli) and integrate information. The evolution of the attachment system made possible the birth of a relatively helpless, larger brained human infant set up for post-birth learning (Bjorklund, 1997). This capacity for learning also extends to learning about feelings and motivational states (Mikulincer and Shaver, 2007). The safeness provided by the parent acts as an affect regulator so that, if the infant/child is threatened from the outside or is inwardly distressed, the soothing of the parent calms the infant's threat system.

We know that the love and affection a children receive in their early lives has an impact on gene expression (Belsky and Pluess, 2009), and the maturation of the brain and neurophysiological systems, especially the frontal cortex, that are important for affect regulation and capacity to integrate self-relevant information (Carlson, Yates and Sroufe, 2010; Cozolino, 2007; Schore, 1994, 2009). Keys to the attachment system are endorphin and oxytocin which are very important for the experience of affiliative relationships (Carter, 1998; Dunbar, 2010; Depue and Morrone-Strupinsky, 2005; MacDonald and MacDonald, 2010). We also know that there are oxytocin receptors in the amygdala such that stimulation of affiliation and oxytocin can down-regulate threat (Kirsch, Esslinger, Chen, Mier, Lis *et al.*, 2005).

Stanley and Siever (2010) argue that much of the phenomenology associated with borderline personality disorder, such as impulsivity, self-harming, emotional instability, aggressive outbursts, sensitivity to rejection, poor self-identity, can be understood in terms of poor regulation of the affiliative system marked by compromise to the oxytocin and endorphin systems. The affiliative system, mediated by endorphin and oxytocin, plays a very important role in stimulating the frontal cortex and in affect regulation.

The role that the affiliative system plays is fundamental to enabling cortical systems to function and to integrate information, whereas the threat system tends to focus on more stereotyped and less integrated defensive responses. Humans have evolved to respond to kindness and affiliation with calming and positive affect; there are specialist neurophysiological systems in our brains that respond to signals of affiliation in caring, and these systems have profound influences on affect regulation, our capacities to learn about and tolerate our emotions and the organization of our sense of self and others.

Compassion-focused therapy (CFT)

CFT uses many established cognitive, behavioural and emotional interventions (e.g. guided discovery, inference chaining, re-scripting, exposure, independent practice, behavioural experiments, mindfulness, imagery etc.). In addition, however, specific interventions aim to activate the affiliative, soothing emotion regulation system that plays a key role in threat regulation. For example, when generating alternative thoughts the CFT therapist ensures that the emotional texture of those thoughts is kind, friendly, supportive and validating as opposed to logical, cold or even aggressive. Therapists might need to work through the fears of compassion and affiliative feeling in order eventually to activate the affiliative system.

We use the term compassion rather than affiliation because compassion is now understood to have a particular focus on suffering and alleviation of suffering (Gilbert, 2005, 2007, 2009a). In its simplest definition it refers to an attentional sensitivity to the suffering of self and others with a commitment to do something about it (Gilbert, 2009a; Gilbert and Choden, in press). To achieve compassion we attend to:

- the degree to which we can be motivated to approach and understand our (and others) distress (including of course the nature of conflicts) as opposed to avoiding it or engaging in various defences
- the motivation, and the cognitive, behavioural and emotional competencies we need to alleviate or tolerate the distress (see Gilbert 2009a, 2010; Gilbert and Choden, in press)

The process of compassion training: switching on the affiliative system

Like Buddhist psychology and more recent mindfulness focused therapies, CFT notes that we often need to train our minds to attend to what is happening in our minds and bodies, and focus on what is helpful using a series of stages, as in Table 14.1.

CFT uses a range of interventions to facilitate the development and accessing of the affiliative soothing system to help balance threat and drive systems.

Table 14.1 Stages of compassion training

- Clarifying the issues and the phenomenology that needs to be addressed
- Developing a safe basis within the therapeutic relationship and preliminary formulation
- Psycho-education to begin a process of de-shaming and helping to reduce self-blame
- Introducing the evolutionary model and the complexity of our evolved mind: brains are designed in such a way that they can be *very tricky* and not work well in high states of threat. Recognizing the *universal* difficulties humans have can be a source of relief
- Explaining the three-circle affect-regulation model: exploring with clients where they tend to operate; which one might be overdeveloped/ underdeveloped
- Developing therapeutic plans around the idea that the affiliative system may require development through practice
- Discussing the nature of compassion, addressing the misunderstanding that it is weak or soft or undeserved – discuss compassion as courage
- Working out the processes for developing compassion capacity
- Bringing the newly developed compassion capacity (e.g. the compassionate self) to the issues to be addressed

Compassionate Mind Training (CMT) refers to specific compassion-focused exercises. Much of the work in CMT is focused on *building compassionate capacity* by:

1   Developing capacity to engage with (unhelpful) threat and drive processes involving avoidance, shame and self-blame.
2   Building capacity to experience positive emotions, particularly affiliation and contentment, without being fearful (Gilbert, McEwan, Gibbons, Chotai, Duarte *et al.*, in press).
3   Multimodal interventions e.g. focussing on soothing rhythm breathing, attentional training (e.g. mindfulness and mindful focusing), addressing cognitive and emotional biases, behavioural avoidance, using imagery and sensori-motor focusing.

Here are a few examples of Compassionate Mind Training exercises:

- *Developing the inner compassionate self:* exercises focus on creating a sense of a compassionate self, just like 'method actors' do if they are trying to get into a role (see http://en.wikipedia.org/wiki/Method_acting). Relax the facial muscles, starting at the forehead and cheeks, and letting the jaw drop slightly, slowing breathing and taking a grounded confident posture. Key here is that the body takes on a 'solid' position, as in Tai Chi, where before moving the body is balanced, stable, centred and inwardly calm – but also alert. Create a compassionate, friendly facial expression and a focus on feelings of kindness and a genuine desire to be helpful and caring. Imagine yourself to be a deeply compassionate person with wisdom (able to reflect and see things from different perspectives, understanding the nature of difficulties), a sense of authority, confidence and calmness, with feelings of kindness and warmth, and being genuinely motivated to be helpful and supportive.

- *Compassion flowing out from the client to others:* from the compassion self we then bring to mind a person (or animal) you care about, wish to see happy and free of suffering. With each out breath, imagine directing compassionate feelings towards that person (or animal). Now focus on a 'heart-felt wish' for their peace and happiness flowing from you to them and the joy it could bring. This type of exercise is common for loving-kindness (*metta*) practice (Kabat-Zinn, 2005; Neff, 2011; Germer, 2009).
- *Compassion flowing into the self:* here the focus is on being open to the kindness of others. It may involve recalling episodes or events when other people were kind to one. Other exercises work on imagining an ideal compassionate being and relating to that image in specific ways.
- *Compassion to self:* here we first spend time cultivating the compassionate self, and getting the solid sense of it, and then we imagine ourselves, or part of our selves (say angry self or anxious self) and focus on a 'heart-felt wish' for that part of us to find peace, or relief from distress (Gilbert, 2009a; Germer, 2009). With practice, and gradual engagement and exposure to these feelings, one can imagine a future self being happy, noticing how that would feel, look and sound and how one would get there. Helping people create positive imagery can have positive effects on mood (Holmes, Lang and Shah, 2009; Tarrier, 2010).

Self criticism

CFT was developed with and for people who suffer from high levels of shame and/or self-criticism. They struggle in standard therapies as their internal self-to-self relationship is primarily threat-based (Bulmash, Harkness, Stewart and Bagby, 2009; Gilbert and Irons, 2005). There is now evidence that self-criticism stimulates threat-processing systems (Longe, Maratos, Gilbert, Evans, Volker *et al.*, 2010). CFT helps people to recognize the origins, forms and functions of self-criticism.

One antidote to self-criticism is to teach people how to be more self-reassuring and compassionate. CFT aims to stimulate the affiliative-soothing system in self-to-self relating that is capable of validating, understanding, being supportive and creating an emotional texture of kindness to oneself (Gilbert, 2009a; Germer, 2009; Neff, 2012). Switching to the affiliative-soothing system has important effects on affect regulation (Gilbert, 2010) and mentalizing (Liotti and Gilbert, 2011).

Complexities: Trauma and threat-affiliative system conflict

Many theorists believe that early trauma can disrupt the smooth integration and operation of threat-affiliative systems and in consequence produce a range of defences to threat (Van der Hart *et al.*, 2006). Trauma-linked dissociation can be the result of overwhelming stress that could not be regulated or integrated even in the context of the safeness of a parent. The parent may be a signal for safeness but also for fear and unpredictability, creating intense approach-avoidance conflict (Liotti and Gumley, 2008). This can create disorganized attachment that might be a vulnerability factor of dissociation (Liotti, 2009; Liotti and Gumley, 2008).

Attachment theory explains the origins of disorganized attachment behaviour in terms of conflict between two different inborn systems, the attachment system and threat systems, which normally operate in harmony (i.e. flight from the source of fear to find refuge near the attachment figure). They conflict in infant–caregiver interactions when the caregiver is at the same time the *source of*, and the *solution for*, the infant's fear, giving rise to approach-avoidance conflicts. When exposed to interactions with a helplessly frightened or hostile and frightening caregiver, or with one who alternates between frightening and frightened, infants are caught in a relational trap. Their defence system motivates them to flee from the frightened and/or frightening caregivers; at the same time their attachment system motivates them, under the influence of separation fear, to approach them. Moreover, comfort would normally be the only source of calming for a young child. Disorganized attachment means the infant risks experiencing 'fear without solution' (Liotti, 2010).

Fears of affiliation

So far the story is that the affiliation system evolved as one of the most powerful regulators of threat and provides the context for a whole range of integrative and mentalizing competencies. These can be compromised, throwing a person back into more basic, earlier-evolved defences. In addition, feelings and desires for affiliation can themselves become a threat. As Bowlby (1980), Gilbert and Irons (2005) and Liotti (2000, 2009) have pointed out, kindness that stimulates the affiliative system will also trigger emotional memories associated with that system, including traumatic experiences. For example, most of us enjoy our sexual feelings and we may try to stimulate them ourselves through fantasy. But if one has been raped, stimulating these systems and bodily feelings can be deeply aversive because this reactivates the trauma memory. What should be positive and approach-based feelings become aversive and activate the threat system. Figure 14.2 shows a simple model.

Understanding how affiliative signals can activate threat can help clinicians who otherwise may be confused by a client acting out, mentalizing insufficiently or even dissociating when the therapist is trying to create a safe affiliative environment (Liotti and Gilbert, 2011).

Kindness from therapist or imagery

Activate attachment system
Activate memories

Fight, flight
shut down

Fight, flight
shut down

Neglect
aloneness

Abuse, shame
vulnerable

Activate learnt and current defences – cortisol

Figure 14.2 Kindness, attachment and threat
From Gilbert (2008), reprinted with permission from Routledge Ltd.

Case Example

Jane is a depressed woman who is self-critical, disappointed in herself and finds it difficult to have feelings of closeness with other people. Previous CBT was helpful to a degree and she 'saw the logic' of trying to refocus her thinking, but didn't feel better. She reported an ordinary family history and no indications of dissociation.

Whilst creating a safe base, the therapist noticed that as Jane talked about any anger towards her mother she went into a mild dissociative state, her mind going blank and losing track of the topic. She sighed and had feelings of being overwhelmed and that the therapy was hopeless. So as angry self was about to emerge it was almost immediately turned off to be replaced by sad and hopeless self. In CFT this can be a sign of beginning to approach attachment feelings and memories, tapping into seriously unresolved conflicts. Her mother had told her how lucky she was to have a loving mother but behaved aggressively and critically towards her daughter. Her threats produced a state of fearful arousal, and emotionally labelling Jane as bad produced shame. Jane was left with no resolution or capacity for soothing contact.

Like others, CFT emphasizes that conflicts are important to the process of dissociation: we can normalize and have empathy for the conflicts. 'Gosh, when your mother behaved like that you must have felt a conflict between being angry and being frightened at the same time'. We try to help Jane acknowledge conflict by talking about the importance of thinking about conflict. In therapy it became clear that Jane's conflicts were multiple, varied and complex (Table 14.2).

Understanding conflicts gave insight into the feelings of depressive collapse and hopelessness triggering the dissociative experience in the face of anger. Learning to monitor thoughts and feelings linked to the dissociative experience, Jane realized that when she talked about her anger she was overwhelmed, thinking 'maybe it was my (Jane's) fault', that she was betraying her mother and

Table 14.2 Examples of Jane's multiple internal conflicts

- Wanting to be loved by her (a) mother yet her mother also stimulated fear and anger in Jane
- Fearing and hating her mother
- Experiencing guilt and self-blame when acknowledging hatred of her mother
- Fear of being shamed, seen as an unloving, ungrateful 'nasty' daughter and abandoned if her negative feelings became known
- Feeling anger generates feelings of being unloving, ungrateful and bad
- Wanting to help and care for her mother, to soothe her so that she wouldn't be an aggressive, fraught mother any more and could turn into the desired loving mother who would appreciate Jane and see her inner goodness
- Acknowledging that she wanted to run away and find a new family generated intense feelings of betrayal and guilt

- As for many with Jane's background, she has two parents – the one that she wanted (set up by our biology as an attachment-based species) and the one that she actually experienced. In letting go of the one she had Jane could grieve for the one she wanted

being bad. Jane noticed that the dissociative experience was linked to emotional body memories or feelings of being left alone in her room when she was frightened and upset. For Jane, identifying the emotions linked to memories of being threatened and sent away was helpful. We could normalize these as horrible but understandable and important to work with here and now. Jane realized that if her threat system was activated in interpersonal contexts, there would often also come a feeling of aloneness. Before therapy she had been unaware of how feeling lonely textured the background of her experience of being in the world.

The therapist gradually helped Jane understand that dissociative experience was linked to conflicts and feelings that were perceived as intolerable. While some kinds of dissociation linked to panic, others were linked to fears of intense loneliness and memories of being threatened and then left alone. The associative learning of fear *with* loneliness is very important, because sometimes in working with fear the therapist neglects working on the intense feelings of loneliness that are rooted in emotional memories of 'being frightened and sent away or left alone'. Through developing her capacity for compassion and her compassionate self, Jane gradually learned to understand, tolerate and engage with those conflicts. So, building the solid base of the compassionate self can aid the engagement with dissociated material and difficulties.

Conclusion

The CFT approach to of dissociation begins with an evolutionary approach to thinking about how our minds evolved in a rather piecemeal fashion and require complex capacities for integration to work smoothly. Integrative abilities become compromised in the context of threat, especially when experienced early in life and with soothing others to create states of mind that facilitate integration. Importantly though, we now know that mammalian attachment and affiliative systems evolved with important threat-regulating functions; e.g. the care of the mother calms the infant. CFT suggests that some aspects of dissociation are linked to the way in which affiliative systems are not able to regulate threat, for the reasons suggested above. One aspect of therapy would therefore be to develop the person's affiliative systems, which may then help them engage with, tolerate, make sense of, integrate and regulate threatening material. More research is necessary to explore these possibilities.

Chapter 15

Trauma-related dissociation

Theory and treatment of dissociation of the personality

Onno van der Hart
Kathy Steele

> '*It is better ... to speak of dissociation of the personality.*'
> William McDougall (1926, p. 234)

The concept of dissociation is often relegated to being merely one among the plethora of symptoms in trauma-related disorders. However, for nearly 200 years many clinicians have considered dissociation as fundamental to the subjective experience of traumatized individuals, and thus it should receive a prominent place in any treatment approach (Van der Hart and Dorahy, 2009). The DSM IV-TR (APA, 2000) defines dissociation as 'a disruption in the usually integrated functions of consciousness, memory, identity, or perception of the environment' (p. 519). However, this is an overly broad and vague definition. Below we propose a definition that clarifies the specific integrative disruptions of the personality found in the dissociative disorders.

Currently, there is relatively wide acceptance that dissociation of the personality is central to the presentation and treatment of complex trauma-related disorders stemming from childhood traumatization, particularly the dissociative disorders (e.g. Brown, Scheflin and Hammond, 1998; Courtois, 2010; Van der Hart, Nijenhuis and Steele, 2006). However, there remains controversy over the degree to which dissociation plays a role in classic PTSD, involving 'simple' or 'Type I' (Terr, 1991) traumatizing events. Nevertheless, several clinicians have proposed that PTSD is a dissociative rather than an anxiety disorder (Chu, 2011; Howell, 2005; Van der Hart *et al.*, 2006). Indeed, the theory of structural dissociation of the personality (TSDP) was not only developed the better to understand and treat clients with complex dissociative disorders, but also to offer a unifying theory that explains all trauma-related disorders, ranging from the simple to the complex (Nijenhuis, Van der Hart and Steele, 2002; Steele, Dorahy, Van der Hart and Nijenhuis, 2009; Steele and Van der Hart, 2009; Steele, Van der Hart, and Nijenhuis, 2005, 2009; Van der Hart *et al.*, 2006).

Briefly, what the DSM IV-TR describes as 'disruption' of usually integrated functions is understood as a dissociation or division of the personality in TSDP, no matter how rudimentary or limited that division may be. The theory holds that integrative failure is definitive in traumatic experiences; without integrative failure, an event is described only as stressful. Unlike contemporary use of the term 'trauma' to denote events, we follow Ross (1941) in defining it not as a particular event, but as the 'breaking point(s)' of personality during or after the traumatizing event, when individuals become too overwhelmed to integrate their experience. TSDP has its roots in historical sources, in particular the seminal writings of Pierre Janet (1859–1947) on dissociation and on his psychology of action, as well as Charles Myers' study of acutely traumatized World War I service men (Myers, 1940), attachment theory, learning theory, cognitive behavioral therapy, affect theory, affective neuroscience, and interpersonal neuro-biology. Following Janet (1889), the theory postulates that dissociation is first and foremost an integrative failure rather than a defence, although it may be utilized as a defence once it becomes an entrenched coping strategy.

A definition of integration

We begin by offering a clearer understanding of integration as the organization of different aspects of the personality into a unified pattern of hierarchical systems of functions. TSDP emphasizes that integration is not a final destination. Rather, it is a series of continuing actions, so that both an integrated personality and sense of self are 'ongoing constructions' (Janet, 1929) that are stable yet flexible, constantly revised to adapt better to life's challenges. So when we refer to a person as being integrated, we imply that there is a relatively cohesive personality organization or structure that is both flexible and stable, and changeable within parameters of consistency.

A well-integrated personality includes a (relatively) unified sense of self, a single first-person perspective, with regulatory and reflective skills that support functioning in daily life and during stressful events. Well-integrated individuals have a consistent sense of who they are across time and contexts, are able to change and adapt, yet experience themselves as the same person. For example, a woman experiences herself as 'me, myself, and I' across various roles as mother, wife, friend, and professional, and also experiences her adolescence and childhood as her own: 'I am me now and then, in everything I do and during all that happens to me.' Individuals who have integrated their traumatic memories and subsequently recall traumatizing events remain grounded in the present and experience recall as an autobiographical narrative memory rather than reliving the past. A person's capacity to integrate experience depends upon social support, developmental factors, context, and genetics, to name a few. The degree of integration varies from time to time. In the field of dissociation, the majority consensus is that adequate integration of one's personality into a cohesive and relatively harmonious whole is important and necessary for effective functioning (International Society for the Study of Trauma and Dissociation (ISSTD), 2011; Kluft, 1993; Van der Hart et al., 2006). Basic levels of integration involve synthesis, including binding (linking) and differentiating (distinguishing) experiences such as sensory perceptions, movements, thoughts, affects, memories, and sense of self. At higher levels, integration involves *realization*, defined as developing an adaptive and congruent perception of reality that may include considering multiple and even contradictory points of views, then effectively responding (Van der Hart *et al.*, 2006). Realization is such an essential component of integration that trauma-related disorders were referred to by Janet (1935) as 'syndromes of nonrealization.'

Realization comprises two complex sets of actions. The first is p*ersonification*, the awareness and acceptance of experience as one's own (Van der Hart *et al.*, 2006). It is the affective experience of realizing 'that is *my* experience; it belongs to me, myself, and I.' Individuals with dissociative disorders do not sufficiently own or *personify* their experiences. *Presentification*, the second component of realization, involves the ability to distinguish between various episodes of one's life, i.e. engage in mental time travel, while still giving the highest degree of reality to the present (Van der Hart *et al.*, 2006). Presentification implies mindful presence with awareness of the impact of the past and expected future, together with the capacity to act effectively in the moment as needed. However, certain dissociative parts (of the personality) typically relive (aspects of) their traumatic experiences, are subsequently unable accurately to discern the present situation, so are unable to engage in actions based on the present. We call this condition '*living in trauma-time*' (Van der Hart, Nijenhuis and Solomon, 2010).

A definition of dissociation of the personality

Nijenhuis and Van der Hart (2011) have developed a comprehensive definition of dissociation of the personality with treatment implications. An abbreviated adaptation of this work follows. Personality is not a thing or entity, but refers to the dynamic, biopsychosocial system as a whole that determines an individual's characteristic mental and behavioural actions (Allport, 1961; Nijenhuis and Van der Hart, 2011). Systems are comprised of subsystems. In an integrated personality, there may be different subsystems that together are congruent and cohesive as a whole, for example, the 'you' that goes to work, the 'you' that is a parent, the 'you' that is a friend, the 'you' of the past. In dissociation of the personality, the personality involves subsystems comprised of discrepant and divided senses of self, behaviors, affects, cognitions, perceptions, etc., separated by psychological barriers, and understood as *dissociative parts of the personality*. Other labels for dissociative parts include ego states, dissociated or dissociative self-states, personality states, modes, identities, and alters.

Although dissociation is often described as a defence against intolerable affects, we believe it is also and foremost an integrative deficit, a 'breaking point' of the personality before, during, or after an event, beyond which integration of experience is not possible at the time. Secondarily, dissociation may serve as a psychological defence, keeping traumatic and related experiences out of conscious awareness. Subsequent breaking points lead to more complex disso-ciation, i.e. more than two dissociative parts. For example, a child can develop a part that experienced the abuse, a part that was fearful and frozen in anticipation of the abuse, a part that fought back (or wanted to), and a part that went to school the next day so that the child could act as though nothing had happened.

Dissociative parts always remain a part of the system of the whole individual, and interact to varying conscious and unconscious degrees. Yet the psycho-biological boundaries between parts remain unduly closed, thus maintaining dissociation. Many parts are rigid and limited, always reacting in the same way, no matter what the context. For example, an abused woman in one part may seem only to react with anger in any relational conflict, while in another she only reacts with fear and appeasement, as if she is about to be abused again. Each dissociative part has its own first-person perspective (which also includes a sense of *'I,' 'me,' 'mine'*) that can be distinguished from that of other parts, at least to a degree.

Each dissociative part is organized according to particular inborn motivational or action systems that direct behaviour, emotion, cognition, and perception, which heavily influence the parameters of a given first-person perspective (Van der Hart *et al.*, 2006). It is hypothesized that there are two basic types of innate action systems: those of daily life and those of defence in the face of threat. By nature, action systems of daily life occur when we feel safe, and include attachment, care-giving, exploration, play, sexuality/reproduction, and energy management (e.g. sleep, food intake) (Van der Hart *et al.*, 2006). For example, energy management directs us to sleep when we are tired and eat when we are hungry. The exploration action system is mediated by curiosity and encourages us to learn about our environment. The attachment system supports us to seek out relationships.

When danger is perceived action systems of defence take precedence over those of daily life. Fight, flight and/or freeze can ensue, which all involve hyperarousal. When actual life threat is perceived, a collapsed state or death feint may occur, involving extreme hypoarousal (Porges, 2011).

Dissociative prototypes

Dissociation typically seems to occur between dissociative parts which function in daily life, and those fixated in various animal defences, as if the past were still present. For example, a man did well in the beginning of his courses at a university, but was quite avoidant of dealing with past severe physical and sexual abuse by an aunt. During the stress of school, each time he saw a woman who reminded him of his aunt, he would find himself in a bathroom or in his car, curled up and paralyzed with fear, crying out like a little boy. These flight and freeze experiences occurred with increasing frequency, and were accompanied by amnesia. They led to increasing inability to get to class and he had to drop out. This example illustrates the prototypical example of one dissociative part that primarily functions in daily life while avoiding reminders of the trauma, while the other is primarily fixed in various defences (fight, flight, freeze, collapse).

These two basic parts of the personality have been called the *apparently normal part of the personality* (ANP) and the *emotional part of the personality* (EP), following descriptions by Myers (1940) of acutely traumatized First World War combat soldiers. Typically EP responds as if threat is current, fixed in defence and not adaptively responsive to the present context; that is, EP lives in trauma time.

Primary dissociation of the personality involves a division of the personality into a single dissociative part functioning in daily life (ANP) and a single dissociative part involved in the traumatic memory and fixated in defence (EP). We believe this characterizes simple posttraumatic dissociative disorders, including many cases of PTSD.

When an individual faces chronic or prolonged overwhelming events, particularly in childhood when integrative capacity is naturally lower due to developmental limitations, dissociation can become more complex and chronic. In *secondary dissociation of the personality* there is also a single ANP, but more than one EP. The division of EPs may often be based on failed integration among relatively discrete defences of fight, flight, freeze and collapse. Others may hold intolerable affective experiences such as shame or loneliness. We consider secondary structural dissociation to be mainly involved in Complex Posttraumatic Stress Disorder, trauma-related Borderline Personality Disorder and Dissociative Disorder Not Otherwise Specified (DDNOS)-subtype1b (DSM IV-TR, APA, 2000), i.e. the subtype most similar to DID.

Finally, *tertiary dissociation of the personality* involves more than one EP, and more than one ANP. Division of ANP may occur when experiences in daily life trigger traumatic memories and/or become overwhelming for the individual. The individual's personality becomes increasingly divided in an attempt to maintain functioning while avoiding traumatic memories. For example, a little girl is sexually abused by her father during the night, during which several EPs are activated. The following morning she must face the perpetrator at the breakfast table and act as though nothing happened. Eventually this morning experience may become sufficiently overwhelming such that an additional division of ANP is developed to cope with going to school after breakfast. The inescapable challenge the child faces at the breakfast table is beyond her integrative capacity, and the addition of an ANP that functions at the breakfast table also has survival value, and involves psychological defence. The child has EPs that endure the abuse, an ANP that avoids the trauma and is quiet and appeasing during morning time with the family, and yet another ANP that goes to school and learns, is social, and plays. The child is, as yet, unable to integrate these very different senses of self and their accompanying affects, cognitions, etc. According to TSDP, this level of dissociation only involves Dissociative Identity Disorder (DID). Often in DID, some dissociative parts gain quite a high degree of autonomy from each other, i.e. function relatively independently of other parts, and have a well-elaborated sense of self and investment in being a separate 'person'; a pseudo-delusion based on an extreme degree of nonrealization.

Primary Structural Dissociation

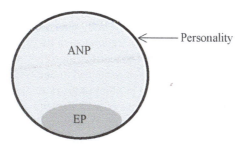

Secondary Structural Dissociation

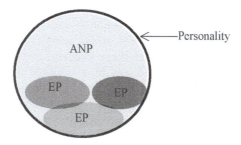

Tertiary Structural Dissociation

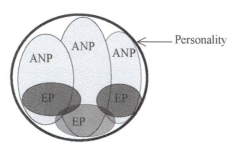

Figure 15.1 Levels dissociation of the personality

Dissociative symptoms

Phenomenologically, the division of personality manifests in dissociative symptoms that can be categorized as negative (functional losses such as amnesia and paralysis, temporary functional loss of certain life skills such as driving a car or doing math) or positive (intrusions such as flashbacks or passive influence of other dissociative parts). Both negative and positive dissociative symptoms can have mental and physical manifestations. Mental, or *psychoform* symptoms include hearing voices, and feeling as though thoughts or emotions which do not belong to you intrude into your mind 'out of the blue.' Physical manifestations, i.e. *somatoform* symptoms involve body experience such as anaesthesia or tics, or somatic sensations related to trauma, such as vaginal pain from a rape in the past (Nijenhuis and Van der Hart, 2011; Steele, Van der Hart *et al.*, 2009; Van der Hart *et al.*, 2006). What is experienced in one dissociative part of the personality is either not experienced in other parts, or experienced as an 'intrusion' not belonging to the prevailing sense of self. Patients may say things like, 'I do not know why I am crying; the tears do not belong to me.' Dissociative individuals often have significant time lapses involving amnesia for the past and often also in the present. They may not be able to account for certain actions, have a subjective inner sense of fragmentation and identity confusion, and experience symptoms of passive influence that were previously considered to be symptoms of schizophrenia (Kluft, 1987).

Many phenomena, such as absorption and imaginary involvement (Butler, 2006), and detachment (Holmes *et al.*, 2005), are regarded as dissociative symptoms. TSDP agrees that these phenomena typically accompany dissociation of the personality and may be a substrate of experience necessary for dissociation of the personality to occur. However, they are also experienced by non-dissociative individuals; hence, they are considered related phenomena, but distinct from dissociation of the personality (Steele *et al.*, 2009; Van der Hart *et al.*, 2006).

Maintenance of dissociation of the personality

Ongoing dissociation of the personality prevents the integration of traumatic memories and is at the roots of the continued existence of different first-person perspectives. We have hypothesized that dissociation of the personality is predominantly maintained by a series of inner-directed phobias (Nijenhuis *et al.*, 2002; Steele *et al.*, 2005; Van der Hart *et al.*, 2006). These phobias involve fear, shame, or disgust reactions to inner experiences that could not be integrated. For example, a person may be very ashamed of dependency needs contained in an EP, disgusted by how an EP participated in abuse in order to survive, or terrified of feeling anger.

Inner-directed phobias include those of mental actions (inner experiences such as certain emotions, feelings, bodily sensations, thoughts, fantasies), dissociative parts, traumatic memories, adaptive risk-taking and change, of attachment and attachment loss, and of intimacy. Overcoming this complex of phobias through building skills such as mentalizing and reflecting, self compassion, increasing the window of tolerance for activation, creating inner safety, and gradual exposure with relapse-prevention, in the context of a stable therapeutic alliance (secure attachment) is a central task of therapy. The treatment of these phobias is discussed briefly below.

Treatment of dissociation of the personality

Treatment strategies should be directed toward raising the individual's integrative capacity to overcome inner-directed phobias, gradually eliminating the need for dissociation, and fostering (re)integration of the personality (Myers, 1940). In cases of complex childhood trauma, standard PTSD treatments are not sufficient (cf. Courtois and Ford, 2009). Although space limitations prevent in-depth descriptions of interventions, treatment approaches for Complex PTSD and Dissociative Disorders can be found in: Chu, 2011; Cloitre, Cohen and Koenen, 2006; Courtois, 2010; Courtois and Ford, 2009; Davies and Frawley, 1994; Follette, Pistorello and Hayes, 2007; Greenwald, 2007 (EMDR); Gelinas, 2003 (EMDR); Howell, 2005; ISSTD, 2011; Kennerley, 1996; Kluft, 1993, 2000; Ogden *et al.*, 2006; Ross, 1997; Steele and Van der Hart, 2009; Steele *et al.*, 2005; and Van der Hart *et al.*, 2006. Where greater degrees of autonomy and elaboration exist in dissociative parts, along with greater degrees of inner conflict and avoidance, more specific intensive work with trauma-related phobias and dissociative parts is needed to develop inner understanding, communication, empathy, and cooperation as a system of the whole individual. A period of stabilization must precede work with traumatic memories.

Phase-oriented treatment

The recommended treatment is based on consensus in the field (Brown, Scheflin, and Hammond, 1998; Courtois, 2010; ISSTD, 2011; Van der Hart *et al.*, 2006), and involves three phases:

1   safety, stabilization,symptom reduction and skills training
2   treatment of traumatic memories
3   personality (re)integration and rehabilitation

The model takes the form of a spiral, in which different phases can be alternated according to the needs of the patient (see Figure 15.2).

Whether the complete phase-oriented treatment is suitable for all clients with complex trauma-related disorders partly depends on the treatment setting (private practice, outpatient clinic, inpatient clinic). Clients who are highly crisis-prone and suicidal probably should not be treated in private practice. *Establishing safety and stabilization are major conditions for further progress.* This is difficult to accomplish when clients are sociopathic or dangerous. Lack of motivation or insight might be contraindications for outpatient treatment, but part of early assessment involves exploring the reasons behind these. Often fear, shame, and skills deficits are amenable to treatment. Therapy is seriously hampered by ongoing abuse, which may evoke serious crises and the need to maintain dissociation. If the therapist chooses to work with such a client, Phase 1 Treatment involving least some skills training could be considered. However, the therapist

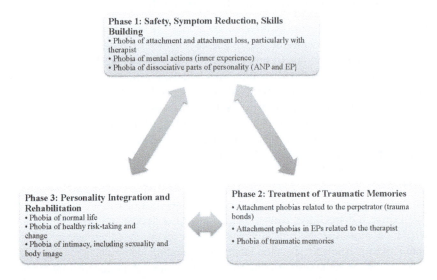

Figure 15.2 Phases of Treatment and Trauma-Related Phobias

Adapted from Arja Antervo

should be aware that some skills are safer than others under these circumstances. For example, a battered woman who tries to be more assertive without being willing to leave the relationship could be seriously hurt by her abuser. The major focus should be on getting out of the situation safely, and traumatic memories should not be approached.

Overcoming trauma-related phobias

The need for phase-oriented treatment is based on the fact that more severe and earlier traumatization in childhood leads to greater adverse developmental effects and more complexity of dissociation and co-morbidity. The majority of patients need to develop specific skills prior to the arduous challenges of integrating traumatic memories and their personality. Stabilization skills include the ability to regulate arousal and impulses, to reflect on one's inner experience and patterns of thinking and feeling; to manage a balance between work, rest, and play; to be assertive and maintain boundaries in relationships, and manage normal relational conflicts; to organize, prioritize, plan and manage time; and to develop empathic and cooperative relationships among dissociative parts (for more specific interventions, see Boon, Steele and Van der Hart, 2011; Chu, 2011; Courtois and Ford, 2009; Van der Hart *et al.*, 2006). Some existing approaches, such as Dialectical Behavioural Therapy (DBT) for clients with borderline personality disorder (Linehan, 1993a), are oriented mainly to skills development, with one approach specific to individuals with dissociative disorders (Boon *et al.*, 2011). However,

Table 15.1 Trauma-Related Phobias in Phase-Oriented Treatment

---

Phase 1: Symptom reduction and stabilization

Overcoming the phobia of therapy
Overcoming the phobia of attachment and attachment loss, particularly with the therapist
Overcoming the phobia of mental actions (i.e. inner experiences such as feelings, thoughts, sensations, wishes, fantasies)
Overcoming the phobia of dissociative parts of the personality (ANP and EP)

Phase 2: Treatment of traumatic memories

Overcoming attachment phobias related to the perpetrator(s)
Overcoming attachment phobias in EPs related to the therapist
Overcoming the phobia of traumatic memories

Phase 3: Personality integration and rehabiliation

Overcoming the phobia of normal life
Overcoming the phobia of healthy risk-taking and change
Overcoming the phobia of the body
Overcoming the phobia of intimacy, including sexuality

---

skills alone generally do not lead to complete integration of the personality when the treatment of traumatic memories remains overlooked, and when dissociation is not addressed.

We refer the reader to the clinical literature for further discussions of standard of care treatment (Chu, 2011; Courtois, 2010; ISSTD, 2011; Van der Hart *et al.*, 2006). Below we will briefly describe principles of treatment involved in overcoming the inner-directed phobias in the context of dissociation of the personality.

Phase 1: safety, stabilization, symptom reduction, and skills training

In this (often) lengthy phase of treatment, the therapist helps the client begin to address several major phobias: phobia of attachment and attachment loss, of mental actions (i.e. inner experiences), and of dissociative parts (see Table 15.1). There may be a need to return to this phase should the client become overwhelmed in later phases.

Overcoming phobia of attachment and attachment loss

Dissociative clients exhibit disorganized/disoriented patterns of attachment involving abrupt and confusing alternations between relational approach and avoidance (Liotti, 2006). Phobias of attachment and of attachment loss evoke different action systems (e.g. proximity seeking, attachment cry, flight, fight, freeze, submission), which can lead to the development of different dissociative parts of the personality. Dissociative parts displaying phobias of attachment and attachment loss form the core of multiple and contradictory transference phenomena (e.g. Kluft, 2000; Liotti, 2006; Ross, 1997; Van der Hart *et al.*, 2006), manifesting in the 'I hate you-don't leave me' conflict so common in individuals traumatized as children.

Relational interventions are first directed towards the 'adult' and most functional part(s) of the individual (ANPs) in order to strengthen daily life functioning and support skills for overcoming phobias. For example, the client as ANP can be encouraged to work collaboratively with the therapist in therapy, rather than be passive, and can learn skills to be assertive with the therapist (as well as others). She or he can be supported in acknowledging dependency yearnings while being helped to contain them via the predictability of the therapist and a boundaried therapy frame.

Overcoming phobia of trauma-related mental actions

Some of the most difficult work in therapy is helping clients recognize, accept, and personify the mental actions which they have strenuously avoided, consciously or unconsciously, i.e. emotions, thoughts, body sensations, fantasies, needs, and memories. These mental actions may be connected in some way to traumatic experiences. Sustained learning and practice of regulatory, mentalizing, and relational skills are usually necessary in Phase 1 to overcome phobias of mental actions (cf. Boon *et al.*, 2011). For example, clients can learn to identify the level of intensity of feelings and practice breathing and refocusing attention to regulate themselves. They can learn to step back and reflect on how they experience their emotions rather than just be in the emotions, to understand and empathize with dissociative parts and their functions, to understand that others may think or feel differently than they do, and learn assertiveness skills that support more healthy relationships.

Survivors need to accept their mental actions such as feelings and thoughts, without assigning value-judgements to them, and learn first to notice and accept, then prevent, shame, fear, or disgust in reaction. Clients are routinely encouraged to be aware of and explore their *present experience*, i.e. to be mindful, and to act reflectively in order to foster presentification.

Overcoming phobia of dissociative parts

The therapist begins treatment of the phobia of dissociative parts and their many manifestations with the most adult part(s) of the client, typically ANP(s). ANP(s) are first strengthened through the teaching of grounding in the present (Boon *et al.*, 2011; Kennerley, 1996), regulation, and reflective functioning skills, with the goal of improvement of daily functioning. When there is more than one ANP, the therapist supports some positive form of communication and cooperation among these parts, always with the goal of helping the client function in a more integrated fashion in the present. For example, the therapist can encourage a part that goes to work to help with problem solving and activities at home, to support an overwhelmed part that tries to function at home, and for the part that functions at home to remind the work part to engage in more self-care, so that there is more energy after work. Each part learns more empathy for the needs of other parts, and also how to engage in a wider range of adaptive feelings, thoughts, and behaviors.

The therapist firmly supports the responsible participation of clients in recognizing, accepting, and being responsible for the actions of various parts, particularly those that tend to be most avoided. In stepwise fashion, the client as ANP becomes consciously aware of other dissociative parts (EPs). As awareness develops, clients work first to diminish avoidant reactions to parts, orient them to the present, and develop understanding and empathy for their various roles. When a degree of empathy and communication is established, clients work to facilitate cooperation among parts in daily life functioning (ANPs), then between ANP(s) and EPs, which are also helped to become more oriented to the present, and *only then to integrate traumatic memories among parts*. Interventions to contain and delay sharing of traumatic memories are typically needed during this phase of treatment, for example assisting the client to construct imaginary vaults or boxes in which the traumatic memories can be placed for the time being (e.g. Van der Hart *et al.*, 2006).

Trauma survivors can become destabilized if both therapist and client (as ANP) are not aware of angry and perpetrator-imitating EPs and how these parts are involved in resistance to change. However, if consciously accessed, understood, and engaged in constructive ways, all EPs can be integrated.

When the integrative capacity of clients has been raised such that they are able to maintain a more stable awareness of ANP(s) and key EPs in the present, can tolerate, understand, and regulate mental actions, and experience a degree of internal empathy and cooperation, Phase 2 treatment is initiated.

Phase 2: integrating traumatic memories

This phase only begins when a considerable degree of stabilization, safety, capacity for mentalizing and reflection, and tolerance of arousal has been established, along with a cooperative therapeutic alliance. There must also be a degree of cooperation among dissociative parts. The therapist should be extremely cautious in initiating this phase in cases of current acute life crises or times when extra energy and focus is needed in normal life; extreme age, physical or terminal illness; psychosis; or severe characterological problems that interfere with the development of a boundaried and effective therapy; or uncontrolled switching among ANPs and EPs. Transient crises or the need to give full attention to other issues may temporarily reduce integrative ability and work can revert to Phase 1 for periods of time. The major phobia addressed in Phase 2 is that of traumatic memories. However, disorganized attachment to abusive and neglectful family members must also be addressed, since these unresolved relational experiences may affect relationships in the patient's current life, and manifest in negative transference toward the therapist.

Treatment of insecure attachment to the perpetrator

Various dissociative parts of the individual may simultaneously hold contra-dictory and strong feelings of hatred, love, loyalty, anger, shame, neediness, or terror toward parents or significant caregivers who were abusive (Steele *et al.*, 2005). The therapist must empathically explore *all* the client's conflicted feelings and beliefs related to perpetrators, evenhandedly respecting the feelings of all parts, and encouraging each part to understand the others, while simultaneously maintaining safety and reducing the risk of harm.

Overcoming phobia of traumatic memory

This is one of the most difficult phobias to overcome, requiring high and sustained integrative capacity. The intensity and duration of exposure must be matched to the patient's overall integrative capacity. Exposure, which involves *guided synthesis*, requires several steps to ensure full realization of traumatic memories in dissociative patients (Van der Hart *et al.*, 2006). It is not exposure to the traumatic memory *per se* that promotes integration, but rather a series of guided realizations when confronted with the memory that is integrative. Ideally, the therapist and client first plan collaboratively, deciding on a specific memory or group of memories to address, and whether all parts will participate, or only some. Other clients may be unable to know enough about a memory to make such decisions. Some clients have sufficient integrative capacity to tolerate sharing a traumatic memory throughout the entire personality at once. Other clients may need a more graduated approach with some parts participating, and others only at a later time when their integrative capacity is sufficient. These latter parts may be asked to 'sleep' or be in a 'safe place' where they cannot hear during the guided synthesis. The client should agree that no part should be 'forced' to participate or not (e.g. Van der Hart *et al.*, 2006). The therapist must be aware that the inability of some parts to tolerate a memory may signal a larger integrative deficit that might preclude work on traumatic memories, and should carefully assess this possibility before proceeding. In some clients, an observing or caring part is able to indicate which parts are not yet ready for the guided synthesis, or it can be decided between the client and therapist using their best judgement and under-standing of various parts.

Guided synthesis

This involves the sharing of traumatic memories that have been dissociated up until that time and are linked with specific EPs. In all cases, the therapist might direct the process of sharing the traumatic memory, or some dimension of it, punctuated by suggestions to temporarily stop for a moment, regulate, and be present in the moment. Contact with the therapist and the present should be maintained at all times during the synthesis.

Synthesis is the necessary beginning of a difficult and longer course of realization that involves accepting, owning, and adapting to what was and what is. This involves personification ('That happened to *me*;' 'These are *my* feelings and *my* actions') and presentification ('I am *here, now* and I am aware how my past affects me in the present and in my future expectations'). Realization continues throughout Phase 2 and long into Phase 3.

Phase 3: integration of the personality and rehabilitation

Though begun early in Phase 1, resolution of the phobia of healthy risk-taking and change becomes a more targeted focus of Phase 3. As clients make efforts to be more involved in present life, they increasingly experience conflict between the desire to change and intense fears of doing so. In fact, adaptive change in this phase of treatment requires some of the most difficult integrative work of painful grieving. Clients must grieve what has happened, what they have lost, and what they may never have. They need much support in learning to live a more 'normal' life, with an integrated personality, ongoing struggles to engage in the world in unfamiliar ways and new coping skills that demand a high integrative capacity. They must learn to take calculated and adaptive risks that have the chance of improving their lives, instead of always maintaining the status quo. For example, clients might take a risk to develop a new relationship, get out and engage in more activities, or go for a job interview to get a better job.

Seriously abused individuals often have a profound phobia of their bodies. Although the therapist supports more bodily awareness in the earlier phases of treatment, it is often only in Phase 3 that clients come to more comfortable acceptance of their body, its resources and limitations, as well as their sexuality. Phase 3 requires a return to the phobia of attachment and attachment loss in the form of developing new healthy relationships and risking intimacy. Clients who cannot successfully complete Phase 3 often continue to have difficulty with normal life, despite significant relief from traumatic intrusions. It is common for additional traumatic memories and dissociative parts to emerge in Phase 3 in response to a growing capacity to integrate. During such times, Phase 1 and Phase 2 issues need to be revisited.

Summary and Conclusion

This chapter presents a brief summary of the theory of dissociation of the personality. With emphasis on trauma-induced dissociation of the personality, the theory may help clinicians understand and treat the inner experiences of survivors with complex trauma-related disorders.

We have described how failure to integrate traumatic experiences affects personality and sense of self. PTSD resulting from single incidents typically involves an apparently normal part of the personality which enables the client to continue activities of daily life, while an emotional part of the personality enables the client to contain but also involves 're-living' of the trauma. 'Complex' PTSD, and other trauma-related disorders of the personality involve more than one emotional part of the personality. DID involves several apparently normal parts of the personality as well as several emotional parts of the personality.

We have described a number of clients' difficulties in terms of trauma-related phobias, which maintain dissociation and other symptoms. We have shown how treating these phobias in three phases involving stabilization, treatment of traumatic memories, and integration can offer the possibility for a more meaningful, stable, and adaptive life.

Using the language of Janet's psychology of action (e.g. Janet, 1919/25), TSDP provides a rational, progressive, and phase-oriented treatment approach to the many problems of complex traumatization.

Chapter 16

Dissociation

Perceptual control theory as an integrative framework for clinical interventions

Warren Mansell
Timothy A. Carey

Using Perceptual Control Theory (Powers, Clark, and McFarland, 1960a, b; Powers, 1973, 2005, 2008), this chapter focuses on the phenomena that are described under the umbrella of 'dissociation' and concentrates on defining when, how, and why, these phenomena would be significant problems.

It is widely accepted that dissociative experiences lie on a continuum with normal experiences (Ray, 1996). This chapter provides a framework for these normal processes, illuminating when they present as significant problems and how to treat them. We conclude that dissociation represents functional splits within the mind. These splits become a clinical problem when they disrupt the individual's capacity to realize important personal goals (e.g. to maintain a social identity, to form close relationships, to keep safe).

Therapy involves helping the person to become more aware of the dissociation process and to let go of rigid ways of controlling it (e.g. social withdrawal, self-criticism). Techniques from Method of Levels cognitive therapy (Carey, 2006) are designed for this purpose, as well as established techniques. Awareness allows more *flexible* control over dissociative experiences, so that the experiences and attempts to manage them no longer inhibit pursuit of important life goals.

What are the phenomena of dissociation that need explaining?

'Dissociation' is usually defined as an altered state of consciousness where one experiences full or partial disruption to the normal integration of experiences (Dell and O'Neil, 2009). This may be felt as separation of consciousness from one's feelings (emotional numbing), from one's body (depersonalization; out-of-body experiences), or from the environment (derealization). The first author of this chapter contributed to an article establishing that dissociative experiences can be discriminated as either *compartmentalization* or *detachment*, functionally distinct processes which can occur separately (Holmes *et al.*, 2005). Examples of compartmentalization are dissociative identities, functional amnesia and somatization. Examples of detachment are states of depersonalization and derealization. This chapter will claim that both compartmentalization and detachment reflect different processes in a control system account. We ask why these experiences might be problematic and seek to explain the 'clinical' features of dissociative disorders and disorders involving dissociative states, suggesting that they involve distress about the experiences and/or significant disruption to life goals.

Perceptual Control Theory (PCT)

Perceptual Control Theory (PCT) was developed by the medical physicist and control systems engineer, William T. Powers (Powers *et al.*, 1960a and b; Powers, 1973, 2005, 2008).The control theory framework has been applied to depression (Hyland, 1987), obsessive compulsive disorder (Pitman, 1987), addiction (Webb *et al.*, 2010), bipolar disorder (Mansell, 2010), and dissociative identity disorder (Johnson, 2009), as well as transdiagnostic processes (Carey, 2008; Mansell, 2005, 2012; Watkins, 2011) and used to develop highly accessible and flexible interventions (Carey, 2006; Carey *et al.*, 2009).

Propositions of PCT

Essentially, PCT continues to explain the functioning of living systems from the point where biological explanations of homeostasis leave off. A homeostatic system (Cannon, 1932) is a *negative feedback control system*. It controls a physical variable (e.g. body temperature, hormone levels, blood glucose levels) within a survivable range, generating outputs that act *against* disturbances that might change the variable. A *reference value* represents the optimal value of the variable. For example, when the glucose level in blood deviates from a safe range, the body acts to restore it to within the normal range. Eating sugary foods increases glucose concentration that requires offsetting by the release of insulin; starvation can decrease glucose concentration, needing offsetting by releasing stored sugar. This process of control occurs constantly in our bodies, mostly outside our awareness.

Human beings must engage in *behaviours* to maintain these systems. Thus, we seek out food, water, safety, and comfort. Homeostatic systems lead to the development of brains that can act to provide what the systems need to keep physical variables at reference values. In the newborn, brain systems involve crude ways of communicating that the homeostatic systems (from here they will be called 'intrinsic' systems) are out of balance. The growing child develops more complex brain systems that enable her to carry out behaviours to regulate reference variables and keep her intrinsic systems satisfied. For example, learning to co-ordinate limbs will eventually enable her to feed herself. Development involves processes of control that become increasingly sophisticated and flexible. This account fits broadly with our knowledge of neuroanatomy: intrinsic systems are located within the lower brain structures (e.g. the reticular formation); other structures (e.g. the thalamus, hippocampus, and amygdala) mediate between the intrinsic systems and 'higher level' control structures of the prefrontal and frontal lobes (Fogel, 2009).

PCT states that 'behaviour is the control of perception' (Powers, 1973). Just as intrinsic systems control physiological variables (e.g. body temperature, blood glucose levels) within optimal limits, behaviour controls perceptual variables within optimal limits, so that the intrinsic systems are satisfied. For example, when a baby is cold, the discrepancy between the current body temperature and the body temperature specified by an intrinsic reference value will be detected, and the baby will engage in whatever behaviours she can to remove this discrepancy. This could involve wriggling, crying, or even dressing, depending on her developmental stage. Although the behaviours can vary, the variable that is controlled (the 'controlled variable') – say body temperature of 37° Celsius – is the same. From a PCT perspective, control is primary, learning is a way to achieve control, and the brain systems involved are known as *perceptual control systems*. Learning allows the person to perform flexible, goal-directed action so that exactly the right behaviour occurs at just the right time. A range of empirical, quantitative studies of animals and humans supports this account (Pellis and Bell, 2011; Bourbon and Powers, 1999; Marken, 1986; Powers, 1978).

One major clinical implication of PCT is that learning during treatment and recovery is unlikely to depend upon learning a specific behaviour that is triggered by a particular situation. It involves an internal change leading to the capacity to be more flexible in the means and processes of control.

Three propositions of PCT upon which an explanation of dissociation will be based are summarized below:

1   A mechanistic understanding of 'control' provides the foundation of development. Control involves keeping a variable within a desired range, by reducing the *error* between a *reference value* (internal standard) and an *input signal* (current perception).
2   Humans are born with *intrinsic systems* that maintain survival via sensing critical internal experiences (such as body temperature). *Intrinsic error* is registered when these variables deviate from the intrinsic set points (or intrinsic reference values). For example, a sensed body temperature of 25° Celsius produces intrinsic error of 12 degrees from the set point of 37° Celsius.
3   Intrinsic error drives the development and change of *perceptual control systems*. These systems allow a baby to learn to control her perceptions of herself and the world to reduce intrinsic error. These perceptions are learned and include, for example, being able to identify people who are safe to be close to. Intrinsic systems use the perceptual control systems as their means of affecting the environment to minimize intrinsic error (see Figure 16.1).

The next section explains how perceptual control systems develop. These five propositions will be explained in more detail in the next section.

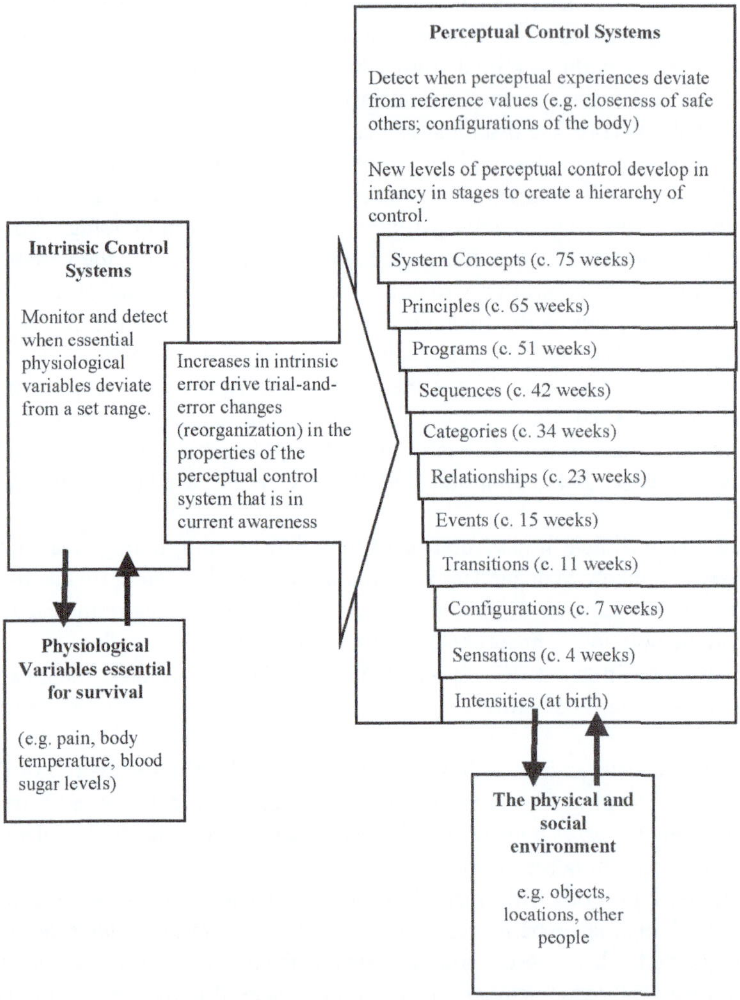

Perceptual Control Systems

Detect when perceptual experiences deviate from reference values (e.g. closeness of safe others; configurations of the body)

New levels of perceptual control develop in infancy in stages to create a hierarchy of control.

System Concepts (c. 75 weeks)

Principles (c. 65 weeks)

Programs (c. 51 weeks)

Sequences (c. 42 weeks)

Categories (c. 34 weeks)

Relationships (c. 23 weeks)

Events (c. 15 weeks)

Transitions (c. 11 weeks)

Configurations (c. 7 weeks)

Sensations (c. 4 weeks)

Intensities (at birth)

Intrinsic Control Systems

Monitor and detect when essential physiological variables deviate from a set range.

Increases in intrinsic error drive trial-and-error changes (reorganization) in the properties of the perceptual control system that is in current awareness

Physiological Variables essential for survival

(e.g. pain, body temperature, blood sugar levels)

The physical and social environment

e.g. objects, locations, other people

Figure 16.1 This diagram illustrates how the intrinsic systems detecting physiological changes in the body that are important to survival drive the development of increasingly sophisticated levels of perceptual control in the infant and child. This forms a hierarchy of perception of the self and others that reflects the adult's personality structure.

4   Perceptual control systems develop as a *hierarchy*. Their sequential growth can be observed as periods of regression and leaps during the first two years of life – infants show periods of increased distress (regression) that predict the acquisition of a new skill (leap). Within PCT, this leap is considered to be evidence of the arrival of a new perceptual level – the ability to perceive

more complex environmental variables – that permits increased interaction with the environment and improved control – e.g. recognition of patterns and sitting upright (holding the body in a specific arrangement) are seen to develop in tandem (Van den Riijt and Plooij, 2003).

5   The *reference values* of perceptual control systems are past perceptions that are stored in a distributed memory throughout the perceptual hierarchy.

6   A key skill a baby learns during development is how to reduce *conflict* between perceptual systems so that intrinsic needs are met.

7   Conflict is reduced by a learning process known as *reorganization* involving internal trial-and-error changes to perceptual control systems when intrinsic error increases.

8   This adaptive development occurs through interpersonal environments. These environments help the child to develop ways of regulating multiple conflicting goals. They promote development of a new system controlling a different class of perception at a deeper (more abstract or complex) level. This allows the child to regulate the conflicted systems. Helpful interpersonal environments involve: safety, containment, acceptance of a wide range of behaviours, limited attempts to control what the child is learning, and playful recognition that new ideas and behaviours, however unusual or odd, are part of life and the learning process. These environments contrast with those proposed to be linked with later dissociation, i.e. attempts by the caregiver to suppress, manipulate, or ignore the emotional needs of the child, often because they trigger memories of loss and trauma in the caregiver (Fearon and Mansell, 2001).

Development of hierarchies

According to PCT, perception is controlled. 'Perception' is formed from the way signals from our senses are transformed into further signals as they pass through our nervous system. The functional anatomy of the nervous system shows that there are two major branches to and from the senses (see also Powers, 1973) – an external branch detecting and controlling sensing of the outside world, and an internal branch detecting and controlling perceptions of internal bodily states. Phenomenological accounts show that people can control perceptions of the world – independently *of* the world – imagery, imagination, planning and inner speech. To understand how this wide range of experiences can be controlled, the PCT model has a hierarchical structure with a functional basis. While the idea of a hierarchy in psychology, psychiatry, and neuroscience is not new (Hughlings Jackson, 1882; Kortlandt, 1955; Selfridge, 1959), the structure of the perceptual hierarchy in PCT is unique, and expressed in functional terms.

Powers (1973, 1992) specified eleven levels of perception developing from conception, each new layer providing a new way of regulating the reference values of the level below. The primatologist Frans Plooij (1984) recorded developmental stages of infant chimpanzees and found that they progressed, after a period of regression where they were more distressed, through discrete skills stages. At each stage following the regression period they could control a new kind of perception. For example, newborn chimpanzees find their mother's nipple by ascending a gradient of warmth until they reach their 'target' and satisfy their need for food. At this age they cannot tolerate being removed from the nipple and become distressed if they are removed. At a later stage, they regulate their search for the mother's nipple as part of a larger set of controlled perceptions, as they explore their environment. The work that Plooij (1984) began has been elaborated around PCT and forms a framework for understanding developmental stages of human children: the development of a new 'skill' is the capacity to control a more sophisticated perception. Van den Riijt and Plooij (2003) explain how at around 11 weeks a child learns to perceive and control smooth transitions: they observed a reduction in the jerky movements of previous weeks and development of smoother coordination of limbs. Each new class of skill (a leap) is preceded by periods of regression (fussiness, distress) as the new level of control is initially trialed by the infant. There is increasing evidence from developmental research to support Plooij's account (Sadurni and Burriel, 2010).

Development of the perceptual hierarchy in PCT provides increasingly abstract levels, each new level being defined and grounded by the levels below. For example, one can pursue a *principle*, such as 'to be honest' through the way that one engages in a range of *programs*. The perception of honesty could be achieved by 'speaking true statements', 'being open with feelings', and 'sharing information'. It is proposed that the complex hierarchies we develop as adults are the personality structure of goals that we build in order to keep our intrinsic needs met in the long term. For most adults, these highest level goals, around self-identity and the kind of world we want to live in, end up transcending the intrinsic systems much of the time as people settle into supportive communities and a regular routine of activities. However, periodically, when intrinsic systems are challenged (e.g. a death in the family; a trauma), the personality structure will need to change to adapt and regain control. The process of change is known as *reorganization*, which will be covered later.

Memory and imagination in a perceptual hierarchy

Powers's (1973) work describes how *memory* involves a wide range of psychological processes that could be considered to be forms of 'dissociation'. Our suggestion is that these are helpful processes that allow people to fulfill their goals when they are controlled *flexibly*. But when they are used *rigidly* to serve one set of goals without regard to others, they indicate *conflict*. This stifles goal progress, and may mean that intrinsic needs are not met, the individual becomes increasingly compartmentalized and separate sections of their mental processes drift out of control.

Figure 16.2 illustrates how a hierarchy can be compartmentalized in a flexible and adaptive manner. There is evidence from social psychology that effective functioning in social contexts involves having multiple identities (Kessler and McRae, 1982); this is particularly effective when identities are 'integrated' with one another (Thoits, 1983). For example, people describe being a 'different person' when they are at work from when with their friends. Within a PCT model, an overarching level of control regulates different aspects of the self according to context. Although different 'selves' are compartmentalized for all of us, awareness and control of these social-selves ensures that 'vertical splits' in the hierarchy do not conflict. The different selves are adaptive, allowing individuals to achieve constant results in variable social environments. People are successful at work *and* when socializing because they have flexibility to alter their behaviour.

Powers (1973) describes how levels lower down the hierarchy can become disengaged from levels above to allow a person to control perceptions of themselves and the world 'as if' they are occurring right now. This explanation

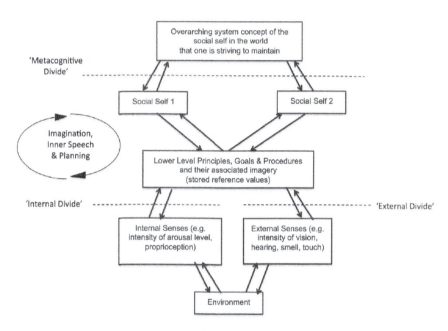

Figure 16.2 **Dissociation involving flexible, adaptive control.** Different compartmentalized social selves are used flexibly in different social contexts through the awareness provided by an overarching concept of the self in the world. Detachment is used to disengage effectively from current feelings and the current environment, when this facilitates imagination, problem-solving, and planning with respect to personal goals. Re-engagement with the internal and external environment in order to implement planned goals is controllable. Intrinsic needs generally remain fulfilled but, when environmental challenges create sudden changes, reorganization of this hierarchy will occur until control is regained.

is used to account for planning, rehearsing, imagining, day-dreaming, and so on. We propose that it is a form of detachment, that this time involves horizontal, rather than vertical, splitting of the hierarchy. For example, while driving we can visualize what we want to eat for dinner; a prisoner can imagine ways to escape or imagine life outside captivity; someone with social phobia can visualize the embarrassment of public speaking. Powers (1973) provides more detail but essentially this relies on taking memories from past experiences and using them as substitutes for the current experience. For example, being inspired by another person may work this way – we recall a person in our own lives, or in a fictional story, who reflects the principles we hold, and carry out acts that make us more like that person. Using this capacity, future goals can be planned through simulation of the real event. At a higher level, verbal thoughts can be substituted for more abstract goals (e.g. 'to be successful'; 'to be loyal'). When the individual is ready to implement their plan (a program in PCT), the higher levels re-engage the lower levels and action in the outside world proceeds – for example, we decide to keep a secret to be loyal to a friend. The brain's capacity to dissociate in this way produces a diversity of mental skills, allowing goals to be achieved more smoothly, and also disruptions to control are pre-empted and managed. We can plan all kinds of future actions in situations we are not currently experiencing, all at the same time as seeing through current goals. Thus, compartmentalization is a functional mechanism that may be essential and ubiquitous to the human psyche.

We propose that detachment can also be functional. A control hierarchy is a *latent* structure that operates outside awareness, just like the concept of a schema. The fact that complex goal structures of this kind operate outside awareness is now commonly accepted, following a wide range of experimental research (Bargh and Morsella, 2008). Nevertheless, at any one time, a proportion of these structures will be in the spotlight of awareness. We propose that when compartmentalization is affecting the content of current awareness, this phenomenological shift is felt as detachment. Essentially, compartmentalization represents the fact that mental structures are separated and may not be in awareness at the present time whereas detachment describes the phenomenological experience within current awareness. This can be explained using two examples – one where compartmentalization is present but not having an impact within current awareness, one where compartmentalization causes detachment. Many clients describe a 'side of themselves' that they hide from others or try to suppress. It may be a more fearful, vulnerable and critical side of themselves. When this compartmentalized side is not relevant to the situation – for example, no obvious threats are present – little effort is required to keep it outside awareness, and no detachment is experienced. In a threatening environment, this side is relevant to the goals of the situation and becomes activated. This may be experienced as feelings and thoughts intruding into awareness. The client may struggle to suppress these experiences, and consequently feel detachment such as emotional numbing or even an out-of-body experience. This example illustrates that detachment can emerge because of compartmentalized self-structures (e.g. different self-identities switching within awareness). Evidence suggests detachment can also be triggered by factors such as acute trauma (Putnam, 1985). Thus, detachment and compartmentalization are closely related but distinct processes.

Our model distinguishes between functional and dysfunctional features of detachment. For example, a new doctor tries to suppress feelings of horror at a serious injury, experiencing this as emotional numbing. If she also finds herself numbing her emotions in close relationships *and* she desperately wants a relationship, this will be a problem. Here it is not detachment *per se* that is problematic. The *conflict* with other life goals makes the detachment a problem. The conflict might be worse if the doctor regarded her emotional awareness as an indication of how affectionate she is – in therapy she might report her emotional numbing as indicating that she is 'cruel and heartless'. Using PCT we have explanations of the process itself and of why it might be a problem.

The development of loss of control in a compartmentalized mind

Figure 16.3 illustrates how a perceptual hierarchy can reach a dysfunctional state characterized by chronic separation of its parts, conflict between them, and ultimately loss of control of normal functioning. Figure 16.3 represents one extreme of a continuum, the other extreme is represented by Figure 16.2. Most individuals can be represented by a combination of both figures; therapy aims to transform processes in Figure 16.3 into those in Figure 16.2. In Figure 16.3, the individual experiences intrinsic error because basic biological needs have not been met. The focus is on short-term, rigid and/or extreme methods of control (known as arbitrary control; Mansell, 2005, 2012; Powers, 1973). This leads to actions that merely maintain or increase conflict. For example, blocking out emotions can increase a sense of control in the short term. But then emotional states cannot be used for functional reasons – such as signaling danger or prompting assertive action. The arbitrary control strategy is met by a rebound effect when goals depending upon emotion for their execution regain prominence. The doctor suppresses her emotions and can deal with horrific injuries but loses her ability to maintain close relationships. The key to recovery lies in developing and reorganizing systems regulating the conflicting selves.

Clinical implications

Here we describe how PCT can be used to understand dissociation in clinical practice, inform why existing therapeutic strategies work, and develop a novel approach to therapy for dissociation.

Case formulation

Here is a clinical example illustrating Figure 16.3. Marjorie, a 35-year-old woman, has received various diagnoses, including bipolar disorder, borderline

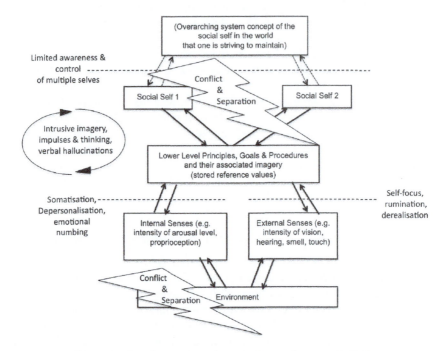

Figure 16.3 **Dissociation involving chronic loss of control.** Different compartmentalized social selves compete and conflict with little awareness, acceptance, or acknowledgement of one another or any overarching self concept. Detachment is implemented by one social self in an attempt to rigidly control the competing self, and the process is often felt as uncontrollable. Intrinsic needs generally remain unfulfilled, and attempts to reorganize this hierarchy are met by rigid and extreme attempts to prevent change. The person remains unable to regain control when challenged by sudden changes in the environment.

personality disorder, and schizoaffective disorder. She described at least two different 'social-selves'. Her 'anxious self' would withdraw from the world, ruminate, and criticize herself. In this mental state she was in touch with her feelings, kept safe, and 'real'. Yet the anxiety was often unbearable. Marjorie's 'tough self' would not experience negative emotions, and was strong. In this state she felt 'unreal' and often got into fights or psychotic or manic states. Both sides of the 'self' (involving vertical splits in the hierarchy) had developed to protect her (the overarching goal at the top of Figure 16.3), yet neither was sustainable. She was in conflict over which side of herself to present and oscillated uncontrollably between them. Each side was associated with a different 'horizontal splitting' (a form of detachment) of the hierarchy at any one time. The 'anxious self' was consumed by imagined scenarios and feelings and yet separated from the physical world. In contrast, the 'tough self' was engaged with the physical world but cut off from internal sensations and emotions. Owing to the extreme advantages *and* risks of each of the sides of herself, Marjorie found it hard to identify 'dissociative' processes that were helpful to her (e.g. imagination, planning as shown in Figure 16.2). The experience of dissociation was instead experienced as an uncontrollable threat.

Theoretical rationale

The principles of PCT have direct clinical implications. Since compartmentalization and detachment may be functional and adaptive processes, dissociation would not automatically be identified as the problem. A clinician practicing within a PCT framework is interested in the *distress* associated with the behaviours and symptoms the person describes rather than the behaviours and symptoms themselves. The focus is on identifying aspects of the individual's life that are not controlled as well as the individual would like them to be – essentially their important goals. The clinician explores the distress experienced: how long has the person been distressed, are they distressed more at some times than others, what reduces the distress, how does it manifest in their body, are there associated images and thoughts, etcetera.

The PCT clinician is alert to indications of conflict within the individual, such as struggling or fighting with themselves, feeling torn between alternatives, being in a dilemma, and feeling stuck. Systematic and specific questioning helps highlight the conflict and expand the individual's awareness so that they are able to appreciate both sides. An optimistic attitude underpins this clinical work through appreciation of the robust and constructive nature of reorganization. Reorganization is the mechanism that produces the changes in control systems necessary for the individual to feel less distressed and more in control. The individual does not need advice about how to behave differently but benefits from sensitive and curious questioning. Through in-depth questioning around both sides of the conflict and careful attention to thoughts occurring during the questioning, the clinician helps the individual's awareness move *from the distress* that is currently in focus to *higher-level systems* that are the source of distress. With sustained attention to higher-level systems, reorganization will occur and bring relief and a sense of contentment and satisfaction. PCT utilizes a therapy known as Method of Levels (MOL; Carey, 2006, 2008) to facilitate this process. MOL uses questioning (1) to help the client to keep talking and (2) to notice disruptions and present-moment processes as they emerge. Questions include enquiries about changes in affect, body language, eye movement, and those that redirect attention to processes such as fleeting thoughts, imagery, and conflict in goals. Examples of MOL are provided below.

Due to the trial-and-error nature of the reorganizing process the first solutions generated may not be the best. The individual may feel some things are worse than they were before. This is analogous to periods of regression experienced by infants prior to developing new control abilities (cf. Plooij, 1984). The therapist assists the distressed individual to continue exploring their conflict until they find a satisfactory solution.

Interventions

Because MOL uses the client's own frame of reference, we are not constrained by the assumptions or terminology of the therapist. In the following vignette we see how questions targeted at helping the client talk about their problems, noticing disruptions and exploring conflict can cover a wealth of approaches within traditional therapies. Look out for the following:

- appraisals of detachment experiences
- formulating different 'self-states'
- use of different cognitive and behavioural processes
- managing risky or out-of-control states

We have coded 'C' for client and 'T' for therapist, with each utterance numbered as C1, T1, C2, T2, etc.

C1:   *I numb myself to everything when I get stressed out – it's my only way of coping.*

T1:   *Tell me more about what 'numbing' yourself involves?*

C2:   *I switch off, cut off my feelings, my emotional pain – it is scary at times. It worries me!*

T2:   *Describing it like that, how does it sound to you?*

C3:   *Sounds desperate, not how I want to be. But what else can I do?*

T3:   *How do you want to be when you are stressed out?*

C4:   *Calm, but in touch with my feelings.*

T4:   *How does that sound?*

C5:   *[look of shock] Sounds like I would get walked over, manipulated by people. Can't see it working.*

T5:   *What happened there, when you said that?*

C6:   *I got a thought of what people would do to me if I was just calm – nasty.*

T6:   *You've told me about numbing yourself as one option and being calm but in touch with your feelings as another option. How are these looking right now?*

C7:   *Both look bad. Either I am cut off, tough, lose a sense of who I am and drink to keep it going, or I keep in touch with my feelings but get abused by people. I can't win.*

T7:   *What is it about being in touch with feelings and getting abused?*

C8:   *What do you mean?*

T8:   *Does one follow the other, do they happen at the same time, or what?*

C9:   *Never really thought of that. They seem the same thing – if I open up to my feelings I open myself up to other people.*

T9:   *How does that sound?*

C10: *Doesn't sound quite true actually. Mmmm…*

T10: *What's with the 'Mmmm'?*

C11: *I thought when I open up here and show my feelings – just some of them – you don't take advantage.*

T11: *How does that work?*

C12: *Well, I feel in control of what I open up to, and I know that I can numb them out if I want, but I don't.*

T12: *Right. What is it about control that's important?*

C13: *That's all I want really – to feel in control – especially when I am stressed out. I don't feel in control when I numb myself out – things can get a lot worse in that state. I need another way to be in control with people who might harm me, some way to be less vulnerable [smiles].*

T13: *What's making you smile?*

C14: *Ah, oh, I just saw myself working as a caterer, years ago, before things got bad. I was in control then, but I could tell people how I felt. I got respect.*

T14: *How clear is this picture?*

C15: *I see this time when I dealt with a nasty customer. I'm really animated. The image is clear until I get angry then it seems to fade. I did get my way with him but I can't remember how.*

T15: *What are you thinking now as you have this image?*

C16: *That there's another way of being, of dealing with stress, by being in touch with how I feel. Don't want to be a really angry person – that would make me as bad as them.*

T16: *How angry do you think is about right?*

C17: *That's an odd question. Is there a right amount of anger? I had never really thought there was. Do you mind if I think about that?*

T17: *Are you OK there if we leave it there for today then?*

Here, the therapist is helping the client to talk about her problem and tracking any disruptions that are linked to her current experiences – often involving themes of conflict. Traditional therapies might explain parts of this session in various ways. A cognitive approach might emphasize exploring appraisals of dissociated states. A cognitive analytic approach might regard this session as formulating different self-states. A metacognitive processes approach might identify the regulation of worry, emotion suppression, and alcohol use. We might prioritize risk assessment and developing better coping strategies. In the vignette, a new strategy becomes apparent in C12 – bringing a memory of coping in a different way to mind. This could be construed as an imagery restructuring procedure – familiar to schema therapists. Interventions designed directly for dissociation, such as 'grounding' using a physical object, may help the client to maintain control when emotions and thoughts seem out of control. While we do not use such techniques in MOL, their utility might be explained by PCT.

For Marjorie, therapy involved monitoring her thoughts, feelings, behaviours, memories, and social contexts with which they could be identified. Basic formulations were developed of the kinds of actions that would bring a specific social self into awareness. For example, emotion suppression tended to enhance the 'tough self' whereas worry tended to encourage the 'anxious self'. The therapist was curious as to the perceived goals of each self in current awareness, and how they related to overarching goals. Marjorie became increasingly able to articulate her own needs and her values for living, and consider how to achieve them.

The questioning was guided by the assumption that the process Marjorie described could be part of a helpful way of relating to the self and the world (as in Figure 16.2). For example, mental imagery was used as a way of problem-solving imagined scenarios, so they became less frightening. Emotions were discussed as potential signals for action rather than threats to be suppressed. The therapist would enquire as to the usefulness of these strategies in achieving Marjorie's overarching goals to feel safe and feel connected to other people.

The clinician needs to be alert to any preconceived ideas they might have about the nature of the ideal solution. Solutions can be unexpected and even seem mundane. The individual's experience is the crucial test; small shifts in perspective can bring about big changes in outlook and attitude. Standardized questionnaires, for example, are not always sensitive to changes experienced through subtle cognitive realignments. For example, Marjorie suddenly said, 'You know, my tough self and anxious self don't need to be fighting. Maybe they've both got something to offer.' This seems obvious, and tempting to suggest to Marjorie, but until she has reorganized her way to this insight, it will not make sense to her. Afterwards, she might wonder why she didn't think of it ages ago. People achieve insights, realizations, and epiphanies in their own time. According to PCT, attempts to steer this process through suggestions and strategies may distract and slow down the reorganizing processes.

Conclusions

We provided an account of dissociation, making 'control' central to whether dissociative processes are helpful or problematic. The perceptual control hierarchy is served by multi-layered memory stores, and serves basic biological needs. Chronic conflict within this hierarchy is the hallmark of 'disordered' dissociation. Clinical interventions facilitate the client's awareness of these dissociative processes alongside the wealth of experiences in their lives, and their deepest values – the 'higher-level systems'. Questioning using Method of Levels helps clients navigate awareness towards these life goals. Reorganization produces changes that make clients more adaptive – contrasting with inflexible strategies (e.g. chronic avoidance, suppression of emotions) that maintain distress. A future direction is to explain the perceptual changes during dissociation using PCT and to build working models to test this account.

Further Resources

If you want to use this approach and learn more about this therapy, the resources we would suggest are:

Carey, T. A. (2006). *Method of Levels: How to Do Psychotherapy without Getting in the Way.* Living Control Systems Publishing. Available at http://tinyurl.com/MethodOfLevels

Mansell, W., Carey, T. A. and Tai, S. J. (2012). *A Transdiagnostic CBT Using Method of Levels Therapy: Distinctive Features.* Routledge: Hove.

Mansell, W. & Hodson, S. (2009). Imagery and Memories of the Social Self in People with Bipolar Disorders: Empirical Evidence, Phenomenology, Theory and Therapy. In L. Stopa (ed), *Imagery and the Threatened Self: Perspectives on Mental Imagery and the Self in Cognitive Therapy.* London, UK: Routledge.

www.PCTWeb.org. This website provides and introduction and links to the research and applications of Perceptual Control Theory.

www.youtube.com/user/InsightCBT. This YouTube channel hosts an array of videos introducing and explaining Method of Levels.

Chapter 17

Dissociation from an acceptance-oriented standpoint

Fugen Neziroglu
Katharine Donnelly

We preface this chapter by addressing the paucity of research in the area. As dissociation is beginning to receive attention among mental health professionals, psychological treatments will emerge with more research. Acceptance-oriented approaches have generated new dialogue regarding treating dysfunctional behavior patterns. Research linking dissociation to acceptance is lacking, but a strong theoretical foundation indicates links between the phenomenon of dissociation, and acceptance-oriented treatment. This chapter elucidates the theoretical links and describes mindfulness and acceptance strategies for managing dissociation and depersonalization.

The phenomenon of dissociation according to acceptance-oriented approaches

According to the *Diagnostic and Statistical Manual of Mental Disorders* – Fourth Edition –Text Revision (DSM IV-TR, APA, 2000), dissociative disorders include depersonalization disorder (DPD), dissociative identity disorder (DID), dissociative amnesia, and dissociative fugue. Depersonalization disorder refers to unrelenting feelings of numbness or unreality; dissociative identity disorder to the presence of one or more 'alter egos'; dissociative amnesia involves inability to recall details of trauma; and dissociative fugue involves sudden disruption in personality and patterns of behavior; see DSM IV-TR (APA, 2000) for more detail. Dissociation is included in diagnostic criteria for other disorders, such as post traumatic stress disorder (PTSD). For the purposes of this chapter, 'dissociation' is defined as a psychological numbing reaction involving some disruption in a person's perception of the present moment, insight into this disruption varying across disorders. While those with depersonalization disorder may be acutely aware of this disturbance, those with dissociative identity disorder or dissociative fugue may be less aware of symptoms in the present moment. Current research suggests dissociation may arise after exposure to trauma, as an adaptive mechanism numbing the individual to the emotional intensity of the trauma. Because this automatic or involuntary reaction dulls experiential awareness of trauma, it follows that this is an adaptive or protective mechanism. Like most psychological symptoms, the average person will experience sub-clinical dissociation from time to time. We refer below to both clinical and sub-clinical manifestations of dissociation. Intervention strategies are aimed at those who meet criteria for a dissociative disorder.

ACT and experiential avoidance

Acceptance and commitment therapy (ACT; Hayes, Strosahl and Wilson, 1999) addresses qualities of the human experience that relate directly to the phenomenon of dissociation. ACT argues that the human brain has the natural tendency to avoid aversive experiences and pursue pleasurable ones. While this avoidance is useful for many environmental problems (e.g. removing a splinter from your hand) it may exacerbate emotional problems (e.g. distancing from aversive emotional experiences through dissociation). Though dissociation itself may be useful and protective in short-term/acute situations, it may become insidious over longer durations. Whether avoidance is deliberate (e.g. compulsive behavior) or automatic and uninvited (e.g. dissociation), the human brain seems hard-wired for experiential avoidance. Avoidance itself is natural and adaptive; avoidance of stimuli not posing legitimate threats to physical or emotional safety may serve to develop and maintain many psychological problems. Evolutionary psychological theories see maladaptive behaviors originating from behaviors that typically serve some adaptive function. Dissociation and related disorders (e.g. DPD and DID) fit this model, in that the ability to dissociate is necessary for survival. Qualitatively, dissociation is not pathological; quantitatively, it can be. ACT emphasizes the need to contact sources of avoidance and analyze behaviors according to their function or dysfunction for the individual. Acceptance of the discomfort that arises in this process is encouraged, as it relates to a mechanism that is necessary: dissociation is natural; we cannot simply get rid it.

ACT emphasizes the importance of contacting avoided internal content (thoughts, feelings, memories, etc.) while pursuing personal values. Avoidance of unpleasant internal content may represent an explanation for the phenomenon of dissociation. As an automatic reaction, dissociation may achieve emotional distance, allowing coping with intense feelings. ACT may offer a means of managing dissociation symptoms. Below we describe core processes of ACT relating to dissociation. We describe acceptance oriented strategies and exercises for managing dissociation.

Core processes of psychological dysfunction according to ACT

ACT sees psychological dysfunction as six core processes contributing to an overall orientation somewhere along the psychological flexibility-inflexibility continuum. *Psychological flexibility* is willingness to experience sensations, emotions and thoughts, and engage in varied activities, contributing to a rich life peppered by discomfort as a natural consequence of staying engaged in important life activities. The litmus test for psychological functioning is not how good an individual *feels* but how *willing* he/she is to endure both pleasant and unpleasant experiences. Assessment of functioning is determined by a person's behavior. Emotional urges may encourage actions that will not result in well-being (e.g. avoiding social situations due to feelings of depersonalization). Increasing psychological flexibility does not remove emotional urges but adjusts their dominance in guiding behavior choices. Six specific qualities (see below) contribute to an inflexible orientation. These patterns are 'part of the human condition', they are psychological traps that beset all people and are not exclusively associated with dissociation or psychopathology. When dysfunctional patterns dominate, significant difficulties may arise (e.g. functional impairment stemming from dissociation).

1. Cognitive fusion

Cognitive fusion is 'buying into' what the mind presents. Being 'fused' with a thought implies thought content is believed. Thoughts, descriptive or evaluative, vary in accuracy, relevance, and importance. Thoughts may guide towards productive or unproductive behaviors. When someone buys a thought, they act consistently with it. This is an important survival mechanism. For example, believing thoughts or perceptions and acting accordingly is important if someone hears a burglar. Here, *not reacting* is potentially devastating. However, believing thoughts can also guide people in the wrong direction emotionally. For example, believing the thought 'the party will be terrible' guides the person not to go. Thoughts generally do not reflect objective reality. Even if accurate, emotionally guided behavior may result in undesired outcomes and long-term dysfunction.

People with dissociative symptoms may experience thoughts about inability to tolerate or 'sit with' the symptoms themselves or events that triggered them. These thoughts may dominate behavior, producing avoidance of situations or events. With regard to depersonalization, deliberation on symptoms frequently produces fear that the symptoms mean something more serious (dementia, losing your mind, losing control, etc.). Cognitive fusion may be evident among individuals with dissociative symptoms: the mind, constantly alarmed by unusual perceptions, believes these perceptions require immediate attention. People may buy into the thought that feelings resulting from dissociation are important and need to be focused on in order to return to normal functioning. The individual becomes more vulnerable to becoming behaviorally inhibited when dissociative experiences arise.

2. Self as content

All people have the tendency to describe themselves in terms of thought patterns (e.g. 'I am obsessive'), feelings (e.g. 'I am depressed'), labels (e.g. 'I am depersonalized'), and evaluations (e.g. 'I am a good person'). Notice how all these sentiments include the verb 'am'. Labels lock us into roles: if you *are* dissociated, there is no way to feel or act in opposition to this label. It is hard to imagine that there is a distinction between the *self* and the activities of the brain. Evaluations, interpretations and feelings are inseparable from how an individual experiences the world. Yet, how can I *be* the content of my thoughts and feelings if they are so changeable?

Seeing the self as the content of one's thoughts often leads to inflexible patterns of behavior. If I identify with thoughts about myself, it is difficult to act contrary to them. If a person experiencing dissociation buys into the label of being disso-ciated, it becomes permissible to act in a dysfunctional manner (i.e. it is more of a challenge to try new behaviors when I already knows who I am and what limits me). This does not imply people with dissociation are malingering. Rather, behavioral therapeutic goals often guide individuals towards patterns of behavior that contradict the inclinations of the disorder. Establishing an attitude that under-mines the importance of beliefs about oneself can help.

3. Lacking experiential awareness or mindfulness

People with dissociation or depersonalization (or any persistent psychological distress) tend to be very focused on things that are not necessarily relevant to what's going on in front of them at this very moment. Psychological suffering is characterized by ruminative focus on psychological distress and excessive worry about events that have yet to transpire. *Lack of mindful awareness* involves rumination and/or obsession with distressing topics, and distractibility; both are relevant to dissociation.

An example of dissociation and *lack of mindful awareness* is driving from point A to point B, not remembering specific details of the journey. I may be consumed by distressing thoughts; I may be talking to someone in the car, or going over my grocery list. This example illustrates mild or common dissociation. People with DPD describe inability to 'tap into' the present moment; feeling as if present experiences are unreal. In DID or dissociative fugue, loss of time or acting without one's own consent may mimic this common dissociative experience. Dissociation may be behaviorally defined as lack of mindful awareness: one is engaging in internal dialogue rather than observing current experiences. Thinking back on the drive, I may be able to recall an idea my mind was absorbed with, neglecting the present moment. Pathological perceptual processing (dissociation) is associated with lack of mindful awareness. Practice of mindfulness or acceptance skills may override symptoms of dissociation as mindfulness and dissociation seem to be dichotomous.

Michal *et al.* (2007) investigated the relationship between mindfulness and depersonalization symptoms among members of the public and non-malignant pain patients. Results showed a significant inverse relationship between DP symptoms and mindfulness, so mindfulness and dissociation may represent competing psychological constructs. The authors suggest that mindfulness may facilitate sensitization to present moment experiences, often a target of treatment for dissociation. A practical application of mindfulness is described below.

4. Experiential avoidance

Experiential avoidance is anything that is done to avoid or escape unpleasant internal experiences (thoughts, feelings, sensations, etc.). Acceptance and commitment-therapy researchers emphasize the influence of experiential avoidance efforts in psychological dysfunction. This includes obvious avoidance (such as agoraphobia) or subtle avoidance (such as distracting oneself from thinking about something). Self-medicating using alcohol is an example of how experiential avoidance can become counterproductive: the immediate result is relief from discomfort, the long-term result is stagnancy, abuse or dependence. Ultimately, experiential avoidance perpetuates psychological dysfunction.

Dissociation can function as experiential avoidance, it may be experienced in place of extreme emotions. The trauma hypothesis of dissociation (e.g. Michal *et al.*, 2007) suggests dissociation after exposure to a traumatic event serves the purpose of avoiding intense unpleasant feelings and immediate emotionally guided decision making. *Peritraumatic dissociation* refers to dissociative symptoms experienced during a traumatic event (Gershuny, Cloitre and Otto, 2003). This is not considered pathological and is not associated with symptom severity among trauma survivors (Panasetis and Bryant, 2003), while chronic dissociation following trauma predicts symptom severity. Peritraumatic dissociation is an adaptive mechanism that allows deliberate action despite exposure to trauma, but a prolonged dissociative reaction may contribute to psychological dysfunction, rather than alleviate it. The emotional/experiential numbness of depersonalization may help distance intense unpleasant experiences. In DID, alter egos may allow individuals to survive trauma or abuse by providing an experiential forum for abuse memories, without threatening the pre-morbid identity.

If dissociation produces psychological distancing, it can be seen as an unintentional experiential avoidance mechanism. When people contact avoided internal content, the result may be a relaxing of the avoidance mechanism. Contacting avoided internal content is a common target for acceptance-oriented therapies, the behavioural rationale being that individuals habituate to discomfort after a prolonged exposure to the discomfort-eliciting stimulus, as in basic exposure and response prevention techniques.

The post traumatic stress disorder (PTSD) literature (e.g. Land, 2010; Marx and Sloan, 2004) increasingly shows the relationship between experiential avoidance and dysfunctional reactions to trauma. Dissociation is often associated with PTSD, symptoms including acute/episodic dissociative re-experiencing of trauma, or *flashbacks*. Those with PTSD may experience perceptual lapses, characterized by intense re-experiencing of emotionally evocative memories.

Flashbacks may themselves be considered dissociative, as they represent disruptions in normal perceptual integration. This deviates from the understanding of dissociation as serving a 'psychological defensive function', as flashbacks are certainly not protecting an individual from acute psychological distress (Van der Hart, Nijenhuis, Steele and Brown, 2004). However, flashbacks are dissociative according to the DSM IV-TR definition of dissociation as a 'disruption in the usually integrated functions of consciousness, memory, identity, or perception.' (APA, 2000). People with PTSD also commonly experience emotional or psychological 'numbing', similar to depersonalization or derealization. Due to this conceptual overlap and the shared symptoms of dissociation and trauma response, the role of experiential avoidance in PTSD will be elaborated briefly below.

Although flashbacks themselves are not considered experiential avoidance, experiential avoidance may follow: efforts may be made to banish traumatic memories (e.g. distraction) or avoid flashback triggers (e.g. not driving through an area where an assault occurred). Experiential avoidance may be related to severity of PTSD symptoms. Tull, Gratz, Salters and Roemer (2004) explored the influence of experiential avoidance and thought suppression on PTSD symptoms. Increased experiential avoidance was associated with depression, anxiety, and somatization; thought suppression (a variety of experiential avoidance) was correlated with posttraumatic symptom severity. Marx and Sloan (2004) and Plumb, Orsillo and Luterek (2004) also found increased experiential avoidance related to increased posttraumatic stress symptom severity. As all studies had correlational designs, it is unclear whether predisposition to experiential avoidance hinders recovery from trauma or if exposure to trauma causes increased experiential avoidance. Regardless, the role of experiential avoidance in PTSD symptoms implies an avenue for investigation into experiential avoidance as it relates to dissociation.

5. Lacking clarity of values

According to ACT, *values* are 'chosen life directions' (Hayes and Smith, 2005, p. 154). Values are *chosen* because they are conscious and deliberate, and are demonstrated through one's behavior; they are *life directions* because they help to guide behaviors. ACT refers to values clarification as 'setting the point on the compass' (Hayes and Smith, 2005, p. 155): through determining one's core values, one can set a direction and pursue it, accomplishing milestones along the way.

If I do not have a sense my values, certain difficulties may arise. Because discomfort and preoccupation with internal experiences tend to dominate the lives of people with dissociative experiences or DPD, they may lack clarity of values. It is easy to become fixated on the thoughts, feelings, and motivations that accompany dissociation or depersonalization, while awareness of what is *truly* meaningful to the individual may become obscured.

6. Narrow behavioral repertoire

Narrow behavioral repertoire refers to neglecting to allow one's values to guide one's behaviors. If I value creativity but do not pursue creative activities, I have a narrow behavioral repertoire. People with dissociation usually cite various reasons for not pursuing activities that are important to them because of discomfort in situations which inspire unpleasant emotional and perceptual experiences. When these sources of discomfort are allowed to guide behavior, the range of behaviors that an individual is willing to experience becomes narrowed, and stagnancy follows.

Acceptance-oriented strategies for treatment of dissociation

While ACT has not been empirically validated for use with dissociation, the techniques and exercises below may be beneficial, due to a theoretical overlap between dissociation and other disorders of experiential avoidance, which have been shown to respond to ACT. The six core dysfunctional processes previously described correspond to opposing functional processes, namely, *cognitive defusion, mindfulness, acceptance/willingness, self as context, clarity of values,* and *committed action.*

Cognitive defusion

ACT distinguishes between observing your thoughts (cognitive *de*fusion) and observing *from* your thoughts (cognitive fusion). The mind *fused* with thoughts sees no distinction between thoughts and reality, and runs rampant, making judgements, evaluations, and interpretations. Subsequent actions usually reflect fused beliefs. If I believe a thought is true, I will be likely to act according to what the mind is urging. When a thought occurs, and it is seen as 'just a thought' (just something the mind generates), I have more flexibility; I am free to choose how to act rather than blindly following emotional urges. The goal of cognitive *de*fusion is to provide a 'bit of breathing room' so that I may recognize and *experience* thoughts as just thoughts, with no necessary bearing on my environment or actions. The following exercise demonstrates cognitive *de*fusion, as a means to achieve control of behaviors without attempting to control internal events.

'Soldiers in a parade' meditation

This ACT exercise is intended to achieve 'cognitive breathing room,' allowing the mind to focus on whatever it will while you focus on the experience of thinking, rather than getting caught up in the specific content of thoughts (Hayes, Strosahl and Wilson, 1999). It involves observing each thought as it occurs, one after the other. The idea is to notice whenever there is a shift from looking *at* your thoughts to looking *from* your thoughts. You will be aware this has happened when you find that you are no longer engaged in the exercise but following some train of thought. Thought observation is relatively simple in explanation, but it is nearly impossible to maintain!

Imagine there are little soldiers marching out of your left ear and down in front of you in a parade. Imagine you are up on the reviewing stand, watching the parade go by. Each soldier carries a sign, and each of your thoughts is a phrase written on one of these signs. Some people have a hard time putting thoughts into words because they see thoughts as images. If that applies to you, put each image on a sign being carried by the soldiers. If you don't like the image of soldiers, use the image of leaves floating by in a stream. Pick the image that seems best for you.

Now here is your task: simply watch the parade go by without making it stop and without jumping down into it. Just let it flow. It is very unlikely that you can do this without interruption, which is the key part of the exercise. You will have the sense that the parade has stopped, that you have lost the point of the exercise, or that you are down in the parade instead of observing from the reviewing stand. When that happens, back up a few seconds to see if you can catch what you were doing right before the parade stopped. Then go ahead and put your thoughts on the signs again until the parade stops a second time, and so on. The main objective is to notice when the parade stops for any reason and to see if you can catch what happened right before it stopped.

The purpose of this exercise is not to keep the mind from 'wandering off' nor to change thought content, but merely to notice the behavior of the mind: what it thinks about, and what carries it away. With practice, individuals may be able to foster an 'observer' orientation towards thought content, empowering behavioral (as opposed to emotional) control. This may be especially important for people with dissociation, as experiential avoidance is a destructive coping mechanism and may be a function of dissociation. Bringing awareness to the pull of experiential avoidance facilitates deliberate action, providing an important leverage point in recovery.

Mindfulness

Mindfulness means being present to experiences while they are being experienced. As in the driving example, people experience mild dissociation when they 'mindlessly' complete activities or are lost in thought for some length of time. In chronic dissociation the ability to experience immediate awareness is the very mechanism that is impaired. Practice of mindfulness may be useful for treatment of dissociation.

Here is an example of a 'sitting meditation.' Participants are instructed to notice the sensations associated with one of the simpler human experiences: sitting and breathing in the moment. As with the former exercise, you are not expected to judge or criticize your response to the exercise, but merely notice the sensations associated with being still and breathing. Clinicians may use these instructions to guide people with dissociative symptoms, but it is worth noting that mindfulness practice is a universally useful method, which most people may benefit from.

Sitting meditation

Assume a comfortable position, and close your eyes. Let go of any thoughts or worries that might presently come to your awareness, and bring your attention to your breathing. Notice the sensation of air traveling into your nose or mouth. Notice the coolness of the air as it passes through these areas. Now feel the air travelling deeply into your lungs and abdomen. This is a vital behavior of the body, which is constantly working with or without deliberate awareness. Notice the benefit of breathing, notice that the only time that attention is ordinarily brought to this process is when some problem is occurring (i.e. shortness of breath, anxious breathing, etc.) But despite the absence of 'warning cues,' you are still able to tap into the sensation of breathing. Maintain your attention on the sensation of this experience. If you notice that your mind has wandered away from this task, just gently redirect your awareness back to the instruction to maintain mindful awareness of breathing. Some find it helpful to count their breaths from one to ten, and then repeat, as a means if staying present to the activity.

If practiced, this skill allows individuals to bring awareness of the 'here and now' thereby reinforcing a skill that tends to be a struggle for those with dissociative experiences.

Acceptance and willingness

The approach of engaging in life despite discomfort is not one that generally sits well with most people who live with chronic suffering. It may be important to consider the difference between *just* and *functional?* A common sentiment is, 'I shouldn't *have* to do it without feeling it; I shouldn't *have* to live this way; I just want it to go *away*!' As true as this is, it is not necessarily useful: whereas decisions made on principle always guide people in the right direction.

When someone is willing to engage in a range of experiences (even if they are experienced in a numb way, as for those experiencing depersonalization), increased opportunities are available. Suffering is a natural consequence of a rich existence (you are bound to encounter disappointment, self-consciousness, and rejection if you engage in the things that are meaningful to you).

Many people with dissociation are searching for ways to make feelings go away. But feeling good does not necessarily translate to psychological health. For example, giving a speech is something many would find intimidating: prior to getting up in front of an audience, everything in my body tells me to get out of the situation immediately (the fight or flight reaction). This response is generated by a primitive emotion-driven part of the brain, and deliberate thought allows human beings to override this urge. Deliberate thought helps me go through with the speech, despite discomfort. The deliberate response is often the more functional: completing speeches is a professional and academic obligation; while the mind and body might protest, awareness of values serves to circumvent emotional reactions. Essentially, acceptance is just that: willingness to experience discomfort as valued activities are pursued.

There are consequences to getting involved in important activities when one lives with dissociation. For someone with DPD, going to a party may produce feelings of disorientation and alienation, but the benefit may be meeting new people or sowing the seeds of a relationship. In order to move towards values areas in life, discomfort must be confronted, and *willingness* to experience discomfort reduces psychological suffering.

ACT suggests we see willingness as 'jumping'; it cannot be done timidly, and must be done in one motion (you cannot jump across a canyon in two steps). The aim is to come into contact with the feelings associated with a challenging activity, without avoidance. In working with dissociation, the purpose can be to come into contact with the feeling of numbness, feelings or thoughts related to traumatic events. Here is an exposure exercise for confronting trauma, emphasizing acceptance of thoughts and feelings.

Willingness to confront a traumatic event

1   Choose an event, noticing what the mind brings up when you consider exploring it: thoughts (e.g. 'I don't want to do this'), feelings (e.g. dread), urges (e.g. avoid this exercise). Bring to mind answers to: why are you willing to do this? What is valuable about confronting this event? On a scale of 1–10 take note of how anxious you feel at the outset, '1' indicating low anxiety, '10' indicating high anxiety.
2   Bring to mind details of the scene of the trauma. Sit safely in this imagery; notice that you can let go of the reins and make room for the thoughts without detriment. What do you see, hear and smell? What tactile sensations are you aware of? Just take in the scene, and again, notice you are capable of sitting with the discomfort. Notice that thoughts associated with trauma are simply mental events like any other activity of the mind.
3   Linger on one particular image. Choose something that you are willing to focus on. Not necessarily the most upsetting image; just something you are willing to fully experience in this moment. Stay with the feelings associated with this image, bringing to mind the value of confronting it. Note your anxiety on a scale of 1–10 at the end of the exercise.

Clinicians may carry this further if the participant is willing, incorporating events of the trauma in sequential order, targeting anxiety or shame-eliciting imagery. The purpose is to confront traumatic events and the feelings that originally inspired dissociation, with an accepting disposition.

Self as context

Self-as-context means conceptualizing the *self* as the 'point from which observations are made' rather than defined by the content of one's thoughts, feelings, experiences, labels, roles, etc. ACT asks participants: where or what is the you that is *you*? ACT provides this: the *self* is an unchanging observer remaining stable under the surface. This meditation may help people experiencing dissociation to move towards self as context.

Self as observer meditation

Bring your attention to your surroundings; take notice of what is around you and realize there is a distinction between what you are looking at and the 'you' that is looking. Try to feel the line that is drawn between 'you' and the world. Pay attention for a minute to the experience of observing. Now turn your attention to the objects that you are touching; feel the chair that is supporting you. Notice the distinction between these objects you are interacting with and the 'you' that experiences them. Notice for a minute the sensations of objects you are touching. Now notice your body. Your body is yours, but it is not 'you'. Notice that you can tap into cues from different parts of your body; 'you' are observing your body. Notice the distinction between your body that you feel and see, and the 'you' that is observing. For a minute, concentrate on what it feels like to feel your body; and any sensations that your body is informing you of.

Now turn your attention to your feelings and thoughts. You have much personal investment in these; they may have given you grief as you have tried to manage feelings of dissociation. Like cues from your body, thoughts and feelings inform you of things that may be important for you to know. Notice that also like your body, your thoughts and feelings are not 'you.' Notice that you can experience your thoughts and feelings, and notice the 'you' that is noticing. Turn your attention to firmly held ideas about who you are; traits you possess, roles you fulfill, the type of person you believe you are, etc. Notice you can feel like an 'honest' person, an 'isolated' person, or a 'worthless' person. Notice how you may be more or less invested in these labels at different moments. Sometimes you are a 'student'; sometimes you are a 'daughter'; sometimes you are an 'employee'. Notice how each of these roles is situation specific, the only constant here is something in you underlying the transience of thoughts, feelings, roles, self-concepts, scenery, etc. See if you can notice the distinction between what you believe about yourself and what the 'you' believes.

Finally notice the 'you' that is the point from where all of these observations are made. It is the only place that can truly be called 'here' or 'now'. It is your point of reference, and the only thing that has remained constant throughout your whole life; not the objects in your environment, not your body, not your thoughts or your feelings, not even your roles, or your strongly held beliefs about yourself. The only thing that stays with you through all of it is the 'here' or 'you' that is observing. Rather than the 'self' being the *content* of your experiences (environment, thoughts or feelings, sensations, beliefs, etc.), it is truer to say that 'you' are the *context* of your life, the context where all of this stuff plays out. Notice that the things that you've been struggling with and trying to change are not you anyway. See if you can let go a little bit, knowing you have been you through everything you have been through, and that you need not have such an investment in all this psychological content as a measure of your life.

Values clarification

ACT emphasizes shifting behavioral impetus from emotional impulse to deliberate or mindful reasoning. *Values* are the personalized important life areas that guide deliberate action. Common values identified by ACT theorists include: romantic relationships, children, other family members, friends, professional pursuits, creativity, health, spirituality, citizenship, etc. Participants in a values-clarification exercise are asked to determine the *importance* of each area on a scale of 1–10. They are asked to rate their *success* within each area. Discrepancies between importance and success help identify areas needing increased commitment. For example, I value my friends at '9,' but find I am unable to make time for them so rate my success '4'; an ACT therapist may help me evaluate what interferes with demonstrating commitment to this value. As in other psychological disorders dissociation often interferes with pursuit of one's values.

Committed action

Committed action refers to acting according to valued life areas. ACT clients are asked to let behaviors be guided by what is important to them. Dissociative clients may be emotionally urged to avoid situations or circumstances that evoke symptoms. For example, a person who values professional advancement and experiences depersonalization/derealization might avoid extreme sensations (such as heat, cold, light, loud noise, etc.) in order to avoid the dull intensity that is often experienced as a result. Should this person act according to emotional impulse, professional responsibilities might be abandoned as fleeting comfort is achieved. It is easy to see how this may limit a person's experiences, and decrease their quality of life. Committed action would involve pursuing activities in line with the value of professional advancement despite experiential discomfort. Committed action is a behavioral (observable) rather than attitudinal shift. In a clinical context, committed action may be achieved through increasing willingness to experience discomfort.

The research evidence for ACT

Although there is no body of evidence supporting ACT for dissociation, it is arguable that ACT techniques are most applicable to psychological problems associated with experiential avoidance, of which dissociation is one. An extensive body of literature explores the therapeutic benefit of ACT for disorders of experiential avoidance, including posttraumatic stress disorder, obsessive compulsive disorder, eating disorders, and substance abuse. This literature may contribute to a theoretical foundation for the use of ACT for treatment of dissociation, as similar psychological mechanisms may be implicated in other disorders of experiential avoidance.

Published case studies and research studies (Orsillo and Battan, 2005; Battan and Hayes, 2005; Ulmer *et al.*, 2006; Williams, 2006) have shown reductions in experiential avoidance and thought suppression in PTSD. Decreased thought suppression was associated with decreases in dissociative experiences among veterans (Ulmer *et al.*, 2006).

Experiential avoidance is associated with OCD symptom severity. Twohig *et al.*, (2010) explored the use of ACT compared to progressive relaxation training for treatment of OCD, with ACT producing better OCD outcomes, as well as reducing experiential avoidance. Experiential avoidance may also motivate substance abuse. Twohig, Shoenberger, and Hayes (2007) demonstrated the use of ACT for marijuana dependence and Hayes *et al.*, (2004) for polysubstance/methadone-maintained opiate addicts. These positive outcomes for the effectiveness of ACT in reducing experiential avoidance should encourage further investigation of ACT with dissociative presentations.

Recommendations for clinicians and researchers

ACT may offer a system for managing symptoms of dissociation. One purpose of this chapter was to provide a theoretical rationale for the applicability of acceptance oriented theory to the phenomenon of dissociation; accordingly, we hoped to provide an introduction to the use of ACT methods suited to this population. Interested readers may refer to *ACT Made Simple: An Easy to Read Primer on Acceptance and Commitment Therapy* (Harris and Hayes, 2009) or *Acceptance and Commitment Therapy: An Experiential Approach to Behavior Change* (Hayes, Strosahl, and Wilson, 1999). Those with symptoms of dissociation may benefit from the workbook, *Get Out of Your Mind and Get Into Your Life: The New Acceptance and Commitment Therapy* (Hayes and Smith, 2005) and from the techniques described in *Overcoming Depersonalization Disorder: A Mindfulness and Acceptance Guide to Conquering Feelings of Numbness and Feelings of Unreality* (Neziroglu and Donnelly, 2010). Future research must evaluate the efficacy of acceptance-oriented treatments for dissociation. Randomized controlled clinical trials must advance the theoretical foundation offered here. Empirical investigations must determine whether ACT will provide clinically significant improvements in dissociative presentations and how acceptanceoriented strategies compare to other viable treatment approaches.

Chapter 18

Summary and conclusions

Fiona C. Kennedy
Helen Kennerley
David Pearson

This book has aimed to bring cognitive perspectives to bear on the many seemingly disparate manifestations of dissociation: unconscious and conscious processes, hallucinations and intrusive imagery, somatoform, cognitive and affective symptoms and presentations involving disturbances in identity such as BPD and DID. In doing so a rich seam of previously unexploited material has been uncovered, with significant implications for clinical practice and future research.

We began the book with a brief overview of the development of the concept of dissociation since the sixteenth century. The story began with possession, travelled through hypnosis, animal magnetism and automatic writing, to hysteria and conversion symptoms. We saw Janet's marvellous and still relevant pioneering work, and how psychodynamic theorists such as Freud first embraced and then moved away from dissociation as a mechanism for repression of memories. The narrative comes up to date with the contributions from psychodynamic and structural theorists, along with DSM III and DSM IV categorizations of the dissociative disorders, their separation from somatoform disorders and the lack of mention of dissociation in other mental disorders, with the exception of BPD. As we await publication of DSM-5 we hope some of these gaps and inconsistencies will be addressed.

Kennedy's cognitive model of dissociation, which is based on an existing CBT model of personality and psychopathology, progresses our understanding of the disparate presentations of dissociation. The model incorporates many symptoms described in the dissociation literature, ranging from hallucinations and intrusive imagery, through somatoform, cognitive and affective symptoms to presentations involving disturbances in identity such as BPD and DID. Along with the WDS scale to assess the type of dissociation, Kennedy's chapter provides a relatively simple means to understand and formulate clinical presentations. The theory underlying the model is well researched, is consistent with what we know about the neuropsychology of dissociation and with other well-known models of PTSD and of personality problems. However, like all recent concepts the model itself and the measure still need further research and debate.

Childhood challenges are often seen as holding the key to future adult mental disorders. Pearson very usefully looked at how abuse and neglect skew normal development. The child without safety and security must somehow still progress through pre-programmed developmental stages. Abnormal and fragile developmental pathways produce an adult psyche built like a house of cards, vulnerable to collapse when the environmental wind blows. Phenomena which society sees as acceptable and appealing in young children (such as imaginary friends) are re-framed as mental disorder in adults. Not only individuals, but their social world, have an implicit understanding that increased capacities to self-regulate, reflect and distinguish reality from unreality are needed and expected from adults – the very capacities with which dissociation interferes.

In search of a definition of dissociation, many authors made use of the distinction between detachment and compartmentalization originally proposed by Holmes, Brown *et al.* (2005). It is an extremely helpful and clinically relevant distinction and one which has been explored very fully in this text. Kennerley and Kischka described neurological structures and processes which may mediate these basic processes. Detachment prevents encoding of information and compartmentalization seems to involve active inhibition of access to stored information. So there are two different routes to psychogenic amnesia, the fragmented memory phenomena outlined by Huntjens, Dorahy and Van Wees-Cieraad. Armed with this knowledge and some brain basics, the clinician can help the client understand their memory problems, working towards integration of compartmentalized memories and coming to terms with gaps in memory where detachment has prevented encoding. Of course, further clinical formulations of these processes are needed, along with research into what kinds of intervention are most effective, but we have compelling theoretical starting points. Research into the neurological correlates of these detachment and compartmentalization processes will help us develop a more accurate understanding of the complexities of dissociative processing of traumatic information which can only benefit our patients and inspire more research.

Alongside memory fragmentation, mental imagery plays a transdiagnostic role in maintaining dissociation. Stopa showed how imagery can occur in all sensory modalities and is closely associated with emotional responding. Intrusive and distressing imagery is a feature of many mental health problems including anxiety, PTSD, psychosis and depression. It is also associated with our sense of self. The clinician can assess for the presence of mental images, explain their relationship with distress and work with techniques to change imagery. Again, research is needed to investigate specific relationships between dissociative symptoms and imagery, but again we have seen that we have exciting theoretical foundations.

This book has aimed to offer a contemporary overview of dissociation and to demonstrate the relevance of dissociation to many mental health problems, including PTSD, eating disorders, psychosis, borderline personality disorder (BPD), somatoform disorders and depersonalization. PTSD is discussed in detail in the chapters by Kennerley and Kischka, and PTSD case examples can be found in many other chapters. Existing CBT models of PTSD mention dissociation as maintaining PTSD by preventing integration of traumatic material, but have not as yet been clear as to what 'dissociation' is or how it prevents integration. We hope the book has contributed to filling in some of this gap.

Eating disorders (EDs), in particular bulimia nervosa, often involve significant dissociation. Mountford explored the role and function of dissociation in the eating disorders and cited research showing that dissociation is indeed associated with EDs and is more severe among individuals with bulimic psychopathology. A new theoretical model shows how dissociation may occur in patients with EDs through somatoform disruptions and/or the need to escape from self-awareness. As the eating pathology develops, interactions between specific triggers, bulimic and restrictive behaviours and physiology (i.e. bingeing driven by restriction) occur. These behaviours are reinforced by subsequent reductions in emotional intensity: a fast reduction for binge/purge behaviours and a slow-acting mechanism in eating restriction. Clinicians are advised to ask about levels of dissociation before, during and after binge-eating and to encourage patients to monitor emotional states and levels of dissociation. Then formulations can incorporate dissociation along with ED behaviours. Kennerley and Kischka note that other emotional regulation behaviours such as self-harm or drug abuse are likely to be associated with dissociation and, once more, the clinician is advised to assess for this and to acknowledge the relevance in case conceptualizations and behaviours.

Long ago, Janet formulated hallucinations as intrusive trauma imagery, along with fantasies, nightmares and phobias relevant to traumatic experience. Cognitive understandings of psychosis have rarely taken this approach. In this book we have had the opportunity to really consider Janet's perspective in the twenty-first century. Newman-Taylor and Sambrook have integrated cognitive understandings of psychosis with those of dissociation and produced a chapter arguing that hallucinations are often dissociative in nature. The task for clinicians is to recognize early trauma, where this is relevant, name dissociative processes maintaining distressing voices, delusions and disorganized behaviour, and address these therapeutically.

Labelled early as 'hysteria' and later as 'conversion disorder', somatoform disorders, those mysterious and puzzling phenomena involving physical symptoms (convulsions, paralyzes, sensory disturbances, pain and gastrointestinal problems) for which no medical cause can be found, was explored by Richard Brown. His integrated cognitive model account of dissociation helps us break free from the notion that pathological dissociation is always a response to trauma or unregulated emotion, making use of the concept of compartmentalization. The model introduces the notion of 'rogue' schemata, with low trigger thresholds, responsible for somatoform (and other) dissociative symptoms. Brown shows how the clinician can help the client understand seemingly mysterious symptoms and formulate the role of dissociation in each case to allow effective selection of interventions.

Haaland and Landrø reviewed the literature on dissociation and borderline personality disorder, demonstrating that the role of dissociation in BPD deserves a great deal more attention. Increased levels of dissociation occur in around 75 per cent of those with BPD, and may be a marker for biological vulnerability to stress. Dissociation in BPD is associated with self-harming, suicidal behaviour, depression, anxiety, PTSD and alcohol abuse. Reduced executive functioning, lower IQ scores and memory impairments in people with BPD and dissociation suggest the need for careful clinical assessment. Emotional learning in patients with BPD has been found to be slower during dissociative states. Clinical interventions for BPD require information processing abilities, and often focus on reducing avoidance and relearning emotional reactions, so these findings have important clinical implications. Specific interventions for dissociation in the context of BPD may be needed. Further research might explore the relationship between neurobiological mechanisms underlying BPD and those underlying dissociation.

Elaine Hunter's chapter took us into the realm of dissociative disorders, examining depersonalization disorder (DPD) and presenting a CBT model of DPD. She illustrated how chronic derealization and depersonalization are found in so many mental health problems, including PTSD, depression, panic, OCD, hypochondriasis, dissociative disorders and all personality disorders. In the CBT model of DPD, the symptoms of DPD can be triggered by a range of affective and situational events. The central processes maintaining normally transient depersonalization/derealization experiences are the catastrophic appraisal of the meaning of the phenomena, and the causal attributions made. These produce a vicious cycle of heightened arousal and DPD symptoms. This understanding can inform our conceptualizations of DPD and begin to guide our interventions.

In a chapter-length case example, Cowdrill illustrates a CBT therapist's journey with a patient with DID, from the confusion as to how to conceptualize the case at the outset, to a shared formulation with the client and success in achieving control over high-risk behaviours. The chapter provides a map for therapists wishing themselves to embark on such a journey, but it also reminds us of the importance of keeping our formulations dynamic and being prepared to re-formulate as our understanding of the patient grows.

The high rates of co-morbidity between disorders classed in DSM IV-TR as dissociative and other disorders, including those in this book, leads us to hope that future classification systems such as DSM-V will highlight their co-occurrence. The separation of somatoform disorders from the dissociative disorders in classification systems de-emphasizes the essential dissociative nature of these disorders and is particularly unhelpful. Dissociation as a response to trauma, loss and neglect in childhood and adulthood seems key in the development of so many pathological presentations that it should surely be part of routine clinical assessment in every case. Existing correlational studies need complementing by longitudinal examinations of the dissociative patterns and processes affecting personality and identity development as well as vulnerability to different mental health problems.

The later chapters in this book are from authors with different but related perspectives on the psychological processes underlying dissociative phenomena.

Gilbert, from an evolutionary psychology point of view, discussed three types of affect regulation systems: threat focused self-protection systems, attachment/ affiliative systems and goal-driven achievement systems. Dissociation, he suggests, can be understood as an inability to regulate threat and over-activation of the threat-focused systems, producing seemingly unresolvable inner conflicts. Compassion-focused therapy can assist therapist and client to observe and describe the thoughts, emotions, physiological responses and memories associated with these conflicts and gently allow the client to 'switch on' their affiliative systems so as to relate to themselves and others in new, more balanced and compassionate ways.

Van der Hart and Steele's contribution describes an up-to date-version of the theory of structural dissociation of the personality, building on their many years of experience as theorists, clinicians and researchers in the field. They define personality integration as the organization of different aspects of the personality into a unified pattern of hierarchical systems of functions. There is a relatively cohesive personality organization or structure. Personality and sense of self are 'ongoing constructions' that are stable yet flexible and constantly revised. In a similar approach to Gilbert's, they stress how unresolvable conflicts between different basic survival systems such as attachment and self-defence can lead to a failure to integrate experience, producing breaking points in the personality structure. This dissociated personality structure can be used to theoretically explain difficulties in linking thoughts, memories and feelings, disturbances to the sense of self as well as confusion about the reality of the outside world. The dissociated structure may serve the function of keeping traumatic events outside of awareness and allowing the person to conduct a 'pseudo-normal' existence. Therapeutic intervention involves three phases: safety, stabilization, symptom reduction, and skills training; treatment of traumatic memories; and personality (re)integration and rehabilitation. This is conceptualized as a spiral where the clinician can alternate phases to suit the patient's needs. Overcoming fears of attachment and loss, of the traumatic memories themselves and of living a normal life are all part of the treatment of dissociative presentations from simple through complex PTSD to DID.

Using Perceptual Control Theory as a framework, Mansell and Carey describe a closely related approach. Development creates a perceptual control hierarchy, where the child learns more and more complex methods of regulating internal emotional states and interactions with the outside world. Flexibility and integration are key to the effective functioning of the adult. Dissociation of structures within the perceptual control hierarchy is normal and necessary: for example, we all have aspects of ourselves we use in some situations and not in others; we all need to switch off from the here and now in order to imagine, plan things or write concluding chapters. Dissociation becomes problematic when it interferes with the person's goals, for example emotional numbing prevents closeness or I am unable to access certain aspects of myself when I need to. The method of levels is the therapeutic approach derived from perceptual control theory and assists therapist and client to notice disruptions in consciousness and observe conflicts. In this way therapists form an observational collaboration with their clients similar to the alliance fostered in Gilbert's approach.

Last but not least, Neziroglu and Donnelly apply the acceptance and commitment therapy (ACT) approach to dissociation. ACT focuses on the problems caused by emotional (or experiential) avoidance. Whether avoidance is deliberate (e.g. compulsive behavior) or automatic and uninvited (e.g. dissociation), the human brain seems hard-wired for experiential avoidance. While avoidance itself is natural and adaptive; avoidance of stimuli which do not actually pose realistic threats is part of the development and maintenance of many psychological problems. Evolutionary psychological theories see maladaptive behaviors originating from behaviors that normally serve an adaptive function. Dissociation is one of these behaviours: the ability to dissociate is necessary for survival. ACT emphasizes the need to identify and formulate with the client sources of avoidance and to contact avoided internal content (thoughts, feelings, memories, etc.) while pursuing personal values. Acceptance of the discomfort that arises in this process is encouraged, as it relates to a mechanism that is necessary: dissociation is natural – we cannot simply get rid of it.

These latter theoretical chapters and the neurological chapters share a developmental and evolutionary perspective that places dissociation firmly among the mental processes human beings need to survive. In this way they help resolve the continuum vs category debate which we have visited in the book: there may be different types of dissociation (categories), but whatever the category, dissociation is natural; it only becomes a problem when it persists or is exaggerated, causing distress, maintaining mental health problems and preventing a person fully experiencing life and fulfilling their potential in the world. These chapters also bring a wealth of theory and knowledge to the cognitive understanding of dissociation which is a treasure trove for future investment in research and debate.

We are very grateful to all the contributors to this book for their enthusiasm and inspiration as we worked with them, and we hope that the ideas contained herein will sow seeds which will grow into a forest of knowledge in the future.

Glossary

Adrenaline also called epinephrine, a hormone released by the adrenal glands that prepares the body for action. It also plays a small role as a neurotransmitter in the sympathetic nervous system and the brain.

Affiliative relationships relationships that involve belonging to a bigger group or system e.g. a family.

Alexithymia a personality trait in which the individual has difficulty in identifying, processing and describing emotions.

Amygdala also called amygdaloid nucleus. An almond-shaped mass of gray matter in the frontal part of the temporal lobe of the cerebrum. It is part of the limbic system and has strong connections with the hypothalamus, the hippocampus and the cingulate gyrus. The amygdala is involved in the processing and expression of emotions, especially anger and fear, and memory. It plays an important role in storing emotional memory and in motivation and emotional behaviour. In particular, the amygdala is implicated in the fear response: 'fight, flight, freeze'.

Analogue studies studies that attempt to replicate or simulate, under controlled conditions, a situation that occurs in real life.

Anterior cingulate cortex (ACC) the frontal part of the cingulate cortex, positioned in the medial portion of the frontal lobes. The ACC probably plays a central role in the processing of emotions and feelings.

Arbitrary control (particularly in Perceptual Control Theory (PCT)) – also known as 'inflexible control'. This concept was initially defined by Powers (1973) and refers to the attempt to control an experience without regard to, or awareness of, other systems that are controlling the same experience. In a clinical context, it typically involves engaging in a process (e.g. detaching from emotions, suppressing memories, expressing a 'side of oneself') that conflicts with capacity to achieve important personal goals (e.g. to grieve, to understand oneself, to be 'normal').

Autobiographical memory a form of explicit memory which is a fusion of general and specific recollections about the self. It holds our emotional history, facts which are personally relevant and personal beliefs, and is fundamental to our sense of self, memories of events or information about one's life.

Awareness the capacity to notice experiences. Reflection involves awareness, meta-cognition involves awareness, and keeping your car on the road involves awareness. Awareness can be of any time within our life experience. Events from long ago can appear in awareness just as we are preparing for an important meeting for example. Many symptoms of psychopathology seem to involve awareness. Rumination is the process of not being able to move awareness away from particular thoughts. Flashbacks occur when awareness returns to upsetting experiences from times past. Dissociation involves being only aware of a portion of our experiences (or self concept) without being aware of their connection to other experiences (or self concepts).

Basal ganglia a group of neurones deep within the forebrain, consisting of four parts: the striatum, pallidum, subthalamic nucleus and substantia nigra. The main function of the basal ganglia is their involvement in the regulation of movements.

Body image vulnerability difficulties in knowing one's own body image, often manifesting as internalization of the thin-ideal, increased body comparison attitudes and behaviours and/ or body dissatisfaction.

Bulimia nervosa a mental health problem characterized by subjective binge eating at times, followed by extreme compensatory behaviours such as eating too little, misusing laxatives, excessive exercise.

Catatonic behaviour a state of neurogenic (nervous-system generated) physical immobility or difficulty in initiating movement which is associated with a range of both psychiatric and medical disorders; the person may pose in an inflexible and rigid manner.

Categorical model the view that an experience or concept moves from one position to another in discrete steps or gradations without a smooth transition in between, so that there are different classes or categories e.g. normal vs. pathological or red vs. black.

Classical conditioning paired association of an unconditioned stimulus with a conditioned stimulus to produce a conditioned response. This was originally made famous by Pavlov who conditioned dogs' salivation response to a bell ringing. Because a bell was always rung when food was presented, the dogs' unconditioned response to food (salivation) became a conditioned response to the bell. Classical conditioning involves physiological systems.

Cognitive restructuring Beck's CBT technique of reviewing thoughts about a situation or self, with a view to evaluating and testing their validity. The ultimate goal is to generating more realistic thoughts, aiding the resolution of emotional difficulties and appropriate problem solving.

Co-morbidity a mental health problem occurring at the same time as another; this can lead to dual diagnosis, e.g. depression and anxiety.

Compartmentalization a form of dissociation in which there is a partial or even complete failure to control deliberately processes or actions that would normally be amenable to such control (e.g. dissociative amnesia, unexplained neurological symptoms characteristic of conversion disorder and somatoform dissociation).

Conflict the situation that arises when two incompatible responses are simultaneously stimulated. For example, wanting to speak one's mind but also wanting the approval of others; experiencing rage towards one's mother whilst also craving her love; aspects of personality (self-states, e.g. angry self vs. loving self) and evolved psychobiological systems (e.g. for self-preservation vs. attachment) can also be in conflict.

Consciousness see awareness

Continuum model the view that an experience or concept gradually moves from one position to another in a smooth transition e.g. from every-day through odd to pathological or from cold through warm to hot.

Control (particularly in Perceptual Control Theory (PCT)) – a natural phenomenon in which variables are maintained in certain states despite conditions and circumstances that would otherwise change the variable's current state. Maintaining a car's speed at 50 mph, maintaining body temperature at 37 degrees Celsius, and maintaining warmth and affection in a relationship are all control processes.

Controlled variable some changeable aspect of the environment that is prevented from changing. Length of hair is a controlled variable for some people and appointments are made at hair salons to help control this variable. Television volume can be another controlled variable that might be reduced when the ads come on and increased when someone else in the room starts talking on the phone. Scientific experiments attempt to control variables by holding conditions steady or by having comparison (control) groups where only one variable changes.

Control groups an experimental device used to control for unwanted variation which might confuse the picture. Often groups of people are matched for age, gender and other relevant variables, and only one group undergoes the true experiment (e.g. one group receives medication, the other a placebo). The experimental effect is the difference between the two groups.

Correlation links statistically one variable (event, measure etc.), to another and indicates the strength of that relationship. Does not imply a causal connection between the two variables, although one may exist. The price of lamb may rise at the same rate as the number of red cars sold – these are *not* related but show high correlation. The temperature of water rises the longer it stays on the heat from a cooker – these two *are* related and the rise in temperature is caused by the heat of the cooker.

Cortisol a steroid hormone released by the adrenal gland under stress. It is involved in the metabolism of glucose, proteins and fat, the regulation of blood pressure, and the immune system.

Critical periods a set time in development when a skill has to be acquired or a psychological process has to happen to prevent permanent damage or dysfunction. For example, infants who do not practice a particular sound during their 'babble phase' are not later able to reproduce that sound or distinguish similar sounds. See also 'sensitive period'.

Delusions beliefs held with strong conviction despite good evidence to the contrary.

Detachment a form of dissociation characterized by the subjective experience of an altered state of consciousness. May prevent encoding of information.

Dialectical Behaviour Therapy (DBT) developed by Marsha Linehan for suicidal individuals with borderline personality disorder (BPD), DBT has been adapted as a treatment for multiple problems and emotional dysregulation difficulties. The standard treatment modalities include individual therapy, skills training, phone consultation and team supervision.

Diffusion tensor MRI (diffusion tensor imaging, DTI) a refinement of magnetic resonance imaging (MRI) that measures the flow of water and tracks the pathways of white matter in the brain thus allowing examination of the integrity of nerve fibre pathways.

Disorganized behaviour unusual behaviour where a person acts in a silly, irrelevant or childlike way which is hard for others to understand. It is assumed that this is due to disrupted thinking and emotional responses in psychiatric disorders. Disorganized behaviour can cause severe problems in the person's ability to function and maintain relationships in daily life.

Disorganized speech speech that is hard to understand and follow. It is assumed that this is due to loose cognitive associations, so that people jump from one idea to another even though the two ideas are not connected in any way that would be logical to others.

Dissociative amnesia a psychogenic inability to recall voluntarily aspects of an event. It is different from normal forgetting.

Disturbances (particularly in Perceptual Control Theory (PCT)) – conditions, events, and circumstances that could change a controlled variable independently of the actions of the controlling entity. Wind blowing across the highway would change a car's position if someone wasn't holding the steering wheel, and other people can be disturbances to an individual's goals – for example by assuming a person has a single identity when their goal is to maintain multiple identities.

DSM Diagnostic and Statistical Manual of Mental Disorders, a diagnostic manual commonly used in the mental health field. Several editions are quoted in this book.

Electromyogram a graph of the electrical activity of a muscle generated during muscle contraction. Small electrodes are placed on or in the skin. The recording process is called electromyography.

Emotional learning the acquisition and development of the skills and ability to recognize, understand and manage emotions

Empirical investigation an investigation that systematically gathers data and then bases its conclusions on the results; the foundation of evidenced based treatment.

Epidemiology the study of the distribution and patterns of health events, health characteristics and their correlates in well-defined populations.

Epigenetic processes by which modifications in gene function occur without a change in the sequence of the DNA. An epigenetic change may indirectly influence the expression of the gene.

Epinephrine see *Adrenaline*

Error (particularly in Perceptual Control Theory (PCT)) – the difference between the way something is and the way we desire it to be. If your appointment is for 3.15 pm and you're actually called in at 3.24 pm that's an error of 9 minutes (it's also an error of 9 minutes if you're called in at 3.06 pm!). Wanting piping hot soup and tasting a lukewarm broth will also register as an error.

Experimental error the inaccuracy found in the effort to experimentally measure the effect of a variable.

Experimental error the inaccuracy found in the effort to experimentally measure the effect of a variable. *Evolutionary psychology* – a branch of psychology that considers the effect of evolution on psychology and behaviour.

Externalizing (of experience) the perception that an event(s) is (are) beyond the control of the individual.

Failure to thrive when a child does not grow as expected, as measured on a growth chart. Failure to thrive can have an organic (e.g. disease) or non-organic (e.g. abuse) cause. In reality there is often a mixture of organic and non-organic causes e.g. food being withheld from a child by a care-giver.

Fight-or-flight reaction a response generated by a primitive emotion-driven part of the brain, when a human or animal responds to threat by either running away or defending its position. This response is both psychologically and biologically driven.

Flashbacks intrusive, vivid perceptions of emotionally evocative past events that have a feel of reality to them, often linked to past trauma. The experience can be so vivid that people say it's as if they are 're-living' it. All flashbacks are dissociative.

Flexible control (particularly in Perceptual Control Theory (PCT)) – the opposite of inflexible control. It involves controlling an experience whilst being aware of the potential impact on other experiences. Typically, flexible control is driven by higher-level goals in a hierarchy so that lower-level goals can be regulated to achieve long-term goals. For example, flexible control of detachment might involve noticing when it is beginning to occur and using it only when it might help one's work as a fire fighter, but not in close relationships.

Fragmentation reduced coherence and a lack of integration.

Fragmented memories memories that are incomplete or confused and which may lack a sense of reality.

Functional splits (particularly in Perceptual Control Theory (PCT)) – in a hierarchy of goals, 'horizontal splits' allow abstract thinking and planning to occur at higher levels while low-level action (e.g. walking, driving) is executed at lower levels. This is functional when used in a controlled manner, but can be dysfunctional; for example it may be involved in feelings of depersonalization and derealization. 'Vertical splits' involve having separate goals at the same level in a hierarchy. Normally the different goals are regulated smoothly by a higher-level system, but can cause conflict when they are not. For example having multiple 'social selves' facilitates flexible functioning when controlled, but can be distressing when uncontrolled.

Functional symptoms one of a number of terms used to describe physical symptoms for which no medical explanation can be found (also called hysterical, conversion and somatoform symptoms).

Glutamatergic system glutamate is the main excitatory neurotransmitter in the central nervous system. It is responsible for the fast synaptic transmission of information between different parts of the central nervous system (CNS).

Grounding technique a therapeutic tool used to help a client learn to stay 'in the present' and in touch with their environment. Used in situations where a person is detached from reality or prone to become so. Grounding techniques include the use of signals (finger click, hand clapping) to prompt the person to return to reality, and tactile, olfactory and other stimulation (using a squeeze ball, smelling lavender oil) to intensify sensory experience. Also routines where the person looks around and notices/names things around them, names the day of the week etc.

Habituation a situation where the nervous system stops responding to a stimulus due to the stimulus being repetitive. A common example is not noticing the ticking of a clock in your lounge unless it suddenly stops.

Hallucinations perceptions that occur in the absence of an external stimulus. Hallucinations can occur in any modality, and include visual, auditory, tactile, olfactory and gustatory experiences, with a compelling sense of their reality.

Hemispheres the left and right sides of the brain, which are networked together by the corpus callosum. The left hemisphere is the more 'verbal' and analytical one.

Hierarchy (particularly in Perceptual Control Theory (PCT)) – the proposed functional organization of networks of control systems and, therefore, our experiential world.

Hippocampus an area of cerebral cortex of the temporal lobe of the brain. It has the shape of a seahorse in cross section. It functions as part of the limbic system and is involved in the processing of emotions and memory.

Horizontal splitting see functional splitting.

Hot spot a term used to describe the most emotionally evocative traumatic part of a recollection of an event.

Hyperarousal becoming physiologically and emotionally aroused very quickly, and often to an unexpectedly high level, in response to an event or thought.

Hypoarousal becoming physiologically and emotionally aroused more slowly, and often to a lower level than would be expected, in response to an event or thought.

Hypothalamic-pituitary-adrenal (HPA) axis activation of the hypothalamus (e.g. by emotions such as fear) triggers a sequence of hormone releases that results in the secretion of cortisol into the bloodstream. The HPA axis is the complex of neural structures supporting this sequence.

Hysteria an early term for conversion or somatoform disorder.

Iatrogenic the idea that a symptom or disorder has been inadvertently produced by those trying to treat it, for example a patient may learn that dissociation is expected in certain conditions, or an inpatient ward environment may inadvertently reinforce violent behaviour.

Imagery re-scripting a cognitive technique aimed at changing unhelpful meanings of past events through manipulating the associated imagery content. The therapist coaches the person, helping to 're-script' the memory. It is not intended to deny the past but to generate new and more helpful understandings.

Implicit memory memories expressed by an automatic behavioural or physiological response. We do not necessarily have words to describe them and they often occur unconsciously: our ability to ride a bicycle (a procedural memory), an automatic physiological response to a trigger (a conditioned response), sensitization/habituation to a dripping tap (non-associative learning), the ease and speed with which we process familiar or anticipated information (priming). Implicit memory describes information processing which occurs outside awareness: recall does not require conscious awareness and it can sometimes take a person by surprise, for example when a conditioned physiological response seems to come out of the blue or a primed response kicks in without apparent warning. If we are fortunate, these are pleasant memories, but so often with our patients they are traumatic recollections which seem to be outside their control.

Input signal (particularly in Perceptual Control Theory (PCT)) – the signal that is controlled in a control system according to the value specified by the reference signal. If you want to see your son smile with delight when he opens his birthday present but he frowns instead, then frowning will be the signal coming into the control system where smiling is specified. And so an error will be generated and action taken to make the input signal – frown – be more like the reference signal – smile.

Integration the embedding of an event within the temporal context of immediate previous and subsequent autobiographical experiences.

Internalizing (experiences) the perception that an event(s) is (are) the responsibility of the individual with the perception that the event(s) could have been influenced by the individual.

Intrinsic error (particularly in Perceptual Control Theory (PCT)) – intrinsic control systems maintain critical variables for survival within an appropriate range. Examples include body temperature, pain and arousal. These systems would detect intrinsic error, for example, when body temperature deviates from 37 degrees Celsius.

Intrinsic systems (particularly in Perceptual Control Theory (PCT)) – see intrinsic error.

Invalidating environment an environment in which a child's or adult's experiences and communications are met with erratic, unpredictable or extreme responses, resulting in the invalidation of experience and subsequent confusion about sense of self, relationships, etc.

Latent structure (particularly in Perceptual Control Theory (PCT)) – cognitive structures or control systems that are not currently in awareness but nonetheless operate to manage one's experiences. Sometimes referred to as schemas.

Leap (particularly in Perceptual Control Theory (PCT)) – a term used to describe the arrival of a new level of perceptual complexity for the developing infant such that the infant now experiences the world in a new way.

Levels of perception (particularly in Perceptual Control Theory (PCT)) – it is proposed that different degrees of perceptual complexity are arranged in hierarchical levels to account for the experiential world we control. Perceptions at one level are comprised of perceptions from the level below. To perceive relationships such as 'on', 'under' and 'beside', for example, you must be able to perceive configurations or shapes.

Limbic system (areas) a group of brain areas that are thought to be involved in the experience and modulation of emotions. The anatomical definition has undergone changes over the recent decades, but most authors include the amygdala and the hypothalamus, with involvement of the orbitofrontal cortex and the anterior cingulate cortex.

Longitudinal data data that is collected over a length of time, e.g., data collected from individuals from childhood to adulthood or from pregnancy to delivery. Produces a body of data spanning a specific time period so that change over time can be explored. Contrasts with data comparing groups in a cross-section of time – e.g. from children compared with adults in 1994.

Mediates/mediator/mediating variable a mediating variable is a necessary (but not necessarily sufficient) variable which affects the relationship between two other variables, for example, dissociation mediates the statistical relationship between trauma and abuse.

Medically unexplained symptoms symptoms for which no medical explanation can be found, which include somatoform disorders.

Mental blanking being unable to think.

Mentalizing the ability to recognize our own and others' mental states. Includes being able to think about thoughts, emotions, wishes, desires, and needs in oneself and other people, and to see that these internal events may have an impact on the actions that are taken, but are separate from those actions.

Method of Levels a transdiagnostic cognitive therapy in which disruptions in awareness are identified and explored in order to shift a person's attention to higher-level attitudes, beliefs, and ideas. The source of the person's psychological distress is thus modified through reorganization of lower cognitive levels in line with higher level goals.

National Institute for Clinical Excellence (NICE) the body responsible for assessing and recommending to the UK government clinical treatments of all kinds.

Negative feedback control system (particularly in Perceptual Control Theory (PCT)) – a system that brings a sensed quantity closer to a specified quantity. Cruise control systems on cars are negative feedback control systems and so are household heating thermostats. The term 'negative' indicates that the difference between the two quantities are reduced.

Negative reinforcement a consequence of a response which results in the avoidance or escape from an aversive stimulus. For example, self harm can be negatively reinforced because it distracts a person from experiencing unbearable emotion or replaces that emotion with another.

Neurobiology the description of biological processes involved in brain activity.

Neuro-imaging the production of pictures of brain activity.

Neuroplasticity the innate ability of the nervous system to reorganize itself by changing existing neural connections or forming new connections. This occurs constantly through learning in healthy individuals, but also after injury to the brain.

Neuropsychology the description of psychological processes and abilities in relation to the brain areas involved.

Nocebo effect negative counterpart to the placebo effect, in which physical symptoms are reported following a sham medical procedure that is presented as having symptom-inducing properties.

Noradrenergic system a neuronal system responsible for the synthesis, storage, and release of the neurotransmitter norepinephrine.

Norepinephrine, also known as **noradrenaline** the primary neurotransmitter released by the sympathetic nervous system, existing in the central as well as the peripheral nervous systems. It has been associated with several brain functions, including sleep, memory, learning, and emotions.

Normal population hallucinations hallucinations that are experienced by people without mental health problems which are commonly quite simple e.g. hearing your name said when there is nobody there.

Normalizing changing a perception so that an experience can be understood as normal or expected for a given event or situations. For example, it is normal (expected) that you will feel cold and shiver if you go outside in winter without a coat. Being cold and shivering in that situation are not abnormal or pathological.

Olfactory pertaining to the sense of smell.

Operant conditioning the linking of a consequence to a behaviour in such a way as to influence the likelihood that the behaviour will re-occur. For example, relaxation from drinking a glass of wine results in drinking another. Getting a shock from an electric fence results in avoiding the fence in future.

Orbitofrontal cortex part of the pre-frontal cortex (PFC). The area of the cerebral cortex located at the base of the frontal lobes above the orbits (eye sockets). Involved especially in social and emotional behaviour including decision-making.

Organic damage physical damage to organic or biological structures or systems as opposed to psychological dysfunction.

Paranoia an unfounded or exaggerated distrust of others, sometimes reaching delusional intensity in which the person believes that others are intending to harm them.

Parasympathetic nervous system part of the vegetative (autonomous) nervous system, in charge of preparing the organism for rest by decreasing heart rate, respiration etc., using the neurotransmitter acetylcholine.

Parietal cortex one of the four lobes of the brain. Associated with sensory and spatial processing.

Passive-aggressive interpersonal behaviour where a person feeling hostile expresses themselves in a non-assertive fashion. Commonly the term reflects being aggressive in a covert manner: for example being stubborn or being manipulative.

Perception (particularly in Perceptual Control Theory (PCT)) – refers to experience or sensation. The sense of coolness from a summer breeze is a perception and so is the coolness from an offended colleague. The activity of living is a process of varying actions (including thought activity) to create and maintain desired perceptions.

Perceptual control systems (particularly in Perceptual Control Theory (PCT)) – functional arrangements within living things that are organized to maintain sensed conditions in specific states. Perceptual control systems are developed to control perceptions of the world in ways that meet one's fundamental needs.

Perceptual Control Theory (PCT) a rigorous and robust scientific theory of living things that was originated in the 1950s and 1960s by William T. Powers. PCT contends that living things control their experiences by varying their actions to produce specified perceptual experiences.

Peritraumatic occurring around the time of a trauma.

Peritraumatic dissociation alterations of perception during a traumatic event, e.g. time slowing, reduction in awareness of one's surroundings, out-of-body experiences, altered pain perception, emotional numbing, and experiencing the event as if unreal.

Phase orientated treatment an approach recommended for chronically traumatized individuals: phase 1 – stabilization, symptom reduction and skills training; phase 2 – treatment of traumatic memories; phase 3 – personality integration and rehabilitation.

Plasticity the ability of a neurological system to take over the function of another, e.g. following traumatic damage such as a stroke.

Positive reinforcement a consequence of a behaviour that strengthens the behaviour, e.g. enjoyment of eating a chip makes it more likely one will eat another. It is not necessary for a person to be aware of the connection between the behaviour and its reinforcing consequence.

Pragmatism using behaviour or thoughts that have a practical outcome. Doing what works.

Precuneus part of the parietal cortex.

Prefrontal cortex (PFC) part of the frontal cortex, located at the front of the brain. It is highly developed in humans and is associated with the regulation of complex cognitive, emotional, and behavioural functioning including executive functions.

Primary attentional system (particularly in the Integrative Cognitive Model of dissociation) – a putative cognitive system that generates a working model of the environment by combining sensory data with information in memory (i.e., primary representations).

Primary Representation (particularly in the Integrative Cognitive Model of dissociation) – a putative mental representation that serves as a working model of the environment and the basis of all experience and goal-directed behaviour.

Principle (particularly in Perceptual Control Theory (PCT)) – the level of perception that organizes programs of action to transcend the specific situation. For example, a principle of 'being honest' entails lower-level goals including saying what is on one's mind and suppressing the urge to lie.

Programs (particularly in Perceptual Control Theory (PCT)) – are a set of 'if... then...' contingencies that validate one's principles. For example, 'If I experience my mood dropping and I am in company, then I want to be alone'.

Psychogenic non-epileptic seizure (PNES) resembles an epileptic attack but is not accompanied by epileptic discharges in the brain and is thought to result from psychological (dissociative) processes.

Psychological dissociation dissociation in which there is a disruption in cognitive or emotional processes (e.g. absorption, amnesia, depersonalization, derealization).

Psychometric measures quantitative measures of psychological variables.

Psychosis a generic term for mental states in which thought and perception are severely impaired; psychotic experiences include delusions, hallucinations, and disorganized speech and behaviour.

Psychosomatic symptoms that appear organic but do not have an underlying organic cause.

Qualitative data non-number based information e.g. answers to the question 'what were the feelings you people had about [an event]?'.

Quantitative data number-based measures, e.g. how many people said they would help a person in distress; scores on a quantitative measure such as an IQ test.

Randomized controlled clinical trials (RCTs) clinical trials which fulfil two criteria: (i) randomly allocating participants to different treatment groups to avoid selection bias (ii) inclusion of a control group, a comparison group which is not receiving the active treatment in the clinical trial – these might be patients on a waiting list or patients receiving placebo treatment, for example.

Rebound effect the empirical finding, and clinical observation, that trying to suppress a thought leads it to come back into awareness, sometimes with greater intensity.

Reference value (particularly in Perceptual Control Theory (PCT)) – the value of a variable that specifies the state to which perceptions must be brought. The reference value can be thought of as a goal, standard, belief, value, attitude, dream, or desire.

Regression within developmental psychology, a period during which an infant (or adult) experiences a loss of skills, increased distress and a need for closeness, and regression to an earlier developmental state is evident. It may occur under extreme stress and also while learning a new skill.

Reorganization (particularly in Perceptual Control Theory (PCT)) – the most fundamental form of learning that does not, itself, need to be learned (as other learning strategies such as brainstorming or cost/benefit analyzes need to be learned). A trial-and-error process of altering aspects of control systems so that error associated with variables important to the survival of the creature is reduced.

Rogue representation a memory representation that is disproportionately active relative to incoming sensory information; regarded as the source of compartmentalization phenomena in the Integrative Cognitive Model of dissociation.

Rorschach test an assessment where a random ink blot pattern is shown to an individual to elicit their interpretation. The interpretations produced are analyzed to help understand the individual's thought processes.

Schema a cognitive framework that helps organize and interpret information. The term schema is used with subtle differences by different theorists.

Schizophrenia a diagnosis of mental disorder characterized by auditory hallucinations, paranoid or bizarre delusions, and disorganized speech and behaviour, and associated with significant social or occupational impairment. The diagnosis is controversial and its value in predicting aetiology and course of the disorder and effectiveness of treatments has been questioned.

Schizotypy a continuum of personality characteristics related to schizophrenia, ranging from odd cognitive and perceptual experiences to extreme states indicative of psychosis. The schizotypy continuum model is in contrast to a categorical view of psychosis in which people are assumed either to experience psychotic states or not.

Secondary attentional system (particularly in the Integrative Cognitive Model) – putative attentional system that controls novel behaviour and is associated with self-awareness.

Sensitive periods describes a time in development when it is important for a skill to be acquired or for a psychological process to happen at a set time. If the skill is not acquired or the process does not happen during this sensitive period there will be knock-on effects that can be difficult to deal with, for example difficulties in cognition, emotion regulation and appropriateness, behavioural self-control and relationships. See also 'critical period'.

Socratic method a method of enquiry which enables the gathering of information and the generating of new conclusions in a way which is neither directive nor didactic. In therapy the therapist does not lead, but facilitates and assumes that, with assistance, the client has the ability to solve their problems.

Somatoform dissociation the somatoform component of dissociation in which there is disruption to the normal integration of physiological, kinaesthetic and sensory processes. Symptoms may be positive (e.g. pain, loss of motor control, alteration of senses) or negative (e.g. anaesthesia).

Standard deviation in statistics and probability theory, standard deviation shows how much variation or 'dispersion' exists from the average (mean, or expected value) in a given population or set of data. A low standard deviation indicates that the data points tend to be very close to the mean, whereas high standard deviation indicates that the data points are spread out over a large range of values.

Sympathetic nervous system the part of the vegetative (autonomous) nervous system that is in charge of preparing the organism for activity by increasing heart rate, breathing etc, using the neurotransmitter noradrenaline.

Syndrome a group of symptoms that are indicative of a specific disorder.

Taxon a category or group, most often used in biological classification or taxonomy. In psychology, taxonomic analyzes can be used to identify subcategories of psychological constructs, such as the pathological dissociation category within the Dissociative Experiences Scale.

Transdiagnostic processes a cognitive or behavioural process that maintains distress and is shared across a range of psychological disorders. For example, people with anxiety disorders, dissociative disorders, psychosis or substance abuse disorders each tend to report engaging in worry and rumination, and individuals who do this more frequently and intensively report more distress several months later.

Type I trauma acute, unexpected, often single-incident trauma.

Type II trauma chronic and/or anticipated trauma, includes intra-family child abuse.

Vertical splitting see 'functional splitting'.

Voices a form of auditory hallucination involving the perception of people talking.

Wise Mind (particularly in dialectical behaviour therapy) – the first of seven skills taught in Mindfulness Practice. Wise Mind is a blending of 'emotional' mind and 'logical, reasonable mind' embedded within intuitive wisdom. The patient learns to access this state in order to make balanced decisions and act in line with values.

References

Ackner, B. (1954a). Depersonalization. I. Aetiology and phenomenology. *Journal of Mental Science, 100*, 838–57.

—(1954b). Depersonalization. II. Clinical syndromes. *Journal of Mental Science, 100*, 858–72.

Allen, J. G. (2001). *Traumatic relationships and serious mental disorders*. New York, NY: John Wiley and Sons.

—(2002). *Traumatic Relationships and Serious Mental Disorders*. Chichester: Wiley and Sons.

Allen, J. G., Console, D. A. and Lewis, L. (1999). Dissociative detachment and memory impairment: Reversible amnesia or encoding failure? *Comprehensive Psychiatry, 40*, 160–71.

Allen, J. G. and Coyne, L. (1995). Dissociation and vulnerability to psychotic experience: The Dissociative Experiences Scale and the MMPI-2. *Journal of Nervous and Mental Disease, 183*(10), 615–22.

Allen, J. G., Coyne, L. and Console, D. A. (1996). Dissociation contributes to anxiety and psychoticism on the Brief Symptom Inventory. *Journal of Nervous and Mental Disease, 184*, 639–41.

—(1997). Dissociative detachment relates to psychotic symptoms and personality decompensation. *Comprehensive Psychiatry, 38*, 327–34.

Allen, J. H., Fonagy, P., and Bateman, A. W. (2008). *Mentalizing in Clinical Practice*. Washington DC: American Psychiatric Association.

Allport, G. W. (1961). *Pattern and growth in personality*. New York: Holt, Rinehart and Winston.

American Psychiatric Association (2000). *DSM IV-TR – Diagnostic and Statistical Manual of Mental Disorder*. 4th edition, Text revision. Washington, DC: American Psychiatric Association.

American Psychological Association (1996). *Final report of the working group on investigation of memories of childhood abuse*. Washington, DC: American Psychological Association.

Anderson, M. C., Ochsner, K. N., Kuhl, B., Cooper, J., Robertson, E., Gabrieli, S. W., Glover, G. H. *et al.* (2004). Neural systems underlying the suppression of unwanted memories. *Science (New York, N.Y.), 303*(5655), 232–5.

Ansell, E. B., Sanislow, C. A., McGlashan, T. H. and Grilo, C. M. (2007). Psychosocial impairment and treatment utilization by patients with borderline personality disorder, other personality disorders, mood and anxiety disorders, and a healthy comparison group. *Comprehensive Psychiatry, 48*(4), 329–36.

Arntz, A. and Van Generen, H. (2009). *Schema therapy for borderline personality disorder*. Chichester: Wiley-Blackwell.

Arntz, A. and Weertman, A. (1999). Treatment of childhood memories: Theory and practice. *Behaviour Research and Therapy, 37*(8), 715–40.

Azam, A. (1876). Le dédoublement de la personnalité, suite de l'histoire de Félida X. *Revue Scientifique, IIième série*, 265–9.

Baddeley, A. (1996). *Your memory: a user's guide*. London: Prion.

Baer, R. A. (2003). Mindfulness training as a clinical intervention: A conceptual and empirical review. *Clinical Psychology Science and Practice, 10*, 125–43.

Baker, D., Hunter, E. C. M., Lawrence, E., Medford, N., Sierra, M., Lambert, M., Phillips, M. L., Senior, C. and David, A. S. (2003). Depersonalization disorder: Clinical features of 204 cases. *British Journal of Psychiatry, 182*, 428–33.

Baker, D., Hunter, E. C. M., Lawrence, E. and David, A. S. (2007). *Overcoming depersonalization and feelings of unreality: A self-help guide using cognitive behavioural techniques*. London: Robinson.

Ballard, C. G., Mohan, R. N. C. and Handy, S. (1992). Chronic depersonalization neurosis au Shorvon: A successful intervention. *British Journal of Psychiatry, 160*, 123–5.

Barach, P. M. (1991). Multiple personality disorder as an attachment disorder. *Dissociation: Progress in the Dissociative Disorders. 4*(3), 117–23.

Bargh, J. A. and Morsella, E. (2008). The Unconscious Mind. *Perspectives on Psychological Science, 3*, 73–9.

Barrett, T. R. and Etheridge, J. B. (1992). Verbal hallucinations in normals, I: People who hear 'voices'. *Applied Cognitive Psychology, 6*, 379–87.

Bartlett, F. (1932). *Remembering*. Cambridge: Cambridge University Press.

Bateson, D. C., Thompson, E. R., Seuferling, G., Whitney, H. and Strongman, J. A. (1999). Moral Hypocrisy: Appearing moral to oneself without being so. *Journal of Personality and Social Psychology, 77*, 525–37.

Battan, S. V. and Hayes, S. (2005). Acceptance and Commitment Therapy in the treatment of comorbid substance abuse and post traumatic stress disorder: A case study. *Clinical Case Studies, 4*(3), 246–62.

Battle, C. L., Shea, M. T., Johnson, D. M., Yen, S., Zlotnick, C., Zanarini, M. C. and Morey, L. C. (2004). Childhood maltreatment associated with adult personality disorders: findings from the Collaborative Longitudinal Personality Disorders Study. *Journal of Personality Disorders, 18*(2), 193–211.

Bazanis, E., Rogers, R. D., Dowson, J. H., Taylor, P., Meux, C., Staley, C. and Sahakian, B. J. (2002). Neurocognitive deficits in decision-making and planning of patients with DSM-III-R borderline personality disorder. *Psychological Medicine, 32*(8), 1395–405.

Beato, L., Cano, T. R. and Belmonte, A. (2003). Relationship of dissociative experiences to body shape concerns in eating disorders. *European Eating Disorders Review, 11*(1), 38–45.

Bebbington, P., Hurry, J., Tennant, C., Sturt, E. and Wing, J. K. (1981). Epidemiology of mental disorders in Camberwell. *Psychological Medicine, 11*, 561–79.

Bebbington, P., Marsden, L. and Brewin, C. R. (1997). The need for psychiatric treatment in the general population: The Camberwell needs for care survey. *Psychological Medicine, 27*, 821–34.

Bebbington, P., Bhugra, D., Brugha, T., Singleton, N., Farrell, M., Jenkins, R., Lewis, G. Meltzer, H. (2004). Psychosis, victimisation and childhood disadvantage. *British Journal of Psychiatry, 185*, 220–26.

Beck, A. T. (1996). Beyond belief: a theory of modes, personality and psychopathology. In P. M. Salkovskis (ed.), *Frontiers of cognitive therapy*, London: Guilford Press.

Beck, A. T. and Clark, D. A. (1997). An information processing model of anxiety: Automatic and strategic processes. *Behaviour and Research Therapy, 35* (1), 49–58.

Becker-Lausen, E., Sanders, B. and Chinsky, J. M. (1995). Mediation of abusive childhood experiences: Depression, dissociation and negative life outcomes. *American Journal of Orthopsychiatry, 65,* 560–73.

Bell, V., Oakley, D. A., Halligan, P. W. and Deeley, Q. (2011). Dissociation in hysteria and hypnosis: evidence from cognitive neuroscience. *Journal of Neurology, Neurosurgery and Psychiatry, 82*(3), 332–9.

Belsky, J. and Pluess, M. (2009). Beyond diathesis stress: Differential susceptibility to environmental influences. *Psychological Bulletin, 135,* 885–908.

Bendall, S., Jackson, H. J., Hulbert, C. A. and McGorry, P. D. (2007). Childhood trauma and psychotic disorders: A systematic, critical review of the evidence. *Schizophrenia Bulletin, 34*(3), 568–79.

Benner, D. G. and Joscelyne, B. (1984). Multiple personality as a borderline disorder. *The Journal of Nervous and Mental Disease, 172*(2), 98–104.

Benoit, J., Coolbear, J. and Crawford, A. (2008). Abuse, neglect and maltreatment of infants in M. M. Haith and J. B. Benson (eds) *Encyclopaedia of Infant and Early Childhood Development*, pp. 1–11. San Diego: Academic Press.

Bentall, R. P. (2003). Madness Explained: Psychosis and Human Nature. London: Penguin.

Berger, D., Saito, S., Ono, Y., Tezuka, I., Shirahase, J., Kuboki, T. *et al.* (1994). Dissociation and child abuse histories in an eating disorder cohort in Japan. *Acta Psychiatrica Scandinavica, 90*(4), 274–80.

Bernstein, E. M. and Putnam, F. W. (1986). Development, reliability, and validity of a dissociation scale. *Journal of Nervous and Mental Disease, 174,* 727–35.

Besiroglu, L., Akdeniz, A. N., Agargun, M. Y., Calka, O., Oxdemir, O. and Bilgili, S. G. (2009). Childhood traumatic experiences, dissociation and thought suppression in patients with 'psychosomatic' skin diseases. *Stress and Health, 25,* 121–5.

Bisson, J. I. (2007). Pharmacological treatment of post-traumatic stress disorder. *Advances in Psychiatric Treatment, 13*(2), 119–26.

Bjorklund, D. F. (1997). The role of immaturity in human development. *Psychological Bulletin, 122,* 153–69.

Bleuler, E. (1950). *Dementia Praecox or the Group of Schizophrenias.* Michigan: International University Press.

Blue, F. R. (1979). Use of directive therapy in the treatment of depersonalization neurosis. *Psychological Reports, 45,* 904–6.

Boddy, J., Skuse, D. and Andrews, B. (2000). The developmental sequelae of nonorganic failure to thrive. *Journal of Child Psychology and Psychiatry, 41*(8), 1003–14.

Bogels, S. M., Mulkens, S. and De Jong, P. J. (1997). Task concentration training and fear of blushing. *Clinical Psychology and Psychotherapy, 4*(4), 251–8.

Bohus, M., Haaf, B., Stiglmayr, C., Pohl, U., Boehme, R. and Linehan, M. (2000). Evaluation of inpatient Dialectical-Behavioral Therapy for Borderline Personality Disorder-A prospective study. *Behaviour Research and Therapy, 38*(9), 875–87.

Bohus, M., Schmahl, C. and Lieb, K. (2004). New developments in the neurobiology of borderline personality disorder. *Current Psychiatry Reports, 6*(1), 43–50.

Boon, S., Steele, K. and Van der Hart, O. (2011). *Coping with trauma-related dissociation: Skills training for patients and therapists.* New York and London: W. W. Norton and Co.

Bourbon, W. T. and Powers, W. T. (1999). Models and their worlds. *International Journal of Human-Computer Studies, 50*, 445–61.

Bowlby, J. (1969). *Attachment: Attachment and Loss, Vol. 1*. London: Hogarth Press.

—(1980). *Loss: Sadness and Depression. Attachment and Loss, Vol. 3*. London: Hogarth Press.

Bowman, E. S. (2006). Why conversion seizures should be classified as a dissociative disorder. *Psychiatric Clinics of North America, 29*, 185–211.

Braakmann, D., Knackstedt, F. and Schweiger, U. (submitted). Das Wessex Dissoziations-Inventar (WDI). Theoretische Entwicklung und psychometrische Charakteristika der deutschen Version. The Wessex Dissociation Scale (WDS). Theoretical development and psychometric characteristics of the German version. *Zeitschrift für Klinische Psychologie und Psychotherapie.*

Braakmann, D., Ludewig, S., Milde, J., Stiglmayr, C., Hüppe, M., Sipos, V. and Schweiger, U. (2007). Dissoziative Symptome im Verlauf der Behandlung der Borderline-Persönlichkeitsstörung [Dissociative Symptoms During Treatment of Borderline Personality Disorder]. *PPmP – Psychotherapie Psychosomatik Medizinische Psychologie, 57*, 154–60.

Braun, B. G. (1988). The BASK (behaviour, affect, sensation, knowledge) model of dissociation. *Dissociation, 1*, 4–15.

Bray-Haddock, D. (2001). *TheDissociative Identity Disorder Sourcebook.* Contemporary Books.

Bremner, J. D. (2010). Cognitive processes in dissociation: Comment on Giesbrecht *et al.* (2008). *Psychological Bulletin, 136*(1), 1–6.

Bremner, J. D., Krystal, J. H., Putnam, F. W., Southwick, S. M., Marmar, C., Charney, D. S. and Mazure, C. M. (1998). Measurement of dissociative states with the clinician–administered dissociative states scale (CADSS). *Journal of Traumatic Stress, 11*(1), 125–36.

Brewerton, T. D. (2007). Eating disorders, trauma, and comorbidity: Focus on PTSD. *Eating Disorders: The Journal of Treatment and Prevention, 15*(4), 285–304.

Brewin, C. R. (1996). Scientific status of recovered memories. *British Journal of Psychiatry, 169*, 131–4.

—(2001a). A cognitive neuroscience account of posttraumatic stress disorder and its treatment. *Behaviour Research and Therapy, 39*, 373–93.

—(2001b). Memory processes in post-traumatic stress disorder. *International Review of Psychiatry, 13*(3), 159–63.

—(2003). *Post-Traumatic Stress Disorder: Malady or Myth?* New Haven: Yale University Press.

—(2006). Understanding cognitive behaviour therapy: A retrieval competition account. *Behaviour Research and Therapy, 44*, 765–84.

—(2007). Autobiographical memory for trauma: Update on four controversies. *Memory, 15*, 227–48.

Brewin, C. R., Dalgleish, T. and Joseph, S. (1996). A dual representation theory of posttraumatic stress disorder. *Psychological Review, 103*, 670–86.

Brewin, C. R., Gregory, J. D., Lipton, M. and Burgess, N. (2010). Intrusive Images in Psychological Disorders: Characteristics, Neural Mechanisms, and Treatment Implications. *Psychological Review, 117*(1), 210–32.

Brewin, C. R. and Holmes, E. A. (2003). Psychological theories of posttraumatic stress disorder. *Clinical Psychology Review, 23*, 339–76.

Briere, J. and Armstrong, J. (2007). Psychological assessment of posttraumatic dissociation. In E. Vermetten, M. Dorahy and D. Spiegel (eds). *Traumatic dissociation: Neurobiology and treatment* (259–74). Arlington: American Psychiatric Publishing Inc.

Briere, J., Scott, C. and Weathers, F. (2005). Peritraumatic and persistent dissociation in the presumed etiology of PTSD. *American Journal of Psychiatry, 162*, 2295–301.

Briquet, P. (1859). *Traité Clinique et Thérapeutique de L'hystérie* (2 vols.). Paris: J.-P. Bailliére and Fils.

British Psychological Society (2001). *The Nature of Hypnosis*. BPS: Leicester.

Broadbent, D. E. (1977). Levels, hierarchies, and the locus of control. *Quarterly Journal of Experimental Psychology, 29*(2), 181–01.

Brodsky, B. S., Cloitre, M. and Dulit, R. A. (1995). Relationship of dissociation to self-mutilation and childhood abuse in borderline personality disorder. *American Journal of Psychiatry, 152*(12), 1788–92.

Brooks, R., Bryant, R. A., Silove, D. *et al.* (2009). The latent structure of the Peritraumatic Dissociative Experiences Questionnaire. *Journal of Traumatic Stress, 22*, 153–7.

Brown, D., Scheflin, A. W. and Hammond, C. D. (1998). *Memory, trauma treatment, and the law.* New York and London: W. W. Norton and Co.

Brown, L., Russell, J., Thornton, C. and Dunn, S. (1999). Dissociation, abuse and the eating disorders: Evidence from an Australian population. *Australian and New Zealand Journal of Psychiatry, 33*(4), 521–8.

Brown, R. J. (2002a). The cognitive psychology of dissociative states. *Cognitive Neuropsychiatry, 7*, 221–35.

—(2002b). Epilepsy, dissociation and nonepileptic seizures. In M. R. Trimble and B. Schmitz (eds), *The neuropsychiatry of epilepsy.* Cambridge: Cambridge University Press.

—(2004). Psychological mechanisms of medically unexplained symptoms: An integrative conceptual model. *Psychological Bulletin, 130*, 793–812.

—(2005). Dissociation and conversion in psychogenic illness. In M. Hallett, S. Fahn, J. Jankovic, A. E. Lang, C. R. Cloninger and S. C. Yudofsky (eds), *Psychogenic movement disorders: Psychobiology and treatment of a functional disorder* (131–43). Philadelphia: Lippincott, Williams and Wilkins.

—(2006a). Different types of 'dissociation' have different psychological mechanisms. *Journal of Trauma and Dissociation, 7*(4), 7–28.

—(2006b). Medically unexplained symptoms. In N. Tarrier (ed.), *Case Formulation in Cognitive Behaviour Therapy: The Treatment of Challenging and Complex Cases* (263–92). London: Brunner-Routledge.

Brown, R. J. and Oakley, D .A. (2004). An integrative cognitive theory of hypnosis and high hypnotizability. In M. Heap, R. J. Brown and D. A. Oakley (eds), *The Highly Hypnotizable Person: Theoretical, Experimental and Clinical Issues* (152–86). London: Brunner-Routledge.

Brown, R. J., Cardena, E., Nijenhuis, E., Sar, V. and Van der Hart, O. (2007). Should conversion disorder be reclassified as a dissociative disorder in DSM-V? *Psychosomatics, 48*, 369–78.

Brown, R. J. and Lewis-Fernández, R. (2011). Culture and conversion disorder: Implications for DSM-5. *Psychiatry, 74*, 187–207.

Bryant, R. A., Brooks, R., Silove, D., Creamer, M., O'Donnell, M. and McFarlane, A. C. (2011). Peritraumatic dissociation mediates the relationship between acute panic and chronic posttraumatic stress disorder. *Behaviour Research and Therapy, 49*, 346–51.

Bryant, R. A., Friedman, M. J., Spiegel, D., Ursano, R. and Strain, J. (2011). A review of acute stress disorder in DSM-5. *Depression and Anxiety, 28*, 802–17.

Bryant, R. A., Harvey, A. G., Dang, S. and Sackville, T. (1998). Assessing acute stress disorder: Psychometric properties of a structural clinical interview. *Psychological Assessment, 10*, 215–20.

Bulmash, E., Harkness, K. L., Stewart, J. G. and Bagby, R. M. (2009). Personality, stressful life events, and treatment response in major depression. *Journal of Consulting and Clinical Psychology, 77*, 1067–77.

Buss, D. M. (2003). *Evolutionary Psychology: The New Science of Mind. Second edition.* Boston: Allyn and Bacon.

Butler, L. D. (2006). Normative dissociation. *Psychiatric Clinics of North America, 29*, 45–62.

Butler, R. W., Mueser, K. T., Sprock, J. and Braff, D. L. (1996). Positive symptoms of psychosis in posttraumatic stress disorder. *Biological Psychiatry, 39*, 839–44.

Camuset, L. (1882). Un cas de dédoublement de la personnalité: Période amnésique d'une année chez un jeune home. *Annales Médico-Psychologiques, 40*, 75–86.

Cannon, W. (1932). *The Wisdom of the Body.* New York: W. W. Norton and Co.

Cardeña, E. (1994). The domain of dissociation. In S. J. Lynn and J. W. Rhue (eds), *Dissociation: Clinical and Theoretical Perspectives.* New York, NY: Guilford Press.

Cardeña, E. and Spiegel, D. (1993). Dissociative reactions to the San Francisco Bay Area earthquake of 1989. *American Journal of Psychiatry, 150*, 474–8.

Carey, T. A. (2006). *Method of Levels: How to Do Psychotherapy without Getting in the Way.* Living Control Systems Publishing.

—(2008). Perceptual control theory and the Method of Levels: Further contributions to a transdiagnostic perspective. *International Journal of Cognitive Therapy, 1*, 237–55.

Carey, T. A., Carey, M., Mullan, R. J., Spratt, C. G. and Spratt, M. B. (2009). Assessing the statistical and personal significance of the method of levels. *Behavioural and Cognitive Psychotherapy, 37*, 311–24.

Carlson, E. A., Yates, T. M. and Sroufe, L. A. (2010). Dissociation and the development of self. In. P. F. Dell and J. A. O'Neil (eds), *Dissociation and the Dissociative Disorders: DSM-V and Beyond* (39–53). London: Routledge.

Carlson, E. B. and Putnam, F. W. (1993). An update on the Dissociative Experiences Scale. *Dissociation: Progress in the Dissociative Disorders, 6* (1), 16–27.

Carter, C. S. (1998). Neuroendocrine perspectives on social attachment and love. *Psychoneuroendrinology, 23*, 779–818.

Carter, R. (2008). *Multiplicity: The New Science of Personality.* London: Little Brown.

Cassano, G. B., Petracca, A., Perugi, G., Toni, C., Tundo, A. and Roth, M. (1989). Derealization and panic attacks: evaluation on 150 patients with panic disorder/agoraphobia. *Comprehensive Psychiatry, 30*(1), 5–12.

Cassell, W. A. and Dubey, B. L. (2007). Restructuring Rorschach pathological body symbolism in the Somatoform Disorders with truth serum behaviour therapy. *Journal of Projective Psychology and Mental Health, 14*, 20–9.

Cassidy, J. and Mohr, J. J. (2001). Unsolvable fear, trauma, and psychopathology: Theory, research, and clinical considerations related to disorganized attachment across the life span. *Clinical Psychology: Science and Practice, 8*(3), 275–98.

Cattell, J. P. and Cattell, J. S. (1974). Depersonalization: Psychological and social perspectives. In S. Arieti (ed.), *American Handbook of Psychiatry* (767–99). New York: Basic Books.

Cavanna, A. E. and Trimble, M. R. (2006). The precuneus: a review of its functional anatomy and behavioural correlates. *Brain, 129*(3), 564–83.

Chadwick, P. D. J. (2006). Person-Based Cognitive Therapy for Distressing Psychosis. Chichester: Wiley.

Chaffin, M., Hanson, R., Saunders, B. E., Nichols, T., Barnett, D., Zeanah, C. *et al.* (2006). Report of the APSAC Task Force on attachment disorder, and attachment problems. *Child Maltreatment, 11*(1), 76–89.

Charcot, J.-M. (1887). *Leçons sur la maladies du système nerveux faites a la Saltpêtrière.* Paris: Progrès Médical, Delahaye et Lecrosnie.

Chu, J. A. (2011). *Rebuilding shattered lives: The responsible treatment of complex PTSD and dissociative disorders* (2nd edn). New York: John Wiley and Sons.

Chu, J. A. and Dill, D. L. (1990). Dissociative symptoms in relation to childhood physical and sexual abuse. *The American Journal of Psychiatry, 147*(7), 887–92.

Chugani, H. T., Behen, M. E., Muzik, O., Juhász, C., Nagy, F. and Chugani, D. C. (2001). Local brain functional activity following early deprivation: a study of postinstitutionalized Romanian orphans. *NeuroImage, 14*(6), 1290–301.

Claes, L., Vandereycken, W. (2007). Is there a link between traumatic experiences and self-injurious behaviours in eating-disordered patients? *Eating Disorders, 15*(4), 305–15.

Claridge, G. S. (1990). Can a disease model of schizophrenia survive? In R. P. Bentall (ed.), *Reconstructing Schizophrenia* (pp. 157–83). London: Routledge.

Clark, D. M. (1986). A cognitive model of panic. *Behaviour Research and Therapy, 24,* 461–70.

Clark, D. M. and Ehlers, A. (2005). Posttraumatic stress disorder. From cognitive theory to therapy. In R. H. Leahy (ed.), *Contemporary cognitive therapy*. New York: Guildford Press.

Clarkin, J. F., Widiger, T. A., Frances, A., Hurt, S. W. and Gilmore, M. (1983). Prototypic typology and the borderline personality disorder. *Journal of Abnormal Psychology, 92*(3), 263–75.

Cloitre, M., Cohen, L. R. and Koenen, K. C. (2006). *Treating Survivors of Childhood Abuse: Psychotherapy for the Interrupted Life*. New York: Guilford Press.

Cloitre, M., Stovall-McClough, K. C., Nooner, K., Zorbas, P., Cherry, S., Jackson, C. L., Gan, W. *et al.* (2010). Treatment for PTSD related to childhood abuse: a randomized controlled trial. *The American Journal of Psychiatry, 167*(8), 915–24.

Combs, D. R. and Penn, D. L. (2004). The role of subclinical paranoia on social perception and behaviour. *Schizophrenia Research, 69* (1), 93–104.

Conklin, C. Z. and Westen, D. (2005). Borderline personality disorder in clinical practice. *American Journal of Psychiatry, 162*(5), 867–75.

Conway, M. A. (1996). Autobiographical memory. In E. L. Bjork, and R. A. Bjork (eds). *Memory: Handbook of Perception and Cognition* (165–96). San Diego: Academic Press Incorporated.

—(2005). Memory and the self. *Journal of Memory and Language, 53,* 594–628.

Conway, M. A. and Pleydell-Pearce, C. W. (2000). The construction of autobiographical memories in the self-memory system. *Psychological Review, 107*(2), 261–88.

Conway, M. A., Singer, J. A. and Tagini, A. (2004). The self and autobiographical memory: Correspondence and coherence. *Social Cognition, 22*(5), 495–537.

Coon, D. (1992). *Introduction to Psychology: Exploration and Application*: 6th edn. New York: West Publishing Company.

Coons, P. M. (1996). Clinical phenomenology of 25 children and adolescents with dissociative disorders. *Child and Adolescent Psychiatric Clinics of North America, 5*(2), 361–73.

Corbett, S. S. and Drewett, R. F. (2004). To what extent is failure to thrive in infancy associated with poorer cognitive development? A review and meta-analysis. *Journal of Child Psychology and Psychiatry, 45*(3), 641–54.

Cormier, J. F. and Thelen, M. H. (1998). Professional skepticism of multiple personality disorder. *Professional Psychology: Research and Practice, 29*, 163–7.

Corrigan, F. M., Davidson, A. and Heard, H. (2000). The role of dysregulated amygdalic emotion in borderline personality disorder. *Medical Hypotheses, 54*(4), 574–9.

Corstorphine, E. (2006). Cognitive-emotional-behavioural therapy for the eating disorders: Working with beliefs about emotions. *European Eating Disorders Review, 14*(6), 448–61.

Courtois, C. A. (2010). *Healing the incest wound: Adult survivors in therapy* (2nd edn.). New York: W. W. Norton and Co.

Courtois, C. A. and Ford, J. D. (eds) (2009). *Treating complex stress disorders: An evidence-based guide.* New York: Guilford Press.

Cox, B. J., Swinson, R. P., Endler, N. S. and Norton, G. R. (1994). The symptom structure of panic attacks. *Comprehensive Psychiatry, 35*, 349–53.

Cozolino, L. (2007). *The Neuroscience of Human Relationships: Attachment and the Developing Brain.* New York: W. W. Norton and Co.

Csikszentmihalyi, M. (1987). For some people half a day is spent in fantasy. *New York Times*, (December 15, 1987).

Cummings, J. L. (1993). Frontal-subcortical circuits and human behavior. *Journal of Psychosomatic Research, 44*(6), 627–8.

Dalenberg, C. J. and Palesh, O. G. (2004). Relationship between child abuse history, trauma and dissociation in Russian college students. *Child Abuse and Neglect, 28*(4), 461–74.

Dalenberg, C. J. and Paulson, K. (2009). The case for the study of 'normal' dissociation processes. In. P. F Dell and J. A O'Neil. (eds), *Dissociation and the Dissociative Disorders: DSM-V and Beyond.* (145–54). London: Routledge

Dalle Grave, R., Rigamonti, R., Todisco, P. and Oliosi, E. (1996). Dissociation and traumatic experiences in eating disorders. *European Eating Disorders Review, 4*(4), 232–40.

Davidson, J. R. T., Book, S. W., Colket, J. T., Tupler, L. A., Roth, S., Hertzberg, M., Mellman, T., Beckham, J. C., Smith, R. D., Davison. R. M., Katz, R. and Feldman, M. E. (1997). Assessment of a new self-rating scale for posttraumatic stress disorder: the Davidson Trauma Scale. *Psychological Medicine, 27*, 153–60.

Davidson, J. R. T., Kudler, H. S., Saunders, W. B. and Smith, R. D. (1990). Symptom and co-morbidity patterns in World War II and Vietnam veterans with posttraumatic stress disorder. *Comprehensive Psychiatry, 31*, 162–70.

Davies, J. and Frawley, M. G. (1994). *Treating the adult survivor of childhood sexual abuse: A psychoanalytic perspective.* New York: Basic Books.

De Bellis, M. D., Keshavan, M., Baum, A., Birmaher, B., Clark, D. B., Casey, B. J., Giedd, J., Boring, A. M., Frustaci, K. and Ryan, N. D. (1999). A. E. Bennett Research Award. Developmental traumatology, Part I and II: biological stress systems and brain development. *Biological Psychiatry*, 45, 1259–84.

De Bellis, M. D., Spratt, E. G. and Hooper, S. R. (2011). Neurodevelopmental biology associated with childhood sexual abuse. *Journal of child sexual abuse, 20*(5), 548–87.

Dell, P. (1998). Axis II pathology in outpatients with dissociative identity disorder. *The Journal of Nervous and Mental Disease, 186*(6), 352–56.

Dell, P. F. and O'Neil, J. A. (2009). *Dissociation and the Dissociative Disorders: DSM-V and Beyond.* London and New York: Routledge.

Demitrack, M. A., Putnam, F. W., Brewerton, T. D., Brandt, H. A. and Gold, P. W. (1990). Relation of clinical variables to dissociative phenomena in eating disorders. *American Journal of Psychiatry, 147*(9), 1184–8.

Depue, R. A. and Morrone-Strupinsky, J. V. (2005). A neurobehavioral model of affiliative bonding. *Behavioral and Brain Sciences, 28*, 313–95.

Devor, H. (1994). Transsexualism, dissociation, and child abuse: An initial discussion based on nonclinical data. *Journal of Psychology and Human Sexuality, 6*(3), 49–72.

Dixon, A. K. (1998). Ethological strategies for defense in animals and humans: Their role in some psychiatric disorders. *British Journal of Medical Psychology, 71*, 417–45.

—(1981). *Preconscious processing.* Chichester: Wiley and Sons.

Dominey, P., Decety, J., Brousolle, E., Chazot, G. and Jeannerod, M. (1995). Motor imagery of lateralized sequential task is asymmetrically slowed in hemi-Parkinson's patients. *Neuropsychologia, 33*, 727–41.

Dorahy, M. J. and Huntjens, R. J. C. (2007). Memory and attentional processes in Dissociative Identity Disorder: A review of the empirical literature. In E. Vermetten, M. Dorahy, and D. Spiegel (eds), *Traumatic Dissociation: Neurobiology and Treatment.* Washington, DC: American Psychiatric Press, pp. 55–75.

Dorahy, M. J. and Van der Hart, O. (2007). Relationship between trauma and dissociation: A historical analysis. In E. Vermetten, M. Dorahy and D. Spiegel (eds). *Traumatic dissociation: Neurobiology and treatment* (3–30). Arlington: American Psychiatric Publishing Inc.

Drayton, M., Birchwood, M. and Trower, P. (1998). Early attachment experience and recovery from psychosis. *British Journal of Clinical Psychology, 37* (3), 269–84.

Dunbar, R. I. M. (2010). The social role of touch in humans and primates: Behavioural function and neurobiological mechanisms. *Neuroscience and Biobehavioral Reviews, 34*, 260–8.

Dunbar R. I. M. and Barrett, L. (2007). *The Oxford Handbook of Evolutionary Psychology.* Oxford: Oxford University Press.

Ebner-Priemer, U., Badeck, S., Beckmann, C., Wagner, A., Feige, B., Weiss, I. and Bohus, M. (2005). Affective dysregulation and dissociative experience in female patients with borderline personality disorder: a startle response study. *Journal of Psychiatric Research, 39*(1), 85–92.

Ebner-Priemer, U., Mauchnik, J., Kleindienst, N., Schmahl, C., Peper, M., Rosenthal, M. and Bohus, M. (2009). Emotional learning during dissociative states in borderline personality disorder. *Journal of Psychiatry and Neuroscience, 34*(3), 214–22.

Egeland, B. and Susman-Stillman, A. (1996). Dissociation as a mediator of child abuse across generations. *Child Abuse and Neglect 20*(11), 1123–32.

Ehlers, A and Clark, D. M. (2000). A cognitive model of posttraumatic stress disorder. *Behaviour research and therapy, 38*(4), 319–45.

Ehlers, A., Hackmann, A., Steil, R., Clohessy, S., Wenninger, K. and Winter, H. (2002). The nature of intrusive memories after trauma: the warning signal hypothesis. *Behaviour research and therapy, 40*(9), 995–1002.

Ehlers, A., Hackmann, A. and Michael, T. (2004). Intrusive re-experiencing in post-traumatic stress disorder: Phenomenology, theory, and therapy. *Memory, 12*, 403–15.

Ellason, J. W., Ross, C. A. and Fuchs, D. L. (1996). Lifetime Axis I and II comorbidity and childhood trauma history in dissociative identity disorder. *Psychiatry: Interpersonal and Biological Processes. 59*, 255–66.

Engelberg, M. J., Steiger, H., Gauvin, L. and Wonderlich, S. A. (2007). Binge antecedents in bulimic syndromes: An examination of dissociation and negative affect. *International Journal of Eating Disorders, 40*(6), 531–6.

Engelhard, I. M., Van den Hout, M. A., Kindt, M., Arntz, A. and Schouten, E. (2003). Peritraumatic dissociation and posttraumatic stress after pregnancy loss: A prospective study. *Behaviour Research and Therapy, 41*, 67–78.

Epstein, D. (1982). The unconscious, the preconscious and the self-concept. In J. Suls and A. G. Greenwald (eds), *Psychological Perspectives on the Self.* Hillsdale, NJ. Lawrence Erlbaum Associates.

Erdelyi, M. H. (1994). Dissociation, defense and the unconsious. In D. Spiegel (ed.), *Dissociation: Culture, mind and body* (pp. 3–20). Washington, DC: American Psychiatric Press.

Essex, M. J., Klein, M. H., Cho, E. and Kalin, N. H. (2002). Maternal stress beginning in infancy may sensitive children to later stress exposure: effects on cortisol and behaviour. *Biological Psychiatry, 52*(8).

Everett, B. and Gallop, R. (2001). *The Link Between Childhood Trauma and Mental Illness: Effective Interventions for Mental Health Professionals.* Thousand Oaks: Sage.

Everill, J. and Waller, G. (1995). Disclosure of sexual abuse and psychological adjustment in female undergraduates. *Child Abuse and Neglect, 19*(1), 93–100.

Everill, J., Waller, G. and Macdonald, W. (1995). Dissociation in bulimic and non-eating-disordered women. *International Journal of Eating Disorders, 17*(2), 127–34.

Fahy, T. A. (1988). The diagnosis of multiple personality disorder: a critical review. *British Journal of Psychiatry, 153*, 597–606.

Fairburn, C. G. (2008). *Cognitive Behavior Therapy and Eating Disorders.* New York: Guilford Press.

Farb, N. Segal, Z. V., Mayberg, H., Bean, J., McKeon, D., Fatima, Z. and Anderson, A. K. (2007). Attending to the present: mindfulness meditation reveals distinct neural modes of self-reference. *Social Cognitive and Affective Neuroscience, 2*(4), 313–22.

Faure, H., Kersten, J., Koopman, D. and Van der Hart, O. (1997). The 19th century DID case of Louis Vivet: new findings and re-evaluation. *Dissociation, 10*(2), 104–13.

Fearon, R. M. P. and Mansell, W. (2001). Cognitive perspectives on unresolved loss: insights from the study of PTSD. *Bulletin of the Menninger Clinic, 65*, 380–96.

Feelgood, S. R. and Rantzen, A. J., (1994). Auditory and visual hallucinations in university students. *Personality and Individual Differences, 17*(2) 293–6.

Ferster, C. B. (1973). A functional analysis of depression. *American Psychologist, 28*, 857–70.

Fertuck, E. A., Lenzenweger, M. F., Clarkin, J. F., Hoermann, S. and Stanley, B. (2006). Executive neurocognition, memory systems, and borderline personality disorder. *Clinical Psychology Review, 26*(3), 346–75.

Fine, C. G. (1992). Multiple personality disorder. In A. Freeman and F. M. Dattilio (eds) *Comprehensive Casebook of Cognitive Therapy.* New York: Plenum Press.

—(2007). *A mind of its own: how your brain distorts and deceives.* Cambridge: Icon books.

Foa, E. B. and Hearst-Ikeda, D. (1996). Emotional dissociation in response to trauma: An information-processing approach. In, L. K. Michelson and W. J. Ray (eds), *Handbook of dissociation: Theoretical, empirical, and clinical perspectives*, (pp. 207–24). New York, NY: Plenum Press.

Foa, E. B. and Kozak, M. J. (1986). Emotional processing of fear: exposure to corrective information. *Psychological Bulletin*, 99, 20–35.

Fogel, A. (2009*). The Psychophysiology of Self-Awareness: Rediscovering the Lost Art of Body Sense*. New York: W. W. Norton and Co.

Follette, V., Pistorello, J. and Hayes, S. (2007). *Finding life beyond trauma: Using acceptance and commitment therapy to heal from post-traumatic stress and trauma-related problems*. Oakland, CA: New Harbinger.

Fonagy, P. (1991). Thinking about thinking: Some clinical and theoretical considerations in the treatment of a borderline patient. *International Journal of Psychoanalysis*, 72, 639–56.

Forrest, K. (2001). Toward an etiology of dissociative identity disorder: a neurodevelopmental approach. *Consciousness and Cognition*, 10(3), 259–93.

Fowler, D., Freeman, D., Smith, B., Bebbington, P., Bashforth, H. and Garety, P. (2006). The Brief Core Schema Scales (BCSS): Psychometric properties and associations with paranoia and grandiosity in non-clinical and psychosis samples. *Psychological Medicine*, 36, 749–59.

Frankel, F. H. (1994). International Journal of Clinical and Experimental Hypnosis The Concept of Flashbacks in Historical Perspective. *International Journal of Clinical and Experimental Hypnosis*, 42(4), 321–36.

Freeman, D. and Garety, P. A. (2004). *Paranoia: The Psychology of Persecutory Delusions*. Hove: Psychology Press.

Freeman, D., Garety, P. A., Bebbington, P. E., Smith, B., Romlinson, R., Fowler, D., Kuipers, E., Ray, K. and Dunn, G. (2005). Psychological investigation of the structure of paranoia in a non-clinical population. British Journal of Psychiatry, 186, 427–35.

Freud, S. (1893/2001). Some points for a comparative study of organic and hysterical paralyzes. In, J. Strachey and A. Strachey (eds), *Standard edition of the complete psychological works of Sigmund Freud, 1*. London: Hogarth Press.

—(1896). The aetiology of hysteria. In, J. Strachey and A. Strachey (eds), *Standard edition of the complete psychological works of Sigmund Freud, 3*. London: Hogarth Press.

Frith, C. D. (1992). *The Cognitive Neuropsychology of Schizophrenia*. Hove: LEA.

Frodl, T. and O'Keane,V. (in press). How does the brain deal with cumulative stress? A review with focus on developmental stress, HPA axis function and hippocampal structure in humans. *Neurobiology of Disease*.

Fuller-Tyszkiewicz, M. and Mussap, A. J. (2008). The relationship between dissociation and binge eating. *Journal of Trauma and Dissociation*, 9(4), 445–62.

Garety, P. A. and Hemsley, D. R. (1994). *Delusions: Investigations into the Psychology of Delusional Reasoning*. Oxford: Oxford University Press.

Garety, P. A., Kuipers, E., Fowler, D., Freeman, D. and Bebbington, P. E. (2001). A cognitive model of the positive symptoms of psychosis. *Psychological Medicine, 31*, 189–95.

Gary, M., Manning, C. G., Loftus E. F. and Sherman, S. J. (1996). Imagination inflation: Imagining a childhood event inflates confidence that it occurred. *Psychonomic Bulletin and Review, 3*, 208–14.

Geary, D. C. (2000). Evolution and proximate expression of human parental investment. *Psychological Bulletin*, 126, 55–77.

Gelinas, D. J. (2003). Integrating EMDR into phase-oriented treatment for trauma. *Journal of Trauma and Dissociation,4*(3), 91–135.

Germer, C. (2009). *The Mindful Path to Self-Compassion: Freeing yourself from destructive thoughts and emotions.* New York: Guilford Press.

Gershuny, B. S., Cloitre, M. and Otto, M. W. (2003). Peritraumatic dissociation and PTSD severity: Do event-related fears about death and control mediate their relation? *Behavior Research and Therapy, 41*, 157–66.

Giesbrecht, T., Lynn, S. J. and Lilienfield, S. O. (2008). Cognitive processes in dissociation: An analysis of core theoretical assumptions. *Psychological Bulletin, 134*, 617–47.

Giesbrecht, T., Merckelbach, H., Van Oorsouw, K. and Simeon, D. (2010). Skin conductance and memory fragmentation after exposure to an emotional film clip in depersonalization disorder. *Psychiatry Research, 177*, 342–9.

Giesen-Bloo, J., Van Dyck, R., Spinhoven, P., Van Tilburg, W., Dirksen, C., Van Asselt, T., Kremers, I., *et al.* (2006). Outpatient psychotherapy for borderline personality disorder: randomized trial of schema-focused therapy vs transference-focused psychotherapy. *Archives of General Psychiatry, 63*(6), 649–58.

Gilbert, P. (1989). *Human Nature and Suffering.* Hove: Lawrence Erlbaum Associates Ltd. New York: Guilford Press.

—(1992). *Depression: The Evolution of Powerlessness.* Hove: Lawrence Erlbaum Associates Ltd. New York: Guilford Press.

—(2000). Social mentalities: Internal 'social' conflicts and the role of inner warmth and compassion in cognitive therapy. In P. Gilbert and K. G. Bailey (eds.). *Genes on the Couch: Explorations in Evolutionary Psychotherapy* (118–50). Hove: Brenner-Routledge.

—(2005). Social mentalities: A biopsychosocial and evolutionary reflection on social relationships. In M. W. Baldwin (ed.). *Interpersonal Cognition.* (pp. 299–335). New York: Guilford Press.

—(2007). *Psychotherapy and Counselling for Depression.* 3rd edn. London: Sage.

—(2009). *The Compassionate Mind.* London: Constable-Robinson. Oaklands, CA.: New Harbinger.

—(2010). *Compassion Focused Therapy: The CBT Distinctive Features Series.* London: Routledge.

—(2012). Compassion Focused Therapy. In W. Dryden (ed.), *Cognitive Behaviour Therapies.* (140–65). London: Sage.

Gilbert P. and Choden (in press) *The Transforming Power of Mindful Compassion.* London: Constable Robinson.

Gilbert, P. and Irons, C. (2005). Focused therapies and compassionate mind training for shame and self-attacking. In P. Gilbert (ed.). *Compassion: Conceptualisations, Research and Use in Psychotherapy* (263–325). London: Routledge.

Gilbert, P., McEwan, K., Gibbons, L., Chotai, S., Duarte, J. and Matos, M. (in press) Fears of compassion and happiness in relation to alexithymia, mindfulness and self-criticism. *Psychology and Psychotherapy.*

Gilbertson, M. W., Shenton, M. E., Ciszewski, A., Kasai, K., Lasko, N. B., Orr, S. P. and Pitman, R. K. (2002). Smaller hippocampal volume predicts pathologic vulnerability to psychological trauma, *Nature Neuroscience, 5*(11), 1242–7.

Gillanders, D., Potter, L. and Morris, P. G. (2012). Pain related-visual imagery is associated with distress in chronic pain sufferers. *Behavioural and Cognitive Psychotherapy,* 1–13. http://dx.doi.org/10.1017/S1352465812000045

Gmelin, E. (1791). *Materialen für die Anthropologie, 1.* Tubingen: Cotta

Gold, S. R. and Minor, S. W. (1983). School related daydreaming and test anxiety. *Imagination, Cognition, and Personality, 3*, 133–8.

Goldberg, E. (2002). *The Executive Brain: Frontal Lobes and the Civilized Mind.* New York and Oxford: University Press.

Goldstein, L. H., Chalder, T., Chigwedere, C., Khondoker, M. R., Toone, B. K. and Mellers, J. D. C. (2010). Cognitive-behavioral therapy for psychogenic nonepileptic seizures: A pilot RCT. *Neurology, 74,* 1986–94.

Goldstein, L. H., Deale, A. C., Mitchell-O'Malley, S. J., Toone, B. K. and Mellers, J. D. (2004). An evaluation of cognitive behavioral therapy as a treatment for dissociative seizures: a pilot study. *Cognitive and Behavioral Neurology, 17*(1), 41–9.

Goodman, M. and Yehuda, R. (2002). The relationship between psychological trauma and borderline personality disorder. *Psychiatric Annals, 32*(6), 337–45.

Grabe, H-J., Rainermann, S., Spitzer, C., Gänsicke, M. and Freyberger, H. J. (2000). The relationship between dimensions of alexithymia and dissociation. *Psychotherapy and Psychosomatics, 69,* 128–31.

Gray, J. A. (1979). *Pavlov.* London: Fontana.

Gray, M. J. and Lombardo, T. W. (2001). Complexity of trauma narratives as an index of fragmented memory in PTSD: A critical analysis. *Applied Cognitive Psychology, 15,* S171–86.

Greenwald, R. (2007). *EMDR: Within a phase model of trauma-informed treatment (Maltreatment, trauma, and interpersonal aggression).* New York: Haworth Press.

Grey, N. (2009). Imagery and psychological threat to the self in PTSD. In L. Stopa (ed.). *Imagery and the threatened self: Perspectives on imagery and the self in cognitive therapy.* London: Routledge.

Grey, N., McManus, F., Hackmann, A., Clark, D. and Ehlers, A. (2009). Intensive cognitive therapy for post-traumatic stress disorder: case studies. In N. Grey (ed.). *Casebook of cognitive therapy for traumatic stress reactions* (pp. 111–30). East Sussex: Routledge.

Gros-Jean (1855). *Seconde letter de Gros-Jean á son évêque au sujet des tables parlantes, des possessions, des Sybilles, du magnetism et autres diableries.* Paris: Ledoyen.

Grosjean, B. and Tsai, G. E. (2007). NMDA neurotransmission as a critical mediator of borderline personality disorder. *Journal of Psychiatry and Neuroscience, 32*(2), 103–15.

Gumley, A. and Schwannauer, M. (2006). Staying Well after Psychosis: A Cognitive Interpersonal Approach to Recovery and Relapse Prevention. Hove: Wiley and Sons.

Gunderson, J. G. and Singer, M. T. (1975). Defining borderline patients: an overview. *American Journal of Psychiatry, 132*(1), 1–10.

Gusnard, D. A., Raichle, M. E. and Raichle, M. (2001). Searching for a baseline: functional imaging and the resting human brain. *Nature Reviews Neuroscience, 2*(10), 685–94.

Haaland, V. Ø. and Landrø, N. I. (2007). Decision making as measured with the Iowa Gambling Task in patients with borderline personality disorder. *Journal of the International Neuropsychological Society, 13,* 699–703.

—(2009). Pathological dissociation and neuropsychological functioning in borderline personality disorder. *Acta Psychiatrica Scandinavica, 119*(5), 383–92.

Haaland, V. Ø., Esperaas, L. and Landrø, N. I. (2009). Selective Deficit in Executive Functioning among Patients with Borderline Personality Disorder. *Psychological Medicine, 39*(10), 1733–44.

Hacking, I. (1995). *Rewriting the soul: Multiple personality and the science of memory.* Princeton, NJ: Princeton University Press.

Hackmann, A. (2011). Imagery rescripting in post traumatic stress disorder. *Cognitive and Behavioural Practice, 18,* 424–32.

Hagenaars, M. A., Van Minnen, A. and Hoogduin, K. A. (2010). The impact of dissociation and depression on the efficacy of prolonged exposure treatment for PTSD. *Behaviour Research and Therapy, 48,* 19–27.

Halligan, S. L., Clark, D. M. and Ehlers, A. (2002). Cognitive processing, memory, and the development of PTSD symptoms: Two experimental analogue studies. *Journal of Behavior Therapy and Experimental Psychiatry, 33,* 73–89.

Halligan, S. L., Michael, T., Clark, D. M. and Ehlers, A. (2003). Posttraumatic stress disorder following assault: The role of cognitive processing, trauma memory, and appraisals. *Journal of Consulting and Clinical psychology, 71,* 419–31.

Hallings-Pott, C., Waller, G., Watson, D. and Scragg, P. (2005). State dissociation in bulimic eating disorders: An experimental study. *International Journal of Eating Disorders, 38*(1), 37–41.

Hamner, M. B. (1997). Psychotic features and combat-associated PTSD. *Depression Anxiety, 5,* 34–8.

Hamner, M. B., Frueh, B. C., Ulmer, H. G. and Arana, G.W. (1999). Psychotic features and illness severity in combat veterans with chronic posttraumatic stress disorder. *Biological Psychiatry, 45,* 846–52.

Harris R. and Hayes, S. (2009). *ACT made simple: An easy-to-read primer on acceptance and commitment therapy.* Oakland: New Harbinger Publications.

Hartt, J. and Waller, G. (2002). Child abuse, dissociation and core beliefs in bulimic disorders. *Child Abuse and Neglect, 9,* 923–38.

Harvey, A. G. and Bryant, R. A. (1999). A qualitative investigation of the organization of traumatic memories. *British Journal of Clinical Psychology, 38,* 401–5.

Hayes, S. C., Strosahl, K. and Wilson, K. G. (1999). *Acceptance and Commitment Therapy: An experiential approach to behavior change.* New York: Guilford Press.

Hayes, S. C. and Smith, S. (2005). *Get out of your mind and into your life: The new acceptance and commitment therapy.* Oakland: New Harbinger Publications.

Hayes, S. C., Wilson, K. G., Gifford, E. V., Bissett, R., Piasecki, M., Batten, S. V., Byrd, M. and Gregg, J. (2004). A preliminary trial of twelve-step facilitation and acceptance and commitment therapy with polysubstance-abusing methodone-maintained opiate addicts. *Behavior Therapy, 35*(4), 667–88.

Hayward, V. (2008). A brief taxonomy of tactile illusions and demonstrations that can be done in a hardware store. *Brain Research Bulletin, 75,* 742–52.

Heaps, C. and Nash, M. (1999). Individual differences in imagination inflation. *Psychonomic Bulletin and Review, 6*(2), 313–18.

Heatherton, T. F. and Baumeister, R. F. (1991). Binge eating as escape from self-awareness. *Psychological Bulletin, 110*(1), 86–108.

Heim, C. and Nemeroff, C. B. (2009). Neurobiology of posttraumatic stress disorder. *CNS Spectrums, 14*(1 Suppl 1), 13–24.

Hemsley, D. R. (1993). A simple (or simplistic?) cognitive model for schizophrenia. *Behaviour Research and Therapy 31,* 633–45.

—(1994). A cognitive model for schizophrenia and its possible neural basis. Acta Psychiatrica Scandinavica, *90*(384), 80–6.

Hendin, H. and Haas, A. P. (1991). Suicide and guilt as manifestations of PTSD in Vietnam combat veterans. The *American Journal of Psychiatry, 148,* 586–91.

Henning, K. R. and Frueh, B. C. (1997). Combat guilt and its relationship to PTSD symptoms. *Journal of Clinical Psychology, 53,* 801–8.

Herman J. L. (1992a). Complex PTSD: A syndrome in survivors of prolonged and repeated trauma. *Journal of Traumatic Stress, 5*(3) 377–91.

—(1992b). *Trauma and Recovery.* New York: Basic Books.

—(2011). Posttraumatic stress disorder as a shame disorder. In R. L. Dearing and J. P. Tangney (eds), *Shame in the therapy hour* (pp. 261–75). Washington, DC: American Psychological Association.

Herman, J. L., Perry, J. C. and Van der Kolk, B. A. (1989). Childhood trauma in borderline personality disorder. *American Journal of Psychiatry, 146*(4), 490–5.

Herpertz, S. C., Kunert, H. J., Schwenger, U. B. and Sass, H. (1999). Affective responsiveness in borderline personality disorder: A psychophysiological approach. *American Journal of Psychiatry, 156*(10), 1550–6.

Herpertz, S. C., Sass, H. and Favazza, A. (1997). Impulsivity in self-mutilative behavior: psychometric and biological findings. *Journal of Psychiatric Research, 31*(4), 451–65.

Hilgard, E. R. (1974). Towards a neo-dissociation theory: Multiple cognitive controls in human functioning. *Perspectives in Biology and Medicine, 17,* 301–16.

—(1977). *Divided consciousness: Multiple controls in human thought and actions.* New York: Wiley.

Hill, D. M., Craighead, L. W. and Safer, D. L. (2011). Appetite-focused dialectical behaviour therapy for the treatment of binge eating with purging: A preliminary trial. *International Journal of Eating Disorders, 44,* 249–61.

Holmes, E. A., Brewin, C. R. and Hennessy, R. G. (2004). Trauma films, information processing, and intrusive memory development. *Journal of Experimental Psychology: General, 133,* 3–22.

Holmes, A., Brown, R. J., Mansell, W., Fearon, R. P., Hunter, E. C., Frasquilho, F. and Oakley, D. A. (2005). Are there two qualitatively distinct forms of dissociation? A review and some clinical implications. *Clinical Psychology Review, 25,* 1–23.

Holmes, E. A. and Bourne, C. (2008). Inducing and modulating intrusive emotional memories: A review of the trauma film paradigm. *Acta Psychologica, 127,* 553–66.

Holmes, E. A., Grey, N. and Young, K. (2005). Intrusive images and "hotspots" of trauma memories in Posttraumatic Stress Disorder: an exploratory investigation of emotions and cognitive themes. *Journal of Behaviour Therapy and Experimental Psychiatry, 36*(1), 3–17.

Holmes, E. A., Lang, T. J. and Shah, D. M. (2009). Developing interpretation bias modification as a 'cognitive vaccine' for depressed mood: Imagining positive events makes you feel better than thinking about them verbally. *Journal of Abnormal Psychology,* 118, 76–88.

Holt L. E. (1897). *The Diseases of Infancy and Childhood.* New York: D. Appleton and Company.

Holzer, S. R., Uppala, S., Wonderlich, S. A., Crosby, R. D. and Simonich, H. (2008). Mediational significance of PTSD in the relationship of sexual trauma and eating disorders. *Child Abuse and Neglect, 32*(5), 561–6.

Honig, A., Romme, M. A. J., Ensink, B. J., Escher, S. D. M. A. C., Pennings, M. H. A. and deVries, M. W. (1998). Auditory hallucinations: A comparison between patients and non-patients. *Journal of Nervous and Mental Disease, 186*(10), 646–51.

Hopper, J. W., Frewen, P. A. and Lanius, R. A. (2007). Neural Correlates of Reexperiencing, Avoidance, and Dissociation in PTSD: Symptom Dimensions and Emotion Dysregulation in Responses to Script-Driven Trauma Imagery. *Journal of Traumatic Stress, 20*(5), 713–25.

Horney, K. (1951). *Neurosis and human growth: The struggle towards self-realization.* London: Routledge and Kegan Paul Ltd.

Hornstein, N. L. and Putnam, F. W. (1992). Clinical Phenomenology of Child and Adolescent Dissociative Disorders. *Journal of the American Academy of Child and Adolescent Psychiatry, 31*(6), 1077–85.

Howell, E. F. (2005). *The dissociative mind.* Hillsdale, NJ and London: The Analytic Press.

Howlett, S. and Reuber, M. (2009). An augmented model of brief Psychodynamic Interpersonal Therapy for patients with nonepileptic seizures. *Psychotherapy: Theory, Research, Practice and Training, 46,* 125–38.

Hughlings Jackson, J. (1882). On some implications of dissolution of the nervous system. *Medical Press Circular 2,* 411–14.

Hunter, E. C. M., Baker, D., Phillips, M. L. Sierra, M. and David, A. S. (2005). Cognitive behaviour therapy for depersonalization disorder: An open study. *Behaviour Research and Therapy, 43* (9), 1121–30.

Hunter, E. C. M., Phillips, M. L., Chalder, T., Sierra, M. and David, A. S. (2003). Depersonalization disorder: A cognitive-behavioural conceptualisation. *Behaviour Research and Therapy, 41* (12), 1451–67.

Hunter, E. C. M., Salkovskis, P. M. and David, A. S. (under review, *Behaviour Research and Therapy*). Cognitive biases in Depersonalization Disorder, *Psychological Medicine*.

Hunter, E. C. M., Sierra, M. and David, A. S. (2004). The epidemiology of depersonalization and derealization: A systematic review. *Social Psychiatry and Epidemiology, 39,* 9–18.

Hyland M. E. (1987). Control-theory interpretation of psychological mechanisms of depression: Comparison and integration of several theories. *Psychological Bulletin, 102,* 109–21.

Hyman, I. E. and Pentland, J. (1996). The role of mental imagery in the creation of false childhood memories. *Journal of Memory and Language, 35,* 101–17.

International Society for the Study of Dissociation (2005). [Chu, J. A., Loewenstein, R., Dell, P. F., Barach, P. M., Somer, E., Kluft, R. P., Gelinas, D. J., Van der Hart, O., Dalenberg, C. J., Nijenhuis, E. R. S., Bowman, E. S., Boon, S., Goodwin, J., Jacobson, M., Ross, C. A., Sar, V, Fine, C. G., Frankel, A. S., Coons, P. M., Courtois, C. A., Gold, S. N. and Howell, E.]. Guidelines for treating Dissociative Identity Disorder in adults. *Journal of Trauma and Dissociation, 6*(4) pp. 69–149. Available online at www.infor maworld.com doi:10.1300/J229v06n04_05)

International Society for the Study of Trauma and Dissociation [ISSTD] (2011). Guidelines for treating dissociative identity disorder in adults, third revision. *Journal of Trauma and Dissociation, 12,* 115–87.

Irle, E., Lange, C., Weniger, G. and Sachsse, U. (2007). Size abnormalities of the superior parietal cortices are related to dissociation in borderline personality disorder. *Psychiatry Research: Neuroimaging, 156*(2), 139–49.

Jackson, C., Knott, C., Skeate, A. and Birchwood, M. (2004). The trauma of first episode psychosis: the role of cognitive mediation. *Australian and New Zealand Journal of Psychiatry*, 38: 327–33. doi: 10.111/j.1440-1614.2004.01359.x

Jackson, C., Smith, J., Birchwood, M., Trower, P., Reid, I., Townend, M. *et al.* (2004). Preventing the traumatic sequelae of first episode psychosis: A randomised controlled trial. Cited by Jackson, C. and Birchwood, M. (2006). Trauma and first episode psychosis. In W. Larkin and A. P. Morrison (eds). *Trauma and Psychosis: New Directions for Theory and Therapy.* Hove: Routledge.

Janet, P. (1889). *L'automatisme psychologique: Essai de psychologie expérimentale sur les formes inférieures de l'activité humaine.* Paris: Félix Alcan. Reprint (1973). Paris: Société Pierre Janet/Payot.

—(1893). *L'Etat Mental des hystériques: Les Stigmates Mentaux.* Paris: Ruef et Cie.

—(1907). *The major symptoms of hysteria.* London and New York: Macmillan. Reprint of 1920 edition (1965). New York: Hafner.

—(1919). *Les médications psychologiques.* Paris: Félix Alcan. (English edition: *Psychological healing.* New York: Macmillan, 1925).

—(1929). *L'évolution psychologique de la personnalité.* Paris: A. Chahine.

—(1935). Réalisation et interprétation. *Annales Médico-Psychologiques, 93,* 329–66.

Jassen, I., Krabbendam, L., Bak, M., Hanssen, M., Volebergh, W., DeGraaf, R. *et al.* (2004). Childhood abuse as a risk factor for psychotic experiences. *Acta Psychiatry Scandinavia, 109,* 35–45.

Jaynes, J (1976). *The Origin of Consciousness in the Breakdown of the Bicameral Mind.* Massachuesetts: Houghton Miffin.

Jenkins, A. and Mitchell, J. P. (2010). Mentalizing under uncertainty: dissociated neural responses to ambiguous and unambiguous mental state inferences. *Cerebral Cortex, 20,* 404–10.

Jerschke, S., Meixner, K., Richter, H. and Bohus, M. (1998). Zur Behandlungsgeschichte und Versorgungssituation von Patientinnen mit Borderline-Personlichkeitsstorung in der Bundesrepublik Deutschland. *Fortschritte der Neurologie – Psychiatrie, 66*(12), 545–52.

Johns, L. C., Singleton, N., Murray, R. M., Farrell, M., Brughs, T., Bebbington, P. *et al.* (2004). Prevalence and correlates of self-reported psychotic symptoms in the British population. *British Journal of Psychiatry, 185,* 298–305.

Johns, L. C. and Van Os, J. (2001). The continuity of psychotic experiences in the general population. *Clinical Psychology Review, 21* (8), 1125–41.

Johnson, J. G., Cohen, P., Kasen, S. and Brook, J. S. (2002). Childhood adversities associated with risk for eating disorders or weight problems during adolescence or early adulthood. *American Journal of Psychiatry, 159*(3), 394–400.

Johnson, R. (2009). The intrapersonal civil war. *The Psychologist, 22,* 300–3.

Johnston, C., Dorahy, M. J., Courtney, D., Bayles, T. and O'Kane, M. (2009). Dysfunctional schema modes, childhood trauma and dissociation in borderline personality disorder. *Journal of Behavior Therapy and Experimental Psychiatry, 40,* 248–55.

Jones, B., Heard, H., Startup, M., Swales, M., Williams, J. M. G. and Jones, R. S. P. (1999). Autobiographical memory and dissociation in borderline personality disorder. *Psychological Medicine, 29*(6), 1397–1404.

Jones, C., Harvey, A. G. and Brewin, C. R. (2007). The organization and content of trauma memories in survivors of road traffic accidents. *Behaviour Research and Therapy, 45,* 151–62.

Jones, S. H., Hemsley, D. R. and Gray, J. A. (1991). Contextual effects on choice reaction time and accuracy in acute and chronic schizophrenics: Impairment in selective attention or in the influence of prior learning? *British Journal of Psychiatry, 159,* 415–21.

Judd, P. H. (2005). Neurocognitive impairment as a moderator in the development of borderline personality disorder. *Development and Psychopathology, 17*(4), 1173–96.

Kabat-Zinn, J. (2003). Mindfulness-based interventions in context: Past, present, and future. *Clinical Psychology Science and Practice, 10,* 144–56.

—(2005). *Coming to our Senses: Healing Ourselves and the World through Mindfulness.* New York: Piatkus.

Kaye, W. H., Frank, G. K., Bailer, U. F. and Henry, S. E. (2005). Neurobiology of anorexia nervosa: Clinical implications of alterations of the function of serotonin and other neuronal systems. *International Journal of Eating Disorders, 37,* S15-S19.

Kelman, H. C. and Hamilton, V. L. (1989). *Crimes of Obedience*: New Haven: Yale University Press.

Kennedy, F., Clarke, S., Stopa, L., Bell, L., Rouse, H., Ainsworth, C., *et al.* (2004). Towards a cognitive model and measure of dissociation. *Journal of Behaviour Therapy and Experimental Psychiatry, 35,* 25–48.

Kennerley, H. (1996). Cognitive therapy of dissociative symptoms associated with trauma. *British Journal of Clinical Psychology, 35,* 325–40.

—(2000). *Overcoming childhood trauma.* Constable Robinson: London

—(2009). Cognitive therapy for post traumatic dissociation. In Grey, N. A. (ed.), *Casebook of Cognitive Therapy for Traumatic Stress Reactions.* London: Routledge.

Kessler, R. C. and McCrae, J. A. (1982). The effects of wives' employment on the mental health of married men and women. *American Sociological Review, 47,* 216–27.

Kessler, R. C., McLaughlin, K. A., Green, J. G., Gruber, M. J., Sampson, M. A., Zaslavsky, A. M. *et al.* (2010). Childhood adversities and adult psychopathology in the WHO World Mental Health Surveys. *British Journal of Psychiatry, 197,* 378–85.

Kihlstrom, J. F. (1992). Dissociative and conversion disorders. In D. J. Stein and J. Young (eds), *Cognitive Science and Clinical Disorders* (pp. 247–270). San Diego, CA: Academic Press.

Kihlstrom, J. F., Glisky, M. L. and Angiulo, M. J. (1994). Dissociative tendencies and dissociative disorders. *Journal of Abnormal Psychology, 103,* 117–24.

Kikuchi, H., Fujii, T., Abe, N., Suzuki, M., Takagi, M., Mugikura, S., Takahashi, S. *et al.* (2010). Memory repression: brain mechanisms underlying dissociative amnesia. *Journal of Cognitive Neuroscience, 22*(3), 602–13.

Kilcommons A. and Morrison A. P. (2005). Relationships between trauma and psychosis: An exploration of cognitive and dissociative factors. *Acta Psychiatrica Scandinavica, 112*(5), 351–9.

Kindt, M. and Van den Hout, M. (2003). Dissociation and memory fragmentation: experimental effects on meta-memory but not on actual memory performance. *Behaviour Research and Therapy, 41,* 167–78.

Kindt, M., Van den Hout, M. and Buck, N. (2005). Dissociation related to subjective memory fragmentation and intrusions but not to objective memory disturbances. *Journal of Behavior Therapy and Experimental Psychiatry, 36,* 43–59.

Kirk-Smith, M. D., Van Toller, C. and Dodd, G. H. (1983). Unconscious odour conditioning in human subjects. *Biological Psychology, 17,* 221–31.

Kirsch, P., Esslinger, C., Chen, Q., Mier, D., Lis, S., Siddanti, S., Gruppe, H., Mattay, V. S., Gallhofer, B. and Meyer-Lindenberg, A. (2005): Oxytocin modulates neural circuitry for social cognition and fear in humans. *The Journal of Neuroscience, 25,* 11489–93.

Kisiel, C. L. and Lyons, J. S. (2001). Dissociation as a mediator of psychopathology among sexually abused children and adolescents. *American Journal of Psychiatry, 158,* 1034–9.

Kleim, B., Wallott, F. and Ehlers, A. (2008). Are trauma memories disjointed from other autobiographical memories in posttraumatic stress disorder? An experimental investigation. *Behavioural and Cognitive Psychotherapy, 36*(2), 221–34.

Kleindienst, N., Limberger, M. F., Ebner-Priemer, U. W., Keibel-Mauchnik, J., Dyer, A., Berger, M. and Bohus, M. (2011). Dissociation Predicts Poor Response to Dialectical Behavioral Therapy in Female Patients with Borderline Personality Disorder. *Journal of Personality Disorders, 25*(4), 432–47.

Klonsky, E. D. (2007). The functions of deliberate self-injury: a review of the evidence. *Clinical psychology review*, *27*(2), 226–39.

Kluft, R. P. (1987). First-rank symptoms as a diagnostic clue to multiple personality disorder. *American Journal of Psychiatry*, *144*, 293–8.

—(1993). Clinical approaches to the integration of personalities. In R. P. Kluft and C. G. Fine (eds), *Clinical perspectives on multiple personality disorder* (pp. 101–33). Washington, DC: American Psychiatric Press.

—(2000). The psychoanalytic psychotherapy of dissociative identity disorder in the context of trauma therapy. *Psychoanalytic Inquiry*, *20*, 259–86.

—(2007). Applications of innate affect theory to the understanding and treatment of dissociative identity disorder. In E. Vermetten, M. J. Dorahy, and D. Spiegel (eds), *Traumatic Dissociation: Neurobiology and treatment* (pp. 301–16). Arlington, VA: American Psychiatric Press, Inc.

Koerner, K. (2012). *Doing Dialectical Behavior Therapy: A Practical Guide*. New York: Guilford.

Kortlandt, A. (1955). Aspects and prospects of the concept of instinct. (Vicissitudes of the hierarchy theory). *Archives Ne´erlandaises de Zoologie, 11*, 155–284.

Korzekwa, M. I., Dell, P. F. and Pain, C. (2009). Dissociation and borderline personality disorder: An update for clinicians. *Current Psychiatry Reports, 11*(1), 82–8.

Korzekwa, M., Dell, P. F., Links, P. S., Thabane, L. and Fougere, P. (2009). Dissociation in Borderline Personality Disorder: A Detailed Look. *Journal of Trauma and Dissociation, 10*(3), 346–67.

Kosslyn, S. M., Thompson, W. L., Costantini-Ferrando, M. F., Alpert, N. M. and Spiegel, D. (2000). Hypnotic Visual Illusion Alters Color processing in the Brain. *Psychiatry: Interpersonal and Biological Processes*, 157, 1279–84.

Kraepelin, E. (1919). *Dementia praecox and paraphrenia*. Chicago: Chicago Medical Book Co.

Kring. A. M. and Sloan, D. M. (2010). Emotion Regulation and Psychopathology: A Transdiagnostic Approach to Etiology and Treatment. New York: Guilford Press

Kroenke, K. (2007). Efficacy of Treatment for Somatoform Disorders: A Review of Randomized Controlled Trials. *Psychosomatic Medicine, 69*, 881–8.

Kroenke, K. and Swindle, R. (2000). Cognitive-behavioral therapy for somatisation and symptom syndromes: a critical review of controlled clinical trials. *Psychotherapy and Psychosomatics, 69*, 205–15.

Kroger, C., Schweiger, U., Sipos, V., Kliem, S., Arnold, R., Schunert, T. and Reinecker, H. (2010). Dialectical behaviour therapy and an added cognitive behavioural treatment module for eating disorders in women with borderline personality disorder and anorexia nervosa or bulimia nervosa who failed to respond to previous treatments. An open trial with 15-month follow-up. *Journal of Behavior Therapy and Experimental Psychiatry, 41*, 381–8.

Kuyk, J., Van Dyck, R. and Spinhoven, P. (1996). The case for a dissociative interpretation of pseudoepileptic seizures. *Journal of Nervous and Mental Disease, 184*(8), 468–74.

Kuyk, J., Spinhoven, P. and Van Dyck, R. (1999). Hypnotic recall: A positive criterion in the differential diagnosis between epileptic and pseudoepileptic seizures. *Epilepsia, 40*, 485–91.

Kuyken, W., Padesky, C. A. and Dudley, R. (2009). *Collaborative Case Conceptualization: Working Effectively with Clients in Cognitive-Behavioural Therapy*. London and New York, NY: The Guilford Press.

La Mela, C., Maglietta, M., Castellini, G., Amoroso, L. and Lucarelli, S. (2010). Dissociation in eating disorders: Relationship between dissociative experiences and binge-eating episodes. *Comprehensive Psychiatry, 51*(4), 393–400.

Lacey, J. H. (1986). Pathogenesis. In L. J. Downey and J. C. Malkin (eds), *Current approaches: Bulimia nervosa.* Dupar Laboratories Limited.

Land, K. M. (2010). Examining the role of experiential avoidance specific to post-trauma symptoms. Unpublished doctoral dissertation. Alliant International San Francisco Bay, CA: University.

Lange, C., Kracht, L., Herholz, K., Sachsse, U. and Irle, E. (2005). Reduced glucose metabolism in temporo-parietal cortices of women with borderline personality disorder. *Psychiatry Research: Neuroimaging, 139*(2), 115–26.

de Lange, F. P., Roelofs, K. and Ivan, T. (2007). Increased self-monitoring during imagined movements in conversion paralysis. *Neuropsychologia, 45*, 2051–8.

Larkin, W. and Morrison, A. (2006). *Trauma and Psychosis.* London: Routledge.

Larkin W. and Read J. (2008). Childhood trauma and psychosis: Evidence, pathways, and implications. *Journal of Postgraduate Medicine, 54*, 287–93.

Layden, M. A., Newman, C. F., Freeman, A. and Byers-Morse, S. B. (1993*). Cognitive therapy of borderline personality disorder. Psychology practitioner guidebooks* Boston: Allyn and Bacon.

LeDoux, J. (1998). *The Emotional Brain.* London: Weidenfeld and Nicolson.

—(1998) Fear and the Brain: Where have we been and where are we going? *Biological Psychiatry, 44, 1129–1238.*

Lee, W. E., Kwok, C.H. T., Hunter, E.C. M., Richards, M. and David, A. S. (2012). Prevalence and childhood antecedents of depersonalization syndrome in a UK birth cohort, *Social Psychiatry and Psychiatric Epidemiology, 47*(2), 253–61.

Lensvelt-Mulders, G., Van der Hart, O., Van Ochten, J. M., Van Son, M. J. M., Steele, K. and Breeman, L. (2008). Relations among peritraumatic dissociation and posttraumatic stress: A meta-analysis. *Clinical Psychology Review, 28*, 1138–51.

Lenzenweger, M. F., Lane, M., Loranger, A. and Kessler, R. (2007). DSM-IV Personality Disorders in the National Comorbidity Survey Replication. *Biological Psychiatry, 62*(6), 553–64.

Leverich, G., S. (2002). Early physical and sexual abuse associated with an adverse course of bipolar illness. *Biological Psychiatry, 51*(4), 288–97.

Lieb, K., Zanarini, M. C., Schmahl, C., Linehan, M. M. and Bohus, M. (2004). Borderline personality disorder. *The Lancet, 364*(9432), 453–61.

Liepert, J., Hassa, T., Tüscher, O. and Schmidt, R. (2011). Motor excitability during movement imagination and movement observation in psychogenic lower limb paresis. *Journal of Psychosomatic Research, 70*, 59–65.

Lindell, H. S. (1947). The Experimental Neurosis. *Annual Review of Physiology, 9*, 569–80.

Lindsay, D. S. and Briere, J. (1997). The controversy regarding recovered memories of childhood sexual abuse: Pitfalls, bridges, and future directions. *Journal of Interpersonal Violence, 12* (5), 631–7.

Lindsay, D. S. and Read, J. D. (1995). Memory work and recovered memories of childhood sexual abuse: scientific evidence and public, professional and personal issues. *Psychology, Public Policy, and the Law, 1*, 846–908.

Linehan, M. M. (1993a). *Cognitive behavioural treatment of borderline personality disorder.* New York: Guilford Press.

—(1993b). *Skills training manual for treating borderline personality disorder.* New York: Guilford Press.

Linehan, M. M., Bohus, M. and Lynch, T.R. (2007). *Handbook of Emotion Regulation.* New York: Guilford Press.

Liotti, G. (1999a). Disorganisation of attachment as a model for understanding dissociative psychopathology. In J. Solomon and C. George (eds). *Attachment disorganization* (pp. 291–317). New York: Guilford.

—(1999b). Understanding the dissociative processes: The contribution of attachment theory. *Psychoanalytic Inquiry, 19,* 757–83.

—(2000). Disorganised attachment, models of borderline states and evolutionary psychotherapy. In P. Gilbert and B. Bailey (eds), *Genes on the Couch: Explorations in Evolutionary Psychotherapy.* (232–56). Hove: Brunner-Routledge.

—(2006). A model of dissociation based on attachment theory and research. *Journal of Trauma and Dissociation, 7*(4) 55–74.

—(2009). 'Attachment and dissociation' in P. F Dell and J. A O'Neil (eds), *Dissociation and the Dissociative Disorders: DSM-V and Beyond.* (53–66) London: Routledge.

Liotti. G. and Gilbert, P. (2011). Mentalizing, motivations and social mentalities: Theoretical considerations and implications for psychotherapy. *Psychology and Psychotherapy, 84,* 9–25.

Liotti, G. and Gumley, A. (2008). An attachment perspective on schizophrenia: The role of disorganized attachment, dissociation and mentalization. In A. Moskowitz, I. Schafe, and M. J. Dorahy (eds), *Psychosis, Trauma and Dissociation* (117–33). Chichester: Wiley and Sons.

Loftus, E. F. (1993). The reality of repressed memories. *American Psychologist, 48,* 518–37.

Longe, O., Maratos, F. A., Gilbert, P., Evans, G., Volker, F., Rockliffe, H. and Rippon, G. (2010). Having a word with yourself: Neural correlates of self-criticism and self-reassurance. *NeuroImage, 49,* 1849–56.

Looper, K. J. and Kirmayer, L. J. (2002). Behavioral Medicine Approaches to Somatoform Disorders. *Journal of Consulting and Clinical Psychology, 70,* 810–27.

Ludäscher, P., Bohus, M., Lieb, K., Philipsen, A., Jochims, A. and Schmahl, C. (2007). Elevated pain thresholds correlate with dissociation and aversive arousal in patients with borderline personality disorder. *Psychiatry Research, 149*(1–3), 291–6.

Lyttle, N., Dorahy, M., Hanna, D. and Huntjens, R. J. C. (2010). Conceptual and perceptual priming and dissociation in chronic posttraumatic stress disorder. *Journal of Abnormal Psychology, 119,* 777–90.

Lyubomirsky, S., Casper, R. C. and Sousa, L. (2001). What triggers abnormal eating in bulimic and nonbulimic women? The role of dissociative experiences, negative affect, and psychopathology. *Psychology of Women Quarterly, 25*(3), 223–32.

MacDonald, K. and MacDonald, T. M. (2010). The peptide that binds: A systematic review of oxytocin and its prosocial effects in humans. *Harvard Review of Psychiatry, 18,* 1–21.

Macfie, J., Cicchetti, D. and Toth, S. L. (2001). The development of dissociation in maltreated preschool-aged children, *Development and Psychopathology, 13,* 233–54.

Mackner, L. M., Starr, R. H. and Black, M. (1997). The cumulative effect of neglect and failure to thrive on cognitive functioning. *Child Abuse and Neglect, 21*(7), 691–700.

Mann, B. J. and Sanders, S. (1994). Child dissociation and the family context. *Journal of Abnormal Child Psychology, 22*(3), 373–88.

Mansell, W. (2005). Control theory and psychopathology: An integrative approach. *Psychology and Psychotherapy: Theory, Research and Practice, 78,* 141–78.

—(2010). Bipolar Disorders. In A. Grant and M. Townend (eds), *Cognitive Behavioural Therapy in Mental Health Care* (2nd edn.). London: Sage Publications.

—(2012). The transdiagnostic approach. In W. Dryden (ed.), *CBT Approaches to Counselling and Psychotherapy.* Sage.

Marcel, A. J. (1983). Conscious and unconscious perception: An approach to the relations between phenomenal experience and perceptual processes. *Cognitive Psychology, 15,* 238–300.

Marken, R. S. (1986). Perceptual organisation of behavior: A hierarchical control model of coordinated action. *Journal of Experimental Psychology: Human Perception and Performance, 12,* 267–76.

Marmar, C. R., Weiss, D. S. and Metzler, T. J. (1997). The peritraumatic dissociative experiences questionnaire. In J. O. Wilson and T. M. Keane (eds), *Assessing psychological trauma and PTSD* (412–28). New York and London: Guilford Press.

Maruff, P. and Velakoulis, D. (2000). The voluntary control of motor imagery: Imagined movements in individuals with feigned motor impairment and conversion hysteria. *Neuropsycholgia, 38,* 1251–60.

Marx, B. P. and Sloan, D. M., (2004). Peritraumatic dissociation and experiential avoidance as predictors of posttraumatic stress symptomology. *Behavior Research and Therapy, 43,* 569–83.

Mathew, R. J., Wilson, W. H., Humphreys, D., Lowe, J. V. and Weithe, K. E. (1993). Depersonalization after marijuana smoking. *Biological Psychiatry, 33,* 431–41.

Mayer-Gross, W. (1935). On depersonalization. *British Journal of Medical Psychology, 15*(2), 103–26.

McDougall, W. (1926). *An outline of abnormal psychology.* London: Methuen and Co.

McElroy, L. P. (1992). Early indicators of pathological dissociation in sexually abused children. *Child Abuse and Neglect, 16*(6), 833–46.

McGlashan, T. H. (1987). Recovery style from mental illness and long-term outcome. *Journal of Nervous and Mental Disease, 175*(11), 681–85.

McGorry, P. D., Chanen, A., McCarthy, E., Van Riel, R., McKenzie, D. and Singh, B. S. (1991). Post-traumatic stress disorder following recent-onset psychosis: an unrecognized post-psychotic syndrome. *Journal of Nervous and Mental Disease, 179,* 253–8.

McGuire, P. K., Cope, H. and Fahy, T. A., (1994). Diversity of psychopathology associated with methylenedioxymethamphetamine ('ecstasy'). *British Journal of Psychiatry, 165,* 391–5.

McGuire, M. T. and Troisi, A. (1998). *Darwinian Psychiatry.* New York: Oxford University Press.

McLaughlin, K. A., Green, J. G., Gruber, M. J., Sampson, N. A., Zaslavsky, A. M., Kessler, R. C. *et al.* (2010). Childhood adversities and adult psychiatric disorders in the National Comorbidity Survey Replication II: Association with persistence of DSM-IV disorders. *Archives of General Psychiatry, 67*(2), 124–32.

McManus, F. (1995). Dissociation and the severity of bulimic psychopathology among eating disordered and non eating disordered women. *European Eating Disorders Review, 3,* 185–95.

McManus, F. and Waller, G. (1995). A functional analysis of binge-eating. *Clinical Psychology Review, 15*(8), 845–63.

McNally, R. J. (1999). Posttraumatic stress disorder. In T. Millon, P. Blaney, and R. D. Davis (eds) *Oxford Textbook of Psychopathology*, (pp. 144–65). Oxford: Oxford University Press.

—(2003). *Remembering trauma*. Cambridge, MA: Belknap Press/Harvard University Press.

—(2004). The Science and folklore of traumatic amnesia. *Clinical Psychology: Science and Practice*, 11(1), 29–33.

McShane, J. M. and Zirkel, S. (2008). Dissociation in the binge-purge cycle of bulimia nervosa. *Journal of Trauma and Dissociation, 9:4*, 463–79.

Medford, N., Baker, D., Hunter, E., Sierra, M., Lawrence, E., Phillips, M. L. and David, A. S. (2003). Chronic depersonalization following illicit drug use: A controlled analysis of 40 cases. *Addiction, 98*, 1731–36.

Mellor-Clark, J., Barkham, M., Connell, J. and Evans, C. (1999). Practice-based evidence and standardized evaluation informing the design of the CORE system. *European Journal of Psychotherapy and Counselling, 2*(3), 357–74.

Merckelbach, H., Rassin, E. and Muris, P. (2000). Dissociation, schizotypy, and fantasy proneness in undergraduate students. *Journal of Nervous and Mental Disease, 188*, 428–31.

Merskey, H. (1995). Multiple personality disorder and false memory. *Journal of Psychiatry, 166*, 281–3.

Meyer, C., Waller, G. and Waters, A. (1998). Emotional states and bulimic psychopathology. In H. W. Hoek, J. L. Treasure and M. A. Katzman (eds), *Neurobiology in the treatment of eating disorders*. (271–89) Chichester: Wiley and Sons.

Michael, T. and Ehlers, A. (2007). Enhanced perceptual priming for neutral stimuli occurring in a traumatic context: Two experimental investigations. *Behaviour Research and Therapy, 45*, 341–58.

Michal, M., Beutel, M. E., Jordan, J., Zimmermann, M., Wolters, S. and Heidenreich, T. (2007). Depersonalization, mindfulness and childhood trauma. *Journal of Nervous and Mental Disease, 195*(8), 693–6.

Mikulincer, M. and Shaver, P. R. (2007). *Attachment in Adulthood: Structure, Dynamics, and Change*. New York: Guilford Press.

Millon, T. (2006). *Millon Clinical Multiaxial Inventory – III: Manual* (3rd edn.). Minneapolis, MN: Pearson Assessments.

Mitchell, S. W. (1888). Mary Reynolds: A case of double consciousness. *Transactions of the College of Physicians of Philadelphia, 10*, 366–89.

Mithoefer, M. C., Wagner, M. T., Mithoefer, A. T., Jerome, L. and Doblin, R. (2011). The safety and efficacy of {+/-}3,4-methylenedioxymethamphetamine-assisted psychotherapy in subjects with chronic, treatment-resistant posttraumatic stress disorder: the first randomized controlled pilot study. *Journal of Psychopharmacology, 25*(4), 439–52.

Mollon, P. (1996). *Multiple Selves, Multiple Voices: Working with Trauma, Violation and Dissociation*. Chichester: Wiley and Sons.

Moran, C. (1986). Depersonalization and agoraphobia associated with marijuana use. *British Journal of Medical Psychology, 59*, 187–96.

Moreau de Tours, J. J. (1845). *Du hachisch et de l'aliénation mentale: Etudes psychologiques*. Paris: Fortin, Masson and Cie. English edition (1973). *Hashish and mental illness*. New York: Raven Press.

Morgan, C. and Fisher, H. (2007). Environmental Factors in Schizophrenia: Childhood Trauma—A Critical Review. *Schizophrenia Bulletin, 33* (1), 3–10.

Morrison, A. P. (2001). The interpretation of intrusions in psychosis: An integrative cognitive approach to psychotic symptoms. *Behavioural and Cognitive Psychotherapy*, *29*, 257–76.

Morton, J., Andrew, B., Bekerian, D., Brewin, C. R., Davies, G. M. and Mollon, P. (1995). *Recovered memories*. Leicester: British Psychological Society.

Moskowitz, A., Read, J., Farrelly, S., Rudegeair, T. and Williams, O. (2009). Are psychotic symptoms traumatic in origin and dissociative in kind? In P. Dell and J. O'Neil (eds), *Dissociation and the Dissociative Disorders: DSM-V and Beyond* (521–33). New York: Routledge.

Moskowitz, A., Schäfer, I. and Dorahy, M. J. (eds) (2008). *Psychosis, Trauma and Dissociation: Emerging Perspectives on Severe Psychopathology*. London: Wiley and Sons.

Mountford, V., Corstorphine, E., Tomlinson, S. and Waller, G. (2007). Development of a measure to assess invalidating childhood environments in the eating disorders. *Eating Behaviors*, *8*(1), 48–58.

Mueser, K..T, Trumbetta, S. L., Rosenberg, S. D., Vivader, R., Goodman, L. B., Osher, F. C., Auciello and P., Foy, D. W. (1998). Trauma and post-traumatic stress disorder in severe mental illness. *Journal of Consulting and Clinical Psychology*, *66*, 493–9.

Murray, J., Ehlers, A. and Mayou, R. A. (2002). Dissociation and post-traumatic stress disorder: two prospective studies of road traffic accident survivors. *British Journal of Psychiatry*, *180*, 363–8.

Mussap, A. J. and Salton, N. (2006). A 'rubber-hand' illusion reveals a relationship between perceptual body image and unhealthy body change. *Journal of Health Psychology*, *11*(4), 627–39.

Myers, A. T. (1886). The life-history of a case of double or multiple personality. *Journal of Mental Science, January*, 596–605.

Myers, C. S. (1940). *Shell shock in France 1914–1918*. Cambridge: Cambridge University Press.

Najavits, L. M. (2002). Seeking safety: A treatment manual for PTSD and substance abuse. *(2002). Seeking Safety: A Treatment Manual for PTSD and Substance Abuse*. New York: Guilford Press.

Narang, D. S. and Contreras, J. M. (2000). Dissociation as a mediator between child abuse history and adult abuse potential. *Child Abuse and Neglect*, *24*(5), 635–65.

National Institute for Health and Clinical Excellence (2009). *Schizophrenia: Core Interventions in the Treatment and Management of Schizophrenia in Adults in Primary and Secondary Care. CG82*. London: National Institute for Health and Clinical Excellence.

Neff, K. D. (2011). *Self Compassion*. London: Hodder and Stoughton.

Nelson, H. (2005). *Cognitive-behavioural therapy with delusions and hallucinations: A practice Manual* (2nd edn.). Cheltenham: Stanley Thornes.

Newman Taylor, K. and Stopa, L. (2013). *The Fear of Others: A Pilot Study of Social Anxiety Processes in Paranoia*. *Behavioural and Cognitive Psychotherapy*, *41*, pp. 66–88.

Neziroglu F. and Donnelly, K. (2010). *Overcoming depersonalization disorder: A mindfulness and acceptance guide to conquering feelings of numbness and unreality*. Oakland: New Harbinger Publications.

Nijenhuis, E. R. S. (2000). Somatoform dissociation: Major symptoms of dissociative disorders. *Journal of Trauma and Dissociation*, *1*(4), 7–29.

—(2004). *Somatoform dissociation: Phenomena, measurement, and theoretical issues.* New York: W. W. Norton and Co.

—(2011). Consciousness and self-consciousness in dissociative disorders. In, V. Sinason (ed.), *Trauma and dissociation: Conceptual, clinical and theoretical issues.* London: Routledge.

Nijenhuis, S. and Boer, J. A. (2009). Psychobiology of traumatisation and trauma-related structural dissociation of the personality. In. P. F. Dell and J. A. O'Neil (eds), *Dissociation and the Dissociative Disorders: DSM-V and Beyond* (337–66). London: Routledge.

Nijenhuis, E. R. S., Spinhoven, P., Van Dyck, R., Van der Hart, O. and Vanderlinde (1996). The development and psychometric characteristics of the somatoform disso-ciation questionnaire (SDQ-20). *Journal of Nervous and Mental Disease, 184*(11), 688–94.

Nijenhuis, E. R. S. and Van der Hart, O. (1999). Forgetting and reexperiencing trauma. In J. Goodwin and R. Attias (eds) *Splintered reflections: Images of the body in trauma.* New York: Basic Books.

—(2011). Dissociation in trauma: A new definition and comparison with previous formula-tions. *Journal of Trauma and Dissociation, 12,* 416–45.

Nijenhuis, E.R. S., Van der Hart, O. and Steele, K. (2002). The emerging psychobiology of trauma-related dissociation and dissociative disorders. In H. D'haenen, J. A. den Boer and P. Willner (eds), *Biological Psychiatry* (1079–98). Chichester and New York: Wiley and Sons.

Nolen-Hoeksema, S. (2000). The role of rumination in depressive disorders and mixed anxiety/depressive symptoms. *Journal of Abnormal Psychology, 109* (3), 504–11.

Noll, J., G. (2008). Sexual abuse of children – Unique in its effects on development? *Child Abuse and Neglect, 32*(6), 603–5.

Norman, D. A. and Shallice, T. (1986). Attention to action: Willed and automatic control of behavior. In R. J. Davidson, G. E. Schwartz and D. Shapiro (eds), *Consciousness and self-regulation. Volume 4: Advances in research and theory* (1–18). New York: Plenum Press.

Noyes, R. Jr. and Kletti, R. (1977). Depersonalization in response to life-threatening danger. *Comprehensive Psychiatry, 18,* 375–84.

Noyes, R., Hoenk, P. R., Kuperman, S. and Slymen, D. J. (1977). Depersonalization in accident victims and psychiatric patients. *Journal of Nervous and Mental Disease, 164,* 401–7.

Nurcombe, B., Scott, J. G. and Jessop, M. E. (2009). Dissociative hallucinosis, In P. Dell and J. O'Neil (eds). *Dissociation and the Dissociative Disorders: DSM-V and Beyond* (pp. 546–55). New York: Routledge.

O'Connor, T. G. and Rutter, M. (2000). Attachment disorder behaviour following early severe deprivation: Extension and longitudinal follow-up. *Journal of the American Academy of Child and Adolescent Psychiatry, 39*(6), 703–12.

O'Kearney, R. and Perrott, K. (2006). Trauma narratives in posttraumatic stress disorder: A review. *Journal of Traumatic Stress, 19,* 81–93.

Ogden, P., Minton, K. and Pain, C. (2006). *Trauma and the Body: A Sensorimotor Approach to Psychotherapy.* New York: W. W. Norton and Co.

Oliner, S. P. and Oliner, P. M. (1988). *The Altruistic Personality: Rescuers of Jews in Nazi Europe.* New York: Free Press.

Orsillo, S. M. and Battan, S. V. (2005). Acceptance and commitment therapy in the treatment of posttraumatic stress disorder. *Behavior Modification, 29*(1), 95–129.

Osgood, C. E. and Luria, Z. (1954). A blind analysis of a case of multiple personality disorder using semantic differential. *Journal of Abnormal and Social Psychology, 49,* 579–91.

Ozcetin, A., Belli, H., Ertem, U., Bahcebasi, T., Ataoglu, A. and Canan, F. (2009). Childhood trauma and dissociation in women with pseudoseizure-type conversion disorder. *Nordic Journal of Psychiatry, 63*(6), 462–68.

Ozer, E. J., Best, S. R., Lipsey, T. L. and Weiss, D. S. (2003). Predictors of posttraumatic stress disorder and symptoms in adults: A meta-analysis. *Psychological Bulletin, 129,* 52–73.

Panasetis, P. and Bryant, R. A. (2003). Peritraumatic versus persistent dissociation in acute stress disorder. *Journal of Traumatic Stress 16*(6), 563–66.

Panksepp, J. (2007). The neuroevolutionary and neuroaffective psychobiology of the prosocial brain. In R. I. M Dunbar and L. Barrett (eds). *The Oxford Handbook of Evolutionary Psychology.* pp.145–62. Oxford: Oxford University Press.

—(2010). Affective neuroscience of the emotional brainmind: Evolutionary perspectives and implications for understanding depression. *Dialogues in Clinical Neuroscience, 12,* 383–99.

Paul, T., Shroeter, K., Dahme, B. and Nutzinger, D. O. (2002) Self-injurious behaviour in women with eating disorders. *The American Journal of Psychiatry. Vol.159*(3), 408–11.

Pearson, D. *et al.* (2001a). Prevalence of imaginary companions in a normal child population. *Child Care, Health and Development, 27*(1), 13–22.

—(2001b). Auditory hallucinations in normal child populations. *Personality and Individual Differences, 31,* 401–7.

—(2008). Auditory hallucinations in adolescent and adult students: implications for continuums and adult pathology following child abuse. *Journal of Nervous and Mental Disease, 196*(8), 634–8.

Pellis, S. and Bell, H. (2011). Closing the circle between perceptions and behavior: A cybernetic view of behavior and its consequences for studying motivation and development. *Developmental Cognitive Neuroscience, 1,* 404–13.

Piper, A. (1994). Multiple personality disorder. *British Journal of Psychiatry, 164,* 600–12.

Pitman, R. K. (1987). A cybernetic model of obsessive-compulsive psychopathology. *Comprehensive Psychiatry, 28,* 334–43.

Plooij, F. X. (1984). *The behavioural development of free-living chimpanzee babies and infants.* (Monographs on Infancy No. 3). Norwood, NJ: Ablex.

Plumb, J. C., Orsillo, S. M. and Luterek, J. A. (2004). A preliminary test of the role of experiential avoidance in post-event functioning. *Journal of Behavior Therapy and Experimental Psychiatry, 35,* 245.

Porges, S. A. (2011). *The polyvagal theory: Neurophysiological foundations of emotions, attachment, communication, and self-regulation.* New York: W. W. Norton and Co.

Posey, T. B. and Losch, M. E. (1983). Auditory hallucinations of hearing voices in 375 normal subjects. *Imagination, Cognition and Personality, 3,* 99–113.

Powers, W. T. (1973; 2005). *Behavior: The control of perception.* New Canaan, CT: Benchmark.

—(1978). Quantitative analysis of purposive systems: Some spadework at the foundations of scientific psychology. *Psychological Review, 85,* 417–35.

—(1992). *Living control systems II.* [Selected papers 1959–90.] New Canaan, CT: Benchmark Publications

—(1998). *Making Sense of Behaviour: The Meaning of Control*. Montclair, NJ: Benchmark Publications.

—(2008). *Living Control Systems III: The Fact of Control*. New Canaan, CT: Benchmark Publications.

Powers, W. T., Clark, R. K. and McFarland, R. L. (1960a). A general feedback theory of human behaviour. Part I. *Perceptual and Motor Skills, 11*, 71–88.

—(1960b). A general feedback theory of human behaviour. Part II. *Perceptual and Motor Skills, 11*, 309–23.

Preeda, N. and Gallardo-Pujol, D. (2011). Neurobiological consequences of child sexual abuse: A systematic review. *Gac Sanit* (on line), 25, 233–9.

Putnam, F. E. (1985). Dissociation as a response to extreme trauma. In R. P. Kluft (ed.), *Childhood antecedents of multiple personality* (pp. 65–98). Washington, DC: American Psychiatric Press.

Putnam, F. W. (1988). The switch process in multiple personality disorder. *Dissociation, 1*, 24–32.

—(1989). *Diagnosis and Treatment of Multiple Personality Disorder*. New Putnam, F. W. (1992). Discussion: Are alter personalities fragments or figments? *Psychoanalytic Inquiry, 12*, 95–111.

—(1997). *Dissociation in children and adolescents: A developmental perspective*. New York: Guilford Press.

Rainey, J. M., Aleem, A., Ortiz, A. M., Yeragani, V. K., Pohl, R. and Berchou, R. (1987). A laboratory procedure for the induction of flashbacks. *American Journal of Psychiatry, 144*(10), 1317–19.

Rainville, P., Hofbauer, R. K., Bushnell, M. C., Duncan, G. H. and Price, D. D. (2002). Hypnosis modulates activity in brain structures involved in the regulation of consciousness. *Journal of cognitive neuroscience, 14*(6), 887–901.

Ray, W. J. (1996). Dissociation in normal populations. In L. K. Michelson, and W. J. Ray (eds), *Handbook of dissociation. Theoretical, empirical, and clinical perspectives* (pp. 51–66). NewYork, NY: PlenumPress.

Read, J. (2006). Breaking the silence: Learning why, when and how to ask about trauma, and how to respond to disclosures. In W. Larkin and A. P. Morrison (eds). *Trauma and Psychosis: New Directions for Theory and Therapy*. Hove: Routledge.

Read, J. and Bentall, R. P. (2012). Negative childhood experiences and mental health: theoretical, clinical and prevention implications. *The British Journal of Psychiatry, 200*, 89–91.

Read, J., Goodman, Morrison, A. P., Ross, C. A. and Aderhold, V. (2004). Childhood trauma, loss and stress. In J. Read, L. Mosher and R. Bentall (eds). *Models of Madness: Psychological, Social and Biological Approaches to Schizophrenia*. London: Brunner-Routledge.

Read, J., Van Os, J., Morrison, A. P. and Ross, C. A. (2005). Childhood trauma, psychosis and schizophrenia. *Acta Psychiatrica Scandinavica, 112*, 330–50.

Resick, P. and Schnicke, M. K. (1992). Cognitive processing therapy for sexual assault victims. *Journal of consulting and clinical psychology, 60*(5), 748–56.

Rhue, J. W., Lynn, S. J. and Sandberg, D. (1995). Dissociation, fantasy and imagination in childhood: A comparison of physically abused, and non-abused children. *Contemporary Hypnosis, 12*(2), 131–6.

Roelefs, K., Näring, W. B., Keijsers, Ger P. J., Hoogduin, C.A. L., Van Galen, G. P. and Maris, E. (2001). Motor imagery in conversion paralysis. *Cognitive Neuropsychiatry, 6*, 21–40.

Roelefs, K., Van Galen, G. P., Keijsers, Ger P. J. and Hoogduin, C.A. L. (2002). Motor initiation and execution in patients with conversion paralysis. *Acta Psychologica, 110*, 21–34.

Romme, M. A. J. and Escher, S. D. M. (2006). Trauma and hearing voices. In W. Larkin and A. P. Morrison (eds). *Trauma and Psychosis: New Directions for Theory and Therapy* (162–93). Hove: Routledge.

Romme, M. A. J., Honig, E. O., Noorthoorn, E. O. and Escher, A. D. M. C. (1992). Coping with hearing voices: An emancipatory approach. *British Journal of Psychiatry, 161*, 99–103.

Root, M. P. and Fallon, P. (1989). Treating the victimized bulimic. *Journal of Interpersonal Violence, 4*, 90–100.

Ross, C. A. (1991). Epidemiology of multiple personality disorder and dissociation. *Psychiatric Clinics of North America, 14*, 503–17.

—(1997). *Dissociative Identity Disorder: Diagnosis, clinical features and treatment of multiple personality* (2nd edn.). New York: Wiley and Sons.

—(2007a). Borderline Personality Disorder and Dissociation. *Journal of Trauma and Dissociation, 8*(1), 71–80.

—(2007b). *The trauma model: A solution to the problem of comorbidity in psychiatry* (2nd edn). Richardson, TX: Manitou Communications.

—(2009). The theory of a dissociative subtype of schizophrenia. In P. Dell and J. O'Neil (eds). *Dissociation and the Dissociative Disorders: DSM-V and Beyond* (pp. 556–68). New York: Routledge.

Ross, C. A., Anderson, G., Fleisher, W. P. and Norton, G. R. (1991). The frequency of multiple personality disorder among psychiatric inpatients. *American Journal of Psychiatry, 150*, 1717–20.

Ross, C. A., Joshi, S. and Currie, R. (1990). Dissociative experiences in the general population. *American Journal of Psychiatry, 147*, 1547–52.

Ross, C. A., Miller, S. D., Reagor, P., Bjornson, L., Fraser, G. A. and Anderson, G. (1990). Structured interview data on 102 cases of multiple personality disorder from four centres. *American Journal of Psychiatry, 147*(5), 596–601.

Ross, T. A. (1941). *War neuroses*. Baltimore: Williams and Wilkins Company.

Ross-Gower, J., Waller, G., Tyson, M. and Elliott, P. (1998). Reported sexual abuse and subsequent psychopathology among women attending psychology clinics: the mediating role of dissociation. *British Journal of Clinical Psychology, 37*(3), 313–26.

Roth, M. (1960). The phobic anxiety-depersonalization syndrome and some general aetiological problems in psychiatry. *Journal of Neuropsychiatry, 1*, 293–306.

Rothberg, M. B., Arora, A., Hermann, J., Kleppel, R., Marie, P. S. and Visintainer, P. (2010). Phantom vibration syndrome among medical staff: a cross sectional survey. *British Medical Journal, 341*, 6914.

Rubin, D. C., Feldman, M. E. and Beckham, J. C. (2004). Reliving, emotions, and fragmentation in the autobiographical memories of veterans diagnosed with PTSD. *Applied Cognitive Psychology, 18*, 17–35.

Ruddy, R. and House, A. O. (2005). Psychosocial interventions for conversion disorder. *Cochrane Database of Systematic Reviews*(4), Art. No.: CD005331. DOI: 005310.001002/14651858.CD14005331.pub14651852.

Rumsfeldt, D. (2002). NATO press conference, NATO H. Q.Brussels, June 6 2002.

Rüsch, N., Weber, M., Il'yasov, K. A., Lieb, K., Ebert, D., Hennig, J. and Van Elst, L. T. (2007). Inferior frontal white matter microstructure and patterns of psychopathology in women with borderline personality disorder and comorbid attention-deficit hyper-activity disorder. *NeuroImage, 35*(2), 738–47.

Ryle, A. (ed.) (1995). *Cognitive analytic therapy: developments in theory and practice.* Chichester: Wiley and Sons.

Sadurni, M. and Burriel, M. P. (2010). The temporal relation between regression and transition periods in early infancy. *Spanish Journal of Psychology, 13,* 112–26.

Salkovskis, P. M. (1996). The cognitive approach to anxiety: Threat beliefs, safety seeking behaviour and the special case of health anxiety and obsessions. In P. Salkovskis (ed.), *Frontiers of Cognitive Therapy* (pp. 48–74). London and New York, NY: Guilford Press.

Salkovskis, P. M., Warwick, H. M. C. and Deale, A. C. (2003). Cognitive behavioural treatment for severe and persistent health anxiety (hypochondriasis). *Brief Treatment and Crisis Intervention, 3,* 353–68.

Sansone, R. A., Levitt, J. L. and Sansone, L. A. (2005). The prevalence of person-ality disorders among those with eating disorders. *Brunner-Mazel Eating Disorders Monograph Series, 13*(1), 7–21.

Sar, V. and Ozturk, E. (2009). Psychotic presentations of dissociative identity disorder, In P. Dell and J. O'Neil (eds). *Dissociation and the Dissociative Disorders: DSM-V and Beyond* (pp. 535–45). New York: Routledge.

Sar, V. and Ross, C. (2006). Dissociative Disorders as a Confounding Factor in Psychiatric Research. *Psychiatric Clinics of North America, 29*(1), 129–44.

Sar, V., Akyuz, G., Kugu, N., Ozturk, E. and Ertem-Vehid, H. (2006). Axis I dissociative disorder comorbidity in borderline personality disorder and reports of childhood trauma. *The Journal of clinical psychiatry, 67*(10), 1583–90.

Sar, V., Yargic, L. and Tutkun, H. (1996). Structured interview data on 35 cases of dissociative identity disorder in Turkey. *American Journal of Psychiatry, 153*(10), 1329–33.

Schachter, D. L. (1999). The seven sins of memory: Insights from psychology and cognitive neuroscience. *American Psychologist, 54,* 182–203.

Schachter, D. L., Adis, D. R. and Buckner, R. L. (2007). Remembering the past to imagine the future: The prospective brain. *Nature Reviews Neuroscience, 8,* 657–61.

Schäfer, I., Harfst, T., Aderhold, V., Briken, P., Lehmann, M., Moritz, S., Read, J. and Naber, D. (2006). Childhood trauma and dissociation in female patients with schizo-phrenia spectrum disorders: an exploratory study. *Journal of Nervous and Mental Disease, 194,* 135–8.

Schauer, M. and Elbert, T. (2010). Dissociation Following Traumatic Stress. *Zeitschrift für Psychologie/Journal of Psychology, 218*(2), 109–27.

Schilder, P. (1939). The treatment of depersonalization. *Bulletin of the New York Academy of Medicine, 15,* 258–72.

Schmahl, C. and Bremner, J. D. (2006). Neuroimaging in borderline personality disorder. *Journal of Psychiatric Research, 40*(5), 419–27.

Schmahl, C., Bohus, M., Esposito, F., Treede, R. D., Di Salle, F., Greffrath, W. and Seifritz, E. (2006). Neural Correlates of Antinociception in Borderline Personality Disorder. *Archives of General Psychiatry, 63*(6), 659–66.

Schore, A. N. (1994). *Affect Regulation and the Origin of the Self: The Neurobiology of Emotional Development.* Hillsdale, NJ: Lawrence Erlbaum.

—(2009). Attachment Trauma and the Developing Right Brain: Origins of Pathological Dissociation. In P. F. Dell and J. A. O'Neil (eds), *Dissociation and the Dissociative Disorders: DSM-V and Beyond.* London, Routledge, 107–41.

Schreiber, F. R. (1973). *Sybil*. New York: Warner Books.

Schupak, C. and Rosenthal, J. (2009). Excessive daydreaming: A case history and discussion of mind wandering and high fantasy proneness. *Consciousness and Cognition, 18*, 290–2.

Schwartz, D. (2000). Failure to thrive: An old nemesis in the new millennium. *Pediatrics in Review, 21*(8), 257–64.

Sedikes, C. and Gregg, A. (2003). Portraits of the self. In, M. A. Hoog and J. Cooper (eds), *The Sage handbook of social psychology* (pp.110–38). London: Sage Publications.

Sedman, G. (1966). Depersonalization in a group of normal subjects. *British Journal of Psychiatry, 112*, 907–12.

—(1972). An investigation of certain factors concerned in the aetiology of depersonalization. *Acta Psychiatrica Scandinavia, 48*, 191–219.

Sedman, G. and Reed, G. F. (1963). Depersonalization phenomena in obsessional personalities and in depression. *British Journal of Psychiatry, 109*, 376–9.

Segui, J., Maruez, M., Garcia, L., Canet, J., Salvador-Carulla, L. and Ortiz, M. (2000). Depersonalization in panic disorder: a clinical study. *Comprehensive Psychiatry, 41*(3), 172–8.

Selfridge, O. G. (1959). Pandemonium: A paradigm for learning. In D. V. Blake and A. M. Uttley (eds), *Proceedings of the Symposium on Mechanisation of Thought Processes*, (511–29), London, 1959.

Selkirk, M., Duncan, R., Oto, M. and Pelosi, A. (2008). Clinical differences between patients with non-epileptic seizures who report antecedent sexual abuse and those who do not. *Epilepsia, 49*, 1446–50.

Sharpe, D. and Faye, C. (2006). Non-epileptic seizures and child sexual abuse: a critical review of the literature. *Clinical Psychology Review, 26*, 1020–40.

Shearer, S. L. (1994). Dissociative phenomena in women with borderline personality disorder. *American Journal of Psychiatry, 151*(9), 1324–8.

Sher, L. and Stanley, B. H. (2008). The role of endogenous opioids in the pathophysiology of self-injurious and suicidal behavior. *Archives of suicide research: official journal of the International Academy for Suicide Research, 12*(4), 299–308.

Shilony, E. and Grossman, F. K. (1993). Depersonalization as a defence mechanism in survivors of trauma. *Journal of Traumatic Stress, 6*(1), 119–28.

Shorvon, H. J., Hill, J. D. N., Burkitt, E. and Halstead, H. (1946). The depersonalization syndrome. *Proceedings of the Royal Society of Medicine, 39*, 779–2.

Siegle, G. J., Thompson, W., Carter, C. S., Steinhauer, S. R. and Thase, M. E. (2007). Increased amygdala and decreased dorsolateral prefrontal BOLD responses in unipolar depression: related and independent features. *Biological Psychiatry, 61*(2), 198–209.

Sierra, M. and Berrios, G. E. (1998). Depersonalization: neurobiological perspectives. *Biological Psychiatry, 44*, 898–908.

Siever, L. J. and Davis, K. L. (1991). A psychobiological perspective on the personality disorders. *American Journal of Psychiatry, 148*(12), 1647–58.

Silberg, J. L. (1998). Interviewing Strategies for Assessing Dissociative Disorders in Children and Adolescents. In *The Dissociative Child: Diagnosis, Treatment, and Management*, 2nd edn., L. J. Silberg (ed.). Sidran Press: Maryland.

Simeon, D. and Abugel, J. (2006). *Feeling unreal: Depersonalization disorder and the loss of the self*. Oxford: Oxford University Press.

Simeon, D. and Hollander, E. (1993). Depersonalization disorder. *Psychiatric Annals, 23* (7), 382–8.

Simeon, D., Gross, S., Guralnik, O., Stein, D. J., Schmeidler, J. and Hollander, E. (1997). Feeling unreal: 30 cases of DSM-III-R depersonalization disorder. *American Journal of Psychiatry, 154*(8), 1107–13.

Simeon, D., Guralnik, O., Schmeidler, J., Sirof, B. and Knutelska, M. (2001). The role of childhood interpersonal trauma in depersonalization disorder. *American Journal of Psychiatry, 158*, 1027–33.

Simeon, D., Knutelska, M., Nelson, D. and Guralnik, O. (2003). Feeling unreal: A depersonalization disorder update of 117 cases. *Journal of Clinical Psychiatry, 64*(9), 990–7.

Simeon, D., Knutelska, M., Smith, L., Baker, B. and Hollander, E. (2007). A preliminary study of cortisol and norepinephrine reactivity to psychosocial stress in borderline personality disorder with high and low dissociation. *Psychiatry Research, 149*(1–3), 177–84.

Simeon, D., Nelson, D., Elias, R., Greenberg, J. and Hollander, E. (2003). Relationship of personality to dissociation and childhood trauma in borderline personality disorder. *CNS spectrums, 8*(10), 755–62.

Singer, J. A. and Salovey, P. (1993). *The remembered self: Emotion and memory in personality.* New York, NY: The Free Press.

Skodol, A. E., Gunderson, J. G., Pfohl, B., Widiger, T. A., Livesley, W. J. and Siever, L. J. (2002). The borderline diagnosis I: psychopathology, comorbidity, and personality structure. *Biological Psychiatry, 51*(12), 936–50.

Skodol, A. E., Siever, L. J., Livesley, W. J., Gunderson, J. G., Pfohl, B. and Widiger, T. A. (2002). The borderline diagnosis II: biology, genetics, and clinical course. *Biological Psychiatry, 51*(12), 951–63.

Sławek, J., Wichowicz. H. M., Cubała, W. J., Soltan, W., Palasik, W., Wilczewska, L. and Fiszer, U. (2010). Psychogenic axial myoclonus: report on two cases. *Neurological Science, 31*, 219–22.

Smith, B., Steel, C., Rollinson, R., Freeman, D., Hardy, A., Kuipers, E., Bebbington, P., Garety, P. and Fowler, D. (2006). The importance of traumatic events in formulation and intervention in cognitive behaviour therapy for psychosis: Three case examples. In W. Larkin and A. P. Morrison (eds). Trauma and Psychosis: New Directions for Theory and Therapy. Hove: Routledge.

Smolak, L. and Murnen, S. K. (2002). A meta-analytic examination of the relationship between child sexual abuse and eating disorders. *International Journal of Eating Disorders, 31*(2), 136–50.

Somer, E. (2002). Maladaptive daydreaming: A qualitative inquiry. *Journal of Contemporary Psychotherapy, 32*(2/3), 197–212.

Sonoo, M. (2004). Abductor sign: a reliable new sign to detect unilateral non-organic paresis of the lower limb. *Journal of Neurology, Neurosurgery & Psychiatry, 75*, 121–5.

Sookman, D. and Solyom, L. (1978). Severe depersonalization treated by behaviour therapy. *American Journal of Psychiatry, 135*, 1543–45.

Southgate, L., Tchanturia, K. and Treasure, J. (2005). Neuropsychological studies in eating disorders a review. In P. Swain (ed.), *Progress in eating disorders.* New York: Nova.

Spiegel, D. (1997). Trauma, dissociation, and memory. *Annals of the New York Academy of Sciences, 821*, 225–37.

Spiegel, D., Koopman, C., Cardeña, E. and Classen, C. (1996). Dissociative symptoms in the diagnosis of acute stress disorder. In L. K. Michelson and W. J. Ray (eds), *Handbook of dissociation* (367–80). New York: Plenum Press.

Spitzer, C., Barnow, S., Freyberger H. J. and Grabe, H. J. (2006). Recent developments in the theory of dissociation. *World Psychiatry 5:2*, 82–6.

Stanley, B. and Siever, L. J. (2010). The interpersonal dimension of borderline personality disorder: Towards a neuropeptide model. *American Journal of Psychiatry*, 167, 24–39.

Startup, M. (1999). Schizotypy, dissociative experiences and childhood abuse: Relationships among self-report measures. *British Journal of Clinical Psychology*, 38, 333–44.

Steel, C., Fowler, D. and Holmes, E. A. (2005). Trauma related intrusions in psychosis: An information processing Account. *Behavioural and Cognitive Psychotherapy*, 33, 139–52.

Steel, C., Hemsley, D. R. and Pickering, A. D. (2002). Distractor cueing effects on choice reaction time and their relationship with schizotypal personality. *British Journal of Clinical Psychology*, 41, 143–56.

Steel, C., Mahmood, M. and Holmes, E. A. (2008). Positive schizotypy and trait dissociation as vulnerability factors for post-traumatic distress. *British Journal of Clinical Psychology*, 47, 245–9.

Steele, K. and Van der Hart, O. (2009). Treatment of complex dissociative disorders: Fostering integration through the resolution of trauma-related phobias. In J. D. Ford and C. Courtois (eds), *Complex traumatic stress disorders: An evidence-based guide* (145–65). New York: Guilford Press.

Steele, K., Dorahy, M., Van der Hart, O. and Nijenhuis, E. R. S. (2009). Dissociation versus alterations in consciousness: Related but different concepts. In P. F. Dell and J. A. O'Neil (eds), *Dissociation and the dissociative disorders: DSM-V and beyond* (pp. 155–70). New York: Routledge.

Steele, K., Van der Hart, O. and Nijenhuis, E. R. S. (2005). Phase-Oriented Treatment of Structural Dissociation in Complex Traumatization: Overcoming Trauma-Related Phobias *Journal of Trauma and Dissociation, Vol. 6*(3) 11–53.

—(2009). The theory of trauma-related structural dissociation of the personality. In P. F. Dell and J. A. O'Neil (eds), *Dissociation and the dissociative disorders: DSM-V and beyond* (pp. 239–58). New York: Routledge.

Steele, M. J., Dorahy, M. J., Van der Hart, O. and Nijenhuis, E. R. S. (2009). Dissociation and alterations in consciounsess: Related but different concepts. In P. F. Dell. and J. A. O'Neil, (eds), *Dissociation and dissociative disorders: DSM-5 and beyond* (155–69). New York: Routledge.

Stein, D. J. and Simeon, D. (2009). Cognitive-affective neuroscience of depersonalization. *CNS spectrums*, 14(9), 467–71.

Steinberg, M. (1994). *Structured clinical interview for DSM-IV dissociative disorders (SCID-D), revised.* Washington, DC: American Psychiatric Press.

Steinberg, M., Rounsaville, B. and Cicchetti, D. V. (1990). The structured clinical interview for DSM-III-R dissociative disorders: preliminary report on a new diagnostic instrument. *American Journal of Psychiatry*, 147, 76–82.

Stiglmayr, C. E., Shapiro, D. A., Stieglitz, R. D., Limberger, M. F. and Bohus, M. (2001). Experience of aversive tension and dissociation in female patients with borderline personality disorder – a controlled study. *Journal of Psychiatric Research*, 35(2), 111–18.

Stiglmayr, C. E., Ebner-Priemer, U. W., Bretz, J., Behm, R., Mohse, M., Lammers, C. H. and Bohus, M. (2008). Dissociative symptoms are positively related to stress in borderline personality disorder. *Acta Psychiatrica Scandinavica*, 117(2), 139–47.

Stone, J., Carson, A., Aditya, H., Prescott, R., Zaubi, M., Warlow, C. and Sharpe, M. (2009). The role of physical injury in motor and sensory conversion symptoms: a systematic and narrative review. *Journal of Psychosomatic Research, 66*, 383–90.

Stopa, L. (ed.). (2009). *Imagery and the threatened self.* London and New York: Routledge.

Stovall-McClough, K. C. and Cloitre, M. (2006). Unresolved attachment, PTSD, and dissociation in women with childhood abuse histories. *Journal of Consulting and Clinical Psychology, 74*(2), 219–28.

Stuss, D. T. and Alexander, M. P. (2000). Executive functions and the frontal lobes: a conceptual view. *Psychological Research, 63*(3–4), 289–98.

Suddendorf, T. and Whitten, A. (2001). Mental evolution and development: Evidence for secondary representation in children, great apes and other animals *Psychological Bulletin, 127*, 629–50.

Suyemoto, K. L. (1998). The functions of self-mutilation. *Clinical psychology review, 18*(5), 531–54.

Taine, H. (1878). *De l'intelligence,* (3rd edn.) Paris: Librairie Hachette et Cie.

Tait, L., Birchwood, M. and Trower, P. (2003). Predicting engagement with services for psychosis: insight, symptoms and recovery style. *British Journal of Psychiatry, 182*, 123–8.

Taylor, E. (1983). *William James on exceptional mental states: the 1986 Lowell lectures.* Amherst, MA: The University of Massachusetts Press.

Tchanturia, K., Campbell, I. C., Morris, R. and Treasure, J. (2005). Neuropsychological studies in anorexia nervosa. *International Journal of Eating Disorders, 37*, S72–6; discussion S87–9.

Terr, L. (1991). Childhood traumas: an outline and overview. *American Journal of Psychiatry, 148*(1), 10–20.

The British Psychological Society, (2000). Guidelines for psychologists working with clients in contexts in which issues related to recovered memories may arise. *The Psychologist, 13*(5).

Thoits, P. A. (1983) 'Multiple identities and psychological well-being: A reformulation and test of the social isolation hypothesis', *American Sociological Review, 48*, 174–87.

Thompson, K. N., McGorry, P. D. and Harrigan, S. M. (2003). Recovery style and outcome in first-episode psychosis. *Schizophrenia Research, 62*(1–2), 31–6.

Tobin, D. L. and Griffing, A. S. (1996). Coping, sexual abuse and compensatory behaviour. *International Journal of Eating Disorders, 20*, 143–48.

Torch, E. M. (1987). The psychotherapeutic treatment of depersonalization disorder. *Hillside Journal of Clinical Psychiatry, 9*(2), 133–43.

Torgersen, S., Kringlen, E. and Cramer, V. (2001). The prevalence of personality disorders in a community sample. *Archives of General Psychiatry, 58*(6), 590–6.

Tull, M. T., Gratz, K. L., Salters, K. and Roemer, L. (2004). The role of experiential avoidance in posttraumatic stress symptoms and symptoms of depression, anxiety, and somatization. *Journal of Nervous and Mental Disease, 192*, 754–61.

Twohig, M. P., Hayes, S. C., Plumb, J. C., Pruitt, L. D., Collins, A. B., Hazlett-Stevens, H. and Woidneck, M. R. (2010). A randomized clinical trial of acceptance and commitment therapy vs. progressive relaxation training for obsessive compulsive disorder. *Journal of Consulting and Clinical Psychology, 78*, 705–16.

Twohig, M. P., Shoenberger, D. and Hayes, S. C. (2007). A preliminary investigation of acceptance and commitment therapy as a treatment for marijuana dependence in adults. *Journal of Applied Behavior Analysis, 40*(4), 619–32.

Ulmer, C., Walser, R. D., Westrup, D, Rogers, D., Gregg, J. and Loew, D. (2006). Acceptance and commitment therapy: Adaptation of a structured intervention for the treatment of PTSD. ACT World Congress, London, July.

Valdiserri, S. and Kihlstrom, J. F. (1995). Abnormal eating and dissociative experiences. *International Journal of Eating Disorders, 17*(4), 373–80.

Van den Bosch, L. M. C., Verheul, R., Langeland, W. and Van den Brink, W. (2003). Trauma, dissociation, and posttraumatic stress disorder in female borderline patients with and without substance abuse problems. *Australian and New Zealand Journal of Psychiatry, 37*(5), 549–55.

Van den Riijt, H., and Plooij, F. (2003). *The Wonder Weeks.* Emmaus, PA: Rodale Books.

Van der Hart, O., Bolt, H. and Van der Kolk, B. (2005). Memory fragmentation in dissociative identity disorder. *Journal of Trauma and Dissociation, 6,* 55–70.

Van der Hart, O., Nijenhuis, E., Steele K. and Brown D. (2004). Trauma-related dissociation: Conceptual clarity lost and found. *Australian and New Zealand Journal of Psychiatry, 38*(11–12), 906.

Van der Hart, O., Nijenhuis, E. R. S. and Steele, K. (2006). *The haunted self: Structural dissociation and the treatment of chronic traumatization.* New York/London: W. W. Norton and Co.

Van der Hart, O., Nijenhuis, E.R. S. and Solomon, R. (2010). Dissociation of the personality in complex trauma-related disorders and EMDR: Theoretical considerations. *Journal of EMDR Practice and Research, 4*(2), 76–92.

Van der Hart, O., Witzum, E. and Friedman, B. (1993). From hysterical psychosis to reactive dissociative psychosis. *Journal of Traumatic Stress, 6,* 43–64.

Van der Kolk, B. A. and Fisler, R. (1995). Dissociation and the fragmentary nature of traumatic memories: Overview and exploratory study. *Journal of Traumatic Stress, 8,* 505–25.

Van der Vegt, E. J. M., Van der Ende, J., Huizink, A. C., Verhulst, F. C. and Tiemeier, H. (2010). Childhood adversity modifies the relationship between anxiety disorders and cortisol secretion. *Biological Psychiatry, 68*(11), 1048–54.

Van Ijzendoorn, M. H. and Schuengel, C. (1996). The measurement of dissociation in normal and clinical populations: Meta-analytic validation of the Dissociative Experiences Scale (DES). *Clinical Psychology Review, 16*(5), 365–82.

Van Minnen, A., Wessel, I., Dijkstra, T. and Roelofs, K. (2002). Changes in PTSD patients' narratives during prolonged exposure therapy: A replication and extension. *Journal of Traumatic Stress, 15,* 255–8.

Vanderlinden, J., Van Dyck, R., Vertommen, H. and Vandereycken, W. (1992). Hypnotizability and dissociation in a group of fifty eating disorder patients: Preliminary findings. In W. Bongartz (ed.), *Hypnosis: 175 years after Mesmer* (291–4). Konstanz: Universitäts Verlag.

Vanderlinden, J., Vandereycken, W., Van Dyck, R. and Vertommen, H. (1993). Dissociative experiences and trauma in eating disorders. *International Journal of Eating Disorders, 13*(2), 187–93.

Vanderlinden, J., Vandereycken, W. and Probst, M. (1995). Dissociative symptoms in eating disorders: A follow-up study. *European Eating Disorders Review, 3*(3), 174–84.

Vanderlinden, J., Vandereycken, W. and Claes, L. (2007). Trauma, dissociation, and impulse dyscontrol: Lessons from the eating disorders field. In E. Vermetten, M. Dorahy and D. Spiegel (eds), *Traumatic dissociation: Neurobiology and treatment* (pp. 317–31). Arlington: American Psychiatric Publishing Inc.

Vannucci, M. and Mazzoni, G. (2006). Dissociative experiences and mental imagery in undergraduate students: When mental images are used to foresee uncertain future events. *Personality and Individual Differences, 41*, 1143–53.

Vogel, M., Spitzer, C., Kuwert, P., Moller, B., Freyberger, H. J. and Grabe, H. J. (2009). Association of childhood neglect with adult dissociation in schizophrenic inpatients. *Psychopathology, 42(2),* 124–30.

Waldinger, R. J., Swett, C., Frank, A., Arlene, F. and Miller, K. (1994). Levels of dissociation and histories of reported abuse among women outpatients. *Journal of Nervous and Mental Disease, 182*(11), 625–30.

Waller, G. and Smith, R. (1994). Sexual Abuse and Psychological Disorders: The role of cognitive processes. *Behavioural and Cognitive Psychotherapy, 22*(4), 299–314.

Waller, G., Babbs, M., Wright, F., Potterton, C., Meyer, C. and Leung, N. (2003). Somatoform dissociation in eating-disordered patients. *Behaviour Research and Therapy, 41*(5), 619–27.

Waller, G., Cordery, H., Corstorphine, E., Hinrichsen, H., Lawson, R., Mountford, V. and Russell. K. (2007). *Cognitive Behavioral Therapy for Eating Disorders: A Comprehensive Treatment Guide.* Cambridge: Cambridge University Press.

Waller, G., Corstorphine, E. and Mountford, V. (2007). The role of emotional abuse in the eating disorders: Implications for treatment. *Eating Disorders: The Journal of Treatment and Prevention, 15*(4), 317–31.

Waller, G., Hamilton, K., Elliot, P., Lewendon, J., Stopa, L., Waters, A. *et al.* (2000). Somatoform dissociation, psychological dissociation, and specific forms of trauma, *Journal of Trauma and Dissociation, 1*(4), 81–98.

Waller, G., Kennerley, H. and Ohanian, V. (2007). Schema-focused cognitive behavioral therapy with eating disorders. In L. P. Riso, P. L. du Toit, D. J. Stein, and J. E. Young (eds). *Cognitive schemas and core beliefs in psychiatric disorders: A scientist-practitioner guide.* (pp. 139–75). New York: American Psychological Association.

Waller, G., Ohanian, V., Meyer, C., Everill, J. and Rouse, H. (2001). The utility of dimensional and categorical approaches to understanding dissociation in the eating disorders. *British Journal of Clinical Psychology, 40*, 387–97.

Waltzer, H. (1972). Depersonalization and the use of LSD: A psychodynamic study. *American Journal of Psychoanalysis, 32*, 45–52.

Warwick, H. M. C. and Salkovskis, P. M. (1990). Hypochondriasis. *Behaviour Research and Therapy, 28*, 105–17.

Watkins, E. R. (2011). Dysregulation in level of goal and action identification across psychological disorders. *Clinical Psychology Review, 31*, 260–78.

Webb, T. L., Sniehotta, F. F. and Michie, S. (2010). Using theories of behaviour change to inform interventions for addictive behaviours. *Addiction, 105*, 1879–92.

Weisberg, D. S., Keil, F. C., Goodstein, J., Rawson, E. and Gray, J. R. (2008). The seductive allure of neuroscience explanations. *Journal of cognitive neuroscience, 20* (3), 470–7.

Wells, A. (1990). Panic disorder in association with relaxation induced anxiety: An attentional training approach to treatment. *Behaviour Therapy, 21*, 273–80.

—(2000). *Emotional disorders and metacognition: Innovative cognitive therapy.* New York, NY: Wiley and Sons.

Wells, A., White, J. and Carter, K. (1997). Attention training: Effects on anxiety and beliefs in panic and social phobia. *Clinical Psychology and Psychotherapy, 4*(4), 226–32.

Wells, A. and Sembi, S. (2004). Metacognitive Therapy for PTSD: A Core Treatment Manual. *Cognitive and Behavioral Practice, 11*, 365–77.

Westbrook, D., Kennerley, H. and Kirk, J. (2011). *An introduction to CBT: Skills and applications* (2nd edn). London: Sage.

Wildgoose, A., Waller, G., Clarke, S. and Reid, A. (2000). Psychiatric symptomatology in borderline and other personality disorders: dissociation and fragmentation as mediators. *The Journal of Nervous and Mental Disease, 188*(11), 757–63.

Wilkinson, R. and Pickett, K. (2009). *The Spirit Level: Why Equality is Better for Everyone.* Penguin Books.

Williams, J. M. G., Watts, F. N., Macleod, C. and Matthews, A. (1997). *Cognitive psychology and emotional disorders* (2nd edn). Chichester: Wiley and Sons.

Williams, J. M. G., Barnhofer, T., Crane, C., Herman, D., Raes, F., Watkins, E. and Dalgleish, T. (2007). Autobiographical memory specificity and emotional disorder. *Psychological Bulletin, 133*(1), 122–48.

Williams, J. M. G., Teasdale, J. D., Segal, Z. V. and Soulsby, J. (2000). Mindfulness-based cognitive therapy reduces overgeneral autobiographical memory in formerly depressed patients. *Journal of Abnormal Psychology, 109*(1), 150–5.

Williams, L. M. (2006). Acceptance and commitment therapy: An example of third wave therapy as a treatment for Australian Vietnam war veterans with post traumatic stress disorder. Unpublished dissertation: Charles Stewart University, Bathurst, NSW.

Wilson, S. C. and Barber, T. X. (1983). Fantasy-prone personality: implications for understanding imagery, hypnosis, and parapsychological phenomena. In A. K. Sheikh (ed.), *Imagery: Current theory, research, and application* (340–87). New York: Wiley and Sons.

Wing, J. K., Cooper, J. E. and Sartorius, N. (1974). *The Measurement and Classification of Psychiatric Symptoms.* London: Cambridge University Press.

World Health Organisation. (1992). *The ICD-10 Classification of Mental and Behavioural Disorders: Clinical Descriptions and Diagnostic Guidelines.* Geneva, Switzerland: World Health Organization.

Young, J. E. (1999). *Cognitive therapy for personality disorders: A schema-focused approach.* Florida: Professional Resource Press.

Young, J. E., Klosko, J. S. and Weishaar, M. E. (2003). *Schema Therapy: A Practitioner's Guide.* New York: Guilford Press.

Zanarini, M. C., Ruser, T. F., Frankenburg, F. R., Hennen, J. and Gunderson, J. G. (2000). Risk factors associated with the dissociative experiences of borderline patients. *The Journal of Nervous and Mental Disease, 188*(1), 26–30.

Zanarini, M. C., Ruser, T., Frankenburg, F. R. and Hennen, J. (2000). The dissociative experiences of borderline patients. *Comprehensive Psychiatry, 41*(3), 223–7.

Zanarini, M. C., Frankenburg, F. R., Hennen, J., Reich, D. B. and Silk, K. R. (2006). Prediction of the 10-year course of borderline personality disorder. *American Journal of Psychiatry, 163*(5), 827–32.

Zanarini, M. C., Frankenburg, F. R., Jager-Hyman, S., Reich, D. B. and Fitzmaurice, G. (2008). The course of dissociation for patients with borderline personality disorder and axis II comparison subjects: a 10-year follow-up study. *Acta Psychiatrica Scandinavica, 118*(4), 291–6.

Zimbardo, P. (2008). *The Lucifer Effect: How Good people Turn Evil.* London: Rider.

Zlotnick, C., Mattia, J. I. and Zimmerman, M. (1999). Clinical correlates of self-mutilation in a sample of general psychiatric patients. *The Journal of Nervous and Mental Disease, 187*(5), 296–301.

Zoellner, L. A. and Bittenger, J. N. (2004). On the uniqueness of trauma memories in PTSD. In G. M. Rosen (ed.). *Posttraumatic stress disorder: Issues and controversies* (pp. 147–62). West Sussex: Wiley.

Zoellner, L. A., Alvarez-Conrad, J. and Foa, E. B. (2002). Peritraumatic dissociative experiences, trauma narratives, and trauma pathology. *Journal of Traumatic Stress, 15,* 49–57.

Zweig-Frank, H., Paris, J. and Guzder, J. (1994). Dissociation in female patients with borderline and non-borderline personality disorders. *Journal of Personality Disorders, 8*(3), 203–9.

Index

*9 7 8 0 4 1 5 6 8 7 7 7 5 *

An environmentally friendly book printed and bound in England by www.printondemand-worldwide.com

PEFC Certified

This product is
from sustainably
managed forests
and controlled
sources

www.pefc.org

PEFC/16-33-415

This book is made of chain-of-custody materials; FSC materials for the cover and PEFC materials for the text pages.

#0165 - 050216 - C0 - 234/156/18 - PB - 9780415687775